John Lehmann

# JOHN LEHMANN
## A Pagan Adventure

Adrian Wright

Duckworth

First published in 1998 by
Gerald Duckworth & Co. Ltd.
61 Frith Street, London W1V 5TA
Tel: 0171 434 4242
Fax: 0171 434 4415
Email: duckworth-publishers.co.uk

A catalogue record for this book is available
from the British Library.

ISBN 0 7156 2871 2

Printed and bound in Great Britain by
Redwood Books Ltd, Trowbridge

for
Terry Dunning
and to the memory of
Barbara Cooper

friendship known and imagined

# Contents

# Preface

If I have one wish for this book it is that it should replace John Lehmann at the centre of the literature to which he gave his life. Let there be no mistake: Lehmann was not at the hub of the English literary world, he *was* the hub. His dismissal to the footnotes of other lives must be one of the great mysteries of our history. Now, it is time for recognition, it is time for disclosure, it is time for homage.

In Lehmann's life stand the colourful and extraordinary: among those playing parts are Michael Redgrave, Lytton Strachey, Leonard and Virginia Woolf, a dying young Greek poet who told Lehmann that his death was 'my present to you', the wife of a French ambassador dressed as a matelot, the emotionally troubled son of one of World War II's most brilliant strategists, a bisexual Austrian shoe-maker, a present-day drama critic of *The Times*, a construction worker presented with the latest electrical drill, Guy Burgess and any number of famous writers – among them Christopher Isherwood (for whom Lehmann had the deepest love) and the 'snarling poodle' Stephen Spender.

One of the most distinguished of the supporting players in Lehmann's life was Sybil Thorndike, the 'Fluffy Dame' (she had a habit on stage of not always remembering the lines the author had given her, but forgot them with exemplary timing). Once in a dressing-room, the Lehmanns were mentioned and somebody said encouragingly 'What a nice family.' The Fluffy Dame looked up. 'Charismatic, talented, yes', she said. 'Nice – no.' With which untypically outspoken judgement Dame Sybil vanishes from our story. It is an opinion that John Lehmann himself might have had some sympathy with, for he was for much of his life the victim of family history. One could not ignore the Lehmanns.

There is a probably apocryphal story that an impressionable visitor, meeting John Lehmann for the first time, was so overcome at the sight of him that he fainted at his feet. There must be a truth here, in that one can imagine it having happened. It was one of John Lehmann's talents to exude a sense of power; one knew one was in the presence of literary influence, of an undisputed *éminence grise*, a man who fixed his companion with piercing blue eyes (Paul Dehn, 'a lovely, warm, beautiful creature', christened him 'The Ice Man Cometh'), a man who bore a resemblance to an S.S. guard (though the Lehmanns were German Jews, a fact of which John did not like to be reminded), a man who when introduced to young men often locked the door behind them.

Before the publication of Lehmann's explicitly sexual memoir, *In the Purely*

*Pagan Sense*, there had been three volumes of autobiography, the first of them particularly distinguished, charting the life of a man at the absolute centre of English literature, written in suitably mandarin prose, detailing his professional and excluding his private life. To Lehmann, it seemed that with this account of his sexual life, the three books of autobiography that preceded it were made complete. The picture would, at last, be whole. The effect was very different, and it is no exaggeration to claim that he was devastated by its reception. This is at least one good reason for the present book, for the distinctions between the professional and private person, though drawn, are brought together. At last, here is a context.

There are many good reasons for this biography. Lehmann's reputation, so overlooked even at the time of his death, deserves new evaluation. He would have wanted it. Lehmann assiduously kept extensive private journals and correspondence, probably in a hopeful knowledge that at some time they would form the basis of a biography. In fact, the Lehmann archive is vast: a huge collection of material mainly dealing with his writing and editorial life at the University of Texas at Austin; another, more alluring, at the University of Princeton in New Jersey. Here, one is as likely to turn up a letter from an old flame ('You may remember that I crack a good whip') as a letter from Saul Bellow. In each, a spark of Lehmann's life lights up.

The biography of John Lehmann can hardly avoid being a *literary* biography, but this is the biography of a person rather than an editor or poet – a person who was an editor and poet, and the reader should hold to the distinction. As an editor, Lehmann's potency is most marked by the *New Writing* series, for it was in the fervid political change of the 1930s and early 1940s that he was most charged, most urgent, most needed and ready.

This is unsurprising because Lehmann had at his centre a simplicity, and his reaction to the war was directly emotional, patriotic, unquestioning. What has surprised me, again and again, in preparing this book, is how his writings of this period have the power to move still. Whatever simplicity Lehmann had, it had the broadness of humanity in it. Turning the pages of his journals, there is a knowledge that here was a man who wanted goodness, who wanted to do the best he could. It was, in Lehmann's case, a wish that transformed itself into a theory that only by intellectual and sexual involvement could he unite himself with the humanity he so needed to be part of. The resultant agonies he suffered need not be imagined, for they are described in the pages that follow.

There may be those who would have preferred a loftier devotion to Lehmann's life as the writers' impresario (a sort of literary Charles B. Cochran) and poet and sterling worker for the betterment of English literature. But such a book would have perpetuated the trick that Lehmann himself worked in his autobiographies, *The Whispering Gallery*, *I Am My Brother* and *The Ample Proposition*. What Lehmann sought throughout life was a fusion of all the elements. It is the least his biographer can do to attempt it: books and boys, and not necessarily in that order.

With a cast of thousands in Lehmann's life, it would make tedious reading to know of them all; I have tried to avoid writing a précis. It would have been too easy to bombard the reader with lists of names; where lists exist, they have seemed unavoidable as, sometimes, in writing of Lehmann's periodicals. The scope of Lehmann's life reached far beyond the confines of Bloomsbury and the gathered darlings of English writers. It is a story that brings the work of Greek, French, Russian, Czechoslovakian writers from their countries, his contribution so pronounced that when foreign authors spoke of Lehmann it was as if, according to the novelist Lettice Cooper, they spoke of England. Creditable it all is, but when there has had, through reasons of space, to be a choice between discussing the plight of writers in Czechoslovakia or detailing an affair of the heart that made Lehmann's life a misery, the heart has invariably won.

Fortunately, Lehmann's private journals, maintained with reasonable consistency (after two schoolboy journals full of 'ripping' adventures) from 1933 until ten years before his death, delineate the fuller picture. They are documents that chart an extraordinary progress, and deserve publication. The reader need have no fear of the verbatim recalled conversations that sometimes occur in this book: they are, in each case, taken from the journals and not the invention of a fanciful biographer.

*

It is as a poet that Lehmann would most have wished to be remembered, perhaps, but long before his death he had recognised this as a forlorn hope. In fact, his achievement was greater, more penetrating, and should even today have its repercussion.

How is Lehmann to be remembered? As the shadowy figure, glimpsed through the indices of so many other biographies, the associate of Isherwood, of Auden, of Spender, whose name merely fell away? (He might, like Cyril Connolly, be seen as a sort of saviour during the years of war: he made words matter, he made their author's voices sound.) As a man who simply made the work of other writers available and, beyond anything we could imagine now, genuinely popular? As a man who did what he could to defend the free world, who believed, for as long as he felt it necessary to believe, in the integration of the masses? As the editor whose work (and nobody could question Lehmann's prodigious industry; his workload would hardly be countenanced today) meant so much to the young airman, soldier and sailor?

When it comes to writing of editors, Cyril Connolly has been remembered and celebrated to an excess that Connolly, so welcoming of excess, would have rejoiced in. There is a case for arguing that Connolly's achievement as an editor was puny compared to Lehmann's. There must be an argument for Connolly remaining in the footnotes of English literature and Lehmann wearing the crown. Connolly himself seems to have been in no doubt that Lehmann was supreme. Besides which, Lehmann remarked, Connolly had dirty fingernails.

Lehmann wrote once:

> The beginning is marked by the end
> And the end is different for every one of us.

These are the words of a man who knew he was one among many, but believed he could affect the fate of the greater number. It was not his fault that such passion became dissipated, that in his last years he was forcibly divorced from his adoration of the natural world, centred forever on his childhood at the family home of Fieldhead. So much was deformed by passing years, the loss of lovers and valiant effort, but Lehmann had a spirit that simply reinvented itself, without perhaps settling on a philosophy that satisfied the disparate strands within him. Ultimately, however, this is a triumphant life, and in moving into it I have sometimes found respect turning into something more.

Lehmann, coming as he does with all the panoply of a long life working at literature, was not an intellectual. His response to literature, as indeed to life, was immediate, built on an absolute knowledge but uncluttered by intellectualism. In a sense, that quality of perception and interpretation confounded his personal life as well as his existence as a writer. How often, years after their relationship had ended, his lovers have been surprised at the intensity with which he wrote of them in his journals. I remember one, standing at his window with his back to me, clearly moved, wondering how different things between him and Lehmann might have been: here, at least, was evidence that Lehmann could indeed inspire affection and regret. Too many of those who knew him in his last years speak of his grandness, his imperious manner, and his legendary meanness: he thought the most economical drink for parties was German champagne served in the smallest possible glasses.

If Lehmann's final years were scarred by ill-health, there was almost no perceptible falling-off in the quantity of work he produced. In not keeping his journals for the last decade of his life (at least, none have been found) perhaps Lehmann was already drawing the veil over what he saw as the best, the most valid. Ends and beginnings: beyond at last attempting to rescue Lehmann from the margins of the literature of which he was once at the heart, this book marks them, and tries to make them one. And now let him reclaim the territory that is rightly his.

# Part I
# GOLDEN LAD

# 1

# Dynasty

Open the *Collected Poems* of John Lehmann and there, the first of the pieces, is 'River Garden'. It is the beginning of evening in an August day, through which a young boy has crept down to where the gardener has been working among the potting sheds. A bonfire burns. The flower-pots are broken. Shaking the branches above him, two ripe nectarines fall at his feet. In his soiled hands he takes the fruit, listening, under the sky, to the music that floats downriver with the last excursion boat.

The child, of course, is Lehmann himself, born into an enchantment at a house called Fieldhead on the banks of the Thames at Bourne End in Buckinghamshire. 'I was born to this house', he wrote. But perhaps he was never quite part of it, just as the young boy with the ripe fruit in his dirtied hands hears the songs of happiness from the river moving away from him.

Behind Lehmann were the dynastic forebears whose portraits stared down from the walls of the great house. From the earliest day, it was obvious that much was expected of him, if he was to earn his place among the whispering gallery of ancestors and friends.

\*

The Lehmanns did not strive for dynasty: dynasty lay in waiting for them. By the beginning of the twentieth century, its fame and responsibility had settled naturally on them from histories in Scotland and Germany. Different but not disparate, the two founding families were destined to forge substantial connections. The maternal branch, the Chambers, provided noted citizens of that most respectable of Scottish towns, Peebles. It was in 1296 that William de la Chaumbre, Baili e Burgois, signed allegiance to Edward I, then fighting not only Scots and Welsh rebels but also the French. In Peebles they had remained, prospering as woollen manufacturers, until the commercial failure of James Chambers which may be traced back to the Napoleonic Wars. Seeking better fortune, James moved to Edinburgh.

His sons, William (born 1800) and Robert (born 1802), reclaimed the success of previous generations. Robert made a stab at teaching, but William, apprenticed to the bookseller Sutherland in Calton Street at 4s. a week and living on porridge, broth and sometimes salt fish, suggested that he should himself set up as a bookseller. They bought premises near the seaport in front of Leith Walk, a busy area where blind fiddlers and one-legged sailors shared the streets with cripples pulled along in dog-carts. Despite the competition, Robert made a living and in 1819, his apprenticeship completed, William put his money into a printing business. As Robert wanted to write, William saw the ideal arrangement: Robert would edit and contribute to a new periodical which he would produce and publish.

William built up the printing works by the successful production of broadsheets and popular songs and other material, while Robert began a long line of works that mined Scottish lore, beginning with *Illustrations of the Author of Waverley*, a collection of portraits of individuals thought to have been the inspiration for various characters in Walter Scott's fiction. Scott became a staunch friend and supporter of Robert, contributing to his researches for *The Popular Rhymes of Scotland*, and the brothers were among the chief mourners at Scott's funeral, a day of national mourning, in the summer of 1832. Robert had a fondness for colourful friends, among them the Ettrick shepherd poet James Hogg, whom he considered more of a prodigy than Burns, perhaps because Hogg had been given almost no education.

Robert had a skill for recognising and exploiting the enormous changes that were happening at the time, signalled in the pulling down of so much of the old Edinburgh. On Saturday 4 February 1832 the firm of W. and R. Chambers published the first of the weekly *Chambers's Edinburgh Journal* for three halfpence, announcing it as 'a meal of healthful, useful, and agreeable mental instruction'. In Scotland alone 30,000 copies were sold within a few days, and its circulation would eventually rise to 80,000. The poet Allan Cunningham told Robert of the *Journal*'s popularity among the Galloway shepherds who left copies of it at appointed times in isolated places for others to pass on in the same manner. His public warmed as much to him as Robert to them – he decided (like John Lehmann) that 'it is possible to lead the life of a literary man without any of those grievances and evil passions which others picture as inseparable from the profession. I envy none, despise none, but on the contrary, yield due respect to all, whether above or beneath me.'

When in 1844 Robert wrote – but did not declare himself the author of – *Vestiges of the Natural History of Creation*, a work about evolution that preceded Darwin's *Origin of Species* by fifteen years, he had already written over thirty books. Rumours spread that it was the work of Prince Albert or Thackeray and the book's success was further helped by appalled churchmen and scientists denouncing it as a notorious attack on accepted thought. Darwin was to write that Robert's work 'had done excellent service' by 'preparing the ground for the reception of analogous views'. Asked why he had written the book, Robert said 'I had eleven good reasons' – eleven children. A prodigious amount of work followed, including a *History of the British Empire* and a *Cyclopaedia of English Literature*, but the crowning glory of Robert and William, by which they became that very real Victorian phenomenon, a household name like Mrs Beeton, was

*Chambers's Encyclopaedia*, a great undertaking begun in 1859 and completed in 1868.

William may not have had the natural popularity that came so easily to his brother, but he was a man of common and sound business sense who meant to do good. In 1865 he became lord provost of Edinburgh, and was largely responsible for the 1867 Edinburgh City Improvement Act that saw the demolition and reconstruction of much of the old city. He was unmarried and worked untiringly for the restoration of St. Giles's Church, dying, three days before its triumphant reopening, in May 1883, before the baronetcy offered by Gladstone could be bestowed.

Robert's professional good fortune was matched by a happy union; Anne Kirkwood gave him three sons and eight daughters. Comfortably established, the couple moved to 1 Doune Terrace in Edinburgh, an address that was soon known as a sophisticated salon to which notable figures of the day made their way. When in 1861 Robert decided he needed to be near the great London libraries, he moved his family to Verulam House in fashionable St. John's Wood. He died in March 1871. His last words seem to have been 'Quite happy – quite comfortable – nothing more.'

*

John Lehmann's paternal great-grandfather, Leo, was working as a portrait painter in Hamburg in the early 1800s when he fell in love with and married Frederika Dellevie. In 1814 the Russians advanced on the French-occupied city and Leo sent Frederika to Kiel where she might more safely be delivered of their first child, Heinrich, later known as Henri. There would be six more children. Like his father, Henri wanted to succeed as a painter and at seventeen he moved to Paris where he became a disciple of Ingres. Only three years later Henri's 'Departure of Tobias' was exhibited at the 1834 Salon. Generous but introspective, fastidious and self-critical, Henri offered to share his Parisian studio with whichever of his brothers also wanted the life of an artist, an opportunity taken up by Rudolf, five years his junior. Together they went, probably at the end of 1838, to study in Rome, where Henri took a studio in the Palazetto Borghese, and made room there for Rudolf, who spent the next six years assiduously copying, studying and painting, mostly peasants.

Henri continued his worship of Ingres, suffering the hospitality eked out by Madame Ingres on Sunday evenings when she would serve the same cake and the weakest of tea. Ingres by now was rather more Roman than French, turning towards Neo-Classicism and against the Romantic headiness of Delacroix. Impressed with Ingres's preference for the probity of drawing over the wildness of colour in painting and marbled passionless nudity, there seems little doubt that Henri's appreciation hampered the development of his own talent. But Henri worked at becoming a highly competent painter of portraits and in 1847, aged only 33, he was named a Chevalier of the Legion d'Honneur, an honour that, over a century later, would also be given to John Lehmann.

Henri had a gift for friendship, too. To Marie d'Agoult and Liszt, with whom she had created a sensation by eloping in 1835, he was endearingly known as 'Clear' or 'Clear Placid', an allusion to Byron's *Childe Harold* in which the poet celebrates Lake Geneva as 'Clear, placid Leman!' Marie d'Agoult assured Henri that 'it was as if we had always been expecting you'. His bond with Mme d'Agoult survived her acrimonious rift with Liszt. In what was possibly his last letter to Henri, Liszt urged his old friend 'Keep for me, my dear Lehmann, your "clear and placid" friendship, and never fear that I shall lose mine for you, however troubled and buffeted by storms my poor life may be.' Mme d'Agoult had her revenge on Liszt by writing a vengeful novel, *Nelida*, exposing an appalling discrepancy between the central character's abilities and ambitions. It was Louis-Napoleon (Napoleon III) who, as President of France, in 1852 commissioned Henri to decorate the Galerie des Fêtes in the Hôtel de Ville in Paris, a work later destroyed by fire.

Yet in spite of these glittering historical connections, it is worth noting that the Vicomte Delaborde detected 'a very genuine anxiety ... concealed under an appearance so very much the contrary of the truth, that those who had neither the time nor the opportunity to look deeper, were tempted to believe that he was not above a certain worldly vanity'. Those 'secret difficulties of an existence the outward appearance of which was so smiling and fortunate' was a characteristic that typified the Lehmanns.

\*

Henri's younger brother Rudolf had his first substantial success at the 1842 Salon. He saw the revolutions of 1847 and 1848 and then lived in Italy, mostly in Rome, from 1856 to 1866. In 1861 he married 'Tuckie' (Amelia), Nina Chambers's sister, and the couple moved that year to Rome where a daughter, Elizabethna, was born in 1862. In Rome, Rudolf's commissions included, wonderfully, an enormous canvas of Pope Sixtus V blessing the Pontine Marshes following the installation of an irrigation works. In 1866 Rudolf and Tuckie settled in London, at Campden Hill, and Rudolf frequently exhibited at the Royal Academy. Tuckie was a well-known amateur singer and, as 'A. L.', a skilful and tasteful arranger of songs; she showed herself as a central member of the Lehmann ménage when she was bridesmaid to Dickens's daughter, Katie, at her marriage to Wilkie Collins's brother, Charles.

Encouraged by Clara Schumann, and the violinist Joachim, Elizabethna, renamed Liza Lehmann, made her professional début as a singer at a Monday Popular Concert in London in 1885. Liza went on to distinguish herself as the composer of several charming song-cycles, among them 'In a Persian Garden' from the *Rubáiyát of Omar Khayyám*. Her settings could be irresistibly arch:

'There are Fairies at the Bottom of my Garden' is still fondly remembered and reveals a scintillating humour. Her score for the musical farce *Sergeant Brue* at the Strand Theatre in 1904 made the *Stage* newspaper feel that she had been 'forced to descend to the conventions of cakewalks and coon songs.' As well as composing songs of ineffable prettiness, her musicianship also revealed a profundity, as in her remarkable setting of verses from Tennyson's *In Memoriam*. She conquered America with two tours, was the first president of the Society of Women Musicians and a professor of singing (also writing a book about it) at the Guildhall School of Music. She had a happy marriage to the painter and, subsequently, composer Harry Bedford, and died in 1918.

\*

Unlike his brothers Henri and Rudolf, Augustus Frederick (always called Frederick) Lehmann did not aspire to be a professional artist. He made his way as a businessman in Huddersfield and then Leith; at Doune Terrace he fell in love with the sister of Rudolf's wife, Nina Chambers, marrying her in November 1852.

Frederick's and Nina's was a match of tremendous happiness. There are countless letters from Frederick's travels in France, Germany, India, Japan, addressed to 'My most deeply beloved wife', 'Most delightful and energetic of all little women', 'Here I am again my pretty little charmer', 'My little blessing', 'My sweet Lily, Snowdrop, Heartsease, and Violet'. Throughout their life together, Frederick was a devoted if often absent husband, desolate and concerned when Nina suffered one of her many bouts of illness and retreated to foreign climates or to their Chine Cottage at Shanklin on the Isle of Wight. After honeymooning in the States, where Frederick needed to be for business purposes, he and Nina moved to Liverpool and then to Eccleshall, Sheffield, where they lived in a house called Fieldhead. It was here that John Lehmann's father, Rudolph Chambers Lehmann, was born on 3 January 1856.

Nina seems to have been an ideal partner. She was a strong-minded woman, a surprise to her father who looked only for acquiescent femininity; small wonder that Nina protested 'Why am I born with reason, and with power to comprehend readily and to argue?' When they moved to 139 Westbourne Terrace in 1859, they inaugurated a salon to which the cream of intellectual society flocked, consolidated three years later when they took Woodlands, a house in Southwood Lane, Highgate, where they remained until they moved to Berkeley Square in the 1870s.

Frederick and Nina were the intimates of a wide circle that included many famous musicians, among them Joachim, the singer Pauline Viardot-Garcia, Meyerbeer, and Carl Hallé, the pianist and founder of the Hallé Orchestra. Arthur Sullivan, of whose work Nina was often less than complimentary, also belonged, as did George Grove, creator of the *Dictionary of Music*. Frederick was perhaps talented enough as a musician to have been a professional violinist, and he belonged to a well-known amateur musical society called The Wandering Minstrels. His connection to Henri and Rudolf no doubt gave him credence when it came to his friendships with prominent artists of his day, notably Landseer, Leighton and Millais. It was with the world of writers that Frederick and Nina made their strongest links. There was 'Pen' Browning, whom they came to know after the death of Elizabeth Barrett, and G. H. Lewes and George Eliot, who first met the Lehmanns when she sat next to them at the Covent Garden Opera in 1864. Edward Bulwer-Lytton, the Liberal and Conservative M.P. and writer of such eagerly-devoured novels as *Pelham*, was thought to be a charming addition, but it was Charles Dickens and Wilkie Collins who brought a real fame to their friendship.

When only six or seven years old, Rudolph (always known as Rudie) was taken by Frederick and Nina to a reading given by Dickens; catching sight of him, the great man took the child in his arms and kissed him. Rudie never forgot the thrill of it. He wept at the account of little Dombey's death and watched amazed as Dickens transformed himself into a pompous and imbecile Justice Stareleigh for the trial scene from *Pickwick Papers*. The Lehmanns also had an enormous fondness for Wilkie Collins, to whom they extended moral and, at times, financial support. After almost twenty years of friendship, Nina could tell him of her pleasure in it, 'always the same, always kind, always interested, always true, always loving and faithful'. Collins frequently stayed at Woodlands. Much of his novel *Man and Wife* was written there, and he dedicated it to them, putting them into the book as the Delamayns – Julius Delamayn is happier to play his violin than to work at his parliamentary ambitions.

It seems likely, too, that in part Nina may have been a model for the admirably resilient Marion Halcombe in Collins's *The Woman in White*. Nina's receptive intelligence is reflected in the playful, fond letters that Collins wrote to her. 'My dear Padrona', he wrote when she was recovering from an illness in 1866, 'But are you learning to take care of yourself for the future? Don't say "Stuff!" Don't go to the piano (specially as I am not within hearing) ... Purchase becoming (and warm) things for the neck and chest. Rise superior to the devilish delusion which makes women think that their feet cannot possibly look pretty in thick boots. I have studied the subject – and I say they can.' Mr Worth of Paris, he assures her, is about to introduce hob-nail boots and comforters for the fashionable woman: 'In two month's time it will be indecent for a woman to show her neck at night.'

We cannot know what Nina thought of the marital and sexual arrangements of Collins or Dickens or the ghastly Bulwer-Lytton who had his troublesome wife Rosina abducted by thugs and incarcerated in a madhouse, arranging to have her certified as insane. (A few weeks later, after a public campaign to rescue her, she was freed. In her novel of 1839, *Cheveley*, she took pleasure in painting a vindictive portrait of Bulwer-Lytton as the brutish Lord De Clifford.) Nina was luckier with Frederick Lehmann, a man whose horizons were broadened by his love of foreign travel, including visits with Collins to Paris and Switzerland, several stays in Cannes (to which he and Nina turned for cures, and became very attached) and in 1869 a voyage around the world. He methodically recorded these adventures in solidly-filled notebooks – tiny, with covers of green silk, or thick and black, the cover embossed with his initials. In the East, he was fascinated to hear the Japanese harp, and in Leipzig he played the violin with the pianist and composer Ignaz Moscheles. And after visiting a mixed sauna in Japan, Frederick decided 'The thing is quite amazing, and proves more decisively than anything that all ideas of morality or propriety are simply questions of latitude.'

Another branch of the Chambers tree was set up in London at 39 Belsize Road and subsequently in Regent's Park Terrace through the marriage of Janet Chambers (William and Robert's sister) to William Henry (Harry) Wills, known as 'The Dodger', a hint to his association with Dickens. Born in 1810, Wills was sending material for publication to Dickens, then editing *Bentley's Miscellany*, in 1837, and in 1841 was in at the birth of *Punch*, becoming its dramatic critic and writing prose and verse for its pages up to 1848. In fact, in 1842 he went to Edinburgh as assistant editor of the *Chambers's Journal*.

It was after marrying Janet Chambers that he moved to London to help Dickens (who resigned after only three weeks) with the *Daily News*. Wills became an industrious sub-editor, commercial manager and fellow proprietor of *Household Words* and *All the Year Round*. He was said by Nina to have 'the heart of a child with the mind of a man'. Thin and slight, it was suggested at a gathering where he went missing that he might be looked for in the flute-case; at dinner, an old woman wrapped her legs around his, thinking it to be the leg of the table. Wills gave Dickens unstinting support and was rewarded by what appears to have been uninterrupted loyalty. He died in 1880 and Janet returned to London and lived twelve years more. She too had always been much admired by Dickens, who liked her wit, her way with a Scottish story or song. 'Will you mention to Mrs. Wills with my kind regard', he asked Harry, 'that I ought to have been born at Peebles, but (owing to the constitutional perversity of my mother) was not?'

Janet Wills could not be kept from the bedside of her niece when Rudie, the first of Frederick and Nina's four children, was born. It was an anxious time. The chloroform given to Nina retarded the baby's birth, and the doctor in attendance pronounced the child dead. Nevertheless, as Janet told Harry, 'they persevered and brought the wee thing round ... Well, he is the sweetest wee lambie, as soft as down, and with a neat face and dark blue eyes and by no means wee.' Frederick was intensely interested in the new arrival. Janet recalled his saying, 'Well, my boy, I'll make the first ten years of your life as happy as it is possible for a creature to be, and after that it will depend on yourself how you go on.'

Rudie's happiness seemed assured. As a boy, he accompanied his father on several foreign excursions, to Heligoland in 1865 and in 1871 to Paris, Metz, Strasbourg, Weimar. On both trips, and in 1869, he travelled to Hamburg to see his grandmother Frederika, and he inherited some of his father's cosmopolitan intelligence. His earliest letters to his father are in German, until he wrote from Elgin House at Highgate School where he went in 1868. In 1875, he began at Trinity College, Cambridge, and was soon spending much of his time at the Boat Club.

In his love of water, Rudie found himself entirely. It was a satisfaction and an obsession that crowded the rest of his life. As well as becoming president of the Union in 1876, Rudie captained the First Trinity Boat Club and rowed for two years in the Trial Eights, besides finding time to win three medals for boxing. Law, not boating, was meant for his profession. In June 1878 he assured Frederick 'I have done a fair amount of legal reading, made myself useful as a coach with pecuniary profit to myself, enjoyed myself labouring at the oar and making bumps.' The following year he was in the University Eight but failed to secure his Blue.

Undeterred, Rudie's passion for rowing found expression not only in the act itself but in writing verses about it, and it was as a prolific writer of that once admired literary genre, 'light verse', that Rudie would become most well-known in the country of his birth. Not only verses on rowing, but animals and, most joyful to the biographer, his family, with whose adventures he regularly jollied up the pages of *Punch*. There was political verse, too, all forgotten today, and decidedly fustian.

Perhaps the inconsequentiality of his poetry was wholly appropriate for a man who seemed to so many such a strange mixture of application, fervour and apathy, a man who was quite content to read the newspapers for hours on end, a man who worked best at the short spurt of creativity. He liked to honour the simplicity of good things: his verse might be 'playful or tender, but it must not be spiteful or mawkish. It may be humorous or regretful, but the humour must not be mere buffoonery and the regret must not become a bitter lamentation ... Refined without affectation, polite without servility; often conventional, but never dull.'

In 1880 he was called to the Bar by the Inner Temple and joined the South Eastern Circuit, but his egalitarian outlook and his belief in Gladstone steered him into politics. Between 1885 and 1892 he contested three constituencies, but failed to get into Parliament. John Lehmann suspected that his father lacked the ambitious edge that might have pushed him further; something reflected by the calmness of the water he loved to travel over.

Long after going down, Rudie became one of the founders of the Cambridge undergraduate journal *Granta* in 1889. By January 1893 he was 'fearfully busy in Cambridge, writing, editing, arranging etc ... The 100th number is out ... I wrote 18 columns out of the 40 it contains myself ... I coached the Cambridge crew on Friday and shall coach them again this week.' Meanwhile, he had also become a frequent and looked for contributor to *Punch*, and was invited to join the *Punch* 'table' in 1890. He was producing formidable amounts of verse, and in 1892 published two books of his pieces, *Mr Punch's Prize Novels* and *The Billsbury Election*.

In 1896 he made the first of many visits to Cambridge, Massachusetts, to coach the Harvard Boat Club, beginning an association that was to give him a transatlantic celebrity (he also coached in Dublin and Berlin). In June 1897 the Americans gave Rudie an honorary degree and, according to the local press, he was 'cheered as few men at Harvard ever were'. When he returned there in November his welcoming ovation in Harvard Square was 'one of the most spectacular scenes in the history of athletics at Harvard'. A month later he was royally fêted in Washington by Mr. Roosevelt and at the White House was presented to President McKinley.

*

It was at Harvard, at the home of his Trinity friend Frank Peabody, that Rudie met the woman that would become his wife. Alice Marie Davis, born in 1874, was governess or, as she would have it, 'teacher-companion' to the three Peabody girls, Martha, Sylvia and Rosamond. Descended on her father's side from the English Burnhams and on her mother's from the American Wentworths, she could claim to be of New English Puritan stock. A noted ancestor was John Wentworth (1737-1820) who had graduated from Harvard to become Lieutenant Governor of New Hampshire and later of Nova Scotia. The Davis family continued to produce distinguished members. There was Owen Gould Davis, who has a claim to being America's most neglected playwright. After working as a geologist and mining engineer he began writing melodramas or 'mellers' for the stage, beginning a prolific string of Broadway successes, including such enticing titles as *Nellie, the Beautiful Cloak Model* (1906) and *Edna, the Pretty Typewriter* (1907). Subsequently he fell under the influence of Eugene O'Neill, writing *The Detour* (1921) about life on a Long Island truck farm, and in 1923 *Icebound*, for which he won the Pulitzer Prize. In later life he wrote for Hollywood, including the Bette Davis vehicle *Jezebel* in 1933. Philanthropically, he worked against state censorship in the theatre, and helped to widen copyright protection for his fellow writers. Alice's uncle Harry Phillips Davis, born in 1868, became known as the father of American radio broadcasting. With Frank Conrad, he made possible the first successful radio broadcast in 1919 and in 1920 they broadcast over a spluttering transmitter the returns of the presidential election.

Like Rudie, Alice held strong liberal sympathies that had been bolstered by her education at Radcliffe College where she had studied English and History, achieving the highest marks ever won by a female student at the college in the subject. She may have had dreams of becoming a writer: there still exists a small sheaf of manuscripts in her hand, a 'storiette' called 'Waking Dreams', and others. She clearly impressed Rudie, who might by now have been considered confirmed in bachelordom.

At their first meeting Alice held her views against his when they discussed the wisdom of female suffrage, and photographs suggest that Alice was a determined character: the chin is firm, the jaw is strong, the eyes are clear. Yet, firmness, strength and clarity, admirable as they are, do not guarantee beauty, and there is photographic evidence that Alice approached plainness. Nonetheless, by 13 June 1898 Rudie was writing to her as 'My own darling', ending his letters 'Goodbye my sweet one, best beloved of all human beings'; by the 20th they were engaged, and the marriage took place three months later, on 13 September, at the Piedmont Church in Worcester. Directly after, the newlyweds sailed to England on the *Majestic*, throughout which voyage they were treated as conquering heroes. Their reception in Buckinghamshire was rapturous, garlanded and cheered. And so Alice moved into Fieldhead, a bachelor's home that was suddenly expected to be a family home.

For Rudie, it was a period of resolution. When the Boer War started in 1899 he had established himself as a Radical Liberal, affronted by the jingoism that rattled all around him. That year he began a series of prose 'Letters to the Celebrated' in *Punch* under the sobriquet of 'The Vagrant', promoting attitudes to the war that were notably out of step with those of the unstoppable Mr Punch. Incensed by the partisan patriotism Swinburne had been publishing in *The Times*, The Vagrant suggested that Swinburne's 'is not the temper in which our soldiers fight their battles ... Brave men themselves, they recognise, they admire the courage of their foes, and when the heights have been won, and darkness comes down on the ghastly work of lead and steel, they will succour their wounded foes no less readily because of Kipling's nursery jingle or Swinburne's disgusting sonnet.'

There was a deep core of human understanding here that would be evident in his son, but it was contradicted by something else in Rudie's personality. Hospitable, kindly and of a generally mild spirit, that sense of beatitude so linked to his love of summer afternoons at the water's edge, there was yet something more. John Lehmann would write of his father's reputation

for a certain intolerant brusqueness of manner and sudden moods of stern displeasure that would transform his more characteristic charm and hu-mour; but he was indulgent and easy-going towards his children, and I cannot remember any occasion on which he was seriously angry with me. There was a kind of affectionate detachment about his attitude which made it difficult for him to see our misdemeanours as anything but absurd and entertaining.

Sir Owen Seaman, *Punch*'s editor, found in Rudie 'a certain masterfulness of manner'. An obituary described him as 'emphatically a "fiery particle", inclined to be dictatorial, intolerant and impatient of opposition ... he was a strange mixture of the fighting man and the hater of war.'

In his modest, hardly startling way, Rudie's life seems always to have been spent in the pursuance of professional or sporting achievement. In 1900, after a brief spell as one of the Liberals who took over the ailing weekly the *Speaker*, his sympathies for the Boer helped him gain Lloyd George's invitation to edit the *Daily News*, but he clashed with one of his fellow managers and took his leave. The following year he was High Sheriff of Buckinghamshire, but it was not until 1906 that his hunger for public service seemed at last to be satisfied when he was returned as Liberal M.P. for the Market Harborough Division of Leicestershire.

At the time of his marriage to Alice he was forty-two, she twenty-four, and there is the slightest hint that a marriage had become necessary to him, for whatever reason. Of his life before Alice, we may see that the camaraderie of the men in the boating crews was central to his happiness. He breathed maleness. By the time he met Alice, Rudie had been a hero in England and in America. A worship of sorts had been his, the due of heroes. Young men looked to him for their instruction and inspiration. As a young man himself, Rudie was extraordinarily handsome, undoubtedly attractive, even alluring in the most masculine manner. There would almost certainly have been a response to Rudie's appeal in some of the men he coached, but there is not a shred of evidence that it ever found expression.

For Rosamond, however, there seems to have been no doubt. She once told her friend and designated biographer Selina Hastings that she had always considered Rudie to be emotionally homosexual. And it may be so; confronted by Rosamond's statement, we suddenly look more carefully at the photographs of Rudie, wondering, as John Lehmann may himself have wondered in later life – as J. R. Ackerley wondered about his own father's sexuality, and his friendships with his fellow soldiers, in his autobiographical *My Father and Myself* – what the secrets of Rudie's orchard might have been.

If we believe Rosamond our perception of the relationship between father and son shifts. Did Lehmann, in adulthood, engage himself sexually in the way that his father, in another generation and milieu, might have? The possibility does nothing to diminish Rudie; the probability adds merely poignancy. For Rudie, the power of his emotional attachment to men would have seemed only natural, intrinsically Edwardian, expected and unsensational. And if we contemplate the dimensions of Rudie's sexuality, the relationship between father and son – with perhaps the father's dawning understanding that his son might grow to be the lover of men – becomes more real, more accessible.

With Alice now in residence at Fieldhead, however, new life began to transform the house. There would be three daughters: Helen Chambers (born 1899), Rosamond Nina (born 1901) and Beatrix Alice (born 1903). The birth of Beatrix was a disappointment because Rudie (and perhaps Alice) had not wanted another girl. She was never called Beatrix, but known as Peggy, although her father called her 'Boy.' The significance of this never left her, clouding her life.

Four years after Beatrix's arrival, at last the son Rudie had always longed for, Rudolf John Frederick, was born on 2 June 1907 at Fieldhead. In recognising that he 'was born to this house', he marked the first great truth of his life. He came on the cusp of good fortune. Rudie had invested much of the family's wealth with a stockbroker friend, in whom he had complete trust. The stockbroker gambled Rudie's money and lost it. The family, as Rudie saw it, was 'all but ruined'. Ruin, of course, is comparative. In Rudie's case, it resulted in modest retrenchment and a reduction in the number of domestic staff and other mild economies. Penury never really threatened, but Rudie had broken the news of their changed circumstances to Alice only a few hours before their son's birth. Perhaps a portent of what his life would be, it had seemed as if the sun had vanished behind clouds, as if the Lehmanns' world was for a moment made brittle.

# 2

# A Burst of the Old Music

Fieldhead was Rudie's making, a fortress, a secret setting for childhood, a melding of earth and water, a retreat and entire world with a perfect exclusivity of enchanted possibilities. It was never ideal. The house seems to have been built awkwardly in its surroundings, few of the windows looking out on views of garden or river. Rather, the house let in glimpses of another, less fortunate world beyond that heaven that made John Lehmann forever yearn to recreate for himself 'a focus of harmony and order, a walled garden of meeting and making'.

If there was carelessness in its design, it may be because Rudie conceived it first as a bachelor home. But there was also something destined, inevitable about its fate. It was in 1892 that Rudie took a 90-year building lease at £40 annual ground rent on a field that led to an old ferry at the edge of the Thames in Bourne End from its owner, Arthur Hammersley. Here he built the house and named it after his parents' home in Sheffield. Its proximity to the water and friends was important. Next door was the late Georgian 'Abney', where Hammersley lived with his wife Violet, whose grandiloquent and unusual beauty could be seen in a gondola propelled by her imported gondolier, Giulio. The Hammersleys were probably Rudie's closest friends. Another close friend was Lord Desborough who lived nearby at Taplow Court near Maidenhead.

New it might be, but Fieldhead yielded nothing in style, sporting its own grandeur as a neo-Queen Anne, post-William Morris confection. Described as 'a dwelling house with Pavilion and Boathouse, flower-garden and orchards' it became grander after Rudie's marriage to Alice. In 1898 he acquired the freehold and in 1906 added a piece of land that the family christened Pegler Park. The library and childrens' wing finally made Fieldhead a family home.

The separateness that distinguished Fieldhead was accentuated as Bourne End developed and lost most of its charm. To John, the ugliness that threatened to spoil the village – the opening of a row of shops along the Parade, and the buildings that gracelessly sprang up wherever there was space for them – was almost invisible, so enclosed did the house seem.

The railway was partly to blame for the changes. At Fieldhead, it crossed the river at the bottom of the garden, with a station and shunting yard on the north side. But for the young Lehmanns such disfigurement brought only romance, the keenness of sound and smell, the reassurance of bodily work forever going on, outside but eternal. They were examples of Railway Children, and there is something in Rudie himself – a remote, kindly fatherliness – suggested in the final pages of Nesbit's novel, when the children's Daddy finally comes back into their lives. Nesbit, of course, would have perfectly understood that precious other-worldliness so essential to the Lehmanns.

In 1950 George Allsop, son of the Bourne End grocer, remembered the calls of the Lehmanns at play. When all was quiet, he and his friends would climb through a hole in the fence and explore Fieldhead's garden. 'I remember the fountains of pampas grass and the festooning roses', Allsop wrote, 'and the eddies in the river at flood-time, as part of my growing up ... it was always a place rather of mystery and remoteness to us, with the occasional presence of your parents and family to bring it to life.'

Lehmann would speak later of the 'magic walls' of Fieldhead, but those walls, intangible as the creeping spoliation of the village around them, contained a garden whose effect on John would be unalterable and indestructible. 'I was born to this house' was a creed as much as a statement. Being perfection, it could never be forgot. It was a central truth that Lehmann recognised, admitted and never regretted, and it made possible the beginning of his life in poetry.

In his first volume of autobiography, *The Whispering Gallery*, Lehmann demonstrates the habit of a lifetime by listing some of the plants that made Fieldhead's garden (and river) irresistible to him: roses, clematis, ceanothus, honeysuckle, violets, daffodils, primroses, narcissus, lilac, syringa, Mexican orange, peony. Whole pages of his personal journals are filled with such catalogues: they stand apart, for he never lost the pride he found in them, marking the seasons as they budded, bloomed and withered. It was a love that seemed to lead Lehmann directly to a pastoral, fully romantic and sometimes romanticized, expression of nature and life.

Perhaps for the young Lehmann the effect was almost too botanical, too prosaic, for in a sense he did not attempt to transfigure what he saw in the natural world of leaf and flower, but put it down rather as a still life is recorded on paper, a distillation of some apparently Edenic happiness. Lehmann never could preconize a subtle changing of the fact of nature into anything other than what it already was.

So often Lehmann represented but did not interpret what he saw in the natural world. The appreciation that Fieldhead had instilled in him, always fond, became cool, architectural, distanced by his hand. Perhaps it was a sign of the intensity he felt towards it as a child. In later life, certainly, he saw that his home had been 'the perfect pattern of earthly arrangements and Fieldhead the very hub of the world, and for a long time I found it difficult to believe that any other real centre of intense life could exist, or that happiness might have to be fought for jealously and ruthlessly'.

\*

That 'very hub of the world', that bewitched island of which Rudie was the

Prospero, had made its patterns by the time John was born. Three daughters had established an almost overpowering influence into which he had to work himself. The femininity was formalised at the Pavilion where Rudie had begun a private education of his girls, a scheme so successful that soon the facility was extended to the children of local friends. In *The Swan in the Evening* Rosamond has left a dazzlingly impressionistic impression of her schooldays within the brick and stucco Pavilion's walls where a truly Froebel regime was introduced by Rudie.

John's education at Fieldhead, begun around 1913, was affected by the fact that shadowed him through childhood: his infancy and gender against what had already been achieved by the strong sisterhood. Behaviour, morals, taste, all had precedent for him to inherit, the right of the family's baby. He was a willing and behaved pupil, never daring to show the comic devilry of Beatrix who could defend herself against Daddy's criticisms: 'I am a cow' she once explained, enacting the fact with movements and expressions that had everyone collapsed into laughter.

So much had happened before he came. There were the kennels, once the homes of long-dead dogs, three of which had been converted into little houses for Helen, Rosamond and Beatrix (it was 1904 when Barrie's Mr Darling first slept in Nana's kennel in *Peter Pan*). Helen probably did not take to hers; Beatrix, in her self-adopted role of 'Lone Scout' which gave her marvellous opportunities for her parodic gifts, exulted in hers; for Rosamond, the kennel's domain was a place where privacy led to knowledge. The kennels were made more wondrous by being close to the kitchen garden, a patch that seemed a world apart to John. It was the place where his young boy stands, nectarine in hand, listening to the floating music from the steamer passing under the railway bridge. When his demands for a kennel of his own became irresistible, the gardener knocked together a contraption that had to serve.

The girls were also united by the Fieldhead Debating Society, at which Beatrix denounced the execution of Mary, Queen of Scots because it had made orphans of her cats and dogs. There was also the Butterfly League, an association formed in cohorts with the Liberal Wedgwood Benn, another friend of Rudie's, though John was eventually allowed membership.

There was always a halo of Byzantine romance around his sisters that John felt he could not match. John idolized Rosamond, and was horrified one day when, like Goethe's Charlotte, he watched as her limp body (she was playing dead, no doubt with Beatrix as a particularly intense pall-bearer) was borne before him on a shutter. He could not bear the thought that death had stopped what he considered her tremendous genius. And he was always open to the teasing that such antics inflicted on him, antics of which Beatrix and Rosamond were masters.

Dogs were essential to Lehmann's happiness. They were an important link between Rudie and his son: when it came to walking them, the man and the boy formed a natural partnership, moving to the river-garden with its particular qualities of light and perfume, or across the water to Winter Hill and down into the boggy Cockmarsh. Winter Hill, a steep ridge of chalk, had little romance about it, but Rudie invented a dragon who lived there – an animal finally exposed in *Punch* as 'A cat, a tortoiseshell mother-cat! / And a very diminutive cat at that!'

Like Beatrix, Lehmann could communicate with dogs in an extraordinary way, which stayed with both of them throughout life. In 1956, when Beatrix was appearing in London in Anouilh's *The Waltz of the Toreadors*, the actor Trader Faulkner heard Beatrix and Taffy (her beloved red setter who was fond of suddenly lunging at a visitor's genitals) through the dressing-room door.

> Sometimes Be's voice could be heard rasping at 'her boy', sometimes croaking, and then the aria would change and the voice would croon softly like a mother with a child. Like 'The Ring' the sung dialogue was decidedly amorous and strangely musical. Be would whoop out 'Hoyo toho, Heiaha!' like some weird primaeval Valkyrie and the dog would make its canine Wagnerian response in a kind of coloratura baritone howl.

Singing dogs were rather a Lehmann speciality: John himself would become known as the owner of Carlotta, a spaniel whose musical interludes delighted Edith Sitwell and all others who fell to her charms.

The Boat-house was another treasured feature of Fieldhead's mystery. Here was mother's skiff, a canoe, a catamaran, an Australian racing-sculler and the 'Water-baby', a randan in which the family would embark equipped with all the impedimenta of summer outings on picnics. The vitality of leisure on water was paramount and it flourished on warm afternoons moving through water, thick with weed and wanding reeds and minnows. The mood was especially tense when it was the Boat Race or, most glorious of all regattas, Henley. When Lehmann conjured these scenes in middle-life, it was as if he could recall no mist across them. He was struck by the impossibility of defining experiences that 'set in motion a tune, a dance of words for images that all the years of adult life have failed completely to recapture or translate'.

Such images have at their edges blurred shadows of the characters that peopled his childhood years: A. A. Milne (whom Rudie recruited for *Punch*); G. K. Chesterton; Alfred Noyes, whose poem 'The Highwayman' was memorised by more than one generation of schoolboys; various members of the *Punch* staff, and John Drinkwater, whose Georgian poetry showed a way forward for John's early efforts. Close at hand were Violet Hammersley's children, Monica, David and Christopher, and an array of relatives and staff.

It was because of the garden that John discovered the relationship that, among the servants, meant the most to him, for the garden was the province of the man who had watched his father create Fieldhead and had helped him fashion it into the paradise it had become.

> I saw your Father's hand obliterate
> The tracks where once the village farmers brought
> Their loaded wagons to the landing-place,
> The inn, the cottage gardens that had pleased
> So many eyes long fastened in the grave
> To make the spacious lawns that now you grieve
> Must vanish too; but all the runes of love
> Will be rubbed out in Time; and only leave
> The river ...

The words are those of the Gardener in Lehmann's dramatic poem 'The House', written for the Third Programme and subtitled 'An Eclogue for the Air on Themes Suggested by Living in an Age of Transition'. It is Goodman, in 'The House', who listens to the Narrator's remembrances, recollections that turn the piece into an apologia, a plea for understanding the fact that the Narrator could not help his class, his privilege, the gift of happy childhood. Like his father before him, he was helpless to alter it, and made every effort to let in the outside world. Earthly, all-seeing and lightly carrying his prime knowledge, the Gardener listens, uncriticising, recounting the planting of tree and shrub and setting of lawn, while from the hidden places of the garden come the long 'Coo-ees' of the playing Lehmann children. 'It is never the same', they call, 'What have we to do, With the people who've changed from The children you knew?'

Goodman was a confidant to John, a man of principle, fiercely committed to his beliefs and a God-fearer. During the Great War his dissatisfaction with the Church dislodged his faith, and he turned his back on Christianity, undergoing a pagan conversion that thereafter had a healthy contempt for organised religion. His political ideas were strong, too. Once a reliable Liberal, he converted to socialism – changes of allegiance that were mirrored in Lehmann's political life. 'I am also haunted', Lehmann wrote over forty years later, 'by an image of him shadowy in the late summer twilight, with the darkening mirror of the water behind him, locking up the changing-rooms and the big roller doors of the Boat-house, suggesting to my imagination some imperishable country god in humble disguise as in the oldest legends, and the river beside him flowing like Time into the night.' In 'The House' Rudie is spoken of, always with affection, praised for his goodness to neighbours and friends, but he does not speak. It is Goodman, the hired help, who listens and explains and marks the passage of years with dignified comprehension of all it means.

Beside Rudie's kindliness, that capacity to be, as his son put it, 'a crusader for the destruction of intolerable woes', there is always around him a sense of withdrawal. In 1910 he had again been returned to Parliament, but his declining health hastened his retirement shortly after, so that by the time John was three years old his father had already begun to move into the shadows that would soon engulf him. Watchful, tolerant, appreciative of his children, Rudie nevertheless believed their upbringing was the duty of Alice and his staff. His easy charm and humour were threatened by the quick moods of anger that seized him without warning, a change of character perhaps brought on by an illness even then at work in him. One of the traumas of Rosamond's childhood was hearing her father shout at her mother. It cut through the hallowed contentment that was meant to pervade Fieldhead. And yet it is as a victim rather than an aggressor that Rudie comes down to us, because he was beginning to be as lost as Lehmann's childhood would always seem lost.

> If I could remember
> If I could find the children we were then,
> If I could question, reconstruct,
> I might know the explanation
> Of more than a one-man sense of loss.

Of his mother, Lehmann would have less to write in autobiography or poem. To the end of his life, he was guarded in what he said of her. His autobiographies offer the merest glimpse of a woman of great natural graciousness and understanding. The glimpses are dishonest.

*

The infrequent buses to Totland Bay stop conveniently for Madeira Road. Pass Inglefield Nursing Home and the Sentry Mead Hotel and a board advertising Turvell's Field ('an open space for use of the general public: S. Henderson, Clerk'), cross Cliff Road with its signposts left to Alum Bay and right to Colwell Bay and Yarmouth, and follow the sign to 'Beach Pier Toilets' along a path, under a bridge, that runs below Stokes Green. It leads to Totland Bay's promenade, almost deserted this afternoon, its rusting pier inaccessible, though a man straddles it, painting the struts. Tea and ice-creams, and a smell of frying hamburgers, can still be had at its entrance.

One family has braved the beach. A boy in a baseball cap tiptoes into the still, very blue sea. His mother wears Colours of Benetton. The man with them, young, tattoed, his arms smooth brown, looks dispirited, stares at sandcastles perhaps made by other hands safely from the water's edge. He shores the defences with a red spade; there is a spade of blue, too, and a yellow bucket: primary colours for the primary activities of the seaside. Two cars above the beach point out to the Solent. One is burned out, ignored, in the other an old man dozes inside an anorak and peaked cap. Some youths pass by, laughing, perhaps to impress the girls they are with. One tells how as a boy he used to crawl through a hole in a Totland garden and come out below the pier. They walk away, towards the closer view of Hurst Castle, surely one of the most abandoned, desolate ruins of England's coast-line: its very aloneness accentuates the compactness and safety of the Isle of Wight.

For Lehmann, Totland Bay, the place where the Lehmanns holidayed for the years of his childhood, always stood for 'a special romance that nothing which has happened since has been able to change ... There was something about it all, a spirit that wouldn't leave one alone. I remember how I used to be almost tormented by the feeling I had to make something out of it, a painting, or a poem, or a thrilling story in which it all played a part, all the landscape and all the people.' Rosamond, who seemed so much older and already on the edge of the adult world, was able to use her sensations; John could only be in awe at the rich, overladen poetry the island inspired in her.

The excitement of the annual excursion from the mainland was intense. For weeks ahead, John collected issues of the *Magnet*, of *Tiger Tim* and the *Children's Magazine* in readiness for the departure by paddle-steamer. A walrus-moustached porter helped load the family's bags on to the boat, sometimes the *Solent*, sometimes the *Spithead*, and the journey began, passed either on deck or in the red-plushed saloon, eating slab cake and drinking black tea. A particular joy was going down into the bowels of the vessel where the engines churned and everything stank of shrimps and salt.

Through the mud flats they would coast into the open channel until the Needles came into view and Totland Pier, then a working structure, was reached. There was still enough afternoon left for the family to find the lodging house in the village of redbrick villas and flint turrets above the promenade, to meet Mrs Scovell the landlady – whose own family were uncomfortably squeezed into the back end of the house for the duration – and apportion beds, and then race down to the shore for the first annual taste of delights to come, bathing and explorations with prawning nets that took them further than the furthest bathing huts in search of hiding shrimps.

And then the days would settle into an endless choice of delights. On afternoon walks they would make for the bays of Colwell or Freshwater or, a favourite destination, Alum, with its cliff faces sandwiched with sand reds, ochres, mustards, yellows, browns, to be etched away and taken back to the lodgings for grinding and arrangement into bewitching patterns. Below Alum's cliffs, that might be reached on foot or by the pleasure boat the *Duchess of Fife*, close by the Needles and lighthouse, they would bathe; Rudie would dance and Peggy would dance. Rosamond was once rowed to Alum Bay by a boy who had invited her and Helen to look through his telescope from his roof and had sung 'Sausages and cherry jam would be nice for tea' at her from a tree. He had taken Rosamond out in his boat one night and showed her phosphorous dancing on the surface of the water. John had been a little nervous of this boy who seemed to be beckoning his sister even closer to adult pleasures.

Beckoning, superior even to the allures of Alum, was Tennyson Down with its great drag upward and across the cliff tops to the place where Tennyson's Cross stood, testament to the Bar crossed, to the Pilot met face to face. If there was the life of poetry anywhere on the island, it was celebrated here, made wild and eternal by sea, wind, sky.

After childhood, the place retained its wonder for Lehmann: 'And I'd climb up to the top of the Tennyson Down, and peer over the sheer white cliff by the Cross – there always seemed to be a tearing gale blowing – and shout out loud to the gulls and the grasses as much as I could remember of Ulysses and "Break, break, break".' By then even youth was beginning to fade. The family no longer emigrated as one, Rosamond no longer ploughed over the downs, burying herself in the deep heather, picnics were no longer packed and immortalised by Daddy ('And Peggy as waitress played her part, And John fell into the gooseberry tart') or teas taken at the refreshment room below Alum cliffs; the children, tired at evening, no longer walked through the turf and watched for the lights of Bournemouth Pier to come out far beyond the sandbanks.

*

There must have been a moment when Lehmann realised his childhood – that irretrievable age of Nesbit – was over, when the quality of everything silently transformed itself into something else. Did this happen at Totland Bay?

The family was there in August of 1914, when, on the 4th, Rudie read to them the declaration of war against the Germans. He conformed to a popular misconception: he told Alice, 'It'll be over by Christmas.' Despite whispers that the Germans were about to overcome the island, the Lehmanns stayed on, defying the popular decision to evacuate. The women of Totland began making clothes for soldiers. Rudie noted that 'One of the marks of patriotism amongst our ladies is the possession of a pair of pyjama legs.' Rumours flew everywhere: the Hun had sunk the British fleet; soldiers were about to be billeted on them; people loitering near one of the island's forts would be shot; spies must be looked for.

Almost perceptibly, innocence was marred. Across the island the sound of gun-practice rattled, and barbed wire marked boundaries and enchanted places now cut off. Marie Hasewitz, a German employed by the Lehmanns as a children's maid, was declared an 'alien enemy' and Rudie had to accompany her to Newport for registration. She returned with him to Totland Bay and settled down to making yet more pyjamas for the Red Cross, just as Helen and Rosamond were knitting khaki mufflers to Lady French's specification in *The Times*: two yards and a half long and twelve inches broad. As with so many happy incidents concerning his children, Rudie communicated all this in the pages of *Punch*. 'There is love knitted into them', he wrote sentimentally of the mufflers, 'and admiration and gratitude, and there are quiet thoughts of beautiful English country-sides and happy homes which our soldiers are helping to guard for us, though they are far away.'

While the girls made for the soldiers, John was doing his own growing-up and beginning to write poems. His earliest efforts are bound together, sewn into a neat little book of folded sheets as 'John's Collected Works': Poem I (inspired by accompanying his mother on exhausting trips to Maidenhead) – Shopping Shopping Never Stoping; Poem 2 – The train / is passing / in the / rain; Poem 3 – There is a cow with my bow-wow. It was in *Punch*, on 26 January 1916, that Rudie communicated another, more ambitious effort of John's, in which he squeezed everything he could from rhymes.

> Summer is coming,
> Then the bees will be humming,
> Birds will be flying,
> And girls will be buying,
> And boys will be running,
> Oh, hail! Summer is coming.
>
> Summer is coming,
> Then the fox will be cunning,
> And all will be glad,
> And none will be sad,
> And I hope none will be mad,
> And I hope none will be bad;
> Oh, hail! Summer is coming.

There is such unsullied romance here, the words of a boy who believes in the inevitability of nature and season, and who can see through his father's insistence that the lean-to shed at Fieldhead (immortalised by Rudie in 1914) is a palace made of ivory and gold and guarded by dragons.

> But John,
> Who's a terrible fellow for chattering on,
> John declares
> They are Teddy-bears;
> And the palace itself, he has often said,
> Is only the gardener's lean-to shed.

There is perhaps a sense in which the war seems not to have affected the living of life at Fieldhead as the girls grew through adolescence into young womanhood, as John turned from baby to boy, obsessed with caterpillars and the plates in *Butterflies and Moths of the British Isles*, by what could be made of Meccano, by postage stamps from far-off countries, by all manner of pursuits that were found in the magazine *Hobbies*. There were still picnics, always the river, and in the winter the paper-chase for which Rosamond tore up *The Times*. And there were dances, strange social gatherings marking the emergence of Rosamond and Helen and Beatrix as women, of which Rosamond wrote in her novel *Invitation to the Waltz*, with its portrait of John as her brother James, James with 'the searching appraisal of his fierce blue eyes. His strength lay in an absolute surface tractability combined with an absolute spiritual reserve and independence.' After Lehmann's death, the writer Lettice Cooper remembered Rosamond's description of John as 'comically ceremonious, lonely'. As a presentiment of what lay ahead, Rosamond's understanding of the essential nature of her brother now seems uncannily accurate.

While Alice gave over much of her time to charitable work, Rudie contributed to the war effort by instructing and drilling the Bourne End Volunteers. It drained so much of his strength, weakened by his writing work and the effect that Parkinson's disease was already having on him. His head trembled as he spoke, he had difficulty writing, his step faltered. For a moment, his disability was the only obvious canker that threatened to spoil what Fieldhead still was, but innocence is only confirmed by its corruption, by change and unlooked for knowledge. Thus is the age of Nesbit smudged, the mirrors frosted, and the magic of the walls exposed as the once-shared belief in a trick.

*

There was suddenly an axis on which, however events turned out, life was forever changed. When the war was young, in 1915, Edward Elgar began writing the music to a play adapted from an Algernon Blackwood novel *A Prisoner in Fairyland*, the story of a happy English family 'wumbled' by their inability to any longer see life through the eyes of a child. In a passionate confession of his feelings about his own childhood, Elgar poured himself into the artifice of *The Starlight Express* while in the real world there were Zeppelin raids on London, slaughter in the Balkans, and Belgium was being besieged. When he first played the music to his collaborators, they were overcome at the beauty of what he had written. With a stabbing poignancy, Elgar had fixed a moment at which change, despite all hope, happens, finishing the piece as the characters wait for a symbol of hope always flowering, the rising of the star. The sentiment seems almost too radiant, almost vainglorious, for its time, for a world where so much hope was being lost.

Just as *The Starlight Express* captured an atmosphere of what had gone before and could be no more, so did the years alter what at Fieldhead had once seemed forever possible. Innocence was broken by discovery. Among a family of Belgian refugees billeted at Fieldhead was a pretty, cheeky boy of about John's age, who one day took John into the bushes

... took his trousers down and sticking out his bum urged me to touch his arse-hole. He giggled a great deal while this was going on, urging me to push my finger just a little further in. He then asked if he could do the same for me ... out of so much that happened in those years, of which no trace remains in memory, I can clearly recollect that boy's bum stuck out at me, his laughing freckled face, and the surprising prettiness of the pink hairless arse-hole.

Transformation had to come. L. A. G. Strong, visiting Fieldhead as the Great War was closing in August 1918, was keenly aware of the qualities there that were shifting and petrifying. All appeared as it had always been. The girls took him out on the river, gracefully punting him across it. They bathed and talked in the sun, John preoccupied with some business of his own, or they took tea at an open window, almost sitting in the branches of a great tree outside it. And he pinned the moment. Three decades later he recalled Rudie's demeanour, the fact that 'Already he showed signs of the ailment which crippled his last years; his hands shook, and his walk was a resolute shuffle. He had a noble head, to which the slight stare of his eyes gave a formidable cast ... The beauty of the two older girls enhanced the radiance of the long, warm days, giving them an aura of romance which held no hint of pain, because the days were like an island. One could stake no claim: one would not come again. It was happiness without desire, a patch of sunlight, unregretted because indestructible.'

The magic walls of Fieldhead seem to have worked on Strong, but the gentle, eternal days of perfection were almost certainly more spoilt than he could ever have supposed. Disclosures beyond anything the laughing, freckle-faced boy had made to John, would begin undercurrents of dissatisfaction and corruption that stayed with him until the end of his life, and almost certainly with Rosamond, too. In his last years, Lehmann confessed to having had sexual relations with her. We do not know how often, or how far their intimacy took them. It may have happened when they were children. Miles Huddleston had a recollection that, if anything happened, it had been when Lehmann was at Cambridge. We cannot expect to find the evidence of it having happened; the proof is in Lehmann's telling of it to others. Whatever the details of it, the terrible knowledge that Lehmann shared with Rosamond can never have forsaken them.

# 3

# Across the Idyll

For each of them, the three girls and John, the moment must come when the walls of Fieldhead had to be breached. It was to Girton that Helen and Rosamond were sent, while Beatrix – perhaps, as Rosamond admitted after her death, the most talented of them – enrolled at the Royal Academy of Dramatic Art. She could not get away from her mother quickly enough, so oppressive was the atmosphere. For the sisters it was a leap into adulthood, for John simply the beginning of another and different sort of childhood. The importance of finding a good preparatory school, and one that would ensure his getting to Eton, was obvious.

Summer Fields in North Oxford had begun in 1864, when its first pupils had been the sons of Shirley Brooks, the editor of *Punch* (which may have recommended the place to Rudie). Its aim was to provide for boys' education and fitness, respectively supervised by its founders Gertrude Maclaren and her husband, on whose gymnastic principles the army based its Physical Training programme. It was four years later that the Maclarens got their first scholar into Eton; by 1916, one boy in three at Eton was an old Summerfieldian. Based on this industry, the school had spread out, apparently haphazardly, from its original building, recalled by Lady Burne Jones as a low white house, its veranda cascaded with roses, and a garden that seemed a small paradise. Across its grounds between the Banbury Road and the River Cherwell was a footpath beaten by the people of Islip hurrying into Oxford in 1555 to see the burning at the stake of Nicholas Ridley and Hugh Latimer.

By the time John arrived at Summer Fields in May 1917, the school was run by the formidable partnership of the headmaster Doctor Williams and his deputy, the Reverend E. H. Alington, both of whom had been at the school since the 1870s. What these two lacked in authentic scholarship they made up for with a keen business sense of what Summer Fields was meant to do: producing candidates for Eton and treating each boy as 'a clever little animal rather than as a miniature intellectual'.

There was certainly no lack of experience in the staff. There were the two Miss Hills, who came in 1903 to take charge of the bottom classes and stayed for 43 years; 'Codfish' Whiting, deaf, but a good teller of ghost stories, who had been Queen Victoria's masseur; W. S. Case, grandson of the composer Sterndale Bennett, who had been assistant music critic for *The Times* and now played the organ and taught the choir, as well as composing operettas, and all for a paltry salary. Case was the only teacher who could stand up to the Doctor's dictatorial 'Mount Sinai' manner. Once, in the presence of the staff, Case loudly informed the Doctor that he was a 'bloody old fool'. Matronly duties were performed by Miss Lilwall Peirce, known as Cussus, who had instituted her regime of encouraging resilient constitutions in 1896 and whose convictions did not extend to believing that little boys could be genuinely ill. There was also the more reassuringly named Nurse Bright.

John's time at Summer Fields was largely spent under the direction of the Reverend Alington who succeeded the Doctor as head of the school in July 1918. His meek, genial, snowy-white appearance belied his nickname of 'Bear', earned because of his bursts of temper. The Bear had strong, if not eccentric, preferences. He abominated 'Cambridge, Roman Catholics, Socialists, the Germans (after 1914) and all aspects of modernity', all this tempered by his distrust of 'the telephone, poverty, overdrafts, contemporary literature, social functions and foreigners'. He exercised discipline, and there were frequent beatings. It was teaching achieved often at the edge of fear, but Summer Fields escaped ever becoming a repository of childhood horrors, instilling memories that, years later, might be mixed but could be recalled with fondness.

There were strict instructions from Alice: 'You are to write to your father or to me every Wednesday and Sunday but you may write very short letters sometimes! Yes, buy a paper, a halfpenny one and ask matron if she will very kindly get you the proper kind of house shoes.' For the first weeks, Lehmann sobbed himself to sleep each night. The war seemed to be to blame for some of his discomfort, for his German name was eagerly picked up by the boys, who called him 'Leh*munn* the *Hun*'. Perhaps war worsened the food, stale bread startled into freshness by steaming, rotting fish and nauseous margarine. The separation from Fieldhead was possibly aggravated by letters from Rudie, letters that have a strange poignancy about them. Within a few days of his arrival, Rudie told him 'I went up to your room the other day and found the new fretsaw looking very melancholy and lonely. It will pick up again when you come home for your first real holidays.'

Rudie did what he could to bridge the divide, passing on news of the dogs and cats, congratulating John on being asked to carry a watering-can for the Head Prefect, telling him that his mother had been saving sugar for jam-making and that Sophy had used it for stewing rhubarb. For Rudie, a new loneliness had opened up: 'I miss you very much. It isn't very often that I get anyone to walk with me and the dogs.' And then there was the news sent by Rosamond and Helen, and Beatrix's witty letters, decorated with comic drawings and rattled off in her carefree way: 'Oh well Beloved … I haven't got a single thing to say and it's only two days to wait so I may as well bottle up.' And for John 'the whole web of childish friendships, passions and dreams, was torn away to become as if it had never existed'.

Summer Fields was, in fact, a tolerable substitution for what had been left behind. There were long walks, swimming and diving, and tending the garden. The Bear was in no doubt, sending a first report that praised 'A charming boy, developing along exactly the right lines ... universally liked.' John had no liking for the Bear or Miss Peirce, but warmed to the Doctor's wife, Mabel (composer of the school song) and, more crucially, to a young master whose arrival at Summer Fields had coincided with his own, Leonard (L. A. G.) Strong.

Twenty-one-years old, already married and working on a novel, published in 1929 as *Dewer Rides*, Strong was also a poet. It was probably due to the approval of Mabel Williams that he had been taken on at £120 a year to teach English (which also embraced History and Geography), Latin, French and Arithmetic. It was fortunate that at this time the English paper began to assume much more importance in the Eton scholarships, a development that partly explains why the Bear rather gave Strong's very individual teaching methods free play. It is possible that Strong became something of a father-figure replacement to John, for he could tell entertaining stories, sketch caricatures, and had a fund of enthusiasm and knowledge about poetry. In later years Lehmann suspected that Strong's interest in him might also have been sexual.

John became ill at Summer Fields in 1918, the year that the influenza pandemic resulted in such large casualties, convincing even Miss Peirce of his serious condition. He nearly died, according to his own ill-defined descriptions in the school history. The illness necessitated his return to Fieldhead where he was nursed back to health and duly despatched back to Summer Fields. Was it at this return that Beatrix, disguised as an old lady, travelled in the carriage with him, only revealing her identity at the end of the journey? His last years at the school were less ravaged by his fondness for home, where the breaking-away of his sisters and himself, and the decline of Rudie, and the effects of war, had altered so much. Transformation had to come.

The Alingtons assured Alice that 'John has settled down again now, he was very sad to leave you and his Father, and told me he could only see the latter very little. I do not think he realises how ill his Father is and it is much better so, for to a child there is such a blackness about things, they cannot see beyond ... John is a very loving soul.' This undated letter suggests that Rudie's condition had considerably deteriorated during John's time at Summer Fields, but he battled against it as well as he could. Throughout, he was keeping his *Punch* readers informed about the boy's doings, and in 1919 wrote a poem 'The Milky Molar', based on John's news that 'Last week one of my back teeth dropped out in the middle of Greek'.

There were still the Totland Bay summer holidays to be written about, and the exploits of the dogs, Winks, Peter, and Puck. Meanwhile, John's imagination worked at the adventures of the Great White Chief Sosoko, whom he had invented to entertain the boys in the dormitory. In October 1920 he edited, with Peter Fairbairn, the first edition of the handwritten *Summer Fields Herald*, with its tantalising headlines: 'Appalling Whiskey Scandal!', 'Awful Orgies Found', and 'Latest in the Divorce Courts'. When he left the school in the summer of 1921 he departed with the Bear's hopes that he would become 'a shining light on the river, as well as a scholar', and the belief that he was 'never likely to do anything dishonourable or mean'.

It is likely that the Bear had given Lehmann and his fellows the statutory lecture on the facts of life, and in their last Summer Fields years they were 'extremely sophisticated about sex, and yet almost totally innocent'. The innocence persisted, though it was obvious that Lehmann's homosexuality was already established. In later life, he perceptibly thought that the strong attachments and admiration he had formed for his mother and his sisters somehow precluded his being able to see women as sexual objects.

*

Summoned into Eton on 20 September 1921, as a King's Scholar, Lehmann's emotional development had not yet had any great confirming physical expression, and he would not find it throughout the years he spent here. He was inhibited by the bed-wetting that would persist beyond Eton (how, one wonders, had Miss Peirce coped with it at Summer Fields?). There was a need for discretion lest the fact became public knowledge that he slept on rubber sheets. At one point in Lehmann's boyhood (we cannot tell when) Alice took him to see the psychoanalyst Ernest Jones, and somehow they began discussing *Hamlet*. 'The penis peeps through', said Jones, a phrase that Lehmann never forgot. The unpredictability and unpleasantness of his condition can have done nothing for the confidence of the fourteen-year old arriving at Eton.

Our understanding of what may have been the cause of his problem can only be limited. The enuresis may have had biological or psychological origins. If psychological, a background of family trauma may often be identified, pressures within a family that find their release in the bed-wetting; the relationship with the father may be at its root. Lehmann had it suggested to him that such uncontrollable urinating was merely a substitute for sexual orgasm. His remarks to Jeremy Kingston leave us in no doubt that his enuresis lasted well beyond the years during which it might usually have been expected to subside; at Cambridge he was still bed-wetting. The regularity of it may have been infrequent, and in those last years the problem may almost completely have disappeared, but the threat of it was still with him.

If research into the causes of enuresis has often been inconclusive, the possible effects on the sufferer seem obvious. A young man wishing to take a partner to his bed cannot feel confident that they will not wake in the morning among, to use Lehmann's words, 'piss-soaked sheets.' The problem distances the young man from his lover, and it is a fact that in many of his sexual relationships Lehmann's partner would be dismissed to another room. The enuresis makes the young man unclean, which he may see reflected in sexual activity.

## 3. Across the Idyll

Something even more potentially damaging may be at work: the separation of emotional and physical feeling. Of this, how often would Lehmann stand accused in the years ahead. Do we see its beginning in the enuresis? In every way it encouraged him to keep himself cut off, contained, against too much closeness. There is the suspicion that it also hampered what might have been a natural sexual development, contributing to his being a late developer. And then there were other problems; the furniture of dynasty, of expectation. At Eton, he was expected very much to prove himself the equal of Rudie (whose reputation, of course, was well-known to all), not least on the river. Meanwhile, Rudie's condition was rapidly deteriorating, so much so that the reins of Lehmann's life had to be taken over by Alice. Matters may not have been helped by the fact that Fieldhead was a mere ten miles from Eton. John had never wanted to leave Fieldhead and had again been taken from it, but it remained tantalisingly close. Returning to it was simple, and visits were frequently made.

Lehmann instantly appreciated Eton's paradisaical qualities, the wonder of Lupton's Tower (whose bell, so close to his room in College, brought sleepless nights), the escape into the 'timeless symbolism' of St George's Chapel, 'the spacious dignity of the eighteenth century' that infused his meetings with the Provost, M. R. James, who would give the boys breakfast, and chatter about detective and ghost stories; but the promised faded rapidly:

> All that was in the early enchanted days at Eton: they were like the upper reaches of a river among delightful and fertile valleys. All too soon the mountains gave way to the plains, and for years one navigated through a flat and dreary landscape, sometimes feeling the floods rise and carry one violently from one's course among the treacherous sandbanks, sometimes baling desperately to keep from sinking as cracks opened wide in the timbers, and still the waters came in; far off in the distance shimmered the famous cities of the delta, achievement, understanding, control; and then the reeds closed in again and the flood sank, and one was lost. I think I disliked myself more than Eton during those years.

The pressures on Lehmann were compounded by his coming into college at the top of his Election, a position from which he could only fall. He had worked hard for his scholarship. Having attained the prime place, he was faced with what was almost an unknown worldliness around him, typified by the figure of Cyril Connolly, who was still at Eton when Lehmann arrived.

There is something threatening in the idea of Connolly, pug faced and smiling, standing in the door of his room opposite Lehmann's in the Sixth Form Passage asking, 'Well, Johnny Lehmann, how are you this afternoon?' Even 34 years later, Lehmann's first account of Connolly suggests an invitation to hedonism, one which Lehmann was quite unready to take advantage of.

Connolly's room was 'notorious among us, dangerous, shocking and exciting', a cavern where Connolly had the company of younger boys at a time when it was not the done thing to form relationships across the different Elections, smoked Turkish cigarettes, spoke of scandalously modern books, night-clubs and liqueurs. It should not be forgotten that Lehmann was describing a boy who was to become one of his great literary opponents, but the inference is clear: at Eton, pleasure and decadence were available to those who sought it. The puritanical sensibilities preferred by Alice were in danger of being challenged; indeed, they had been overthrown by Connolly and his followers in their insouciant pursuit of pleasure.

Along the way, Connolly became a professional Etonian; there was something of the grubby schoolboy about him throughout his adult life. But while Connolly went on to make almost an industry out of having languished under Lupton's Tower, Lehmann left it behind, and was happy to do so. He seems never to have wished to belong to any of the supposed movements that established themselves there. 'Let me glory in the name of aesthete', Harold Acton had pleaded, bringing, with his brother William, a Mediterranean sophistication to the college, a concept radically removed from anything Rudie and Fieldhead had left Lehmann with. The confident smartness of Connolly eluded him, as did the vogue of Eton dandyism. Lehmann's rejection of it was fundamental and healthy: we may trace back to it that egalitarianism that informed the finest of his work, notably his years with *Penguin New Writing*. At Eton, there is a sense in which he did not belong.

*

All this accelerated personal exploration, plagued as Lehmann was by 'a philosophic darkness that swallowed me up, in which nothing seemed to have any secure meaning, no beginning or purpose or end, the darkness being filled with relentless questioning voices'. In writing, he searched for style, voice, and found several.

At fourteen he wrote a poem, 'Shadows', which betrayed a strongly Pre-Raphaelite romanticism with its opening exhortation to 'My Lady Ermyntrude of pallid face', while 'Autumn Night' was an attempt to organise some feelings about the war, with 'The souls of the murdered in battle.' More often, for the generation that had not experienced its horror, a reaction to Ypres and the Somme produced something inadequate and inappropriate. To them nonsense seemed as good a reaction as any. Lehmann wrote 'dotty' plays parodying his Eton contemporaries, 'mellers' such as *Toll for the Brave: A Horrible Tragedy*. There were stories, too, but 'the real object of them was always to paint some natural scene or effect' that somehow had to be wrapped in a plausible context.

Around 1923 Lehmann wrote a story, 'The Household': of course, the household is set on the banks of a river; of course, he is writing of Fieldhead. The consciousness of decay is the most striking feature of it.

## 3. Across the Idyll

It seemed to Arthur that something had gone out of their lives when the household had broken up, as if life had never been so full of purpose and colour since. The light that the household had shed had faded from them, and with it had faded a real but elusive happiness they once had known.

Now, at sixteen, Lehmann mourned the loss of Fieldhead, and the inadequacy of reunion: 'Whenever they come across another, the mask of years dropped from them, and they were as they had been in the great days of the house. And always when they parted the change that had taken place in the life of each showed a little more clearly, a little more poignantly.' It was a vision made the more radiant by its fading, the figures moving 'as in the benediction of a Golden Age'.

It is in a broadsheet poem, 'Dawn', with Lehmann's woodcut of Lupton's Tower, that we find a sudden, unexpected outburst of very real passion. The title suggests another attempt at a description of the rising of the sun and the coming day, but 'Dawn' is merely introduced as something to which the poet's troubled revelation may be compared: we are in the presence of something life-changing; things will never be the same again.

> Your beauty breaks upon me! – like the dawn
> With all her singing train,
> When from the starry wave she leaps and kindles
> Fire on her horse's main.
>
> O drown me in deep waters, where remorse
> May curse me not again,
> Where the blind soul's imperfection shall be hid
> From sin's eternal pain;
>
> Your beauty breaks upon me! – So my flesh
> Suddenly knows its stain,
> And through the anguished night of revelation
> Must burn and burn, in vain.

In 1966 Lehmann revisited Eton with Philip Mansel. They looked at the old group photographs of College that still hang on its walls. Lehmann identified himself and pointed to another boy in the picture, whom he writes of in his journal only as 'D. B. S.' Lehmann whispered to Mansel, 'That's the boy I was in love with!' The only boy with these initials who coincided with Lehmann's time at the college was David Babington Smith, who had started at Eton the year after Lehmann; his brother was already a scholar. Like Lehmann, Babington Smith was in College.

Their relationship had a devastating effect on Lehmann, who in the summer holidays of 1924 reflected how

It is curious how David has drifted from my mind. I hardly think of him now. I s'pose it's 'correct', as it had to be. It's an awfully queer thing, a friendship like that, – and rather interesting. Of course this all sounds as if I don't like him any more. No, but I'm seeing him in a saner light, perhaps, with the dawn of other hopes – e.g. last evening, such a wonder, in a scented mist-rising garden, with a full moon.

What is clear is that 'Dawn' signifies the awakening of homosexual feeling in the adolescent Lehmann, that 'anguished night of revelation'; the need to come to terms with the 'blind soul's imperfection'; 'an awfully queer thing' had certainly happened. The flesh, at last, had been stained. The confrontation is perfectly stated: sexual attraction versus the wonder of nature, the prospect of carnal enjoyment against aesthetic appreciation. It is a recognition that should bestride our understanding of Lehmann's future.

The changes at Fieldhead were only too perceptible when the summer holiday of 1923 began. Rosamond was there with Leslie Runciman, whom she married that year. Helen had married John (Monty) Bradish-Ellames three years before. Beatrix was touring with a theatrical troupe of old Harrovians. Rudie was attended by a Nurse Lewis, but still able to get onto a launch, full of interest, talking and demonstrating.

Much of Lehmann's time was spent roaming the country lanes in search of Bim, a dog who disappeared. With another dog, Bridget, he walked to Winter Hill meaning to sketch but was distracted by a perfect view of the Henley regatta, where 'the sentimental strains of the band are hopelessly intrusive'. Out in the tub-sculler, he and Beatrix rowed while Rosamond coxed. One of his crazes was for the explorer Nansen, and he wanted to go on Arctic expeditions, but settled for some time in North Berwick, seeing the gannets of the Bass Rock in the Fourth Estuary. In the city of his ancestors, Edinburgh, he saw St. Giles and Princes Street and the National Gallery's landscapes, 'all of which nearly I wanted'. Before returning in autumn, he went on to the Runcimans at Doxford, and to the Bradish-Ellames at Minehead, where Monty's mother took him to see a western at the cinema.

\*

At Eton, Lehmann was already being exposed to a circle of writers, beginning literary associations that would last a lifetime. Here were Connolly and Harold Acton before they left for Cambridge; Rupert Hart-Davis, Anthony Powell, Robert Byron and Alan Pryce-Jones before they left for Oxford; Eric Blair (who would become George Orwell) before he left for a job with the Imperial Office in Burma. But his first close working relationship was with Dennis Wrangham with whom he shared the editorship of *College Days* (anonymously; it appeared as 'Edited by Present Etonians'), an occasional periodical that had been published since the end of the war. Lehmann remembered it as an attempt at an Eton *Punch*, to which he and Wrangham managed to attract a string of distinguished contributors, among them Alfred Noyes, Rose Macaulay and John Buchan; rather than moving heaven and earth to discover new talent, the youthful editors preferred age and experience.

Whatever Wrangham and Lehmann's literary talents might be, *College Days* was moribund, only really enlivened by the advertisements for Koh-I-Noor pencils, Aertex underwear and the Windlerosa Tea House in Windsor. In the first Wrangham-Lehmann issue, no. 11, published for St. Andrew's Day in November 1924, Lehmann contributed a poem that shows how he was struggling still with juvenilia. The rhymes come so thickly that one recalls his very first attempts, when rhymes were very nearly all. 'Aunt Jane' tells the story of a presumably elderly relative who takes cocaine and goes insane and drinks champagne which will not clear her brain. It must be either the drug or the drink that encourages Aunt Jane's surrealism.

> Feverish
> She shrieked, 'Explain
> Why passengers mayn't leave the train
>
> While in motion,
> Or again,
> Why the Spaniard
> Comes from Spain!'
>
> Curates soothed her,
> 'Twas in vain;
> 'Soup is soup!'
> Was her refrain.

In the *College Days* for November 1925, there is what E. F. Benson would have called a 'spook' story, 'The Man in the Corner', in which Lehmann tries to whip up a frenzy of diabolical atmosphere, ending up with almost as many ellipses as prose. Conventional and unconvincing, the man in the corner's gruesome death at least upsets the charwoman who discovers the body. In the well-worn below-stairs style so beloved of ill-educated drudges, she bemoans the fact that 'It was 'orrible finding 'im like that when I came in the morning. I shan't forget it in a 'urry.'

Lehmann appreciated he had come to Eton at a 'fortunate' moment, for he had circumvented having to attend Lower School, and his position as head of

Election gave him privileges that were enhanced a year later when he became Captain of Chamber, responsible for discipline. Given the power to punish boys, Lehmann considered himself 'just, but severe because I did not see how I could keep control if I was not', although he was working against his nature 'and sustained only by this quite unsubtle conviction of being in the right'.

He enjoyed the Wall Game. Surprisingly, he was good enough to secure both his 'Mixed Wall Choices' and 'College Wall Choices' for 1924, and the following year again received his Mixed Wall, 12th man, marking him out as one of the top six players in College. In a possibly *risqué* example of the 'Characters of the Wall Elevens' that appeared in the *Eton Chronicle* in November 1925, we are told that Lehmann 'Uses his weight well and goes very hard when roused.' This perhaps concurs with his explanation years later that the Wall Game meant he could get very close to another boy's bottom without anyone realising why he did so.

Of course, it was as an oarsman that Rudie and Alice would have most wished him to excel, but it was not to be. He could never make the Eight. There is an irony in the fact that one of the most haunting photographs of Lehmann, young and full of hope, a Golden Lad that Housman might have eulogised, should be of him in his boating costume for the 1925 procession on the Fourth of June, wearing his hat bearing the name of his boat, the 'Dreadnought.' Alas, the 'Dreadnought' was a Lower Boat. 'I'm a rowing failure', he told Alice, 'and dislike the feel of it.'

Eton could not make Lehmann happy, and there were periods of ill-health, whether physical or mental we cannot discover. In March 1926 he was exhorting Alice to consider, even at so late a moment, his quitting Eton, pleading that 'a perpetual round of the sort of exams and cramming I go through at Eton, and have been going through for the last years, rather warps one's mental powers and balance and also one's completeness of outlook'. He wanted a rest before starting at Cambridge, needed an opportunity to break from the friends and associates he had already spent so much time with. H. K. Marsden, the Master in College, lamented the rather cloistered existence he had led in college; 'Bloody Bill' (as Marsden was aptly called) felt that 'more acquaintance with boys of a lower intellectual level but with other compensating good qualities would have broadened his outlook'.

Marsden's final report to Lehmann's parents of 9 August regretted that so capable a boy should be leaving with 'such a feeling of disappointment. I think he set himself too high ambitions, both intellectual and athletic, and has been too much depressed by his failure to attain them.' Having come into Eton with all the glamour of a distinguished rowing career in front of him, Lehmann had not allowed for the fact that, while he stayed at the top of his Election, he had been by far the oldest of his generation and the younger members of the Election had been able to catch up with him.

The boy, Marsden continued, was friendly and notably unselfish, having devoted much of his time to coaching on the river, but he had grown 'increasingly introspective, thinking a great deal both about abstract things and about himself ... He has very good all-round abilities but I do not think he is going to be brilliant at anything. I do not think that he has been any too well all this year ... worried himself over trifles ... I gather that he occasionally has outbursts of fury.'

It was not an enthusiastic envoi, and the legacy Lehmann left at Eton did not improve in the years that followed. There are too many tales of his plundering the knowledge of Eton scholars to enhance his own works and publishing it without the hint of an acknowledgement. The College's Librarian, Michael Meredith, remembers Lehmann as 'a mean-spirited man'. He never gave Eton a single book or manuscript, preferring to sell both to wealthy American universities, often without gaining the permission of his correspondents whose letters flew the Atlantic. 'He was not', Meredith recalls, 'a good friend to Eton.'

One day, Meredith asked Lehmann if he would sign the title page of a book that Stephen Spender had already signed. Lehmann turned the pages and wrote his name at the end of the book, rather than have his name on the same page as Spender. Once, when Lehmann told Meredith he had a picture of Mrs Benzon (Frederick Lehmann's sister Elizabeth), Meredith asked if he would be good enough to photograph the picture for him. He assured Lehmann he did not mean to publish it. The photograph duly arrived, but had been taken at such an angle as to make its usefulness impossible. Perhaps Lehmann was not a good photographer. Perhaps, by then, the tremor that would afflict him in old age was already at work. But in Meredith's suspicion that Lehmann had deliberately contrived to impair the quality of his gift there hides the feeling that is so often expressed about the man who grew from the Golden Lad of Eton: the feeling that there was an unkindness, or a want of something better.

# 4

# The Romantic Ninny

Lehmann did not seem prepared for Cambridge. Many years later he would write of it as wasted time, feeling that he hadn't begun to understand what life was about. In *The Whispering Gallery* this disappointment is obscured; it was 'a great release and new beginning. I floundered badly during my first term, broke away, and came back, and must have been a spectacle for my friends of overwrought nerves and spiritual confusion.' He had rooms at Trinity overlooking Great Court, shared first with Anthony Martineau and then James Brock, both of whom had been with him at Eton, as had Eddie Playfair; Jolly Boaters all.

At first, Cambridge seemed inhospitable, exposed as he was to the East Anglian cold: 'Knives and circles and snakes round your shoulders at night.' He went out cycling with Martineau, and when Brock acquired a car they explored the country even more. Not enamoured of the quality of teaching at Trinity, Lehmann in effect made up his mind to undertake his own education in English literature. He withdrew from Classics in favour of History and Modern Languages, which he thought might serve him better if, as seemed likely, he was to go into the diplomatic service.

Lehmann was being propelled in another direction, not least by George Rylands, called 'Dadie', a year Lehmann's senior, handsome, appealing, a friend of Rosamond's and with hair that Virginia Woolf thought 'the husk of corn'. He had fleetingly been assistant to Leonard and Virginia Woolf at the Hogarth Press, leaving them in December 1924 to study at King's College, where in 1927 he became the youngest don. Lehmann feasted on his book *Words and Poetry*, published 1928, and was to be both guided and influenced by Rylands' taste in literature.

In emotional matters, too, Rylands felt qualified to advise the younger man. Seventy years later, still living in the same rooms at King's College, Rylands recalls Lehmann as 'a romantic, full of feeling and enthusiasm, always falling in love with people. I was very fond of him. He was passionate by nature, he loved the passions, but he loved suffering too. He was racked with passion for his own sex. Not a first-class brain, not an intellectual, too romantic to be an intellectual. A great reader, and good at admiring other people, but John was old-fashioned where others were go-ahead, he didn't experiment. He was a romantic old ninny.'

It was Rylands who encouraged Lehmann to sit for the Charles Oldham

Shakespeare scholarship, a tremendous undertaking that ate up an entire summer. For that time, Shakespeare became Lehmann's life,

> ... and my mind was changed by the experience. In no other way could I have understood that Shakespeare was the key to the whole of English literature, the master mind that determined its course and depth and vitality so fundamentally that we can hardly conceive what our imaginative life – perhaps even our moral values – would be like without him.

Much of that summer he worked at Kidlington, where Rosamond, now married to the painter and communist Wogan Philipps, lived. It was not too far from Stratford, enabling excursions to see Shakespeare's plays there, the productions too often tatty and the acting hammy, but feeding his appetite. Poetry had altered Lehmann's perception of England. It acted, almost, as an anaesthetic to industrial dereliction and to urban sprawling.

> The river and the wooded slopes around Marlow were filled with the presence of Shelley composing *The Revolt of Islam*, and his magic boats sailed under the willows, reducing to ghostly vanishing point the spooning spivs with their raucous portable gramophones oozing sentimental jazz. [Lehmann never did really understand music.] On the downs of the Isle of Wight the rhythms of *Maud* and *Crossing the Bar* were what sounded in my ears, and not the back-firing, the honking and brake-screeching of the char-a-bancs that carried their loads of trippers on the daily advertised tours down lanes that were made for shepherd and farmer's cart. I lived in a timeless England of ideal presences, where all the centuries joined hands to praise ...

At Cambridge, there was a sympathetic hiding-place from modern ugliness in West Road at 'The Pavilion', where the novelist 'Topsy' (properly E. B. C.) Jones and her husband, the Hogarth poet Peter (F. L.) Lucas lived. Lehmann, like Cecil Beaton before him, was intellectually taken in hand by Topsy Jones, happy that she gloried in being 'profoundly disillusioned and pessimistic about ideas and human folly'. Sexual folly interested her too, and she could be demanding and successful in her probing of a young man's secrets. Over many an afternoon tea, she did loftier things such as introducing Lehmann to the poetry the elderly Yeats was writing. Lehmann took notice and Yeats was added to his heroes. Lucas, often tucked into his study (the marriage did not last), was less forceful but friendly. Like Rylands, he was a fellow of King's, and had been an Apostle.

In fact, it is the personalities of King's (and, more disastrously, Magdalene's) College that impinged rather than those of Trinity – partly no doubt because 'Trinity was too large for the complex web of gossip and scandal that was spun so closely over the denizens of King's'. Certainly, Rylands feels that Lehmann would have been happier had he been a King's man. At root Lehmann meant serious business and already felt bound up in a concern for real life, if he could only be certain of identifying it. How badly he needed to divine what happened to ordinary people; he felt a natural lack of ordinariness, from which Fieldhead had contrived to withhold him. The shadow of the Great War was something to focus the mind, spreading a pall throughout the Cambridge consciousness; hadn't he brought it with him from Eton, where he had tried to put into his poetry the waste of it all?

The mood at Cambridge was pacific. Past wars were condemned, future war was to be eradicated. At a safe distance, it was a time when the English consciousness needed to exercise its accumulated anxieties about what had happened between 1914 and 1918. R. C. Sherriff's *Journey's End* and C. K. Munro's *The Rumour* were two plays that made audiences think about what war was about; Lehmann saw Munro's play at Cambridge's Festival Theatre, then blessed by productions by Norman Marshall and even Ninette de Valois.

It was at Cambridge that Lehmann began his friendship with Julian Bell, a second generation Bloomsbury and without doubt one of the most interesting and attractive of that bunch. His attractiveness, according to Lehmann, was not particularly physical; David Garnett remembered that he had lost his looks when at Cambridge. The photographs of Bell contradict this, and there is something immensely appealing in the thin, strong face, the youthful figure, and the ragged clothes wrapped around or falling off his body. The impression is of a boy who has never grown up, never felt comfortable in Sunday clothes and, indeed, seems not to own any. This was Lehmann's impression when Eddie Playfair introduced them, 'a great, untidy, sprawling figure of a young man, awkward in manner and dressed always in dishevelled clothes with buttons rarely meeting button-holes at the neck and wrists'. But staring from the photographs is a wild glamour.

The elder son of Clive and Vanessa Bell, Julian had gone up to Cambridge in the autumn of 1928 and had rooms in St. Edmund's Passage. The following year he moved into college and was elected to the Apostles. In some notes for a memoir written shortly before his death, Bell felt his had been a happy life, 'unusually' so, in which he might not have achieved much of note, but life had given what he wanted of it. His main wish, he said, was to be in a war. His schooling had left him with a taste for combat – from which he looked always as if he had victoriously recently emerged. At his public school, Leighton Park, a Quaker establishment near Reading, he was bullied and suffered from feelings of physical inferiority. His father wanted to make him a man of the world, and a Francophile, and it was arranged that Julian would go to the Pinault family who lived on the Left Bank. Bell seems to have been happy here from autumn 1926 until the summer of 1927, studying at the Sorbonne and learning about politics, art and literature from Monsieur Pinault (who was secretary of the Louis le Grand *lycée*). More importantly, he began to be a poet.

At Cambridge, there was consolidation and, with Lehmann, the beginning of a friendship that was to be of great significance to Lehmann, and to Bell himself. It was a friendship uncluttered by sexual difficulties: Bell was heterosexual, a disappointment to his fellow-student Anthony Blunt who hoped to deflect him from that course. It did not prevent Lehmann from giving advice on Bell's love-life. In November 1931 he was telling Bell that he had had a long talk with 'Helen' and 'It worried me a lot. I don't believe it's really any good that you should see much of one another for a while, and clearly it must be a final break for both your sakes.' Lehmann was clearly intrigued by the younger man's personality.

> He was a hesitant but obstinate debater, never voluble or overbearing; he was too anxious to discover the truth and too conscious of the importance of good manners in argument to want to gain a victory by the tricks of rhetoric. And yet strong emotions were held in uneasy control under the smile, and his nature was more complex than these discussions at first revealed. At one moment he seemed full of indolent charm, a sensualist who cared only for the good things of life: at the next one saw an entirely different side emerge, ascetic, hard-working, ruthless and battlesome. We kept up an enormous correspondence for years, mostly concerned with problems of poetic technique and the philosophy of poetry.

A substantial book could be written around that correspondence (one half of one has been) but it is enfeebled by the confines of biography. We can catch only a flavour of it

> ... the most detailed arguments and theories about couplets, quatrains, blank verse, free verse, cæsuras, rhythm and counter-rhythm, realism and romanticism, dialogue in verse and description in verse, clarity, obscurity, ambiguity and all the other subjects that two eager apprentice craftsmen in poetry can find to discuss with one another. The light has faded from them, the ashes are dead. And yet it was the most exciting colloquy in the world: the whole future of poetry, we felt, depended on these arguments; we were remoulding English literature nearer to our own hearts, and even our great differences of approach seemed to promise a spark of fusion out of which the new way of writing, the completely modern poem would be made.

Of most interest to us is the fact that the long debate with Bell stimulated new activity and passion in Lehmann's poetry. In a sense it is the root of Lehmann's devotion to it. The years of discussion with Bell did not start a new brilliance in Lehmann's poetry, rather they fed his unquenchable interest in the work of other poets. In this way, we may see Bell as the catalyst to something in Lehmann's editorial life, an opening to Lehmann's editing of poetry.

Ultimately, the outcome of their fevered letters and talks (and how wonderfully disorganised Bell must have looked throughout them all) dissolved into something that might be thought personally disappointing. Lehmann was not to be the great poet he longed to become, and Bell was to die in 1937. But they needed one another, responded, adjusted, pontificated. The arguments fortified Bell's resolve to reject romanticism and the styles that had predominated throughout nineteenth and twentieth century poetry in favour of a return to the eighteenth century. He hitched his star to the heroic couplet, thinking it possible of expressing all emotion. Lehmann was understandably concerned that by adopting so draconian a policy Bell was limiting, even inhibiting, his development. He told Bell 'I think there is something to be said for taking certain 18th century writers as models, as a counterbalance to Romantic licence and exaggeration. But it would be disastrous I think to imitate them.' As poets, however dimly Bell thought of romanticism, they were naturally Romantic, and their friendship, though never physically consummated, was essentially romantic.

Talk did as well as sex, and enabled the relationship to last longer (until Bell's death) than it would have had bed intervened. Lehmann wrote later of their 'endless discussions' as they strolled the Downs beyond the Bell's home at Charleston with his spaniel bitch at their feet, in Bell's rooms at King's College or in Lehmann's rooms, along the Backs of Cambridge, at Fieldhead where the somewhat constrained country-house atmosphere must have come as rather a shock to Bell. At Charleston, he cooked ham omelettes for Lehmann, before they turned again to talking of Pope, Swift, Herrick, the modernists, and assorted pretenders. It did not matter that in one letter Lehmann would be dismissed as a hopeless romantic; the next might insist that his poetry would last for hundreds of years. And, as the years passed, they were united, if not made indistinguishable, by a growing interest in politics, interests that in both cases turned to sorts of obsession.

\*

The *Venture* was the most professionally produced periodical with which Lehmann had yet been associated. Its first issue of November 1928 included one of his woodcuts (of daffodils) but nothing else by him. The contributors included John Drinkwater, Louis MacNeice, Clemence Dane and the poet Humbert Wolfe, the whole edited by Anthony Blunt – 'a bit of a cold fish, and intellectually arrogant' – and, from Magdalene, the twenty-year-old Michael Redgrave.

The magazine had been started 'with only one purpose: to publish Cambridge prose or poetry of any merit, in decent print at a reasonable price [1/6d]'. There had been a slight shift by the time the third number appeared in June 1929: now it would stand as 'a protest against the more licentious forms of Free verse, Surrealism, and Art Without Tears!' Graciously, it carried an advertisement for Oxford's periodical *Farrago*, but none for its rival, *Experiment*, published by

Cambridge's extreme Left and emanating mainly from Magdalene who thought the *Venture* neo-Georgian. The *Venture* was essentially a magazine of the centre; its editors believed that Cambridge in the late 1920s was not over-concerned with politics.

No matter: the *Venture* was well-produced, highly literate, well worth seeking out. A prized number is that containing William Empson's poem 'Camping Out' with its arresting first line 'And now she cleans her teeth into the lake'. (Less startlingly, Empson had also written a book, *Seven Types of Ambiguity*, that was to be of seminal importance to Lehmann's appreciation of poetry.) Other of the *Venture*'s poets included Jacob Bronowski, Kathleen Raine, Julian Bell and Lehmann himself, though he would later see the pieces published there as juvenilia, and drop them from his collected work.

Lehmann had become almost a different creature, for now he was the brother of the novelist Rosamond Lehmann, whose first novel *Dusty Answer* had brought her not only fame but a sort of notoriety when it was published in 1927. Remarkably, not only had Rosamond (through the enthusiasm of Dadie Rylands, who had recommended the novel for publication) won extraordinary fame, she had also become, simultaneously, a woman of tremendous glamour. It seems likely that Lehmann had only admiration for what she had achieved – there is no evidence that he ever felt the sort of jealousy that perhaps Rosamond herself was capable of – but in the shadow of her monumental achievement he can surely only have felt himself trailing behind. For now youth shielded him. He confessed to Alice that he found *Venture* 'very disappointing', its poetry mostly 'monstrously depressing in its straining after oddity and originality'.

*

Michael Redgrave, too, wrote poetry, although he was already getting noticed as an actor (in 1929 he played Edgar in *King Lear* and appeared in Milton's *Comus*, both productions directed by Rylands). Poet or actor, it was obvious that something glittering lay ahead for him. In *The Whispering Gallery*, giving no hint of his longings for Redgrave, Lehmann recalled him: 'Tall, slim, with curly chestnut hair and a romantic profile, he was an engaging embodiment of the ideal conception of what a young poet should look like and how he should behave.' When, the following year, Redgrave became editor of the *Cambridge Review*, Lehmann continued their association by becoming his assistant.

There seems no doubt that at his first meeting with Lehmann in early 1929 Redgrave became fascinated; by the time of their second meeting on Sunday 10 March Redgrave's infatuation was switching to love. On the 11th they lunched together, but probably not alone, though they walked together afterwards. Two days later, Rylands urged Lehmann to write a letter, 'not long but affectionate', to Redgrave; if he did not take this advice (he doubted whether this ever happened) he did not 'deserve to love or be loved'. Rylands continued in a vein that showed an intense interest in Lehmann's emotional life, and a sharp understanding of his personality.

> My dear, you must pull yourself together – *and think more about Michael than about yourself*: he is a dear creature and by that means you will turn his great liking for you into love. You will be no help to Michael if you allow yourself to become so jumpy, divided and neurotic. And pulling oneself together does not mean saying 'it is all utterly ridiculous': because a) it is extremely serious *and if it isn't* then I have no further interest in it or you: b) to dismiss it as ridiculous does not prove that you have a sense of humour (yours is very limited) but the *reverse*. A sense of humour is not needed just now but a sense of values ... In your love for Michael lies your return, your salvation and you have got to be prepared to endure doubts and fears and to make sacrifices.

It seems from this not only that Rylands was keen to influence Lehmann's feeling for Redgrave, but that if a coming-together of the two men could be effected it would be beneficial, in some spiritual way, for Lehmann. Surely here, too, are seeds of the difficulties Lehmann would so often have about relationships. Rylands thought falling in love with Redgrave would be the making of him, and the unmaking of the person he had been – 'jumpy, divided and neurotic'. Rylands thought that Redgrave, though not an intellectual, was cleverer than Lehmann, and could see that Redgrave, a romantic, a poet, essentially Tennysonian, was tremendously attractive to Lehmann.

Redgrave wanted more; when he said goodbye to his new young friend on Trinity Steps he wanted to fix another meeting. Lehmann suggested nothing beyond a vague invitation that Redgrave might call to see him at some time. 'But I will try to be honest', Redgrave told him on the 21st.

> I love and respect you vastly; I want to be with you and talk to you and see you; I think about you a good deal; I miss you. But there is this, which I should tell you: I am not at all what you think me; I am shallow, selfish (horribly), jealous to a torturing degree, greedy, proud and self-centred; I have grasped at people's love and done vain and stupid things to get it; I am at times hideously immoral.

The rich, generous overstatement of a passionate young man, or merely a confession of flawed character? In the same letter, Redgrave also admits to understatement, but he wanted to admit these faults to his new young lover, to be as truthful as he could be. On the previous day, Redgrave had celebrated his twenty-first birthday; the following morning, as he lay in bed, he had opened Lehmann's letter and laughed and cried to have it. 'You seem so straight, and kind, and somehow it seems wrong ... I do love you, John, and want you.'

There was more urging from Rylands, who may well have envisaged Lehmann and Redgrave as a pair that would go through life together. On the 22nd, he wrote

I am very fond of you and very fond of Michael and I am sure that this is a wonderful opportunity for him as well as for you and I don't want to see it missed and muffled. Michael has all your tastes and interests but of course he is not an easy person – what young man worth loving is easy? There is something intangible, elusive about him: he often baffles me: but I believe that by loving him and devoting yourself to him you will surmount that.

And so the relationship was indeed begun, fierce and quick, charted in the sudden flurry of letters that passed between them. On the 22nd, Redgrave was in a train to Reading, conscious that something new was about to happen in his life. Writing at his most arcane and fidgety, he told Lehmann 'There is a bird flying with the train. Where are you going, bird? Are you expectant, too? Why do nuns always have smart umbrellas? And why do fat and beery men in trains invariably have their fly-buttons undone? Everything is a jumble.' He had not realised in those first meetings how attracted Lehmann had been to him. Now he was reassuring him that they could mean everything to one another, while Lehmann gloried in the fact that at last he had found love returned.

They were separated later that month when Redgrave went with a reading party from Magdalene to Mortehoe in North Devon, where he read and dug on the sands after lunch and battled with writing beauteous poems with titles like 'Noon-Sea'. Whatever he did there, Lehmann's letters only had the effect of making the place seem unreal and Redgrave felt confident enough to tell him something of his past. For a full year he had been in love with Michael Garrett, getting nothing back from the devotion he had poured over him, and the infatuation had ended when Garrett himself began a new relationship with another man, denouncing Redgrave as sulky and remote. Something in his passion needed confirmation of his worth and attractiveness: 'O you do love me, don't you?' he pleaded to Lehmann, 'don't you? Why are you so far away?'

Redgrave sent him another poem, 'More Light', but nothing could bridge the separation. 'I feel it so much,' he wrote, 'that at night, when I blow out the candle and let in the starlight, and the smoke of the wick mingles with my breath and sickens me, I could cry for you. Each day makes me find something more in this love, so long forgotten.' Their knowledge of each other was so fresh and rare that at moments Redgrave could barely recall Lehmann's voice or face, as if he glimpsed him in a film, but he exulted in the thought of him, walking for miles along the beach until he came to a quiet place where he hollowed out a bed in the sand and, taking his clothes off, spread himself out to the sun.

# 4. The Romantic Ninny

*

In truth, Redgrave's rapture that protested deep love was muddled with a much more enduring passion for words, poetry and Shakespeare, wonders that he almost immediately knew would be the guiding stars of his life and career, offering that abiding satisfaction that nothing merely sexual could provide. Perhaps Lehmann was simply one of the last infatuations of youth, excused and lovely because lacking in care. April had barely arrived when tensions began to disturb the perfection. Now, we can only catch hints of what these may have been. The mere fact of enforced separation, that would be a constant threat to all of Lehmann's relationships, may have contributed to misunderstandings, or at least to a lessening of understanding.

No doubt exacerbated by the spectre of Garrett, Lehmann was expressing doubts that Redgrave loved him. Still Redgrave insisted that Lehmann was the centre of his existence, so fulsomely that it sometimes spilled over into triteness. 'Our love is beautiful to me, and I pray for the sunshine of you to make it grow; more beautiful, more lovely love. In the quiet of the river we shall be alone, with life only a humming top at our feet. We will talk and dream together. Such dreams do not fade.'

'I grow to love you more every day', Redgrave wrote from the Scole Inn near Diss at the end of May, but by 10 June the relationship began to untangle with unexpected speed. Some argument led to Lehmann shutting his door to him. It was too much for Redgrave, already distracted by the weightier attractions of language and career, and another separation ensued. Then, from Eastbourne on the 13th came the terrible confession that he was still in love with Michael Garrett, notwithstanding Garrett's current affair with a woman.

> It would be foolish to believe that I love you best, now, John. I can't, it isn't in my power – And please see that I would to God I could! You will always be a better friend to me than anyone else, for you come nearer to understanding me than anyone in the world. If you would be my friend still, John, it would help me more than anything. Don't think I am consoling you with this; I need your friendship, my position is every bit as unfortunate as yours. If you are proud again, and withhold it from me it will be blind and selfish of you. Don't think I have been deceiving you. Only occasionally did I suspect that my love for M was not quite dead … Say you will help me. Say you forgive me for such as there is to forgive. I shall always love you, John. M.

We might accuse this letter of dismissal as disingenuous if it was not apparent that it was the best, and most honest, that Redgrave could come up with. Its content is almost a vindication of the character assessment of himself he had offered Lehmann in the first days of their affair. Aware of the 'terrible injury' he had done to Lehmann he begged for an understanding of the terror that had engulfed him.

> Suddenly, the stars change, the whole world changes, and time slips back, back, and I am sick and sold at the inevitability of this awful love, that will not let me be, that I hate, yet cannot kill. I fly to you to help me, but forgetting you have been numbed, and cannot help me now. I could have lied to you and consoled myself, but I love you too much to do that. O John, what shall I do? I have been hurt, and I have hurt you.

There was another shift of feeling on the 20th when, having found Lehmann's letter righteous in tone, Redgrave told him it was best that they did not see or write to one another again. After reading this, Lehmann made a pencilled note on the envelope: 'But now I know you, I might make you love me. I might make something of you – on a quite different basis of love.' It was appropriate that Rylands told him that summer 'You have grown up a great deal since last year: I wish it was not such a painful process.'

Redgrave had rejected Lehmann's love. Now, faced with the prospect of losing his friendship, he told him it would mean his losing the little remaining respect he had for himself. In August, there was another separation when Redgrave went to Capri. When he returned he made what seems to have been an attempt to retrieve Lehmann's affection for him. The business with Garrett was over, for Garrett had brutally, but perhaps justifiably, stated that as well as their love for one another having faded, so had 'that second class article you call your friendship'. Redgrave told Lehmann 'I honestly and really care more for you now than I have ever done', but it was too late.

Whatever letters were written in the next weeks have not survived. When they resume at the end of the year it is as if their closeness had never been: an air of rancour had taken over, and Redgrave compounded the injuries he had served on Lehmann by trying to criticise his work. 'One cannot make a poem out of observation without comparison' he told him, hitting on the seemingly conscious decision of Lehmann's poetry not to alter what it depicted, or, indeed, impair it by any argument. 'Your danger as a poet', Redgrave continued, 'as you must so frequently have been told, is the exotic and fragile quality of your imagery.' Once again Redgrave was treading very near a truth, and, as always when faced by unasked-for criticism, Lehmann bounded back from it.

Preparing his reply to this genial outburst Lehmann scribbled at the bottom of Redgrave's letter 'You write like a person on whom The Light has broken. What has really happened is, I think, that you have ceased to have any ideas of art whatsoever. You never had much.' Responding to 'the bad temper of your letter' Redgrave made one more try at expunging the bitterness; he had only, he said, wanted to make sure that Julian Bell had not influenced his poetry 'for you are a poet worth more than any Julians', but there could be no happy ending now. And so the letters subside into scraps of polite, social gossip.

There remains a record by Lehmann of what may have been the final meeting between them as lovers, written immediately after Redgrave had visited him in his rooms. He asked Lehmann's forgiveness, admitting that he had acted brutally towards him, and though Lehmann gave it he could not accept Redgrave's kiss, 'too false, too hopeless, too reminiscent'.

Hopelessly, they sat on Lehmann's divan together, and one of them (presumably Redgrave) turned out the light. Lehmann could only moan 'It can't end like this' and 'It isn't true' as Redgrave tried to soothe him. Then he sat at Redgrave's feet, clutching on to the man who had become an idol to him; he wanted to embrace him, but knew it would create a wrong impression, falsify the moment. Lehmann said 'Michael is here all the time. This is treachery to him.' Redgrave said 'He knows. And he is not for me.' 'But he is for me', said Lehmann, 'and always will be, and it is treachery on my part.'

Redgrave, perhaps desperate, laughed, and Lehmann lifted himself away from him, looking at Redgrave's face, paled and almost invisible in the dim light, that seemed now infinitely remote. Once more, Redgrave tried to kiss him and broke down in Lehmann's arms, but Lehmann's passion was stilled. 'That's for something else,' he said. 'It is too reminiscent.' There was the cold recognition that Redgrave was no longer behaving naturally, that his kisses had grown cheap, that Lehmann was being cheated. Immediately, Redgrave realised everything had gone and that Lehmann could no longer be cajoled back into anything romantically sexual. He snatched up his hat and gloves and left the room, stopped by Lehmann on the landing. 'This is good-bye then?' he asked, and Redgrave replied 'For a long time.' He ran down the stairs and Lehmann, in silence, let him out.

*

Lehmann's meeting with Redgrave had more or less coincided with an event that had been long expected. Years before, Parkinson's disease had almost removed Rudie from the family circle. When Barry Pain died in 1928, Lehmann asked Alice 'Was R. C. L. at all able to realise it, or didn't you try?' and in letter after letter to her, his father is not mentioned.

Rudie died in January 1929 (the death certificate gave pneumonia as the cause) before Lehmann, summoned to Fieldhead, could see him for the last time. Then, 'We were alone; I had never felt so close to him, nor so strongly the archetypal power of the bond between father and son, at the very instant when it had been broken – for me – for ever.' At Cambridge, flags were flown at half mast, and the Union had a minute's silence. The interment was at Wooburn Cemetery, Rudie's coffin draped in the flag of the Leander Club. It may be that the pain of Rudie's death was muffled by the protracted expectation of it, but in a revealing letter Lehmann showed the anguish he had stored up for the moment, sharpened by the tributes of Rudie that sounded everywhere. 'He seems to me more and more wonderful now', he told Alice, with 'every fresh thing I read. He is really a legend. I have never been able to say it, but I can't tell you how often I'd longed that he'd been in health during my Eton and early Trinity days. I needed his help and advice just as much as a hundred young men he took up in his bachelor days.'

The pain of regret was obvious, and the suspicion, the worst and so often inevitable, that he had not known his father well enough. Now, irrevocably, it was Alice who was left to do whatever needed to be done for their only son, and it was a responsibility that Lehmann probably did not welcome. There seem to have been whole areas of emotion ('I have never been able to say it') that were forbidden between them. Rudie's affection had always seemed more obvious, if a little unspoken.

The break-up of the family (so concerning to Rudie in 'The Household') was hurrying. There was the sudden perception of Fieldhead as a liability. Only two weeks after Rudie's death the house was valued for a possible sale, and in May Alice let it and went to see relations in America. Meanwhile, Lehmann compiled a book of Rudie's pieces, even though he must have suspected that their time had passed; literary fashion had already relegated his father to a backwater.

# 5

# Between Two Worlds

There seemed to be a professional choice available to Lehmann on coming down from Trinity. The first choice – which must have appealed to Alice and was not altogether unappealing to Lehmann – was that he should become a diplomat, a career in which his first cousin Sir Ronald Campbell, then First Secretary in Washington, had succeeded. The alternative was that he should take a post at the British Museum in the Prints and Drawings Department, a vacancy detected by Violet Hammersley. It might have been a perfect solution for someone as fascinated by art as the young Lehmann. Though a job as a curator might allow him time enough for his writing, Lehmann remained unsure. In preparation for such a career, a grand tour of some of the world's great art galleries was organised: in Berlin the Kaiser Friedrich Museum, in Vienna the Albertina, in Paris the Louvre.

In fact, when he returned to Fieldhead in November 1930, his life would take a quite different course. Throughout his travelling he had been working on a collection of poems. Rylands showed this collection to Virginia and Leonard Woolf, and in December Virginia wrote to Lehmann accepting the poems for the Hogarth Living Poets series; they were published the following year as *A Garden Revisited and Other Poems*. Weighed down by the responsibilities with which the successful Press had burdened them, and without adequate professional assistance, the Woolfs were looking for a third person to come into their business, and on 19 December Lehmann was asked if they could meet to discuss the possibility of his joining them.

From the first, Lehmann was aware of the difficulties he might be starting on. Leonard's reputation as an irascible and demanding taskmaster had proved itself in his unhappy relations with the young men who had preceded Lehmann – Strachey's lover Ralph Partridge, Angus Davidson and Rylands himself. Rylands and Julian Bell sounded alarms, but after meeting the Woolfs in January Lehmann's future was settled: now, he was an adjunct to the Bloomsbury set. 'Lehmann may do', Virginia noted, 'a tight, aquiline boy, pink, with the adorable curls of youth; yes, but persistent, sharp.'

The Woolfs drove a hard deal. Firstly, they offered Lehmann a partnership in the Press for an investment in the business of £5,000. It was a very considerable sum, and, despite Alice's willingness to help smooth the way, it could not be reached. Instead of their partner, he would be the Woolfs' manager. As manager Lehmann's brief included meeting authors, designing promotional material, stock-taking, preparing financial statements, fulfilling orders and distributing them, as well as travel up and down the country as the Press's rather hapless commercial traveller (a duty he did not relish, but tried to acquit honourably). Terms were decided and renegotiated: there would be a trial period of eight months with the prospect of a £250 annual salary with ten per cent of the profits – meanwhile, he would receive £100 for the first six months, £150 plus profits thereafter. There would be six weeks holiday, and from April 1933 Lehmann had an option to purchase his partnership.

Lehmann began work at the Press's home, 52 Tavistock Square, on 21 January 1931. It was not the address of an Elysium, not an office that proved the Woolfs' concern for their unfortunate, fully exercised employees. A thoroughly gentle-manly firm of solicitors (Dollman and Pritchard) inhabited the ground and first floor, above which were the Woolfs' living quarters. The Press's business was confined to the basement, the front room of which had once been the kitchen but was now ruled over by Miss Belcher and her assistants the Misses Walton and Strachan. The former scullery was the printing room, in which even now Virginia or Leonard might be found at work, despite the fact that most of the firm's printing was done elsewhere by modern machinery. Redundant galley proofs served as toilet paper in the lightless W.C. The manager's room was nothing more than a cupboard, and had cupboards inside it, an unopenable window and a deficient gas fire: it had once probably been a butler's cubbyhole. When it came to employment, the Woolfs clearly believed in squeezing the lemon. Leonard's temper was short, and his expectations tremendous. Mostly penny-pinching, he had a congenital tremor that worsened when dramas ignited. Miss Strachan probably missed her bus on more than one occasion when staff were detained at the end of the day to account for the mystery of a missing farthing.

Perhaps surprisingly, in the early months (when Lehmann had moved into a studio flat at 9 Heathcote Street), his relations with Leonard were untroubled, even grateful. He was at his most urbane, tutorial and bending, even friendly, and Lehmann listened and learned. At the same time, the Woolfs surely realised that he was ultimately going to prove a good deal less pliable than those who had gone before. It was soon clear that his contribution to the Press's success was considerable, and this was to be one of the most distinguished periods in its long history.

The first months had Lehmann overseeing the publication of titles the Woolfs had accepted before his arrival, such as the flapper-poet Joan Easdale's *A Collection of Poems* (Lehmann was distinctly unconvinced), C. H. B. Kitchin's commercially unsuccessful novel *The Sensitive One* (it sold well, for some reason, in Germany), and John Hampson's *Saturday Night at the Greyhound*. Hampson (a pseudonym for the homosexual writer John Hampson Simpson) had already had another book, *Go Seek a Stranger*, refused by the Press; Virginia identified it as Hampson's sodomitic novel.

Hampson was a writer to whom Lehmann showed allegiance in the years to come, and had been referred to the Woolfs by William Plomer, whose novel *Sado* the Press brought out in 1931. Lehmann's first meeting with the twenty-eight-year-old Plomer was the beginning of a friendship that lasted until Plomer's death in 1973. Indeed, it might be said that Plomer was one of the most constant of Lehmann's circle. Privy to the tangled components of Lehmann's life, Plomer – a homosexual, who never regretted that as a boy of eleven he had been seduced by a sailor *en route* to England in 1914 – had been born in South Africa, and become the most unlikely of sheep farmers.

Of central importance to Lehmann was the publication of *The Waves* (as with everything Virginia wrote, he saw it as the work of a genius), but Lehmann was to be almost shaken in direction by a foreign writer, the poet Rainer Maria Rilke. His *Notebook of Malte Laurids Brigge*, translated from the German, was published by the Press in February 1931. At once, Lehmann had found the inspiration that would fire his longing to write poetry. Rilke had died in 1926, leaving a body of work the majority of which had not been translated into English. For Lehmann, there was the prospect of rising to the challenge Rilke had given his imaginary poet Brigge:

In order to write a single verse, one must see many cities, and men and things; one must get to know animals and the flight of birds, and the gestures that the small flowers make when they open out to the morning. One must be able to return in thought to roads in unknown regions, to unexpected encounters, and to partings that had long been foreseen; to days of childhood that are still indistinct ... and to mornings by the sea, to the sea itself, to oceans, to nights of travel that rushed along loftily and flew with all the stars.

After seven months at the Press, Lehmann's publishing voice was heard for the first time. With Julian Bell he had already hoped to compile a volume of verse and prose by contemporary Cambridge writers, but the scheme had foundered. The idea of a state of the art anthology was revived in September when a poet, Michael Roberts, wrote Lehmann an admiring letter and asked if they might meet. Born in 1902, Roberts, resembling 'a giraffe that had taken to the serious life of learning', had been at Trinity like Lehmann, and was now working as a schoolteacher. Roberts saw in the work of many contemporaries unifying, revolutionary notes that seemed to make them relevant one to another, and finally, Lehmann and Roberts settled on nine poets who between them provided 43 poems; from Cambridge, Julian Bell, the American Richard Eberhart, William Empson and Lehmann himself; from Oxford, Auden, Cecil Day Lewis and Spender. Plomer and A. S. J. Tessimond had no such pedigrees.

The Woolfs accepted Lehmann's suggestion, and *New Signatures: Poems by Several Hands* appeared in February 1932, with a preface by Roberts. For

Leonard, the book was the manifesto of its generation, and there is no doubt that, at an important moment in history, the collection seemed to catch a shared feeling of rebellion and hope, both spurred by socialist fervour. *New Signatures* distinguished itself by seeming to put its contents into a context, even if F. R. Leavis thought its purported homogeneity was in doubt. As Lehmann noted, 'Several of the poets were already known individually; but the little book was like a searchlight suddenly switched on to reveal that, without anyone noticing it, a group of skirmishers had been creeping up in a concerted movement of attack.'

The reception of Lehmann's first collection of poems, *A Garden Revisited*, was quieter, perhaps befitting verses that reflected Wordsworth's definition of poetry as 'emotion remembered in tranquillity'. The *Cambridge Review* saw 'formalized reminiscences' in which 'there is nothing but rhyme and metre in control'; the *Manchester Guardian* thought the first of its two parts 'almost unbrokenly descriptive, and [it] suffers acutely from monotony of cadence, movement, mood and tone'. In the second part, however, 'he becomes active. He handles his forms. His emotion is now stirring … his verse lives and moves.' But too much here is stationary and lacks not only any hint of enlivening danger but transforming thought. It is, indeed, still life, nature as seen and, mostly, delivered raw to the page with classical allusions. The old enchantments of youth are accepted, nothing rifts perfection.

Another poet, one of the most promising of the new generation that made up *New Signatures*, was to offer perhaps the most truthful critique of *A Garden Revisited*. Surely, he asked, Lehmann's life was more interesting than Lehmann himself realised? – interesting enough to make poetry from. Wasn't there a dreamlike quality in the verses? Didn't Lehmann work on the outside edge of his poetic consciousness, retreating from what was real into a sort of genteel embroidery in a Cambridge Nature tone? Why did Lehmann pretend to be heterosexual in his poetry? Did Lehmann really care more for nature than having sex? Couldn't his poetry be more honest?

This was probably not what Lehmann wanted to hear, especially from Stephen Spender – but there are perceptive truths there. One of the problems that beset their long and deeply troubled relationship may have been in under-standing aspects of one another's characters too well; indeed, in seeing each one's personality to some extent mirrored in the other. The men had met for the first time at Christmas 1930, when Rosamond brought Spender to Fieldhead. The Lehmann-Spender link had a dynastic resonance, for Spender's father, Harold, had been Rudie's assistant editor on the *Daily News*. Lehmann and Spender had walked towards Marlow by the river. 'Very tall and slim, with a huge head of curls, he loped along beside me in the mild winter landscape, pouring out his views on the world, on how to find fulfilment and how to write and graphically described the life he had adopted in Germany, where he spent most of his time.'

In 'graphically' telling of his life abroad, Spender obviously spoke of the boys he had sex with, of the whole days spent looking for them, which must have excited Lehmann's interest in what might wait abroad for him. But in almost every sphere Spender was helping to light fires in Lehmann's imagined future. Spender extolled Germany for having emerged from the Great War without having succumbed to the corruption of the West, and it was in Germany, not England, that 'youth had started to live again, free of the shackles of the past, life without inhibition, inspired by hope, natural humanity and brotherhood in the springs of being'. It seemed such a promise; an ideal that might be attained if he could loose himself from Fieldhead and all it meant. Spender's enthusiasm did not end. 'In England we were chained still by guilt, ossifying bourgeois conventions, and philistinism. If only I came out to Germany I would see the beginnings of the new world for myself.' He told Lehmann that his enthusiasm had been sparked by Auden and the novelist Christopher Isherwood, who had left England and now lived in reduced circumstances in Berlin.

Spender brought Lehmann face to face with the presiding difficulty of his life. As across a chasm that separated their successful breaking away from their backgrounds, Lehmann saw the three poised before him: Auden, Isherwood and Spender, writers all. He already had his own credentials as a writer (*A Garden Revisited*, despite what he called its 'soggy' welcome, proved it) but, by his connection with the Hogarth Press, he was becoming the literary mid-wife, the channel through which other authors might get themselves read

> ... like a slowly tolling bell, I was to hear it for the next twenty-one years ... the unresolved dilemma of my life: was I to be the impresario of other people's creative work, or a creative writer myself? Each time I had some success in one direction, I was to feel the need of effort in the other.

It may be that Isherwood and Spender sympathised with Lehmann, but they were uneasy allies. They saw the benefits to themselves of Lehmann concentrating his energies on publishing, but made the right noises about the impossibility of this continuing if it hampered his progress as a poet.

Spender's relationship with Lehmann would always be especially difficult, as new opportunities to rediscover the unsatisfactory elements in each other's personalities came along. There is no doubt that Lehmann worked to further Spender's career. During his early months at the Press, he recommended Spender's novel *The Temple*, a distinctly autobiographical and experimental account of a twenty-year-old Oxford poet's adventures in Germany. He did not believe it would have large sales, but appreciated its quality, and saw accepting the novel as a way of later getting Spender's poetry. As for its homosexuality, 'the author is perfectly calm about it all, there is no attempt to strike a martyred attitude, and above all (from the point of view of publishing) there is nothing "indecent". In fact I believe it might get across.' It was a determined try, but the

Woolfs rejected it. When *The Temple* was at last published by Faber in 1988, Spender – one must say typically – made no reference to Lehmann's efforts to have it taken on by the Press.

For the moment, it seemed that Lehmann wanted to be made in the matrix of the trinity he stood in awe of, but from the beginning the truth was clear: he was the late beginner, the junior partner, the member allowed in the club on the nod of his superiors. And his superiors were not blighted by the dichotomy that he would always feel had damaged him.

One essential lesson at least had been learned: Lehmann must escape from England to the foreign country that would provide for his spiritual, bodily and political needs. His politics were removed from the broad liberalism of his father; by example, he was fixing on, at least, socialism. At the Press, this was almost *de rigueur*, even if Virginia Woolf seemed the sort of woman who complained about shopgirls: like so many of their set, the Woolfs' beneficence to the lower orders was at its most pronounced when theoretical. An adherence to socialism gave validity to the work of the creative writer; better still was communism. A move to the Left made neonates of writers. In August 1931, when Lehmann visited Spender in Salzburg, Spender was on the point of becoming a Communist. There was so much that was admirable in the way he had broken from his roots and expressed his sexuality.

Of course, it is tempting to wonder if another source of the difficulties between the two men was an early love affair or, most probably on Lehmann's part, an attempt to begin a sexual relationship. Spender's letters to Lehmann strongly suggest the latter, but it seems likely that such a move was rebuffed by Spender. Whatever subtext his words might disguise, by September Spender was telling Lehmann that he declined to discuss their friendship and that at present he had no idea of how close they might become. Lehmann, in effect, was told to keep his distance.

A refusal – if refused he was – would have brought its own injury. Lehmann was in his early twenties, and we should not forget his tall, Aryan form, the startling blue of his eyes and the penetrating glare that came from them; beauty borne up by privilege, the final hallmark of the golden lad. Sexually, he may well have thought himself irresistible, the taste of the time. In the years ahead, there is a gradual shift in Lehmann's life, it seems, from being the hunted to being the hunter. What is clear is that already, with Redgrave, the pattern had been set: love, quick with sex, the giving away of the soul and then, smartly, cruelly, disagreement and a drifting away. We should be less clear about the true relationship, in those first meetings, between Lehmann and Spender, and yet there seems the greatest possibility that Lehmann would have invited his new young friend to take the first steps in working out that pattern.

Spender's reluctance to take part was the finest of foundations for the many disagreeable events that punctuated their friendship in the years to come. And when Spender, at the end of his life, had the opportunity to pass comment on

Lehmann, a dismissal of everything he had contributed smacked suspiciously of the paying off of old grudges.

\*

It is doubtful that Lehmann was emotionally fulfilled in the next two affairs he became involved in, experiences that could be gone through without fear of censure, even if the sexual acts were against the law. There was sympathy. Lehmann recalled being brought up – what would Freud have made of his saying that 'when I say brought up I mean from Cambridge onwards'? – in London among the Bloomsbury circle, where 'there was no feeling of hostility or prejudice against homosexuals ... I was lucky to have been brought up in that atmosphere. Leonard and Virginia didn't care tuppence if one loved one's own sex or not.'

Jack Marlowe, the Lehmann-figure of *In the Purely Pagan Sense*, is repulsed by Babington (Babs), a crudely fictionalised Lytton Strachey, who makes love to him as a young man just down from Cambridge; repulsed, but still so excited by his fumblings that he prematurely ejaculates, much to Babs's surprise. Despite efforts – according to Lehmann's fiction – he was never cajoled into Lytton Strachey's bed. A letter from Strachey, one of the only shreds of evidence we have, suggests that this is so.

'I'm afraid this correspondence is not being a great success', wrote Strachey, after receiving a letter from Lehmann that 'reduced me for the moment almost to tears.'

> I rather think that the *outré* nature of some of my remarks may have given a false impression, and that this has led you to impute a 'sinister' interpretation – in more than one case – which the quiet facts don't justify. Truth to tell, I had been hoping that we might get to know each other better ... but ... the general tone of your letters, the lack of any suggestion on your part that we should meet again, to say nothing of the absence of a certain word in both letters ... all this makes me feel rather sad.

In later life, Lehmann remained coy about giving details of his friendship with Strachey, whom he hero-worshipped. When, in 1976, Peter Burton and Denis Lemon asked him how well he had known Strachey, Lehmann was content to offer the vaguest of answers: 'I knew him quite well for a limited number of years, because you must remember that he died early [in 1932] ... and I got to know him soon after – or during – my Cambridge days, and then saw quite a bit of him soon after. He was a most delightful person to know, and enormously kind to young men whom he thought would, you know, appreciate what he was after.' In the face of such praiseworthy but rather lofty waffle, Burton asked 'Did he seduce you?' 'Well', said Lehmann, 'Jack Marlowe's experiences sometimes came rather close to my own.'

Jack Marlowe's lover Duncan is a painter with reddish-blond hair who eventually and somewhat curiously explains away his bisexuality by admitting to being a lesbian. We do not know what Quentin Bell, the younger son of Clive and Vanessa Bell, thought of Lehmann's portrayal of him, or of the fact that Marlowe has his first happy sex with this man (an oblique comment on Lehmann's affair with Redgrave).

Again, we have Lehmann as victim. Through a muddle of undated letters, it is possible to glimpse moments in their relationship. For a time, at least, there seemed no doubt of Quentin's feelings. 'What can I say to you that you will like', he asked. 'I love you. You know that all ready of course but perhaps it's worth repeating. I wonder how much longer you'll endure me? I think I'd have thrown myself over last night if I'd been you. I am too stupid today to think of anything else.' At some point he upset Lehmann, no doubt precipitating one of Lehmann's tantrums. 'Dear dearer dearest Frederick,' pleaded Quentin from Charleston,

> Take Ovaltine, take a holiday, take (if you have nothing better to hand) your humble servant QB ... But oh how could I be so thoughtless as to make that imbecile remark about you being a Jew. What would it matter if you were ... I really am your admiring lover Quentin.

Warnings that he might prove an unsatisfactory partner for Lehmann were given. Julian had told Quentin that Lehmann was 'brittle' – Quentin agreed – and 'it wouldn't be so bad if one knew how to hold you so that you won't break, but alas I, at any rate, don't. As I may have told you before (I think I told you on our first night together) I AM THE VERY DEVIL OF A PERSON TO HAVE AS A LOVER.'

In fact, the affair seems to have collapsed early in 1932. On 8 February Quentin was apologising to Lehmann, hoping that

> I have given some moments of happiness because I'm feeling pretty bloody about the way I've treated you. The truth of the matter of course is, that I am far too much of a womanizer ever to make you or me thoroughly happy for long. I hope your [sic] not too unhappy. Find someone else as soon as possible, someone who can be everything that I was not; it won't be difficult. My love – I wish I could give you more of it. Quentin.

There was more spiritual hope for Lehmann's new friendship with Isherwood, begun (perhaps another source of their discontent) through Spender. At once, Lehmann asked Spender to persuade Isherwood to send the manuscript of his second novel, *The Memorial*, to him in England, and urged its publication on the Woolfs. Leonard disliked it but thought it 'distinctly clever', and Lehmann's persuasiveness triumphed. Accepted in November 1931, the book was published in February 1932, breaking Isherwood's connection with Cape and beginning the relationship with the Hogarth Press that lasted until 1940.

By the time Lehmann met Isherwood briefly at Tavistock Square in August 1932, Lehmann had become restless at the Press. Leonard's attitude and behaviour was a constant source of irritation, even if only a suggestion of what Lehmann would allegedly suffer later at his hands: he nagged, interfered, was impatient and unreasonable. Lehmann considered that the Woolfs had too 'emotional' an attitude to the Press and, it seemed, their manager, who soon might be their partner. The impossibility of such a situation was emphasised by Lehmann's realisation that he simply needed to get away from the office-hour demands of the day, to make room for his development as a writer, to break at last from the stultifying omnipresence of Fieldhead and familial expectation.

In the spring, Lehmann took a holiday that would provide the catalyst for change. From Paris, he travelled on the Arlberg Express to St. Anton in Tirol. It was only his second visit to Austria, and he was enraptured. It was not only the colour and texture of the aesthetic or physical beauty he found there, but a rush of feeling that this was the place where he might live out a destiny as poet and person. He was alone, moving through Innsbruck, dazzled by its light, the fields thick in new flowers, to Salzburg, shimmering in the sun as if the buildings themselves were made of snow. At night in the Mirabel gardens, there was the festivity of watching lovers meeting, kissing, laughing, a rekindling of the sort of magic he had experienced long ago on regatta evenings on the Thames.

Rilke it was who 'had created the illusion that the country itself was more beautiful than any other, the inhabitants more sympathetic, more deeply civilized and yet closer to the natural rhythms of life than anywhere else in Europe. Whatever it was, illusion or reality or childhood haunting, it grew into an infatuation strong enough to turn the whole direction of my life.' He had to steel himself to a process of 'self-loss and self-renewal'.

From Salzburg he went to Hamburg, where his great grandfather's paintings reminded him of his dynastic obligation, of the prestige that must always be associated with the name of Lehmann. Turning away, he saw the misery of unemployment in the harbour and knew he must work for the collapsing of social injustice: that way, he might yet be in touch with real life.

On Ruegen Island, he met Spender. They talked and talked, by day walking over the island's cliffs or through wooded country, by night talking again in a café. There seemed nothing disagreeable between them. Filled with the conviction that it was Austria that could hold him, he knew too that in Vienna the government was working to bring about an improvement in conditions, a redefinition of qualities, without a need of communist interference. Now, it only needed for Lehmann to prick the blister of his old life.

\*

When, the holiday over, Lehmann returned to the Press, it was clear that a new formula had to be found if he was to stay there. Leonard drew up a new arrangement that he hoped would detain his apprentice, despite Virginia's growing dissatisfaction with Lehmann. Never the most generous of patrons, their reversal of opinion as to Lehmann's qualities was so stark as to be discountable. Now, he was hard as nails, fractious, quivering, irritable, grasping. He was not to be forgiven for trying to pluck a reputation of his own from the fire.

Lehmann moved towards settling the differences. He proposed that he would end his day an hour earlier (at 4.15 p.m.), increase his salary by £50 a year, and take an eight-week holiday, as well as having the use of Virginia's studio-store room. Leonard balked at the eight-week holiday. In June a contract that would radically alter his life at the Press was drawn up. As from 1 September, he would work only two hours a day at a minimum salary of £200 (or ten per cent of the Press's profits paid in a monthly advance). It was an optimistic arrangement – how could Lehmann's duties, encompassing almost everything he had done before, be done in so short a space? – but, considering Leonard's reputed meanness, generous.

It did not matter, for the crisis had been reached, and with no warning to the Woolfs, Lehmann absconded, signifying his resignation to Leonard in a letter of 31 August. On that day, he walked from the office saying he would be in again the following afternoon, and disappeared, it seems, to Vienna.

A week later, Leonard informed Rosamond that her brother had deserted him, news that must have horrified Rosamond, for the family clearly knew nothing of it. Leonard's only information had been in Lehmann's letter. 'His behaviour seemed to me to be so either outrageous or childish that I decided to have nothing more to do with him', Leonard told her, 'and simply did not reply, for under the circumstances there is nothing to say but that. However when I went up yesterday they told me that either you or your sister had been ringing up to find out where he was.'

Even as Lehmann was being sought like a truanting schoolboy by his employer and sisters, the tensions that had brought about his debunking were in large part familial. The evidence is unquestionable. The Lehmanns celebrated Christmas Day 1931 with various larks and a levity probably needed to alleviate what Beatrix described as a day 'of endless horror *and* horrors'. The highlight seems to have been when she dressed up as the vicar, a Mr Bull (and one may imagine Beatrix's huge irreverence), and when Lehmann dressed ('the funniest sight of 1931') as Alice. Beatrix assured Rosamond that the stunt 'went hilariously but unfortunately after such "jokes" Mum was obliged as usual to deliver a few inappropriate snubs and "dusty answers" to John ...!!*!! Why, oh, why by all that's Freudian must these things be?...'

Lehmann's defection could hardly have sent more shock waves through the corridors of Fieldhead; he had, after all, had to leave the country to get away from the pressure being exerted on him. He left behind a wealth of concern, of the right sort, in Beatrix. In October, from Dresden, she was telling Rosamond 'it is queer about old John. I'm afraid that his emancipation (on the surface very admirable) has countless neurotic twists, the most unfortunate of which is his antagonism against Mummy.' Beatrix had probably gone to meet her brother in Germany, having sent Alice a telegram on her arrival as if from both herself and her brother, highly annoying Lehmann who considered that Beatrix was pandering to their mother's need to have children who were emotionally dependent on her. 'Perhaps he'll outgrow it', Beatrix wrote to Rosamond, '... It seems so wrong and cruel that this unfair age should have no use (urgent use) for his good brain.' A few weeks later, she was met by her brother on a railway station platform in Dresden, 'and I was *real* glad to see him. *What* a lonely, odd creature it is! He's shabby and a bit tattered but violently determined about vague things.'

Lehmann at least had the sympathy of Wogan Philipps, the eldest son of the first Lord Milford, the shipping magnate, who (despite Alice's disapproval) had married Rosamond in 1928 after the collapse of her first marriage. He seems perfectly to have understood his brother-in-law's predicament. 'I am terribly glad you have done all this. Bravo', he told Lehmann. 'And I heartily sympathise with your quiet get away. I know you have been in an awful worried state, and that to slip away quietly was the only way to escape.' Understandably, Philipps had not told Rosamond he was writing to Lehmann. She would hardly have approved her husband telling Lehmann 'your family seemed to have a queer notion of what you are really like ... I feel so sorry for you struggling in all this network.'

There had been hysterics when his defection had become known at Fieldhead. Alice complained that she could not be left alone there. Beatrix said his absence meant she would not be able to winter abroad and look for film work in Berlin. Rosamond (and one can almost feel the smack of her disapproval) thought it was not the action of a brother. It seems likely that at about this time Alice must have been made aware of her son's homosexuality, even if she chose to overlook the evidence. She was in the habit, after all, of constantly asking him when he was going to get married.

In fact, Lehmann had begun to be what for Rosamond he would always remain: a nuisance to the family. Now, his sex-life presented itself, literally, at the door of Fieldhead. In August, he had sent clothes to a young man, Frank Beresford. The clothes were too big. Staying in the Casual Ward of the workhouse, and 'lodging' on Southend beach, Beresford had to get his own clothes out of pawn 'as those which I have on are terribly dirty with vermin, and I am ashamed'. He sent his insurance cards to Lehmann for inspection, possibly because he hoped Lehmann might help him to find a job, and 'you have been my only friend and I shall never forget it'. In a letter of 3 September, it seems clear that Lehmann had spoken to Beresford about their being together in Vienna. Beresford was hoping to be taken on at Southend's Palace Hotel, but had his passport ready if the call came, 'already to go away at a minute's notice ... if you still want me to come, I give anything to be out there with you'.

A month later, Beresford was at the Church Army in Paddington, and decided to travel to Fieldhead to ask Alice for a loan. Lehmann was outraged and, understandably, nervous of what had been unfolding in his absence. Philipps told him that there was 'a penniless, begging boyfriend of yours, dressed in one of your old suits, who walks about with a letter from you in his pocket, asking alms from your mother'. Conscious of the threat that Beresford's actions posed, Philipps assured Lehmann 'If you are frightened, I do know a solicitor all the boys go to. But I dare say it is all all right.' In mid-October Lehmann sent Beresford money by which he was able to settle his debts; by now, he worked in a small residential hotel. His last extant letter to Lehmann was written a month later from Wormwood Scrubs where he was under observation in the prison's hospital, 'Well I'll say good by,' he finished, 'and I hope to see you soon. Wish me luck, please.'

It is unlikely that the Lehmann women would have been ready benefactors to Beresford or others of his class. For Lehmann, the gifts of money and clothes were simply a factor in the homosexual relationship he had with such men, largesse that further accentuated the differences between him and them. Indeed, it was with the underclass homosexuals that Lehmann had control, where money made a sort of control just possible.

In the 1960s, Bruce Cruickshank was struck by the fact that Lehmann seemed to put his boyfriends in a state of financial dependency on him. When he was a victim, it was usually (if not completely) when he associated with people who were rather more 'us' than 'them'. The social gap between him and so many of his boys gave a different landscape to their association.

Lehmann became particularly and increasingly fond of working-class lovers. The local difficulty with Beresford had not deterred him in the least. By March 1933, Lehmann was preparing to spend a week with Fred Turner, a soldier in the Coldstream Guards; a begging letter from him followed in April. In August Turner was promising 'I have kept away from other fellows as I said I would before you went.'

At some stage, Lehmann seems to have broken from him, and Turner told him he had always been grateful for the money he had scrounged, and 'for your friendship you were best [*sic*] I had. Well John I hope you have found a better boy.' In 1934, Turner got a girl pregnant and married her, 'and I think too much of my wife to play a double game ... I am going to lead a straight life and play the game with her.' Again, Lehmann was paying a penalty of having had sex with a man who went with women, but even now the bonds remained. In February 1936 Turner, still wearing a suit that Lehmann had given him, wrote to apologise for having ended their friendship: 'I have been a liar and a scoundrel to you, who was my best friend.' Couldn't Lehmann give him another chance? It seems he did, for as late as 1939 Turner was thanking him for 'that job you so kindly offered. It really is very good of you to do this for me I'm sure I don't deserve it.'

The letters from Turner tell us another constant about Lehmann: it is there in the soldier's vow to keep 'away from other fellows as I said I would before you went'. The enforced parting for long periods of time that would affect all Lehmann's loves had happened, and Turner had been made to promise that he would be faithful. This was always expected; and it is unlikely that Lehmann, for his part, withheld from sexual activity with other men (indeed, highly unlikely in the periods when he was abroad).

*

From Lehmann's arrival in Vienna in that autumn of 1932, there was new freedom, the restrictions of England had been abandoned. Politics too had a naked force it had lacked in England.

On the one hand I see the moribund state of the culture I have been brought up in. The need to reject its shams and pretences if I am not to become a complete cynic. The need to be transplanted to fresh ground. On the other hand I have been educated in and accustomed to the old culture, my habits and states have been formed by it. My roots are fairly firmly embedded in the exhausted ground. Go and live among the workers, take part in their activities, make friends with them, work with them if you can, refuse to have anything to do with the bourgeois world, says one voice. And another: but practically all your friends belong to that world, you cannot break the old ties. And what's more, you're totally unfitted to think as they think and work as they work; you lack the background and training of circumstances. So we stand between two worlds, uneasily contriving makeshift compromises to placate conscience and reason.

That autumn, Lehmann took a room at a pension in the Josefstadt, surprised that his fellow lodgers (a group of Indians) were so amenable: 'they could not have been more amiable or more indifferent to the fact that I belonged to the race that ruled their country'. He wanted only to be subsumed into Vienna. He studied its language, the grammatically correct, the colloquial, the vernacular, and how to speak *Wienerisch*.

The red flag flew over the city, even as the Austrian Nazis were gaining prominence. Lehmann was in awe of what the Social-Democratic Party had achieved in government, and full of respect for the *Schutzbund*, the defence corps created by the SDP with its young, amateur warriors. Against the scourge of unemployment, there was the almost miraculous achievement of 50,000 flats built, 8,000 houses built, the re-housing at low rents of some 180,000 citizens, eradicating the terrible squalor that had pervaded Vienna before they came to power.

For Lehmann, the scale of what reform could do was typified by the Karl Marx Hof, one of the great tenement settlements the SDP had created (he attended the grand opening of another, the Engels Hof on the banks of the Danube, in July 1933). Here were not only comfortable homes for the working-class, but something like miniature towns, with their own laundries, playgrounds, libraries, kindergarten, lecture-rooms and communal baths.

It seemed almost possible that it was a Utopia beside which the significance of Fieldhead would fade. When Lehmann returned to England that Christmas – and we may imagine the reception that must have awaited him in the drawing-room at Bourne End – he had already resolved to make a home for himself in Vienna, even though he had now left his flat in Heathcote Street and moved back to Fieldhead, where he would establish an office in one of the old nurseries.

It was on his way back to Vienna, in the New Year, that Lehmann decided to spend a month in Germany with his new friend Christopher Isherwood. A week before he arrived in Berlin on 8 February 1933, Hitler had succeeded von Papen as chancellor, leading a coalition of Nazis and Nationalists. There seemed no part of life in Berlin that was not in turmoil. The train into the city was crowded with Polish workers, emigrants to France now being repatriated to almost certain misery and worse. A fat Dalmatian commercial traveller told Lehmann that every day the trains went through with such loads. And yet, when he had left the train and found his way to Isherwood, it seemed as if Lehmann had crossed another frontier, finding a place where existence was heightened, where pleasure was necessary and grasped at every opportunity.

No sooner had they met than Isherwood took him to the Cosy Corner bar for a reunion with a friend made during Lehmann's earlier visit, 'Tiddlywinks'. Isherwood had hinted that the boy had lost his looks, but Lehmann thought not. The boy signalled to him to come to his table. Lehmann sipped cherry brandy as, between embraces, Tiddlywinks drank beer and ate fried eggs. Later, the youth 'looked more exquisite than before without his clothes on, and showed what art he'd acquired as a lover'. After a second night of sex with Tiddlywinks, Lehmann felt bitter than the boy's interest in him was purely mercenary. Lehmann told him their friendship was over; they shook hands at the door. A look of wretchedness crossed the boy's face.

The following night Rico, a young, shy boy with slanting Chinese eyes, was lying on Lehmann's breast after being given an English lesson. Anxious and sleepless, Rico explained that soon he would have no room to live in. Lehmann offered him sanctuary: 'I find it very exciting to make this proposal. I picture the late evening when we come back from the cinema, sleeping together, then my leaving him quietly to go back to my own room again.' Rico admitted that in the past he had prostituted himself when money was short.

Rico's confession touched Lehmann, for whom – inescapably seeing the boy's vulnerability against a political backcloth – his lodging in the Kleiststrasse seemed 'a point from which waste lands extend in all directions, himself a grain of dust on a vast map of Europe'. When they next slept together, Rico made the 'inevitable confession about the woman' (inevitable, perhaps, because the boys circulating the Berlin bars and clubs were almost all bisexual) and, in doing so, created 'the obstacle in the flow'.

Tiddlywinks and Rico were a prelude to four weeks of sexual assignations. When Georg and, later, an ex-Nazi who had promised to meet Lehmann, failed to turn up, Lehmann took Gustav, a man known to Isherwood's friend Gerald Hamilton, to his hotel. Muscular and pugnacious, Gustav stood on his head, balanced a chair on one finger and spoke in a comic English slang, exposing the gaps that various brawls had left in his teeth. He was proud of his spying at Nazi and *Stahlhelm* meetings, but his pitiful income came from working on Saturday nights as a chucker-out at a *lokal*. Gustav was thrilled when Lehmann offered to pay for a room in which he might escape registration. At once, he asked Lehmann to spend the night with him there. Sleeping with a lover until morning was not Lehmann's habit; but he agreed. The next day they made their way to Gustav's room – which he occupied during the absences of a whore – in the Unterwelt, where Gustav said he had to go to the Laterne to earn more money. Upset, Lehmann left, accompanied by a silent Gustav. All was forgiven; on 19 February, Gustav took Lehmann to meet his parents at Osdorf, taking cakes and cigarettes.

It was a means of reaching other glimpses of life, the reality Lehmann had so lacked: the grimy cottage, the smiling, cow-like mother, the kitchen filled with baking and boots, the home-made wireless, the prized book of family photographs. He was taken into Gustav's brother's bedroom and shown the gun kept there, before they returned through the wood heavy and silent in white, to the railway station and Berlin. That night, Gustav's enthusiasm could not be contained. He instructed Lehmann how to steal cars, how to swim the crawl, how to defend himself from attack. When, at last, he was persuaded to bed, he told Lehmann that they would go far into the Urwald and live together.

The attentions of the personable Gustav were not enough. Lehmann was haunted by the face of another boy he had met at the Kleistbar, 'Willi the Mixer'. He suspected their liaison might be

> ... the most successful of all. And yet at the same time I can have these feelings for Rico – Gustav too. Whether one can carry on more than one affair at the same time is as much an affair of the imagination as of the pocket. Each is different. If I can project myself with my imagination completely and separately into each, then all will be a success.

Slim, slightly girlish, freckled, Willi, a substantial history of prostitution behind him, was no less mercenary than Rico or Gustav. They spent an evening at the Silhouette,

> Willi vamping up to me, very sweet, bleeding me white … If he weren't fixed in this no-world, to which I can't make any concessions, and I could see (and afford) him every day, I might fall very deeply in love. At the moment I sway, rather giddy, but still firm-rooted, on the brink.
>
> My instinct is now to hurt him, to make him want me, leave him for a while and see what happens.
>
> As Christopher said this morning when he came in for a long talk, one wants someone whom one can take into one's blood. I can't do this with Willi. Or with Rico.

It was not enough to kill his infatuation with Willi. He bought him a ring, the symbol of constancy.

On 27 February, the Reichstag was burned, the arson blamed on the Communists. The next evening Lehmann learned that any writers of pacifist tendency or those who supported the Left were being arrested by the Nazis. 'I feel absolutely sick in my bowels with loathing and horror', he wrote. 'Now for fascism, now the mask is off, and violence, only violence and the brute-mind rules.'

Typically, his loathing for the new dystopia was melded with his literary and sexual desire. He needed, in some barely delineated way, to have them present themselves as one passion, the lines between each of which had been eradicated. Sexual pleasure was never an escape from the horror of global destruction; it was an act against it. And through sexual union he forged another, stronger link with the classes he needed to identify with.

In sharing his body with the boys of Austria and Germany, Lehmann was absorbed totally into their existence: there could have been no more physically intense statement of his belief and preference. In becoming one with their bodies, he felt himself almost mystically absorbed, not only into their sexuality, but into their class; sex with them was thus a necessary procedure in his journey of change from the person he was to the person he wanted to be.

On the 11th, Isherwood and Lehmann walked through the Tiergarten to a café where Isherwood encouraged him to work on his prose poems. Lehmann wanted to make a new book of poems peculiarly his own, 'in the same way as M. L. Brigge is Rilke's'. In the Nollendorfplatz, Lehmann had passed a pale, melancholy looking boy with white hair who had stared after him: he seemed to personify the young Brigge during his first days in Paris. Lehmann's appreciation of Isherwood was more guarded; in later years, doubts would never be so clearly expressed, even to his journal. Now, there are references to 'His childish vindictiveness, his constant need to assert the belief in his own "power". His rapid hostility and intolerance, his malice.' Against Isherwood's knack of appearing to be 'quite charmingly ridiculous', there was 'his weak chin contrasting with his autocratic nose and intelligent forehead'. Lehmann disapproved of what he saw as Isherwood's unscrupulous behaviour in his affair with Heinz Neddermeyer, and of Isherwood's jealousy; he would never introduce Lehmann to his other friends and sexual partners.

One of the effects of Lehmann's brief stay in Berlin was to increase his disgust for England, ready as he was to be convinced that his true milieu was that of the boy-bars and resistance workers. By the 21st he was complaining 'I've reached a period of extreme crisis and indecision, and that the whole flame of me will be dying out unless I can make up my mind and go forward. The trouble is I can't even make up my mind to go forward into complete lostness.'

Lehmann was repulsed by the ambition and vanity of London life, and always conscious of the manipulation that had been practised on him, notably by Alice and Rosamond, always ready, he thought, to play the 'Abandoned Woman. They play it with such readiness and moral gusto, that it has undoubtedly a sexual origin'. His reckless sex life was one way of repudiating what the Abandoned Women demanded of him; it was something to which Alice turned a blind eye, and of which Rosamond always hugely disapproved.

There was anger in recognising that 'this idea my family has that I want to be a "littérateur" is insane. It is really that they want to see me doing something that the world approves.' Vienna would be his respite, but, more than the city itself, it was his meeting with a young Viennese that was to alter the meaning of his existence. His name was Toni Sikyr. Because of him, for Lehmann Vienna was turned from an indulgence into a necessity.

# Part II
# WARS

# 6

# Vienna

Writing ten years after the end of World War II, Lehmann was perplexed by his inability to remember so much of the detail of his life in Vienna: his telephone number, the registration number of his car, the precise sequence of events that moved Austria into disaster, and, probably, the names of lovers. 'How is it possible that people in the centre of one's happiness in those years should have vanished without a trace', he asked; 'How can it be that so many years of one's life, so full of varied and intense experiences and discovery, in human relations as in intellectual exploration, should be as completely cut off from oneself as an arm or a leg left on the battlefield?'

Now, he meant Austria, specifically Vienna, to be the centre of his existence. While Isherwood was exiled from Germany, Lehmann had the constancy of his association with the great city, where he moved into a small flat, almost bereft of home comforts, close by the Arenberg Park. He exulted in his new intimacy with the places and people, the throng in the Prater, a gift to the Viennese from Josef II, moving in colour, light and music as in a darkened room. He went there, he said, like other people went to the ballet, to watch and be enchanted. By the 1930s, one of its main attractions to a more fun-seeking public was the Clown's Prater or *Wurstlprater*, with its three major attractions: the *Riesenrad* or Giant Wheel, the *Hochschaubahn* (scenic railway) and the Lilliput Railway that made its way beneath the Prater's chestnut trees through into the meadows that lay beyond. There were other diversions – Alpine Toboggans, the Spectre Railway (a ghost train), and Waterdromes – besides the shooting booths, the cafés with their bands of musicians in lederhosen and fetching hats, sailors, soldiers, pickpockets and young men desperately in need of money for an exchange of favours.

It was at the Prater that Lehmann and Toni Sikyr, a handsome twenty-one-year-old Viennese, a shoemaker by trade, had their first assignation. The boy's life had not been easy, and Sikyr seems not to have had a proper home for much of his childhood because his father was in Russia or else living with another woman. Sikyr and his younger brother Karl were educated at a convent, the prey of sadistic nuns who had left him with a hatred of the Church. At a government-run home for orphans Sikyr was almost beaten to death by a half-mad teacher, and regularly escaped over the railings. He went to live with his father but disliked his stepmother and ran away to live with his remarried mother, Frau Chval.

Slim, broad-shouldered, strong-legged, full-lipped, Sikyr might have been shy at what seems to have been his first meeting with an Englishman – and a clever, well-read one at that – but had no sexual inhibition. They ate at one of the Prater restaurants and, part of a brief courtship, took a ride on the switchback and the ghost train, after which Sikyr led Lehmann away into some bushes where they made love.

Love, perhaps the deepest Lehmann had known, was what was begun there, a relationship that was the most important of his Viennese years, chronicled (and sometimes barely altered) in the pages of *In the Purely Pagan Sense*. It would need a thesis of its own to disentangle and delineate the multitude of sexual partners that Vienna provided him with, a wearying exercise, and it is important to remember that his relationship with Sikyr was not sexually exclusive: spiritually, it was more so. It was obvious to Lehmann that Sikyr enjoyed girls, and pursued them, easy about a bisexuality that Lehmann merely thought of as typically Austrian.

Reading Lehmann's account of the boys of Vienna in *In the Purely Pagan Sense*, one has to overcome Lehmann's dead-handed prose, his almost William McGonagall talent for the flat phrase, the over-ready adjective. Here is a world where smiles are always mischievous or playful, eyes are bewitching or laughing (or, as he would write of Isherwood's in a peculiarly repugnant analysis, 'twinkling'): if Lehmann had a pungent understanding of human nature, he did not translate it to the written page.

It is one of the sadnesses of that book that Franzl (the fictional equivalent of Toni) does not stir into life, when the prototype of that life seems to have been so vibrant, so real, so excitable, virile and troubled. Of course, when Franzl and Marlowe quarrel, the light goes out of Franzl's eyes (they had been 'mirth-loving'); they lose their 'sparkle'. Somewhere, lost, is the true Toni Sikyr, blood-brothered to young Karl, fancied by the girls, never bored with his motor-bike, good to his mother, known as a likely lad in the *lokals* and weight-lifting clubs that proliferated in the city.

It was Sikyr's distinction to be the first of Lehmann's many lover-secretaries (and, later, chauffeur, when Lehmann imported a sleek car from England). There would be a great many others, and in this, surely, lies one of the most unattractive things about Lehmann: his readiness, indeed, his expectancy, to have sex with the young men who worked for him. It was really a policy he pursued throughout his life, and was bound to lead to a number of disagreeable conclusions for both parties.

Sometimes, Sikyr would spend the night with a girl while Lehmann was having sex in the flat with a boy Sikyr had recommended to him; but if there was a suspicion that meaningful feelings were developing during such meetings, Sikyr became jealous.

It was an arrangement that suited Lehmann. He knew that the needs of the many boys he was intimate with were as basic as his own. It was a bodily, gentlemanly transaction of lust, and totally necessary to his theory that through sexual activity he might at last reach the inner sanctum of the proletariat. He recognised the overflow of his sexuality, finding, in even the most perfunctory of his boys, memories and emotions that would not easily dissolve. The discoveries seemed endless. It was with another boy that he had his first penetrative sex.

> He started to kiss me passionately and undress me, undressing himself at the same time. When we were both completely naked, after fondling my cock which was growing hard, he flung himself down on the bed on his tummy and invited me to fuck him. He took a tube of Nivea cream from the chair beside the bed, and then handed it to me.... though the student himself disappeared from view for a long time after that night, it aroused in me an urgent desire to find other boys who liked just that.

Meanwhile, there would always be Fieldhead that threatened to pull him back. When Alice was taken ill with a badly affected heart, Beatrix reproachfully (but who could blame her?) instructed her brother to 'be careful what you write home and ask your own conscience what remarks, guaranteed to distress and panic, are best eliminated. She is like that, there it is, and it is high time we lumped it and were considerate ... I think we shall have to consider abandoning this millstone of a house now.' Lehmann resisted the temptation to react as his mother might have wished; the once dutiful son apologised to Beatrix that she was having to cope with a crisis. It was not the first time he had been expected to respond to such events.

> I'm afraid these crises become more pathological each time. It's quite clear – though I wish it weren't – that the feeling that a child has snapped the umbilical cord has again brought it on, though this time it was aggravated obviously by the operation & the 'flu, & the careless way she behaved about both. I simply can't have you ruining chances of work by staying down there, & I insist on your saying it straight out. Helen after all is always pleased to have Mother, & hasn't got the same need to assert independence as we have. I'm really extremely worried about it all, but unless she gets worse, see no sense in dashing to the sickbed. Indeed, to be frank, I'm very doubtful about the wisdom of ever returning to Fieldhead for more than a weekend, since it only produces these crises in the end, & the clutch to retain me stronger each time. It's one of the oldest stories in the world, but I don't suppose Mother sees what happens to V. H. [Violet Hammersley] is exactly what happens to her, though she conceals it more, disguises it instinctively ...
>
> I shall certainly take the greatest care not to alarm her by any mention

of a wild revolutionary life which I don't lead – and anyway couldn't lead at the moment …

Comparing Violet Hammersley's actions to those of his mother was hardly complimentary: Violet had been fiercely protective and overbearing in her adoration of her son Christopher, who had only managed to escape her clutches by marrying an alcoholic and moving to the Virgin Islands (simultaneously, she had contrived to almost totally ignore her daughter Monica, just as, perhaps, Beatrix had been ignored by Alice).

Lehmann felt himself the victim of a monstrous manipulation that he did his utmost to ignore and repudiate. His life had so moved on that his new home high above Vienna seemed like something out of Fritz Lang's *Metropolis*; it was certainly modernistic, angular, almost futuristic, an observatory that hovered in its way above time itself – not without reason did Lehmann sometimes refer to it as his 'Zeppelin cell'. The flat was at the very top of a great building, once the offices of a Czech mining firm, on the Invalidenstrasse.

Lehmann's particular space had been the dining-room of the firm's directors, with a display of deep windows that gave a panorama of the city. It was an eyrie that Lehmann made his own, with the help of a young architect, keen on Viennese *Wohnkultur*, Herr Grünbaum, who transformed the space into something bunker-like, a room that might have belonged to a military commander. Appropriately, Lehmann sometimes fantasised about being the autocrat of a small eighteenth century state, where immorality and the arts flourished. Above the desk of his observatory-platform below the windows, Lehmann had maps wallpaper the room: maps of all those countries whose fates so concerned him and of which he had, almost ineluctably, become citizen. A small bedroom, or a space where the bed was kept, was concealed behind a curtain.

Sikyr at once was part of life in the Invalidenstrasse flat, while Frau Chval became housekeeper, cook, seamstress, cleaner, maid of all work. She became fond of Lehmann and he of her, linked as they were by his being her son's employer and lover. In her unquestioning loyalty and fondness and usefulness she might have been his surrogate mother. When other jobs in the flat defeated her or her son's ingenuity, there was always another boyfriend of Sikyr's who could be called on. An art student, Richard, a friend of Sikyr's girlfriend Gretl, painted excitable and sexually dubious jungle scenes on the back wall of the flat.

Communism was at the core of Lehmann's life from 1933 onwards, so intense because to be anti-fascist almost necessitated Marxism. He would later make his excuses for what he had so believed in then, but we should not question the potency or truthfulness of those beliefs. Lehmann saw that 'Society was sick, it was sick unto death: it had called in the thugs as doctors'; it was a sickness caused by the evils of capitalism, a concept that only the Soviet Union had completely eradicated by its uncompromising Marxist line. So it was that Lehmann was led into appreciating the educational possibilities at the fingertips of Russian peasants, the efficacy of tractors, the wholesomeness of Soviet hotels, the ideal ambience that made Stalin's empire so attractive for the creative temperament. Only later did he see how totally he had been taken in by it all. In 1934 'we astonishingly deluded ourselves in believing that Moscow had not only established all those liberties and opportunities that were the breath of our being, but had established them beyond the possibility of destruction'.

It was in good heart that Sikyr and Lehmann set off for Russia that spring, by which time Sikyr had a firm place in his feelings. 'We discuss the future', Lehmann wrote, 'and he says Yes, he will come anywhere to me at any time.' They left a lilac-filled Vienna for Poland and, by express train, the Russian frontier, arched with the message 'Workers Of The World Unite', and red everywhere, in the flags, the banners, the uniforms, and The Internationale. Their progress through Negoreloe and on the Manchurian Express was punctuated at Minsk by more crowds waving placards, and speeches made by workers' delegates. Russia, it seemed, was in a frenzy of communistic celebration.

In Moscow they were tightly organised by an Intourist guide, whisked from place to place in a Lincoln automobile. Everything they saw was intended to impress: a textile workers' school where they sat through another speech praising the Soviet system; the Udarnik cinema where the unfortunate customers waiting for a film to begin were beguiled with an improving lecture; the Elektro-Kombinat factory (light bulbs were made there) with its 20,000 employees; the S.I.S. motor works, where Sikyr was horrified at the lack of safety precautions. They were told that even the most inefficient of employees was never dismissed, merely put back to less well-paid work. To Sikyr it must have seemed something of a miracle: unemployment had simply been done away with.

They peered, open-mouthed, at the Mayday celebrations in Red Square, at Stalin and Voroshilov, the exiled *Schutzbündlers* taking part in the march past, the advertisements for the new metro (it would open the next year, much of its construction done by unpaid volunteers), the grotesque caricatures of Nazi capitalists paraded before the masses: 'Toni is immensely excited and says that Moscow is undoubtedly the place to be.'

For Lehmann, the trip was useful in helping him to take Sikyr's education in hand; the working-class lover, after all, had to be bettered. His journals of the time are full of such efforts: 'Toni and I talk hard, and I try to explain USSR Baltic policy, war etc'; at meals or in bed Sikyr was instructed on socialism. Surprisingly this does not seem to have dampened Sikyr's enthusiasm, for socialism or Lehmann – even going through the steppes of the Ukraine he was full of a 'sort of tom-cat purring happiness'. At Kharkov they were shown round the Palace of State Industry and a shoe factory (a chance for once for Sikyr to know more of what was going on than Lehmann) with a childrens' nursery: 'as pleasant as Hugo's nursery' Lehmann, perhaps hopefully, noted, comparing the accommodation to the somewhat less regimented surroundings of Rosamond's

son. They drank their first vodka and were surprised at the party-like atmosphere of the divorce courts, where everyone seemed to giggle. Returning
through Simferopol and the bay of Sevastopol, they climbed the Malakoff Hill
where sailors sun-bathed and played balalaikas and accordions, then moved to
Yalta and Odessa (the steps looked grubby). How could Lehmann not be
impressed by 'the enormous complexity, the world by itself of this Russia'?
When he visited it again the next year, he was struck by the 'switchback-holiday
look' of the passengers riding the metro, gliding through this 'amazing new
civilization so rapidly developing here'.

In Vienna, Lehmann had already aligned himself with the communist-based
movement to fight Fascism and the threat of any war, and in Paris had got himself
introduced to the writer and activist Henri Barbusse, originator of the Clarté
group that united writers in a thrust of social and political protest. Barbusse was
convinced by the young Englishman's passion, and agreed that he should
become the secret Viennese correspondent for his organisation.

Suddenly, Lehmann was somewhere at the heart of the resistance, a conduit
through which information from the Austrian underground might find its way
out into what was left of the free world. It was a job for which he was ideally
placed, free as he was to travel between France, England and Austria. He wanted
to be an intimate of Austria and its affairs, and the political tripartite of the
country (Clerico-fascists, Nazis and Social-Democrats and Communists) intrigued him, and 'I felt I could pursue my literary activities and enjoy my life in
Austria far more happily if I had this matter-of-fact association with the new
movement, working in a way for which I intended specially to equip myself.'

It was such consolidation that encouraged him to make a permanent base of
the Invalidenstrasse flat. But all was uncertain. In the bitter cold of February
1934 the workers of Floridsdorf called a strike that led to a short but terrible
Civil War in Vienna, in which socialist forces, fortified by the government's
tenement buildings, stood against the Clerico-fascists, the reactionaries supported by Mussolini in the provinces under the command of Prince
Starhemberg. After four days of fighting

> There only remained the attempts of various groups to escape across the
> Czech frontier, occasional short outbreaks of shooting between the Police
> and desperate bands of insurgents from their lairs, and the macabre
> guerrilla war in the great underground drains. No official dared to name
> the number of victims among the insurgents and it was clear to every one
> that the figure given for those killed on the side of the Army and the Police
> themselves was far below the truth: the total, for both sides, possibly ran
> into several thousands.

Under Dollfuss, Vienna's Social-Democrats had increasingly given way to the
federal government, and when the hastily organised resistance and the

*Schutzbund* collapsed, the Social-Democrats had damaged beyond repair their reputation as an opposition to the Fascists. In an increasingly volatile political climate, Socialists, Communists and Nazis, all of whom had been forced underground, began to work for the ousting of the government.

The events in Vienna were in themselves so complex, and of such importance, that Lehmann was approached by the British government to become a supplier of information to them. 'Spy' would be too strong a word (certainly for Lehmann, who would have found the idea repugnant), but there was an element of spying about it. It was only his well-known homosexuality that prevented his being taken on in a more official capacity for such work: even the police in Vienna had prepared a report on his sexual habits.

The same year there was a failed Nazi *putsch*, but Lehmann knew war would come. His infatuation with Vienna held him to the moment: 'The living truth of Vienna haunted me like the reality of one's beloved.' The murder of Dollfuss at Nazi hands that summer was only a fragment of the terrible reality that he needed to push into his poetry, now disguised as prose. He sees Vienna as from under trees on a distant mountain, imagining its pulsing life hidden to the eye, even if

> A mile away, under the trees, all this has vanished. Even the murder of a Chancellor, the execution of a Socialist, can have happened unheard and unseen. It is strange to imagine, under that still appearance, the despair of the bankrupt shopkeeper, or the student who knows he will find no post, the mixture of curiosity and revolt of the unemployed leather-worker, as he passes the entrance to a fashionable restaurant. And startling to remember the suffering in overcrowded prisons, the words of darkness repeated in court after court ...
>
> And now the lights begin to come out, scattered or in groups and strings, evidence indeed of life but as inexpressive as the stars. Just so they glitter now, while the heavily armed police restlessly prowl the streets and revolutionaries are whispering under their feet, as they would were the city echoing at last to shouts of Freedom, and the tramp of exiles' feet returning.

Such emotions did not find much favour when Lehmann's new collection of poems, *The Noise of History* (what noise, Spender asked, *did* history make?), was published by the Woolfs to a generally unenthusiastic reception in October. The contents, according to Dylan Thomas, were 'as dead as a last year's waltz, as hollow as an empty tumbler with a copy of Mr. Spender's Poems laid on the top'. They were not words to encourage either Lehmann's writing of poetry or his fondness for Spender, but worse was to come. Thomas continued 'He will never be, as he attempts to be, a poet of the masses.' He was 'a minor voiced lyricist, a soft romanticist in a hard age'. For George Stonier in the *New*

*Statesman* it was 'rank and file' stuff. Even the *Daily Worker* could raise no enthusiasm, complaining that 'much of this book suffers from the uncertainty of its images ... at least Lehmann is a real poet writing about real things'. With such discouraging comments, Lehmann's attention turned from poetry to other areas of literature in which he might find more success.

\*

There was also the pressing concern of his fondness for Sikyr, the need to educate him, conscious all the time as he was of the effect of the young man's economic freedom, and thinking in frustration of 'the never-to-be country cottage' where they might live together. When away from Vienna, Lehmann hoped to find a substitute for Sikyr but couldn't, at least not anyone who came up to what Sikyr offered him. Sikyr was too deep in his bones, but still he tried to resist the faithfulness to which such devotion might have led him.

As 1935 ended, 'I suddenly seemed to see the truth about myself – my deepest passion to be in touch with young, confident, family life, life of the masses, and to serve it, and that arising from my frustration as a small boy.' What is suggested, of course, is that he had never enjoyed what he perceived as a happy family life; he had never been allowed near ordinariness.

There was comfort in his love for Sikyr, but Lehmann was threatened by the success of the boy's transformation: two years after their meeting, Lehmann saw in him someone who had developed, matured, stronger and more intelligent than before. Now, he displayed what Lehmann saw as 'the second person'; in a breakdown between them, Lehmann witnessed 'the collapse of the structure, the bitter discussions and black reflections lasting far into the night'. Clearly, the old dog of nagging disagreement over something in their relationship had come between the men, and, as so often with Lehmann, the differences precipitated a crisis.

Lehmann knew that much of the problem was in his having spent so much time away from Vienna, and 'in that time he gets bored, – he plunges into the oddest adventures – when I come back, the return is hard'; but they would not part from one another. They went to see Garbo in *Anna Karenina*, after which Sikyr took Lehmann home and Frau Chval made coffee for them. Lehmann felt it was up to Sikyr to sort out for himself the difficulties between them; from now, there must be a new, readjusted relationship (another constant happening in Lehmann's resolves about his relationships. He was always looking for solutions that would be satisfactory to him.) Somehow, he was left with the 'feeling always, after leaving Toni, of something unsaid, of some vital shade of feeling left unexpressed'.

\*

In the spring of 1936, the first *New Writing*, the publication that would so long be associated with him, appeared, and from now on he was in even more of a welter of reading, writing, meeting and discovering writers and poets, not only from England but from across the world.

As if this workload was not enough, by summer 1937 he had edged himself back into Bloomsbury and approached the Woolfs about a renewed association with the Hogarth Press. Despite the past, the Woolfs agreed to resume operations with him. After various options had been suggested and abandoned (including a plan by which Auden, Isherwood, Lehmann and Spender would run the Press as a co-operative), Lehmann paid £3,000 for a half share, and his partnership was established.

It is not difficult to appreciate the inherent problems that besieged Lehmann at this period of his life, the demands of the Hogarth Press, of *New Writing*, of the *Geographical Magazine* (to which he now regularly contributed), of the many other periodicals he was writing for, of Sikyr and Vienna and, perhaps increasingly, other lovers in England. The most prominent of these was a good-looking youth, Pip Dyer, christened by Beatrix 'the boy with pink hair' (he was a strawberry blond). One evening in 1937 Dyer was hurrying home from his work at Graingers' furniture store in Oxford Street. His way took him through Tavistock Square.

> It was a dreary, drizzling night. At exactly the moment I passed the Hogarth Press out came John. He accosted me instantly, and I suppose I thought 'Oh God, a pick-up', which would certainly have had no appeal to me. He said, 'Haven't I seen you before somewhere?' I thought, 'Oh dear, the old line.' Then he said, 'Outside a café last summer eating wild strawberries' which of course registered at once. Had he approached me in any other way I should have brushed him off and gone on, but with that preamble who could fail to be impressed?

Dyer was already in a relationship with the photographer Hans Wild, but his meeting with Lehmann marked the start of a 'secondary affair' that lasted, sexually, for about a year. Throughout Lehmann was a 'brutal, inconsiderate lover'. Dyer immediately told Lehmann about Wild ('my life wouldn't have been worth living if I hadn't') and Lehmann told Dyer about Sikyr. It seems likely that Lehmann saw him as a possible alternative to Sikyr when Vienna had to be left behind, but over fifty years later Dyer confessed 'It never occurred to me. I was not happy at all about the physical side.' But Dyer was ideal material, a blank page on which Lehmann might make his mark. Here was new education to be undertaken, a taste for reading fostered.

Isherwood, who was conducting two affairs at this time (one with Jackie Hewit, at various times the lover of Guy Burgess and Anthony Blunt), accused Lehmann of betraying Sikyr by his new attachment. It seems that Isherwood was forbidden any meeting with Dyer. Dyer, meanwhile, felt too often (and without reason) 'the ignorant youngster' when in the presence of the great writers. He felt uncomfortable at a party that Spender gave, but Spender and Lehmann 'were extremely kind to me. They said "You've had so many experiences of being brought up in some degree of penury that you've learned a great deal that we still haven't".'

In September 1936 there was a reunion with Isherwood in Brussels after fifteen months of correspondence. Lehmann burst unannounced into the bedroom where Isherwood lay on a camp bed and, in a double bed beside him, Heinz Neddermeyer, stupider, lazier and vaguer than Lehmann had remembered. Isherwood confessed that he felt he had never really lived since leaving Germany. Lehmann thought he had

> not grown less egocentric or superbly (and also at times irritatingly) conceited ... I felt bad, thinking that after all we should drift apart, there wasn't enough harmony of ideas to hold us together over such long absences, our utterly different lives now ... if it wasn't for *New Writing*, perhaps, it occurred to me drearily, we should already be beginning to recede from one another ... and yet he might have meant more than any.

Even with Isherwood, Lehmann blamed the times they were apart for the divisions that came between. As always, Lehmann was investing so much of his emotion in other people, people who would not respond in the manner he most wanted: it seems he had to externalise so many of his needs. And, of course, there is Lehmann's suspicion that 'he might have meant more than any'; here, there must be the suggestion that he would have liked his relationship with Isherwood to have been physical as well as spiritual.

*

When Lehmann and Isherwood met in January 1937, again in Brussels, their moods seemed more in tune. Lehmann considered that Spain was partly responsible for this. The Civil War that had broken out the previous year, precipitated by Franco's uprising against the Republican government and buttressed by German Nazis and Italian Fascists, began the deadly struggle in which the workers' militia was supported by many English intellectuals, among them John Cornford, Spender, John Sommerfield, Orwell and Julian Bell, who served in the International Brigade which, like the Soviet Union, served the Republican cause. It was a conflagration that elicited all the passion and belief in a communist solution, a conflict where ideals of the young and committed would surely win the day.

Julian Bell had resolved to work on behalf of the Republicans, and left China at the end of 1937, despite strenuous efforts by his family to prevent his going.

It was a stark breaking-away from the Bloomsbury that had claimed him for so long. His only concession was that he would not be a combatant, but an ambulance driver with the Spanish Medical Aid organisation, and he set off in early June. His involvement with the cause was brief. On 15 July his ambulance was hit by a bomb. Bell himself was unhurt, and moved to the front where he was in charge of thirty stretcher-bearers. A new lorry was delivered to him on 18 July, the first anniversary of the war. He was driving it along the road outside Villanueva de la Canada when a bomb dropped. Conscious but mortally ill, he was taken to the Escorial hospital. He told those who nursed him that he had always wanted to have a mistress and to fight in a war, and had achieved both ambitions. He then spoke in French, possibly poetry, and lapsed into a coma from which he did not recover. Bell was buried outside Madrid at Fuencarral. He had once written to his mother that he would be happy to die a violent death.

It was inevitable that Lehmann would consider going to Spain and playing his own part, encouraged by Isherwood who was ready to assign roles in the war to his circle, but

I had already chosen mine. I had made up my mind that I was going to see the Austrian drama through to the end: I had created a home in Vienna, I had many friends who were deeply involved, and I believed that in a crisis I might be of help … I could not help feeling the pull of Spain more and more, and a sense of release when I travelled home every few months through Paris and London, a sense of returning to the centre of desperately urgent activities. The wall of civilisation was falling, and I was doing so little, posted at one remote corner, to shore it up.

In 1937 he went to Hungary and Belgrade, where the peasants wore shoes made from old tyres. He hated Bucharest; Romania was 'supremely corrupt'. No place meant as much as poor, troubled Vienna, the links were unbreakable, and 'I know that I can't leave Toni like that, that I must and will find fulfilment with him before I can leave him for any length of time.' The continuity of that emotion could not be interrupted, but the closeness of war made any disaster possible. When the Nazis annexed Austria on 13 March 1938, the resignation of Chancellor von Schuschnigg marked an end to most hope: already, with Austria fallen and the *Anschluss* achieved, Lehmann felt at war.

It was not until September, in Paris, that he again began writing his journal, determined to restart his life, restart 'with all the force of my imagination, the way we must prepare our lives for the future; and to write about Toni, before it is too late.' He knew that they, among millions, were about to be engulfed in Hitler's nightmare. Sikyr's last letter to him had been full of his love for the Attersee where, Lehmann remembered, they had seemed for the first time to cement their relationship – close by it, Sikyr was always 'lyrically happy, he was transformed by the sun diving through its blue waters'. Lehmann wanted Sikyr to get to England, to live with him there, but how could it be done? In October they managed a reunion in a town on the Rhine to which they had never been before. It was only two days, but blissful, before Lehmann flew back to the London fog. If proof was needed, the days showed that 'Toni and I belong entirely to one another, in fact more deeply in spite of time and in spite of distance; and that Toni is growing and deepening as a personality in a way that makes me admire him in an entirely new way.' It was 'a happiness that only the love and quarrels and common experiences of years could have brought'.

Sikyr told Lehmann he would happily pack a rucksack and escape with him out of it all, but he knew he had to stay, whatever battle might come in Vienna. He thought Isherwood had the right idea in wanting to get to America, but he did not want to leave Gretl, who had stood by and had been good to him. Lehmann was pleased when Sikyr said that Gretl knew he was 'on her side: but I was glad, too, when he said if he didn't find work he would leave her for me again, to share life with me in new surroundings, however hard the way'.

But most of all our final lunch together will remain in our mind, when we were discussing the future. He said he felt certain he'd come through somehow, and meanwhile 'I've always got you, I know that. And we shall find one another again in the future somehow.' He went on to talk of Austria now, of the monstrous shamelessness of the regime. I told him again how I had written many articles about it, and he said: 'Write more, more and more. If only enough people can realise just the truth ... the thing will collapse.' And he went on to speak of my books, and said no, not propaganda, that wasn't my business, but to reveal just this real face of life, the human side, that was the great service I could do.

But here it is Lehmann's reputation that is taking on an importance beyond the personal dimension of his love for Sikyr. The moment flits too easily from personal to professional concern, when any more feeling lover might have thrown professional interests and pride overboard.

Is it uncharitable to think that here Lehmann becomes something indispensable, while Sikyr remains merely a cog caught up in the workings – perhaps the *noise* – of history? What did Lehmann's aspirations as a saviour of Vienna matter beside his feelings for his lover? Lehmann seems intrinsically incapable of differentiating the two. Love, for Sikyr, for Dyer, for any of the boys he went to bed with, could not triumph; and what prevented that triumph, was his own. 'My books', 'the great service I could do', the plea that he should write 'more, more and more': everything was his achievement. There was little left for Sikyr. And how could Sikyr have felt at ease with all this? His successors, through the years to come, would not.

Returning to England, he obtained a permit for sending Sikyr monthly payments. So much of his energy was given over to the Hogarth Press, and to what would happen to his beloved Isherwood, all events unrolling against the backcloth of sometimes violent quarrels with Leonard Woolf, these in turn agitated by the Hogarth's poor sales returns. Isherwood seemed on surer ground. He had stated his intention that if war was to come, he meant to have a good one; at least he was being true to his selfishness.

Lehmann, of course, knew that war would come, and invited Isherwood to live with him at his flat. When Munich at last made the inevitable seem so much closer, Lehmann told Isherwood it was the end of the Europe they had wanted. Isherwood replied that it was no longer of concern to him: he would be in America, at which moment a part of Lehmann's world must have collapsed.

Everything Lehmann and Isherwood with his twinkling eyes might have gone on to do trickled between his fingers and was gone. There might yet be a professional retrieval, some literary compensation that could be wrested from the disaster, and the chance came because Isherwood and Auden needed money to finance their emigration. They proposed that the Hogarth Press should commission a travel book to be written by them both, to be called *Address Not Known*, and also that Auden's next collection of poems would go to the Press.

In effect, Lehmann, who paid the advances for the books from his own funds, was duped. *Address Not Known* proved to be a peculiarly appropriate title for a manuscript that never materialised. For his part, Auden knew perfectly well that he was committed to T. S. Eliot at Faber for any new poems (as Eliot subsequently politely pointed out to Lehmann, and paid back the money he had given Auden). To a less devoted disciple than Lehmann, the events might have forever soured relations. For the present, Lehmann hoped still that Isherwood would not leave. There seemed 'a dawning sense in Christopher's own mind that the whole scheme was not "going down very well" – already resulting in a first row [with Auden, presumably] that took a little gilt off the gingerbread'.

In his flat, Lehmann urged Isherwood to realise how mistaken he was to keep up his relationship with Jackie Hewit. Didn't Isherwood know it was the duty, the dignity, of the creative artist to be (except for the allowable Neddermeyer) alone? On and on he went, until Isherwood cried 'For God's sake, someone get me out of this.' Lehmann, of course, wanted to be the one to do just that, and saw the crucial part Auden was playing in Isherwood's plans. To ease the path for them both, he made up his mind to go to his financial limit in helping them. Probably exhausted by it all, Isherwood stayed the night. Lehmann lay alone in his bedroom and 'I shouted to him before falling asleep, through the door: "I can't bear you being out there, thinking different thoughts".'

The following morning, Isherwood went to Tavistock Square to tell Lehmann that he had indeed broken off his relationship with Hewit; perhaps this was a sort of victory for Lehmann. Isherwood's prize, it seems, was to be given a glimpse of the strawberry blond Dyer. Anyway, 'Pip managed it with unconscious brilliance arriving at the last moment as Christopher and I changed taxi after waiting in growing despair, flushed, excited, radiant, more beautiful than ever' (no matter, for a few weeks later Lehmann noted that Dyer was 'slipping away' from him). Next day, Lehmann gave Auden his cheque at a Lyons Corner House, 'while Wystan luridly described his experiences under a rectoscope'.

\*

From Vienna came dismaying news of Sikyr. The flat had been burgled and flooded; 'his bad luck is endless: a first impulse to blame him for losing again, again what had taken so much trouble to provide, – to blame because it hurt so' gave way to a sureness that things would only be right when they were together once more. Lehmann had 'a vivid picture of him in the flat, lugging the coals in, dead tired, falling asleep after supper, – and then in the dismay of the theft, finding pipes bursting all around him'.

The uncontrollable flooding was reflected in the gush of conflict through which Lehmann himself was struggling. And always, throughout his journals, there is the setting-down of good intention, the mapping-out of goals to be achieved, roads gone down, ideals to be fixed. So much was required.

> Wanted: a new kind of journalism in London to drive the elderly softnesses and condescensions of the *New Statesman* and *Spectator* off the stage, and usurp the pretence-new of the pseudo-American;
> Wanted: a new kind of art to blow the spunkless complacencies of Bloomsbury sky-high;
> Wanted: a new kind of writing that has really caught a spark from the true machine of modern life, the machine in the terrible powerhouse just off the boulevard; Christopher a hope, but not good enough yet; in poetry Wystan for certain, a start.

Sikyr was not the only person in Vienna for whom Lehmann felt responsible. Another was Clothilde Schweiger, a Jewish hostess of formidable personality who had been helpful in opening up Viennese society for him, introducing him to Austrian writers and artists. At first she, as so many others, put her faith in the new regime of National-Socialism under the Nazis, confident that it would bring none of the terror that it had meant in Germany. When she and other Jews began to receive anonymous, obscene and threatening telephone calls, such hope was finally abandoned. Eventually, Lehmann helped orchestrate Schweiger's escape to England, where she spent some months at Fieldhead. In October of 1939, she wrote from Paris to ask him for £50

> as I cannot leave otherwise and you will certainly not like to be morally responsible for my being forced to remain in Europe till 1942. For you it means the slight inconvenience to liquidate some tiny investment or to

borrow the money from somebody richer than myself – for me it may mean
to be or not to be.

Lehmann was outraged. Her letter was 'an astonishing insult of which I did
not imagine you capable ... after I have done everything in my power for you
from the moment the Nazis arrived in Vienna eighteen months ago'; he sent her
the money.

As crisis followed crisis or dragged hopelessly into a declaration of conflict,
Lehmann's visits to Vienna were necessarily less frequent and of shorter duration. He was there again in March 1939, only for four days, spending most of
the time with Sikyr, who was now living in the flat, and often, it seems,
accompanied by Gretl. They went to the theatre, restaurants, old haunts, down
to the Danube on the back of Sikyr's motorbike, to drink with friends. Lehmann
bought him books (it had been a real success that Sikyr had grown so interested
in reading), happy to see him still 'closely following and deepening in understanding'. Frau Chval, the great earth mother he would so have benefited from
knowing in his childhood, was so thrilled to see him that she almost knocked
him over.

There would be one more return, that summer, before the curtain fell across
Europe. In Sikyr's arms, after their day together, Lehmann remembered their
past happinesses, the nights in hotels and mountain inns, evenings at the Wiener
Wald's *heuriger* festivals, their journeys to Paris, to Russia, the night of Chinese
lanterns when they had rowed across a lake, out of reach of the other boats, and
their times at the Attersee. In the morning, they drove to the frontier. Sikyr told
Lehmann he had decided to marry Gretl. Lehmann knew it was for the best,
perhaps shook his hand. They embraced, kissing on both cheeks. The S.S. guard
smiled, and Lehmann drove away.

By the autumn, England, the world, was at war. Sorting his papers one
evening, Lehmann came across the last letter Toni had written him 'with all its
warmth and gaiety, – but anxiety in the gaiety, and the feeling that he has really
depended entirely on me the whole time'. It was an unbearable moment, 'But at
least we know we love one another, that always.' At the start of an exile that
would never be rescinded, he felt, more strongly than ever before, that the
feelings he had invested in Vienna and Sikyr were 'something positive and
created in my life, something supremely happy I should never reach again; how
beautiful beyond all memory Austria looked from the train as I passed out of it
for the last time'.

# New Writing

Even at the heart of *New Writing*, a contribution to English literature that remains the most tangible testament to Lehmann's industry, there lies a personal delusion, an air of trickery, that was perhaps dispelled early during its existence. We do not recognise the nature of that delusion in anything Lehmann tells us about *New Writing* in *The Whispering Gallery*, or in anything that Lehmann subsequently wrote. The facts of that delusion could not cloud the achievement of *New Writing*'s survival through a long metamorphoses of style, content and intention, beginning in the spring of 1936 and ending fourteen years later. But there was an inevitability about the outcome of Lehmann's ambition to utilise what was best and current in English and foreign writing, underlit by a determination to repudiate Fascism: a bringing together of literature that might have a political dimension but no political *raison d'être*.

It was a different policy from that of the *Left Review* which, since 1934, had published many of the writers that Lehmann would use in the new anthologies. There were hopes of a new comradeship in the written word, the meeting of middle-class, privilege and university-educated authors with those of the working-class, bringing up their manuscripts from the coal seams of Wales, from the dark, perhaps still satanic mills, from the airless factories of the industrial North, from the hulks of great toiling ships at sea.

From the start, there was in Lehmann's mind the mission that *New Writing* would make the extremes between these two worlds of literature indivisible, though this aim went unmentioned in the 'Manifesto' with which he introduced the first issue. Perhaps the ideal was too remote, too subconscious, too subversive to reveal. The manifesto nevertheless seemed clear enough. *New Writing* would appear twice a year; it would concentrate mainly on the work of young writers and poets, English and foreign, whose contributions might be unsuitable for publication in other anthologies. It would not carry criticism. It welcomed all political parties, but rejected the reactionary and the Fascist.

There is no doubt that another of Lehmann's unstated objectives was the encouragement of the short story, the stunted novella, the European taste for which he wanted to encourage in the English reader. From the start, his concern was for genre as well as content, but the vagueness of the manifesto was something chalked on a board, to be washed out and altered when need arose. The more grandiose concept of a band of writers enabling a prevention of war went unmentioned here, confined to the reflective mood of *The Whispering*

*Gallery*. At the precipice of war, it seemed a time for proving the pen mightier than any sword.

At the beginning, Lehmann had at his elbow two essentially different intellects whose editorial contributions he would later acknowledge: Isherwood and the communist historian and writer Ralph Fox. Fox, whose hopes for the new venture must have been more politicised than Lehmann's, brought with him a wide knowledge of contemporary Soviet writers, a fact reflected in the Russian contingent that spread across *New Writing*'s first issue, distinguished by Boris Pasternak's lengthy poem '1905'. From France came André Chamson's story 'My Enemy', from China, Tchang T'ien-Yih's 'Hatred' with its cool description of a labour-gang worker being eaten alive by ants; from Czechoslovakia, Egon Erwin Kisch's searing account of the widow of a political activist raped by her husband's oppressors while he is forced to look on, singing The Internationale; from Germany, a graphic description of Nazi cruelty against the background of 'The Lord's Prayer', told by Anna Seghers.

Among the most substantial of the English offerings were Isherwood's story 'The Nowaks', rescued by him from his abandoned novel *The Lost*, and eventually to become part of *Goodbye to Berlin*, Edward Upward's 'The Border-Line', extracted from his novel in progress *Journey to the Border*, published 1938, and four Spender poems. Plomer and Lehmann contributed travelogues, respectively on Ireland and Paris, Moscow and the Caucasus, accentuating *New Writing*'s international tilt.

The working-class writer, generally expected to come up with fiction that merged into a documentary realism, was introduced without trumpets in the form of Gore Graham, Charles Harte, John Hampson and Ralph Bates. Struggling, and often lacking the recognition that Lehmann's more statuesque authors brought with them, this new breed perhaps had one identifying characteristic shared between them: they appreciated what Bates, in his story 'The Launch' (the first piece of fiction to be published in *New Writing*), called 'the hardihood of men'.

Consider their credentials. Bates had been a fitter-engineer in England before working in Spanish dockyards, Graham a metal-turner in Yorkshire. In fact, both men had established themselves as writers by the time Lehmann took them up, but their origins marked them out as the genuine article – they had achieved without prejudice of education or wealth. Charles Harte's 'Blackleg' so conjures up a world of Midland Station hotels, stiff blue overalls, dinner-time hooters and foremen, that the brown-grey Britain of the thirties exists in it with complete truth; its prose has a rough poetry that is entirely appropriate. Is its effectiveness shaken by knowing that Harte was educated at Belfast's Queens University? John Hampson already had five novels behind him, having become, with Walter Allen, one of the 'Birmingham Group' of writers. Hampson's qualifications were impeccable, for he had received no university education. After a childhood lived in poverty, he worked as a chef and billiard-maker before writing his first novel,

*Saturday Night at the Greyhound*, in 1931. By the time he came to Lehmann, Hampson brought not only working-class *gravitas*, but a sense of purpose rooted in place – what might be called a positive provincialism. Both were to be useful in the pursuit of Lehmann's Grail.

Perhaps it is salutary to remember that one of the most effective of Lehmann's writers of the working-class story was G. F. (Dick) Green. The fact that his father was an ironfounder is irrelevant, for Green went on to Repton and Cambridge, beginnings that possibly nurtured the extreme sophistication he lavished on his language, for he wrote with a constantly energetic, observant precision in dialogue that makes his work some of the most distinguished to appear in *New Writing*. If there was to be a fusion of the old and new, it seemed that a beginning in which there was tremendous potential had been made.

*

It may partly be due to Lehmann's magpie thievery of all kinds of material in the charged climate of the mid-1930s that he would never really lead the British working-class writer into battle – one for which they were weakened by continually having to rub shoulders with the writer mandarins. The ideal was that Lehmann would bridge (he had considered calling his new venture the *Bridge*) the accepted and the unknown. He intended to break the stronghold that had held good for so many years, to introduce the vernacular. By a labelling of this cogent force he might have strengthened what could be achieved, but the movement, if such it was, remained *ad hoc* and unnamed. He might have defined both intention and limitation had he only given a title to their poaching activities; they were, indisputably, the Trespassers of English Literature.

If what was expected of the Trespassers was underplayed in the early days of *New Writing*, the juxtaposition of foreign with home-spun material held a recognised prominence. Lehmann's hope of opening the English sensibility to the sensibilities of other cultures and peoples was laudable and altruistic, but there was always the danger that too much un-English stuff would affect the balance of the whole. Fox emphasised the importance of the English contribution, telling Lehmann that it was with these that his first duty lay.

In fact, there was no noticeable reduction in the amount of international writing for the second issue, published Autumn 1936. There was no poetry, the only poet, Auden, represented by an Ionesco-like theatrical monologue, 'Alfred', for an old woman preparing sage and onions. There were solid pieces from Orwell (the Burma-inspired 'Shooting an Elephant'), V. S. Pritchett's 'Sense of Humour' and, by Rex Warner, 'The Football Match'. There were some new names among the Trespassers: as well as Bates, Willy Goldman, George Garrett and Leslie Halward. Always, too, there was some manifestation of foreign Trespassers: in this issue, the exiled Viennese Georg Anders, who had been a *Schutzbündler* in the February 1934 Socialists' Rising, the exiled German Bodo

Uhse, and the exiled Italian Ignazio Silone's 'Journey to Paris', a story of Fontamara peasants.

Patterns, altering in their constituents, were emerging. By the third issue, of Spring 1937, Lehmann had obvious cornerstones in 'A Berlin Diary', again plundered from Isherwood's bottom drawer. The Sally Bowles story was also offered to Lehmann, who reluctantly declined it on account of its length – Beatrix always maintained that Isherwood had been fascinated by the model for Bowles, Jean Ross, not because of her physical attractiveness but because of her willingness to describe her most recent sexual adventure to him in the greatest detail. From Upward there was another extract from his novel-in-the-making. Spender's two theatrical poems were eclipsed by Auden's 'Lay your sleeping head, my love', one of his most outstanding lyrics.

As in the first issues, there was a notable lack of American writers, but work from Spain, Russia, France, Poland, some from writers driven from their homeland by Fascism, whose work had first appeared in the anti-Fascist monthly *Das Wort*. There was a pronounced political feel to the third issue, published as a tribute to Fox who in January had been killed in the Spanish Civil War, leading the International Column at Cordova. Lehmann's intention was strongly realised. Under the heading of 'Workers and Fighters', he presented a forceful collection of pieces on the Spanish conflict, Polish oppression, and the great Hunger March of 1922. It seemed that *New Writing* was fulfilling what the *Manchester Guardian* had detected at its beginning, the evolving of 'a literature arising from the violent conflicts of human life in our time'.

With Fox dead, and Isherwood (according to *The Whispering Gallery* at the centre of its existence) in Germany, it was inevitable that Lehmann's control over *New Writing* would swiftly become autocratic. He felt himself skidding with the third issue, appearing at 'a time of great tension for me', not least because Lawrence and Wishart had now taken over publication from the Bodley Head.

Its reception was muted, suggesting 'clear press prejudices against political implications'. As bad, in June, was the reception of his book about Soviet Georgia, *Prometheus and the Bolsheviks*, which left him wounded. With both the book and *New Writing*, 'I had not been prepared for the attitude of the right and the new counter offensive'; besides, the book had been 'brought out in too great a hurry'.

*Prometheus and the Bolsheviks* offered Communist solutions to international problems, advocating the charms of extreme socialism under which all life, and not least the arts, would flower anew. For Lehmann, it was the promulgation of a personal vision, promising far more than a nationalistic Utopia. The intensity of the promise is conveyed at the book's close, when Prometheus, mythic beast of the Caucasus, appears before Lehmann as in a dream. It gives Lehmann the opportunity to tell Prometheus how impressed he is with everything he has seen, the success of the collective farms, the happiness of the peasantry, the availability of work suitable for all gifts, the richness of education, the lack, everywhere, of any discrimination: Lehmann can barely differentiate between the Caucasus and Paradise. Prometheus asks

'... did you feel that literature was appreciated by this new society, and given its proper place in men's lives – literature, I mean, in the most austere sense of the word?'

'Yes, [replies Lehmann] and increasingly so. You see, I've come to believe that uncorrupted people, everywhere in the world, have a natural desire to understand and enjoy art. And here I've felt that the sluice-gates were for the first time being fully opened for this desire, like an immense pressure of waters, to pour through.'

'That is certainly true for the literature of the past. And the literature of the present: Is the young writer, do you think, cared for?'

'His existence,' I answered emphatically, 'is securer than anywhere else in the world.'

'And you did not get the impression that an imaginative writer must adopt a definite outlook before he can succeed? I am not speaking, mind you, of those who write on specifically political problems, but of the creative artist in his own province.'

'On the contrary, I did. But this outlook is so wide that I would willingly submit to it: it is belief in humanity. As the years have gone by, the freedom of artists has steadily grown, and I believe profoundly that as economic security advances and the very real danger of war decreases, the day will approach when this new society will show a variety and richness of literary and artistic achievement as has never before been seen in the world.'

Before vanishing into air, Prometheus tells Lehmann that he has himself decided to join the Communist Party.

The sentiments Lehmann expresses did not find their way into the *New Writing*'s manifesto, but we can better understand Lehmann's preferences. Nevertheless, he was shaken by the mixed reaction to *New Writing* 3, even though reassurance came from Spender, Upward, Kingsley Martin and, after initial carping, Rosamond. He had to 'remain in the steady conviction of the reality of what I'm doing that Nos 1 and 2's reception confirmed'. The pressure of responding to the reception of each issue was considerable, and the responsibility for maintaining a standard his own. In the middle of the fervour, an almost terrifying realisation cut across the weariness he was experiencing. In September 1937 he confided to his journal 'My journalist life and apparatus – at times I realise I only half believe in it, and am playing a part just as hard as I can.' It is the kind of confession that a man makes only to himself.

*

Number 4 of *New Writing* by no means turned its back on the political slant of its forerunners. Lines still came in from the battlefields, notably Alfred Kantorowicz's 'A Madrid Diary' and John Cornford's elegiac 'Three Poems' published after his death in Spain in 1936. Poetry had found its feet, proving Lehmann's assertion that it had performed an evolution towards the spirit of the prose, a trick that may well have been one of his greatest achievements.

*New Writing*'s poetry was to prove consistently interesting. There is a sudden flavour that breaks into it from this issue on, typified here in Auden's frolicsome 'Miss Gee', 'Victor' and 'Under the fronds of life', and in Louis MacNeice's 'June Thunder'. And so the list expands: Day Lewis, Ahmed Ali, who translated his own work from the Urdu, Bertolt Brecht, Federico Garcia Lorca, Walter Allen, E. M. Forster, T. C. (Cuthbert) Worsley. There was probably a strengthening of purpose after Lehmann's break with Lawrence and Wishart, who had held out the promise of beginning a 'Library' of monographs by *New Writing* authors which was never realised.

In his renewed association with the Woolfs, Lehmann saw renewed hope for the future of the war years, and the ensured progress of his magazine under a permanent banner, and it was under the Hogarth imprint that the first number of *New Writing new series* appeared in the autumn of 1938. For the first time, there was a published acknowledgement that Lehmann had edited it 'with the assistance of' Isherwood and Spender.

The settling-in with Hogarth presaged an up-turn in *New Writing*'s fortunes, a consolidation of what had been before. There were photographs: portraits of André Malraux, film stills, two scenes from the Group Theatre's productions, and – taken by Humphrey Spender – glimpses of human life, 'Street Scenes in Whitechapel' and 'Dancing on the Pier'. Clearly, *new series* was opening itself to other arts besides literature, and at once a new tone of criticism and anthropological intensity, was part of it. Its strengths began to seem formidable.

The first issue had poems by Spender, Auden, MacNeice and Lorca, as well as stories by the New Zealander Frank Sargeson, essays on Malraux, French cinema, Spender on the plays of Auden and Isherwood, and Willy Goldman (the first of the Trespassers to turn critic) on 'Literature and the East End'. There was a sharper focus, suggesting that Lehmann's original mix of stories and poems had needed the background that would put them into some sort of perspective, an appreciation of the world the writers and readers inhabited. Vitality was there, and continued to spark the three issues that made up *new series* until it ended in Christmas 1939.

The awareness of a sociological element, ignored by Lehmann's original manifesto, was especially useful in bringing the Trespassers to the fore, for their true value could only be seen in the context of the period (defined by Lehmann as existing between the rise of Hitler and the outbreak of war). In this, they had a corollary in the Documentary Film Movement, which really only existed between these same parameters, and gave a heightened visual evidence to the way the working-class lived.

Mass-observation, though only begun in 1937, was another strand of the same forward thrust with more earnest and scientific purpose, and carried its work through the war. Two of its originators, the poet Charles Madge and the anthropologist Tom Harrisson, would themselves contribute to *New Writing*, where they would have felt comfortable among the writers contributing the fiction-reportage that was now a regular feature. The socially-disadvantaged, and their sympathisers, were having their voice, typified in what Lehmann thought 'the vivid human appeal of these stories, their sensitive, unhysterical truth with a just perceptible undercurrent of stolid bitterness'.

How faintly their names come back to us now: B. L. Coombes, Willy Goldman, Leslie Halward, Sid Chaplin, Gore Graham. In 1937, Coombes was working as an underground ambulance man at a colliery, a defiant, sharp little man whose photograph gives an impression of a stubborn, steadily burrowing animal with blunt claws. His stoicism was almost symbolic. He had his personal stigmata, a piece of blue coal embedded in his nose (Lehmann was astonished when he noticed it for the first time). When Coombes sent his first story to *New Writing*, 'The Flame', it perfectly suited what Lehmann was looking for from a Trespasser – an almost painstaking attention to industrial detail, the whiff of fact that had been forced into fiction. As literature, much of what Coombes wrote verged on the primitive, but it was sharpened and honed by honesty, a direct, unemotional communication, flickering as on a screen (it is no surprise that in the mid-1950s he was writing film scripts, for his writing has an absolutely cinematic simplicity and directness).

The uncluttered depiction of underclass living found an easy response in Lehmann. It is interesting that in his 1940 Pelican *New Writing in Europe*, (in a chapter not altogether reassuringly titled 'The Man in the Street') he expresses an uneasiness with the stories of G. F. Green, their 'elliptic' quality 'so shorn grammatically', apparently unable to see that it is these very characteristics that give Green his unique, musical voice. There must be the suspicion that Lehmann preferred his Trespassers to come with their words untroubled by stylistic individuality.

Lehmann said he was 'inarticulately aware … of the difference between a literature that is an interpretation of its time, and one that transforms it', but it seems that Lehmann never decided on which side his working-class writers, not quite within the bounds of an organised movement, belonged. Youth and dirtied hands sometimes seemed enough, stuff to give credence to the entry in 'Notes on Contributors' that introduced each *New Writing*. Leslie Halward had been diesinker, toolmaker, labourer and plasterer; Gordon Jeffrey a shipwright apprentice; Goldman (who would also help Lehmann on the editing side) a docker and rag-trade worker.

An association with sea-going was often there, most strongly linked by the three 'sailor' writers who by themselves seemed capable of expressing everything that needed to be said about Bates's 'hardihood of men': James Hanley, George Garrett and Jim Phelan. All three made significant contributions both to *New Writing* and the *Left Review*. Hanley never met Garrett (a pseudonym for the even harsher sounding Joe Jarrett) or Phelan, but the men would have understood each other.

Hanley and Garrett both left their Catholic Liverpool homes at an early age to work at sea; Irish-born Phelan left home at eleven, scraping a living around the Dublin slums until he too went to sea. He subsequently joined the I.R.A., and in 1923 killed a man during a post office robbery, a crime for which he was sent to be hanged. The death sentence was commuted, and he stayed in prison until 1937. He was well equipped to write about abuse, cruelty and obsession, and he did so, in stories that have nothing hybrid or apologetic about them. In his 1938 novel, *Ten-A-Penny-People*, he has a young Liverpool boy, Joe Jarrow (surely another pseudonym for Joe Jarrett), refusing to accept his father's insistence that he goes to sea as a stoker. They fight, and Joe is overcome. The father opens his flies and urinates over the boy's face.

Abuse also makes the disturbing centre of much of Hanley's work. His first published story, in 1930, 'The German Prisoner' was an account of English privates sexually torturing, and murdering, a German soldier. In the following year came his novel *Boy*, banned as an obscene book in 1932. The deep power of Hanley's novel is unquestionably brutal, a catalogue of sexual and emotional abuse inflicted on a boy taken to sea. He is raped by sailors, he is smothered to death. Throughout, we believe that Hanley has learned his understanding of such horrors, and needs to communicate them. As a Trespasser, he might have proved one of the most aggressive of Lehmann's army, but he quickly faded from *New Writing*'s pages.

George Garrett's small body of work suggests that he shared some of Hanley's distinctiveness. He had already spent a young life in the stoke-holds of ships but, justifiably if we judge by the few pieces he left, considered himself a writer. His first work for *New Writing*, 'Fishmeal', is strong. We are inside one of the stoke-holds that Garrett knew so well, where Costain lies ill, tortured in mind and body by the terrible conditions under which he works and lives. Unable to tolerate his surroundings, he casts himself into the sea 'so vast, so fascinating, and so inviting', desperate for 'a decent cooler'. When his body is dragged back on deck, 'it hung awry with arms outstretched like a blood-stained Christ'. Garrett, like Hanley, could conjure up a Conradian intensity, and manage the shift into symbolism with aplomb.

Hanley, Garrett, Phelan: all had something uncompromising that might have acted as an agent of change, but were nevertheless in parallel to the less savage of their compatriots. Theirs was almost a contradiction of everything that had gone before; an altered order of things that made what Isherwood had drummed up seem hollow and rootless. There is an impression that to Lehmann the

Trespassers were a vague vogue that he never thought worth bringing to the fore, that they would always be a supporting cast, divertissement not act.

> One must not only see that this great and terrible epoch is coming, but one must see the pattern in it, so that the vision of the meaning and the end can keep one steady – if it can – in the middle of suffering and tension.
>
> And more: all through one must hold on firmly to the ideal of humanism, a new humanism that can help one to stand in the middle of the battle, and not only that but also to prevent the battle changing people into its own evil.
>
> I believe that perhaps I have a real role to play, but only the shape the battle takes can determine what precisely it is. It is necessary now as never to seek power. At moments I feel so urgently convinced of this that I am like a machine roaring aimlessly out of gear; at others I feel I am inflating myself with grossly exaggerated confidence and powers ...
>
> But again I feel that my part as rallying point for the younger writers and intellectuals – particularly those who care about politics as well as art – defines itself always more clearly, and I mustn't shirk my responsibilities ...
>
> And one day may show me that it is all a pack of cards –! And a 'sense of destiny' only one of the ways in which ambition or ripeness makes one drunk.

Lehmann's appreciation of a 'sense of destiny' was accentuated by the publication of his novel, *Evil Was Abroad*, in September 1938. It had begun as a story, 'The Boy who Disappeared', in the late autumn of 1933, was interrupted a few months later by the upheavals in Austria, and taken up again only in the winter of 1937. When he read it, Isherwood urged Lehmann to turn it into a novel, and it is thus developed that *Evil Was Abroad* survives as an intriguing statement of belief and passion at a crucial point, not only in the destiny of civilisation, but in Lehmann's life.

Indeed, it is as autobiography, highly altered as it may be, that the book exists. Peter Rains, an upper middle-class writer, educated at Oxford and making his living from hack (if literary) journalism, has come to Vienna to write the life of the great dead poet whom he reveres. Peter (Lehmann, of course), never gives his poet a name, but we know it must be Rilke, through whom Peter means to make his own reputation. It seems the book's foundations are literary, but these foundations are almost immediately rocked by what Peter begins to discover about his poet's life. Confronted by unpublished manuscripts, he is on the verge of a tremendous re-assessment of his poet, 'a glimpse of an entirely new conception ... of revolutionary significance'.

For a moment, it seems that this novel will concentrate only on what is of literary interest, for it is on this that Peter has fixed his professional fortune. It is a continuing discovery. A photograph of the poet reveals to Peter 'an unexpected look of bold determination, something far more incisive and active, though the whole expression remained sensitive and delightful, than the accepted, almost feminine dreaminess, which had become the popular symbol of the poet's appearance'. Robert K. Martin has noted the importance of this passage,

> … since it amounts to a recognition both that art need not be decadent or 'effeminate' and that homosexuality has its own virility. In both ways Lehmann was significantly altering the dominant image, inherited from the *fin-de-siècle* and Bloomsbury, of an effete, androgynous culture. Against that he poses the 'new' image of an engaged art and an engaged sexuality, both of them infused with a new spirit of the working-class youth.

Lehmann's active, manly attitude may also in part be a reaction to what he had endured at the hands of Strachey, Bell and Redgrave. He was putting an end to subordination; no longer would he be victim.

In Vienna, Peter becomes a natural hunter. At an Automatic buffet, he sees an out-of-work young man, the shoemaker Rudi Slavanek, who follows him home. Peter is instantly attracted to him, and they arrange to meet again; Lehmann has wasted no time in announcing a sexual aspect. Rudi introduces Peter to his handsome friend Bertl, a metal worker and member of the military defence corps (the *Schutzbund*). It is Bertl who discusses politics and the social situation in Vienna, thus establishing the third and final strand of the book – the predominance of politics.

Literature, sex and politics, it is in the inter-relationship of each that Peter must find his way. The effect of Rudi is to activate in Peter feelings that had lain dormant for so long, emphasising the suspicion Peter had already felt at university that he had grown up 'in so narrow a circumference, and to be so deeply ignorant of what most Englishmen were like, what they thought, what they wanted, how they worked and earned'. Any understanding of a real world populated by working men had been remote, 'ideas in the void'. Rudi creates the longing 'to know more details of his life and the life of his friends, to be able to picture it vividly, to live through it in imagination as if to make it part of his own experience'. Peter, in fact, is beginning to see a new life, lived in default of his own, in other people. It is to Rudi and to the sexual obsession that he stirs in him (necessarily obscured in the text's surface meaning), that Peter looks to sort 'the tangle between the ideas on which he had built up his picture of the world while still at school, when Voltaire and Darwin had seemed to him the only prophets, and the confused leaning towards a kind of mysticism that had since troubled those too clear waters'. All of this, of course, blatantly exposes Lehmann's insistence that he had never experienced a normal, real life.

Peter instinctively assumes a responsibility for Rudi's well being: he feels his role is to 'tackle seriously the problems of Rudi's life'. This well-meaning intervention is a characteristic mirrored in all of Lehmann's emotional relationships, from Toni Sikyr onwards. Apart from the sexual element, his friendship was there to effect a *change* in the life of the loved one, a change for the better, and one that contained more than a suggestion of literary 'improvement'. This need to control, even divert, the path of a lover's life was clearly one that Lehmann recognised in himself, without perhaps ever appreciating the difficulties it brought.

But Peter's fascination for Rudi is not exclusive. He is also attracted to Bertl, and indeed to all the young men who float in and out of the novel, always seemingly aware that they are bisexual, and are sometimes only diverted into homosexuality by a need to make some quick money. Affection, in *Evil Was Abroad*, may be prostituted; sexual discovery is everywhere, even suggested in the history of the poet when Lehmann hints at a liaison between the poet and his married friend Richard Horn. The poet's dilemma is mirrored in what is happening to Peter, whose work in progress is 'a direct door into his favourite world, a world inhabited by poets and artists of the past'.

The placidity of that world is shaken by sexual appetite, for Peter is aware, as soon as he meets Rudi, of a disturbance that

> ... had started earlier, seemed only to have reached a sort of crisis in the meeting under the lamp-post: mingling with the recurrent thoughts of the boy's hands moving through their half-frozen gestures, the torn pull-over, the toneless despairing words, were thoughts of the discoveries he seemed to be making in the poet's life, the new aspects of his art they revealed.

Links are thus perceived between male sexuality and the inner meaning of the written word. There is an awareness, suddenly, of the necessity of this two-way arrangement. Later, 'there were two processes at work, and that contact with Rudi and his friends was bringing him new understanding of the poetry, just as much as the poetry was bringing him towards the living'.

Of course, we have to break through the genteel sexual translation forced on Lehmann. Reassuringly, Lehmann himself illuminates the meaning forty years later in his second autobiographical novel *In the Purely Pagan Sense*, where his Lehmann-figure, Jack Marlowe, confesses that his life has been the 'pursuit of illumination through sex'. Even through the gauze of a work of fiction appearing in 1938, however, Lehmann's original philosophy could scarcely be made clearer.

One of the factors that prevent Lehmann, or Peter Rains or Jack Marlowe, from turning that philosophy – 'the pursuit of illumination through sex' – into any sort of enduring happiness is also transparently obvious in *Evil Was Abroad*. Peter decides to travel to Prague to visit his friends Dick and Juliet (either of whom, Lehmann seems to suggest, might have provided an alternative emotional future for his hero), thus abandoning Rudi to his uncertain existence, Rudi who was

> ... entirely without protection, without pretensions or power, and his complete exposure seemed to give him a freshness, an unspoilt quality, that was to Peter like food that you only realise you have badly needed when you happen to taste it. And at the same time it roused in Peter an immense latent desire to protect ...

But even as Peter is struck by the force of this, he leaves Rudi to go to Prague. This act of physical separation was to be another ever-apparent feature of Lehmann's real-life relationships, repeated over and over. There is no evidence that it ever did anything but harm to the lover of the moment; it bedevilled the progress of love. Now, Peter remembers how at university he and Dick and their circle had railed against the English hypocrisy about sex, insisting that

> The great sin was to pretend that any relationship could be deep and strong without an undercurrent of simply physical attraction, entirely natural and inevitable. This was their charter of emancipation, their answer to the mess that previous generations had got themselves into. The world seemed suddenly free and glorious, there were no more corrupting inhibitions and guilt was driven back like a shoddy impostor. Now, he felt with sharpened perception, what they had written on their charter was true indeed, but only the beginning of the truth, too obvious to have made such a stand about, only the first step in the argument to a far more comprehensive and exciting truth about the creative power of all relationships, whether expressed physically or not.

In Prague, Peter becomes convinced that at the heart of his beloved poet's work lies 'a protest against the very foundations of the society they lived in, a protest that developed from an early malaise to a disgust and rejection, an appeal to other values' – a protest that we may perceive in Lehmann as continually emerging throughout his writing life. It is those 'very foundations of society' that are questioned not only in *Evil Was Abroad*, but also throughout his long prose poem 'Christ the Hunter' and *In the Purely Pagan Sense*. We should not forget that of principal concern to Lehmann was the sexual territory he inhabited. We should be refreshed to know that, even in this first novel, there is no shock attached to his awakening knowledge of his own sexuality.

Today, we might see Lehmann as a 'happy' homosexual, in the sense that any unhappiness his condition brought him (and it brought him much) was not caused by any inherent dissatisfaction with his sexual orientation. He seems never to have considered rejecting it. Everywhere, indeed, in *Evil Was Abroad*, is the untroubled conviction that his life will be marked, and indeed distinguished, by his homosexuality. His love of men is a fact that brings no problem with it. The problems are only manifested in Lehmann's, or Peter's, essential personality.

When Peter returns to Vienna, Rudi has disappeared. A long search ensues, through streets, homosexual clubs, tenements. Through another young boy, Peter discovers that Rudi has had a relationship with a girl, Lisl, after which he became ill (Lehmann hints at venereal disease). But Rudi cannot be found. Has he, like so many of the desperate young men of Vienna, killed himself? There can only be disillusion.

> How was it that he, Peter Rains, could feel intimate with some one for weeks, months, to find after all that he had not seen the real person? That plate after plate of coloured glass had been taken away, but there still remained one plate that falsified the whole image.

Again, here is Lehmann recognising, perhaps unconsciously, an element that would cloud his emotional development for the rest of his life: his inability, never to be corrected, of apparently failing to see 'the real person' – a real person, of course, that was anyway immediately susceptible to Lehmann's demand for change. Peter's meeting with Rudi sets in motion the events that would repeat themselves throughout Lehmann's life: sexual attraction quickly consummated and almost immediately given a deep significance, a need to have some controlling influence over the lover's existence, eventually followed by argument or misunderstanding and an inevitable parting.

Throughout the process, it seems that Lehmann was not particularly adept at expressing the depth of the emotion he was feeling for those he was sleeping with. Indeed, his obsession for Rudi, which gives the reason to *Evil Was Abroad*, cannot be overstated. Without him, Peter can only be identified with him through the Austrians rising against Fascism and, as the novel ends, at last he becomes one with the struggling crowds, one of a movement that means to alter the world's history.

At its most effective, *Evil Was Abroad* is a potent autobiographical expression, pinned at a time of great personal and international realisation. It has about it the shape of a journey, for it is Peter's dissatisfaction with his English life that begins his life in Vienna, and it is with the unhappiness that Vienna has brought him that the book ends. Crucial to it is Rudi's disappearance, in which it is not fanciful to see the potential obliteration of Toni Sikyr from Lehmann's life, with Peter the victim of catastrophic events that Lehmann would become. How much of this Lehmann recognised we cannot tell. He saw the book's publication on 26 September 1938 as the appearance of 'a child that strays into a party of loudly arguing grown-ups, completely ignored'.

The book was not ignored by the critics, whose reaction to it was consistent.

Richard Church thought its 'upper' meaning 'immature, the technique and the sympathies clumsy. The "under" meaning is true, gentle and promissory of creative compassion.' To Frank Swinnerton it seemed 'under-emphatic; and the impression it leaves is of an immature talent not yet free of conventional ideas'. Lehmann's old ally from Summer Fields, L. A. G. Strong, complaining that the Prague episode broke the story's flow, suspected that 'Many readers may be impatient with a hero who must go abroad to wake up to facts which with a more robust upbringing he would have known before he was ten', though the author was 'exceptionally sensitive: he can convey his impressions to the last half-shade and undertone'.

*

For Lehmann, the publication of his first novel was synonymous with a great closing down of whole areas of his life. Beyond it

> The shutting of frontiers down there away on the Danube sounds like steel doors violently clanging, and the extinguishing lights in Prague and Vienna is like the final night of hope and happiness while the storm of hate and murder howls up from the horizon to the vault of the sky.

At the forefront of these happenings was the deep personal regret of impending enforced separation from Vienna and Sikyr, thoughts of whom were revealed as 'immensely precious'. Lehmann saw that for too much of their life they had been apart: the very problem that had helped to break Peter and Rudi.

It seemed increasingly unnatural to run *New Writing* from anywhere but England; Vienna was inhibiting its potential. Spender, that 'natural traitor', was perceived as an impediment to these ambitions. It was not only that, having promised that Hogarth would have his first novel, Spender then decided it should go to Faber, his action obliging Lehmann to act like

> ... a grasping business man. But betrayal is necessary to his disease-swollen ego, proved time and again this past year, and will be for the future ... It is only my belief in him as a great poet that holds me to him, though I feel our private relationship is ruined.

Lehmann found in Spender 'a streak of genius in an absolutely pathetic temperament, dementedly egotistical, suddenly inflamed with feverish impulses that can only find satisfaction in wrecking anything in which [he is] collaborating, in biting savagely and unexpectedly at any one who becomes too friendly or too helpful, with the spirit of a snarling poodle'.

Robert Waller, then about to be published by Lehmann as a 'Poet of Tomorrow' ('tomorrow', he recalls, 'never comes') was one day waiting in the Hogarth office when Spender walked in. Spender placed an open notebook on a table and walked out. Lehmann came in, read the open page, said 'Traitor' and, taking no notice of Waller, went back into his office. Waller sped to the notebook and read 'Today I renounce homosexuality.' He sat down 'like a patient in a dentist's waiting room, too astonished to be amused'.

The on-going sexual uncertainties that troubled Lehmann and Spender's relationship was further aggravated when Spender promised allegiance to Cyril Connolly's new magazine, *Horizon*; indeed, Spender would, to all intents, be its co-editor, one of the three central figures (with Peter Watson) in *Horizon*'s future. He was careful that his name should not be seen with Connolly's on the magazine's notepaper, but his involvement was absolute, and the magazine – first published in December 1939 – was run from his flat in Lansdowne Terrace. Cuthbert Worsley informed Lehmann that his three rivals moved in an aura of 'mass-hysteria, with Spender so alarmingly in the centre of it'.

Lehmann was furious when, in February, *Horizon* carried Connolly's announcement that the new magazine would indeed be competing with *New Writing*. By now, it was 'impossible to have a direct and natural relationship with [Spender] as a friend or even close collaborator, pathologically eaten up as he is with jealousy, vanity, egotism, and utterly corrupted by years of extravagant self-deception'. 'I know he is my enemy', Lehmann wrote in April 1940, 'in the deepest sense.'

But by the autumn of 1939 Lehmann was deeply involved in deciding what the war would mean to *New Writing*. The third of the *new series*, published Christmas 1939, announced itself as the last, while promising that its work would in some form or another continue. He was constantly seeing new writers, buoyed up by Roger Senhouse telling him that *New Writing* was 'one of the few things that will count in this decade'. Rosamond assisted at a final party for those that had been involved in its success, but there was the excitement of something about to happen rather than something ended.

\*

What emerged for Autumn 1940 was *Folios of New Writing*, its utility thick pages bereft of illustrations and with a much reduced list of foreign authors: the voices of the far-off oppressed had grown fainter. The time was full of fresh uncertainties and muddle. For Lehmann, there was a feeling that 'so many of the contributors had been moved by the slogans of passion and idealism of the thirties, and now found them inadequate'. New reasons had to be found.

Meanwhile, the revised format benefited by a compression of content, and there was much that was admirable in effort and realisation. Orwell's 'My Country Right or Left', a brief but effective essay on the mysticism of patriotism, advocated changes that could only come with revolution, and a bloody one if necessary. Somehow, Orwell's message already sounded dislocated if hopeful, with his belief that Colonel Blimps might yet be turned into socialists. It was a transformation of the poet, the artist in imagination, that concerned Spender in 'The Creative Imagination in the World Today', urging the utilisation of art in transforming society.

The English fiction included V. S. Pritchett's luminous short story 'Aunt Gertrude', Coombes' 'Sabbath Night', another glimpse of mining life that showed his knack for unsensational dialogue, and a touching 'Fragment of a Diary' by Julia Strachey, the story of a Portuguese boy removed to a bleak English seaside hotel. Laurie Lee, Day Lewis, Rex Warner and Charles Brasch wrote poems. And then there was Virginia Woolf's 'The Leaning Tower', a transcript of a talk given by her at Brighton in May to the Workers' Educational Association.

Lehmann had long wanted Woolf in *New Writing*, a desire she resisted, claiming that she was unhappy to work within the limits of his manifesto. Now, she dealt with the accumulated history of English literature, a history she recognised as rooted in the appreciation of class, its groupings tethered within prescribed hedges. She spoke of writers occupying a raised chair, benefiting from gold and silver, advantages close at hand from the comfort of the raised chair. Even as such a circle gratified, it grew on itself. The boy brought up in a library would become a book worm, the boy brought up in fields an earth worm. It was natural that the writer's art had to be taught, or at least learned. 'To breed the kind of butterfly a writer is you must let him sun himself for three or four years at Oxford or Cambridge so it seems.'

Thus springs up Woolf's Tower, made unsteady by literary underminings that had withheld until war, and youth at the gate, roared up at it. Woolf accused Yeats and Eliot of throwing away the inheritance left them by their predecessors. Auden was a politicians' poet. Now, writers were trapped in the tower from which they could not descend, a calamity that explained 'the violence of their attack upon bourgeois society and also its half-heartedness. They are profiting by a society which they abuse. They are flogging a dead or dying horse because a living horse, if flogged, would kick them off its back.' A need for politics and truth had resulted in autobiography having more validity than any imaginative writing, crippled as it was by a paralysis of the inner mind. And yet, Woolf insisted, she was ready to welcome those who trespassed on the preserves, for literature was common ground; it was for writers to negotiate the gaps that had shaken the tower's foundation. She had sounded an attack on the empirical principles that threatened order.

Three replies to Woolf were published in the subsequent issue of Spring 1941, from Louis MacNeice, Edward Upward and B. L. Coombes. None sympathised with Woolf's implicit suggestion that they and their contemporaries were misguided and compromised by any association with reality. Upward looked to a time when the tower of the middle class would collapse; besides, a writer who praised the society in which he lived as adequate was likely to be a poor specimen: there could be nothing shoddy in the fusion of political belief and creativity. To MacNeice, Woolf was 'inconsistent and unjust' in acidly dismissing the modern writer as 'the embittered and futile tribe of scapegoat hunters'; Woolf was undiscriminating, inconsistent in argument, and they were justified at throwing mud at her old horses.

One can imagine Coombes too wanting no part of Woolf's pretensions. His reply, perhaps with unintentional irony on Lehmann's part, was titled 'Below the Tower', which showed an awareness of the *status quo*. He waved aside Woolf's differentiation between the working-class and the poor, finding them the same. From his lowly position, Coombes heard the muttering that would not be ignored, noises heard by 'leaders in thought' and 'political experts'. He felt Woolf could never be at home in a world thus under revision. If she visited a miner's home, the family would show her into the parlour, and an exception would have been made; if Coombes went, he would be taken into the kitchen and life would go on as if he were not there.

Coombes saw solution enough in workers becoming writers, although their characteristics might be those of an 'alarmed infant', held from the centre by the other classes. He plainly saw that

> ... the Leaning Tower writer starts with a tremendous advantage over us because he has been taught the use of words and the beauty of language and has been trained in the ways of great writers and the manner of getting the right effect. In comparison we are crude and clumsy because our life has made us so, and having no guide we grope into the darkness – often taking the wrong road. Yet I feel we have some advantages because the material for our shaping is very close to our hands.

Coombes is a lone voice here, but surely not typical of the Trespassers. His talent is at heart inferior to those with whom Lehmann identified him. To have Coombes respond to Woolf's tenuously argued philosophising was lopsided, but Coombes could be relied on to be respectful. Cap in hand, he is brought in and given his say. One wonders what response Phelan or Garrett or Hanley had to Woolf's essay – they, perhaps more than any of the Trespassers, would have simply seen it as signalling from across a terrible divide.

Coombes did put up a fight, however. What, he asked, was a writer's capital? Was it not 'all his experiences; his environment; his knowledge of human life and how people live and aspire, love and desire, hate and die?' With a clear-sightedness that makes one wish he had written criticism, Coombes pointed accusingly toward the Tower, whose writer 'will lack the closeness of men who live and work together; who eat the same food at the same time, and who speak the same language ... I want those from the Leaning Tower to come down and teach me what I lack.'

We might guess at the Trespassers' reaction to Woolf, but what can the

Trespassers have made of Lehmann's 'Postscript', made on her behalf since the essay had been published posthumously? It is impossible to see Lehmann's final word as anything other than a dismissal of his fundamental belief in a literary democracy. Hadn't Woolf's words, Lehmann suggested, been merely provocative? He seemed almost to suggest she had been a little tease. He reduced her snobbery to a skittishness. As a socialist, of course she had always been sympathetic to the working-class struggle but, rooted as she was in her own class and culture, could never shift her position; the Trespassers could only expect her borrowed interest. For Lehmann, it was enough that she had never lost her keen interest in new writers. Not only did he not question anything 'The Leaning Tower' had contained – he was all too clearly waving the message across the distance between Woolf and himself and the strugglers of whom she had written.

It was a disappointing performance, four pages of barking up the wrong tree. There was a line beyond which Lehmann's perception could not reach. By linking himself with Woolf he left no doubt that it was the literary establishment that nourished him, and to which he clung. Despite the protestations of bringing the writing man in from the street, he was conscious of the social nicety of what he did, embedded as Lehmann was in classicism and what he unquestioningly saw as 'good' in literature.

Lehmann wanted the bond with the unheard, unkempt voice of the young working-class men, but the truth was that the only way he could achieve this was through having sex with them. The Trespassers might have been forgiven for giving up there and then. Workers all, they trudged on.

By the time Lehmann published the last of Coombes' pieces to appear in *New Writing*, 'Thick Candles', in 1944, the story of a miner unwittingly bringing his wife 'corpse' candles, some of which he had already taken to the widow of a miner killed that day in a pit collapse, the game was up. The miner does not want his wife to know what has happened, but she is alerted, by the thickness of the candles, of an omen. All the hints of Coombes' old bitterness are here, but the time for it to be effective had so clearly passed. It was as if contact had for a fleeting moment been made with beings from a forgotten planet. Coombes, fulfilling Woolf's assessment of biographical confession, wrote his life's story, *These Poor Hands*, published by Gollancz. He continued writing, and found himself fêted as a writer when in 1955 he travelled to Germany, though he seems not to have been an easily likeable man. Three years later, Lehmann helped him secure a pension of £75 a year from the Society of Authors. He retired to a run-down cottage near Seven Sisters in the company of his sheepdog Suzy, neglecting himself and as grumpy as ever, the piece of blue coal, presumably, still locked into his flesh.

\*

It was at the beginning of the war that Barbara Cooper came into Lehmann's life, a life to which she gave everything she had. Her father, the head of a steel and engineering works in the North of England, was a friend of Rudie. All three of his children, Lettice (born 1897), Leonard (born 1900) and Barbara, the youngest, had literary careers. Barbara was born in 1905 at Wetherby in Yorkshire and spent much of her childhood at Roundhay Grange and Carr Lodge at Horbury near Wakefield. Her father had a passion for living in grand houses; if business was poor, he simply moved to a smaller one until finances improved. There was a strong Anglo-Catholic strain in the Coopers, and Barbara was to be a regular churchgoer, High Church, throughout her life. After attending Queen Margaret's at Scarborough she did not, like Lettice and Leonard, go on to university. Her ambition was to be a singer of *lieder*, in which she was encouraged by Julius Harrison, the conductor of the British National Opera Company. After training with Sir Edward Bairstow she gave one or two recitals in Leeds, but it was clear that her voice was too small to fill a hall. Disappointed, she turned to book reviewing for the *Spectator* and the *Yorkshire Post*.

When in late 1939 Barbara moved to London to live with Lettice – then working for *Time and Tide* – in Canfield Gardens, she applied to Lehmann for a job in publishing. Despite her admission that she had no shorthand and could only type in her own fashion, the interview was successful (helped by a recommendation from L. A. G. Strong) and she became his secretary, the start of a twenty-year-long working relationship that would span not only *New Writing* but Lehmann's publishing imprint and the *London Magazine*. Lehmann thought her too good to be true, displaying 'a near-fanatical loyalty, an infallible memory and an unquenchable zest for reading manuscripts, no matter how dreary, pompous, silly, ill-written or ill-typed'. Leonard Cooper felt that his sister's work for Lehmann went largely unrewarded.

> She was more like a partner in the firm. He trusted her to vet material in a way he would trust no one else, but he treated her shabbily. Everything he did was perfect to her: she adored him. She knew about his homosexuality, but Barbara never condemned anybody. I think perhaps she regretted it. She was a born editor, but John never gave her sufficient credit for what she did. She was a very loving, affectionate person, a great friend of mine. I don't think there was ever a romance in her life.

In 1990, Lettice remembered that 'because there was no sexual element, generally a feature of John's relationships with his hitherto male secretaries, it enabled a friendship of trust, dependence and great affection to develop: a relationship of the type often only possible between a homosexual man and a heterosexual woman'.

Had she shown more ambition and less faithfulness to Lehmann Barbara might have become something more than the Amazon Queen of Lehmann's slush-pile: she had the talent to do so. Her novels *Two Walk Together* (1935),

*The Light of Other Days* (1939) and an unfinished romance of the Civil War could have been the beginning of a career as a novelist. Her knowledge of Shelley and Keats, of whom she long cherished hopes to write a study, was peerless, as was her instinct for what was good in poetry. Studying letters, both of acceptance and rejection, signed by Lehmann, one is struck by the fact that so often his words merely echo, often word for word, the verdict that Barbara handed on to him. She was the only person other than he who was allowed to read manuscripts and reject them on his behalf. According to Lettice 'all the credit, kudos and plaudits were for John alone. Perhaps in consolation for his lack of recognition as a creative writer he needed this acclaim.' James Michie defines the truth: 'every firm needs a Barbara Cooper'.

To so many of the young male assistants who worked alongside Barbara she was a figure of fun, a roly-poly pudding (she was once seen to eat a whole packet of digestive biscuits at one sitting). She was almost certainly more conscious of their sexual activities than most of them ever suspected, and was worried about the risks that Lehmann ran as a homosexual, but her nephew Leo Cooper thought she was 'not above a bit of pimping'. When she introduced him to Lehmann as a very young man (unnervingly, Lehmann locked the door of the room behind him) Cooper felt she was 'quite willing to offer me up as a piece of flesh for John'.

\*

Barbara, nonetheless, was left outside the inner circle of Lehmann's life, unlike Isherwood who was cared for but undeserving. Read *The Whispering Gallery*, turn the pages of Lehmann's letters, examine his journals, and there is no doubt that Isherwood was of central importance to him. An impression is freely given of Isherwood's interest, support, encouragement, but where is the evidence? There is a longing for Isherwood's presence that runs the thread of Lehmann's life, pages of worry, admiration and love. Examine the diaries of Isherwood, however.

Perhaps those that Isherwood wrote before he left for America are stuffed with a reciprocal obsession; perhaps. We may never know, for some are lost and none are published. But in his diaries between 1939 and 1947 Isherwood makes not a single mention of Lehmann. At the end of his life, Lehmann published some of their correspondence, presumably thinking it proof of the bond between them. But it does not take a very penetrating eye to see in Isherwood's letters often little more than a polite acknowledgement, no effort required. When, after the war, Isherwood makes diary entries on Lehmann, they are dismissive.

We can only have an impression of Lehmann's dependency on Isherwood. Beguiled into believing that Isherwood was in every way worthwhile, Lehmann could not act when faced by the disappointments Isherwood regularly dispensed. The result was a gratefulness for crumbs that he might throw him.

Lehmann must have felt Isherwood's desertion from *New Writing*, but he had almost invented Isherwood's commitment to it. By December 1938 he was telling Lehmann that he could not come up with anything original that could be used. Lehmann could only mildly protest that he was upset to hear it, torn as he already was by his feelings for Sikyr and the difficulties of his Vienna-England existence. He was suffering from 'moods of almost suicidal gloom'. But something made him insensible to Isherwood's neglect. In September 1939 he told him 'I miss you terribly, nearly all my best friends seem to be so far away. And I don't think I would have let you down ... But don't come back now, – across those barbarous seas. I want someone to survive, I want you to survive.' When Isherwood and Auden left England for America on 19 January 1939, for Lehmann an impenetrable distance opened between them. He could not see that it had always existed.

# 8

# Triumph of the Blood

It was quite by chance that when Lehmann called at the *New Statesman*'s offices on 1 February 1940 its editor, Raymond Mortimer, discovered he had free tickets for that evening's performance by Les Ballets Trois Arts at Hammersmith. It was a night of piercing coldness during which a twenty-year-old male dancer, who was to completely alter the pattern of Lehmann's life, stepped on to the stage. We may trust *In the Purely Pagan Sense* for an accurate description of the boy, 'Of medium height ... beautifully formed legs with strong, full calves, and an almost perfectly proportioned figure, broad shoulders, slim waist, long neck, and yet ... no suggestion of over-developed muscles. Above all, the boy's grace astonished me.' Before the performance had ended, Lehmann had made up his mind that he must get to know this elegant creature, this faun that seemed to have strayed from an enchanted wood. Lehmann went backstage to the dressing room the boy shared with another, diminutive, member of the company, Gordon Hamilton.

Despite an obvious shyness, the boy accepted Lehmann's offer of accompanying him to the Café Royal. But once there he could not be persuaded to take off his galoshes or a thin dark overcoat that he clasped to him. From the Café they took a taxi to Lehmann's flat, where they made love. 'And now', Lehmann wrote four days later, 'I feel as if he may always be part of my life: it was as if we had wanted to meet for years after the first five minutes. I pressed a button, expecting the lift to rise quietly, – and the whole house blew up.'

*

Alexis Rassine had not long known the ways of England. He was born, the second of three brothers, on 26 July 1919 in Kaunas, Lithuania, to Russian parents who gave him the name of Alec Raysman. They seem to have been sympathetic people, anxious to do the best for their children. Raysman *père* was an engraver with a strong love of music and a talent for painting that had developed when he was a German prisoner in Munich for the last three years of the Great War. He spoke no English, his wife spoke Russian and perfect Polish, the families who shared the apartment block where they had an apartment on the top floor provided a polyglot background of Russian, Polish, German and Yiddish, but Alec never did master Lithuanian. Not a pliant schoolboy, he was naturally fascinated by theatrical mystique and at seven years of age would steal cast-off ballet pumps and discarded costumes from the rubbish bins behind the Kaunas Opera House. Only once in childhood did he get inside the bewitched place when an aunt took him to see the ex-Diaghilev ballerina Vera Nemchinova. By the end of the 1920s, Alec's boyhood in Lithuania was over, for his father had moved to Cape Town two years earlier and, around 1930, the rest of the family uprooted and joined him. By now it was clear that Alec's passion for the dance needed food and light. He had already developed an almost absurdly supple back and legs.

Rassine was sent to study with the *doyenne* of the South African dance world, Helen Webb, at the Cape Town Academy of Dancing, which he attended for the next four years. It was probably around 1935 (the dates of Alec's progress are unsure, and often contradicted) that Webb arranged that he should dance the mazurka from *Les Sylphides* for the great Nemchinova, who had taken up residence at the Kaunas Opera in 1930. She was impressed, and persuaded the Raysmans that their son would benefit from a period of foreign study, possibly in Moscow or Leningrad. In fact, he was sent to Paris, where he arrived at the Gare de Lyon in 1938 with two suitcases, £7 in his pocket, and one or two words of French. He was taken up by Olga Preobrazhenska, once the *grande dame* of the Tsarist ballet and star of the Maryinski Theatre. Decades later, he recalled her, a woman in her late sixties, working gruellingly long hours, living, so it seemed, on air and biscuits, and carrying a watering can from which she sprinkled water to prevent her dancers slipping. It was Preobrazhenska who suggested he should change his name from Alec Raysman to Alexis Rassine. At the end of her long days, she would hurry home to her little flat in Passy, fasten her windows and unlatch the doors of her caged birds, which would fly through her rooms.

Rassine wasted no time in Paris, taking classes, making do with hardly any money, watching and learning from dancers at the Paris Opera Ballet, where he admired Yvette Chauvire (with whom he would later have a notable partnership) and his fellow-Russian, the controversial and powerful Serge Lifar, and the Venetian Serge Peretti, soon to be named that theatre's *étoile*. The Opera Ballet would not have him and, during a holiday of 1938, he travelled to London to see the Ballets Russes de Monte Carlo at Drury Lane. Leonide Massine, the company's founder, had invited Rassine to join it, but he bowed to Preobrazhenska's advice that he should complete his training before accepting a professional job. On a second visit to London that year he participated in Marie Rambert's dictatorial classes at the Mercury Theatre, staying for several months (according to Rassine) and sometimes appearing in productions for her, terrorised, as were many of her charges, by her aggressive treatment ('Hold in your monstrous stomach!' she would shout). Then it was a return to Paris and his ballet masters, but his existence seemed rootless, the opportunity for improvement elusive.

England broke the spell. In 1939 Rassine was in London again, and was taken on as Alec Raysman in Marcel Berger's Bal Tabarin revue at the Casino Theatre, a venue that specialised in vulgarised, anglicised Parisian excitement, providing what passed for sophistication for that prolific race, the tired businessman. Nudes (in accordance with the Lord Chamberlain's requirements, they never moved) were grouped into various tableaux. Rassine would stand in the wings joking with the girls who shivered with cold. The spectacle demanded animals, too, horses and a vicious performing chimpanzee with whom, surprisingly, he made friends. Ballet was an essential component of this continental *mélange* of decadence. One was set in the court of Louis XIV, a splendid opportunity for the wardrobe department to overload the cast; another told of a Greek sun god, for which Rassine bronzed his body with make-up and danced almost naked. He was one of the four boys ('one for each arm and leg') who supported the dazzling Pamela Foster, who had recently returned from Berlin where she had danced for Hitler and Goering – she thought Rassine 'a bit dainty for a male dancer'. Momentum starting to build up, Rassine took rooms in Bayswater. He danced in a television production of Capek's *The Insect Play*, broadcast from the Alexandra Palace. It was an Irishman, John Regan, who made his real début possible in Les Ballets Trois Arts, a new company that had its London opening in November 1939 at Hammersmith.

\*

The night with Rassine fixed Lehmann's resolve to do better. It is thus that Rassine enters the story: inspiration as much as lover, an epitome of striving aestheticism, almost as a conduit through which Lehmann's longings as an artist might be made real, or at least possible. Their night underlined what might be achieved in the war; the boy had awakened a reassurance that ahead lay

> ... some great synthesis of writing talent, of imagination, and criticism, beyond New Writing, which by next year might be on the way, might give hope and activity to so many of the younger writers who now seem lost, might discover new talents and rescue talents in danger of being frozen out, might at least make real the new ideal in my mind, – of a new lyricism, and a new 'tragic' mission to literature ...

'Alexis did a very unexpected thing to me: he suddenly reopened a world of pure art existing outside the war, and the way I've been living receded for a few days to the end of a telescope.' It was in this explosion of identification with the boy dancer, that Lehmann began to see Diaghilev as 'the supreme example of the creative type that interests me'.

So the relationship began, and staggered on through those early weeks. From his digs shared with Gordon Hamilton in the provincial towns Les Ballets Trois Arts was now touring through – Blackpool, Southend, Westcliff-on-Sea – Rassine sent off letters to Lehmann in his almost illiterate scrawl. On 8 March Lehmann went to Oxford to see him dance. They met at the Randolph, walked through the town in the spring sunlight, went to a café where they met Hamilton.

Alexis had now become 'Alyosha', a crowning grace on a new love that left Lehmann with the weight of loneliness in his absence. A pattern emerged, with Lehmann waiting up into the small hours of Sunday mornings for his lover to get back from his week's engagement. Watching him dance at Westcliff-on-Sea, he floated in the reflected glory of Rassine's skill, thinking, as so many infatuated others before and since who have been beguiled by the deceits of theatre, that Rassine was dancing especially brilliantly only because he was there with him. There could be no doubt now about their love: 'To feel, like a stabbing wound, that someone is entirely unique in their ways and expression, and that no one knows it so painfully and intimately as I do myself, – that has always been a sign with me that the relationship has reached the fatal and burning stage.'

'Fatal' and 'burning', so strongly associating love with pain, seem to have been well chosen words. Only a few weeks later a letter from Rassine in Harrogate told Lehmann he could not now go with him on a holiday they had planned to take as the company had been booked to appear in Ireland. In sorrow or anger, Lehmann almost felt he would rather not see or write to him again. By 20 April three letters, unanswered, had arrived from Rassine. 'Is it Pride?' Lehmann asked his journal 'Suspicion or jealousy? Or a feeling that I must make him understand that I'm real, and not a dream? Because I feel sometimes as if I'd been swallowed whole into his intense and extraordinary dream'.

Their reunion after Rassine's return from Ireland was a mixture of great happiness and bitter struggle, quick quarrelling ending in love, and the inevitably sometimes uneasy sexual settlement. Prophetically, Lehmann wrote on 28 April

If one could understand the real meaning of pain; there are times when I feel my natural reaction and placing of it is all wrong; I can't know the world in the deepest way until I have found this out.

He thought it might be sensible to 'turn down the tap before the explosion, there's another way that's also happiness, though not the trumpets'. In other, differently lucid moments, Lehmann felt the war itself might be made some sense of if only he could give richly enough, to Rassine and to the young writers whose voices needed to be exercised. How could he realise that even in these earliest days of Rassine a friendship had been forever fixed? 'Our friendship will go on just as long as you want it to', Rassine told him; but Lehmann's thoughts were too often of damages never to be undone, of friendships shattered, of partings never to be healed.

*

By September 1940, the war sleepy and a year long, Lehmann was distressed and puzzled by the lack of any word from Isherwood – somewhere in an America that seemed to Lehmann to be growing immensely remote, as far away and unreachable as Toni Sikyr and Vienna. He told his diary that Isherwood and Sikyr were the two people he held dearest. October brought with it the old melancholy he always associated with that month, and an aching need to have news of old friends. After what seemed to Lehmann an appalling interval of weeks, a letter from Isherwood arrived on 12 October, sharply relaxing him. But rereading it a few days later it struck Lehmann as something so far removed, false or out of contact, in a way that distressed him enormously.

At Fieldhead, Plomer came down for a night and agreed that Auden and Isherwood had taken themselves out of the central experience of their generation and that the gulf could only widen. The pits of that experience and the struggle to construct some kind of thinking that would withstand the onslaught bore no relationship to what was happening to them. Lehmann was suddenly struck by a weakness in Auden's gift, recognising in him something sententious and too much above the battle that others had been left to fight. The fate Isherwood had abandoned him to was becoming more palpable as the real war advanced.

Lehmann wanted to understand the anatomy, the foreign and military policy of the war, intensely, to penetrate to the heart of what it meant, while maintaining the integrity of the artist to make no concessions against the truth, to prepare for a new phase of life, and to find his level in London. All around was the energy of change.

> Young writers in the airforce, – Gully [Mason] writing of the unapproachable heroic world of the pilots; John Sommerfield of the fantastic no-culture of the far stations. And Roy [Fuller] coming back from France longing for more Auden and *New Writing*, but bursting above all to tell me of his first French tart; John L [Lepper] uncertain of himself in the civvy world, more firmly convinced than ever of 'England's destiny', tough yet rather pathetically lost in a way, breaking down when he finds his girl has left him; Jackie [Hewit] subtly changed, growing rapidly into something stronger inside as well as outside; they are all going through a transformation, – deeper even than those who control the machine know.

Lehmann was surprised by the speed with which he seemed to grow a new existence in which the undercurrents were of a sort of grave desire of life for the young men caught up in the conflict; an existence in which the thought of death was always attendant. He longed for closeness to the young heroes making the most of their escapes in London: new faces in old pubs; falling into conversation south of the river with four French sailors who couldn't speak English and couldn't change their money. Happy to be their translator, he was touched when the rest of the company wanted to stand the five of them drinks.

At Victoria, two Grenadier Guard boys poured out what they felt about the war, agreeing with Lehmann that the old men of power must go, and asking what would happen to them when peace came. He looked into the faces of the Belgian and Dutch refugee men in the streets of Bloomsbury, and searched for 'Shakespeare Fred', who eventually turned up, full of racy stories, and was taken back for supper at the flat. He went drinking with the artist John Banting who, transformed by a single Pernod absinthe, became extremely arch and told Lehmann he knew of a 'secret negro dive' but didn't think he should take him to it. He did, leading Lehmann down into a darkly lit billiard hall where they were accosted by a melancholy black man from the Gold Coast who wanted to talk about his conscription. Lehmann admired the signed celebrity portraits on the walls, and took the man away to have sex. The possibilities of gross adventure were everywhere. Turning the pages of Lehmann's journals – with their details of meetings that so often fade out with suggestive ellipses – one can almost feel the blood rising.

Wandering through this homosexual wonderland was not merely an expression of lust. 'I am still looking,' he wrote in April 1941, 'always looking for the friend who will give me the direct, warm and natural, entirely loyal relationship that I dream about, that is the only thing I care about, that I seemed to find once or twice'. Meetings might lead to sex, or news of unheard of friends, or challenging attitudes to the time; it was as if it was all one. One night, he met a young French journalist who gave him hope that André Chamson was alive and well somewhere in France, the first glimmer of hope he had had of Chamson for a year. 'And by poetry,' wrote Lehmann after this meeting, 'I mean a state that almost anything may attain: Soldiers, dancing, a party, a way of life.'

Poetry, sex, beauty, the integration of fucking and fellatio into a bound pattern of good living at the edge of an appreciation of art – Lehmann wanted the threading together of all this, and felt the ripe conditions that the war had brought with it. Against the unperturbed, if changing, glories of Fieldhead's garden, he felt the need to look at the age 'in a more eternal way, one must continue to be outside it even while one is intensely in it'. A love of maleness was a branch of the new existence: his fascination with an airman he gave a lift to; the young railwayman in his tin hat beside the river as they saw out their Home Guard shift by the river at dawn; 'to think in four dimensions, to see things vanishing and what remains, is a secret of calm'.

Always he clung to whatever dimensions made his experiences with attractive men in some way, however slight, physical. Spending a night with a young Irish guard who wanted to talk about the war in France, reminded Lehmann that since the beginning of the war he had found a power to make friends with such people. At Euston station, a young, shabbily dressed, young man accompanied by his mother, got into his carriage. The boy needed someone to talk to and began, always with the same friendly expression on his face, to tell how his father had been killed by a bomb a week before. Their home had been wrecked and now he was called up. It was all told so uncomplainingly, unshakeably, but what so moved Lehmann was the boy's desperate need to describe and confide it all. When the boy had finished, he took Lehmann's hand and another union of male trust had been sanctified.

I want to get out of the purely intellectual life which has claimed me, to be in this war in some way or other with men, men at work, men at sea, men at war.

Lehmann was shocked at Cuthbert Worsley's when a gaggle of camp boys turned up, giggling and kissing each other and chirruping about who they had spotted at the Café Royal. Now such behaviour seemed out of joint, shamelessly removed from the fate of the Irish and Scots soldiers he had once known who had vanished at Dunkirk, and he felt uncomfortably certain that Spender had chosen, and perhaps even helped to create, just such a facile underworld.

If Sikyr's fate was beyond his control, Lehmann yet had the possibility of directing that of his mother and Rassine. Obliged to prepare contingency evacuation plans for the Hogarth Press, he hoped his mother might be persuaded to go to her old home in America; but she would not. He urged Rassine to move to New York. America might promise safety, but Rassine's career, so inconveniently coinciding with the war, was at a crucial point. In the autumn of 1940 he became a principal dancer with the Anglo-Polish Ballet, many of its members Polish refugees, and began establishing himself in works with which he would become strongly identified, including *Le Spectre de la Rose* and *Les Sylphides*. It was in the Anglo-Polish Ballet that he was nicknamed 'Cockadoodle', perhaps because of his rather beaky little nose (the result of a nose-job that had destroyed the aquiline original), or his quick, high-pitched way of speaking in a mid-European dialect coloured with a veneer of South African, or because of what came to be seen by many as a growing flamboyance.

For two nights Rassine listened as Lehmann tried to persuade him to emigrate for the duration, and when Rassine said, 'Of course you will come too, and be with me', Lehmann was left dazzled and, for a moment, infected by the idea, before he realised it was impossible. Rassine was gradually introduced to several of Lehmann's circle, even though in later years there were many close to Lehmann who only caught glimpses of Rassine. In June they went to Brighton to see Beatrix play Abbie in *Desire Under the Elms*, one of her greatest roles. She and Rassine had from the beginning a natural liking for one another; just as well, for it was a friendship that was to prove essential to him in later years. Then, Duncan Grant sketched Rassine in his *Les Sylphides* costume, and painted his portrait. Lehmann bought recordings of *Swan Lake* and *Aurora's Wedding* and Rassine, with 'all the charm of a wild child from some primitive country', played them constantly. Lehmann could hardly imagine what might become of Rassine if the invasion came, just as he found it difficult to imagine what was happening to the men at the lines of the war.

*

Imagination was not to be savoured if sanity was to be preserved. Lehmann had learned of the invasion of the Low Countries from the station-master at Bourne End as he boarded the 8.44 to London. By mid-day, people felt sick in the pits of their stomachs at the anxiety. It was a spring day, still and clean, and a few hundred miles away the world, he knew, had gone mad. He was incensed at the complacency of England's rulers, the decadence of their not having foreseen what would happen. 'And I wake this morning', he wrote on 2 June at Fieldhead, 'and am still alive and thirty three years old, and in the lush summer peace of the house where I was born.'

His first experience of an air-raid came when he was on the 5.30 from Salisbury. Blinds down, the train staggered forward while a battle raged overhead. The passengers put up the blinds and watched. When the all-clear sounded, the girl beside Lehmann sighed and giggled. The time for appointments and assignations slipped by: a soldier had missed his date with a girl in a Gravesend pub, a man was late for work, his wife became hysterical, and soldiers began jumping from the train, nipping through backyards on to the road to look for a bus. Lehmann jumped on to the rails and saw fires burning over Holborn.

When he reached home he drank half a bottle of wine and ate an apple and some chocolate biscuits and, laying fully-dressed on his bed, began to read *Père Goriot*. He had barely settled when bombs began falling and the house was racked with violent concussions. Incendiaries burned in the garden and a great blaze had begun beyond the balloon unit in the Foundling Estate. He was alarmed that it might be near Spender's flat. There was a tremendous explosion, for which the house seemed to clench itself. Looking out, he saw a cloud of grey dust rolling down the road towards him, and a man in pyjamas quietly crossing the street below. A neighbour in a tin hat told him there was an unexploded time-bomb in the garden, and that they were evacuating the shelter. It occurred to him that Byron Court looked different, until he realised he was looking at the tree beyond it, for the Court had been blown away. He was conscious of the presence of death suddenly made vivid, of the arrival of firemen and ambulances and A.R.P. wardens and the blood-transfusion unit, as the tabby persian from No. 40 picked its way across the debris to its favourite porch.

Lehmann was surprised that he was so little frightened and how much more noisy he had imagined it would be. He sat on a step at the shelter's edge, knowing that the Nazis would retreat from the coming light and the ascending English fighters. He talked on and on to an A.T.S. girl. Other girls lay asleep, clasped in the arms of their husbands. Someone produced a novel by Dostoevsky.

Women from Byron Court sat about with powdered hair. The lavatory door banged, reminiscent of falling bombs.

When the all-clear came, Lehmann went to the Athenaeum, had a bath and ordered breakfast, and went to see Rassine. That night, there was the pitiful sight at Paddington of the hordes of families evacuated from the East End, their lives broken open. He remembered what someone had once told him was one of the most haunting images of the Spanish conflict: the wrecked, sodden furniture of the poor tipped against rubble, the exposure of intimate lives. As the raids followed one on another Lehmann thought it might be a good thing if the invasion came without delay and decided England's fate one way or the other. He finished reading *The Good Soldier Schweik* and laughed throughout, revelling in its Austrian atmosphere and convinced by its being an ultimate riposte to War, and the State and Authority 'and all the other horrors that batten on life'. He recognised Sikyr's qualities in Schweik, the face of innocence strong against avengers, the resourcefulness of humour and 'that rock-bottom-ness that will get him through the war if anything can'.

*

The Mecklenburgh Square flat, its door chalked with a cross, had to be evacuated. Lehmann met Willy Goldman who tried to describe to him what the East End had endured, the ruin of Stepney and the Commercial Road, the grieving Jewish families, scarcely one of which had not lost somebody. He was relieved that Spender, looking as wild as ever, came to see him, with Connolly and Peter Watson, and he had coffee at the Athenaeum with Cuthbert Worsley and lunched with Spender, who brought a boyfriend, at an almost deserted Café Royal. On Friday 13 September Buckingham Palace was hit. The raids lasted most of the morning, with the bombers dodging through low clouds.

In the middle of it all he met the Woolfs, just arrived after some fantastic voyage from Rodmell, wandering along Guildford Street; Virginia's lack of concern was more welcome than Leonard's bravado. That afternoon, as he was taking a taxi to Beatrix's flat, the attack increased. Without warning, bombs burst directly ahead of him. People were running, glass flew through the air, trolley buses piled up, and the taxi skidded into a side street whose inhabitants stood gazing with steady curiosity from their doors.

It was obvious that the Hogarth Press could not stay in town, but must be moved to Letchworth to lodge with the Press's chief printers, The Garden City Press – where the Press remained until the end of the war. Most of Lehmann's first night there was spent under the works manager's dining-room table, where the family hid for shelter. He would spend two or three nights in Cambridge, within commuting distance of Letchworth; on his way there he would stop over in London; he would weekend at Fieldhead. Dadie Rylands produced a room belonging to King's College in St. Edmunds Passage. It was close to the Arts

Theatre in Cambridge where he had arrived twelve years before. He wondered 'Why hadn't I learnt how to live then? Why did I take so long to learn even the first steps?' The regular melancholy that came with October brought no answers, but for the next six months the plan of his existence had been worked out.

Lehmann had never seriously considered the luxury of defection that unforgivably, he felt, Isherwood and Auden had rushed at, but an essential part of his nature was distanced by remaining in England, by waiting for and enduring the bombs. He had been at his happiest wandering through Europe, at home in Austria with Sikyr, and there were times when England had seemed little more than a prison to him.

The starting up of a proper war could be blamed, now, for preventing escape; it held him to the narrow focus of the moment. He took a flat at Athenaeum Court, Piccadilly. On his first night there, he laid in bed listening to the gramophone in the next room playing *Swan Lake*, and suddenly he was aware of how much Rassine had already become part of everything. The last words of his 1940 journal tell his 'great revolutionary truth:– not that all men are equal, but that all men are men'. To them, since the beginning of the war, he owed his mission.

> How strange, how quickly this feeling came with the war: of being older, of having a duty towards the young, to help them and illuminate things for them; and consciousness of being so ill-prepared; so much self and carelessness to be burnt away.

The exercise of that duty had a dismaying capacity to pain the giver. The starts of suffering he had already felt had put down roots. It needed only the making of another liaison.

*

It was at the end of 1991 that the *Stroud Defector* mourned the death of one of its most colourful contributors. The photograph of a thick-set, completely bald man, a cigarette dangling from his lips, his eyes squinting against the rising smoke, might be of a Eric Von Stroheim lookalike. Stroud had been left a 'less interesting place' by this man's passing.

Adrian John Liddell Hart had always had an interest in the Navy, and had once expressed a preference for being buried at sea. On arriving at his favourite Stroud pubs, in summer wearing merely a pair of ill-fitting dungarees from which an abundance of pink flesh spilled out, a panama or peaked naval hat and little else, he would be piped aboard by the regulars. At his flat in Stroud Castle, he was a scandalous and entertaining host, generous and mischievous, telling of how he had left the Foreign Legion because they would not give him a clean shirt every day, cooked sausages for the Queen at Buckingham Palace, talked to murderers in their cells, stood for Parliament, worked for the Foreign Office, written a book and served in Vietnam. He was remembered as being kind to his neighbours, playing scrabble with them, fetching shopping, running errands, collecting prescriptions.

Hart was only eighteen years old when Lehmann noticed him one day in the Passage; on 23 October 1940 he sent him an invitation for drinks. He never forgot the memory of that first meeting in a war-torn autumn with the handsome young man in a sky-blue roll-top pullover. Almost immediately the relationship was strongly sexual. 'Did what took place a few evenings ago surprise you, Adrian?' he wrote on 16 November. 'I'll be frank, and say for myself, no: but it was wonderful the way the key turned in the lock, without any fumbling or wrenching, and it made me very happy. Do you like the sensation of setting out on a voyage of discovery, with the sun on the deck and the band playing? Do you have it? I do.'

From the beginning it might have been obvious that Lehmann had taken on a highly troublesome adolescent passenger. The son of the military strategist and historian Basil Liddell Hart, Adrian suffered from a complex parcel of nervous neuroses, turmoil aggravated not only by his uneasy progress through Cambridge via Eton and the war, but also by his sometimes violent outbursts and the difficulties in his relationship with his parents, whose marriage was by now crumbling. With Lehmann, he could joke about his father and what he called the 'Ambleside government' (the family home was there). Hart was a pupil of Rylands, who considered him

> a clever, lively, amusing boy who rather dazzled John. Cleverer than John, and rather flirtatious. He was attractive, but I don't remember him as a raving beauty. I do remember one day John chasing him through the outskirts of Cambridge calling after him.

Never for any length of time was the friendship between Lehmann and his new lover contented. In mid-December, Hart vanished to Devon, telling Lehmann that their relationship was a 'fiasco'. 'You say that all roads have corners', wrote Lehmann. 'I reply that false starts don't mean blind alleys.'

The first devastating blow came in February with the news that Hart, before completing his first year at Cambridge, had enlisted in the Navy, providing a new set of geographical problems like those that had plagued Lehmann's love for Sikyr and Rassine. Soon, Hart was on H.M.S. *Collingwood*. Lehmann's anxiety poured out. Was there somewhere close by where he could discreetly stay for a night or two? Why hadn't they seen each other during Hart's last weekend on shore? Why hadn't he given Lehmann even a photograph of himself? 'Sailors don't care, Adrian', he suggested, 'well perhaps, but I care about sailors, or *a* sailor any way.'

With danger signals already waving over Hart, another friendship ended, adding to a sense of loss that would not retreat. On Friday 14 March 1941 Lehmann met the Woolfs at St. Stephen's Tavern, a meeting at which it was agreed that he should read Virginia's new novel *Between the Acts*, the existence of which had come as a complete surprise to him.

Virginia was full of doubt, Leonard enthusiastic – his praise perhaps so fulsome because he recognised a grave deterioration in Virginia's mental state, and was desperate to rescue her from it. Lehmann recalled forty years later that Virginia was 'in an acutely abnormal state of agitation and anxiety, especially when the novel was mentioned. I remember that with absolute clarity.' Leonard's eagerness to have the book published misled Lehmann into believing that there was no doubt that it would be in the Hogarth Press's list, and he announced the book as forthcoming in the *New Statesman*. On 20 March Virginia wrote to Lehmann asking that he give his casting vote on the novel's future. She thought it should be hidden away: it was 'too slight and sketchy', and that it was 'a mistake from all points of view to publish it'. Lehmann apologised for his slip.

The manuscript arrived from Rodmell on a day when Lehmann was scheduled for a night's Home Guard duty, and before he left the house with his rifle and tin hat he had read it. Ploughing through Virginia's eccentric typing, he felt 'amazed and deeply moved by its poetry – in fact it's more a poem than prose, more so than To the Lighthouse, she has pushed prose to the furthest inch at the frontier – into the no man's land.'

In reply to his ready acceptance of the book came Virginia's decision that *Between the Acts* needed serious revision, and would not be ready at least until the autumn. Enclosed with her letter was another from Leonard, alarmed and despairing of what might befall her. Remembering the awful tension there had been in her in the old days when she was finishing a book, and her last entreaty that she should have something to do (could she do some reading for him, she asked), Lehmann realised there had been a suppressed unease and excitement in her mood at their final meeting.

It was sometime around mid-day on Friday 28 March that Virginia Woolf walked into the River Ouse. She had left Leonard a suicide note. Despite an immediate search, only on 18 April did some bicycling teenagers from Lewes see her body, still in its fur coat, floating in the water near Asheham.

'I could see her so well', wrote Lehmann, 'setting out on her walk to the river, with this thing splitting in her brain, and Leonard's look when he found the letter.' Decades after, in 'The Lady of Elvedon', Lehmann paid a late tribute to his old friend, against a background of remembered lawns and trees, decline and resurgence from earth.

## 8. Triumph of the Blood

Hush: the red funguses and ferns smell strong,
Primeval fir cones fall to rot
Among the grasses; sleeping daws take wing;
And someone, see, will stay to write,

Ransomed as in eternity, between
The two long windows that face the lawn
The gardeners sweep for ever; she has won
The game with death and keeps the crown.

Loss came in more guises. In January 1941 there had been a break with Rassine, 'senseless, inexplicable, an act of pure destruction' – on Rassine's part, presumably. In an attempt at reconciliation they lunched together at the Leicester Square café where they often met, but to Lehmann the meeting had a dream-like quality, as if two friends were talking about another who had failed to turn up.

Lehmann was already sleeping badly, suffered from colds and overworking, but he resolved not to let the disaster with Rassine go to the back of his mind. He knew there must be a re-ordering of his life, listing among his ambitions 'stoic humanism – return to responsibility – pursuit of the elemental'. The problem seems to have been a suspicion of Rassine's unfaithfulness, always anathema to Lehmann who prided himself on his loyalty.

Whatever the details of his doubt may have been, in early February Lehmann was in London pursuing his lonely voyage of exploration about Rassine. In Cambridge, he saw him dance with the Anglo-Polish Ballet and seems to have learned more truths from Rassine's almost habitual companion, Gordon Hamilton. Whatever information he gleaned from Hamilton effected another transformation in his attitude to Rassine. Suddenly, the beautiful faun had become callous, treacherous, and a return to past happiness seemed forever beyond hope. Watching Rassine on stage, he was overcome with melancholy.

Back in London, there was the round of the pubs, the constant parade of men in or out of uniform. He saw the vague sniggers, heard the vaguer endearments, observed the telling poise of a cigarette – 'as unvarying as the steps of a well-trained ballet corps' – and knew the paradox that these men, sissies before Hitler, were serving their country with bravery and accomplishment.

Sometimes the void left by Rassine or Hart or the thoughts of Sikyr could be temporarily filled, with gratifying sexual results. Lehmann took a young musician to a friend's abandoned flat with its collapsed ceiling and furniture covered with dust-cloths. A woman ran up and down the stairs on the landing wailing that the occupant had been a Fifth Columnist. In the dim, they found drinks in a brightly-lit refrigerator, drank and made love. After having sex with a young soldier at Athenaeum Court, the soldier asked if he might have a bath. Time passed, and Lehmann became aware of the continuing silence from the bathroom. Standing on the seat of the lavatory next door and craning his neck out of the top window, Lehmann saw that the soldier lay lifeless in the bath. Concerned that he would be asked to explain the presence of a dead and naked soldier, he threw potatoes at him until one scored a direct hit at the soldier's head. There is no record of what the soldier said.

\*

Still Lehmann lay awake every night, wondering how his feeling for Rassine might be resolved. By early March a new beginning was made,

> ... with Alexis laughing on the bed and devouring sausages happily in my dressing-gown, everything seems to come right as a phrase in music, and the early spring sun breaks through outside ... I made up my mind from now on that my relationship with Alexis must be different; and I think he responded at once to the change ... it made no difference at all to me that Alyosha had deceived me and let me down so cruelly, fundamentally I loved him still as deeply as ever.

For the moment, it seems that this *rapprochement* existed largely in Lehmann's mind. He needed the fact of a single, deep affection rather than (or as well as) the pleasures of casual sexual encounters. By now, the clarity he needed to sort the tangle with Rassine was being hopelessly muddied by the presence of Hart.

Lehmann's desire to shape his lovers' future had lost none of its sharpness. On 30 April 1941 he wrote that Hart's letter

> ... threw some light on the enigma of you, Adrian: and left me with a miserable feeling that I was too far away in space and too remote from your new life psychologically to help much. But I think all the same I do understand a little bit what's happening inside you, as I went through some very curious twilight phases myself between Eton and Cambridge, phases I've always found it very hard to describe to anyone else. It isn't much use saying it'll adjust itself, is it? But it will ... I think the key for me was to get my sensual self flowing: when I had balanced my blood and my sex against my mind, then at last I began to feel power, and sureness in life. That was an idea, a necessity that came in my generation – for Christopher and Stephen and Auden – before politics, and though it got mixed up with politics later many of us have forgotten how important this original 'triumph of the blood' was.

For a time, it seemed that all Lehmann's energies might be poured into keeping Rassine. It was his reason for visiting him in Blackpool that May. As always, Lehmann was exhilarated to be so near the sea. Streams of airmen walked the esplanade, there were English boys, their faces boiled pink and white, Polish boys with fierce eyes and long noses, and men marching and drilling along the sea-front, the barricaded piers behind them.

The passion of his journey, 'an attempt to regain Alexis, the centre of my hopes', succeeded. He had planned Rassine's return with the precision of a military campaign, and triumphed in the long explanations and appeals on the moonlit sea-front, the revelation that the affair with Pip Dyer was finally done with, the declaration of new vows. 'And I keep on remembering those unique and charming gestures, exclamations, glances, flashes of style which I cherish so much and which I know now I have missed unbearably.' Rassine had now to accept the fact that Lehmann could spend days and nights of idyllic sexual delight with Hart.

\*

When Lehmann and Hart parted after a visit to Cambridge in late May, they were almost on the verge of tears, but a few days later Hart was in London and made no attempt to see his new lover. When they met, Hart poured out the problems with his parents – whom Lehmann considered had already done their son tremendous harm – and his philosophical struggles. The coming together of Lehmann and Hart seemed too often to resemble a collision, but by the beginning of June it seemed as if a plateau might have been reached. From barracks at Portsmouth, Hart wrote

> When I remember how it started, those words of yours about the band playing on the river ... This very deep sense of failure has, I know, affected my life in a way nothing else has; if it wasn't for our relationship I don't think I should be where I am now. I sometimes feel that that band has meant shipwreck, but you must realise how much you have meant in my life, more than anyone else, how much I depend on you and want you. I realised my ideal, that I found the answer to what I'd thought insoluble, that unity of qualities, and I gave you what I'd never really given before, admiration.

Their affair had started as an incidental pleasure which, hard-boiled, they had assured one another would never grow into anything meaningful, but Lehmann was too ready to make Hart an emblem of what love and sex and a lust for literature might create when an older man loved a younger: Hart, ideally, was a young victim of the war, too, rocked by its misadventures, lured unthinkingly into its crux. Lehmann was consumed

... with joy and unhappiness, a foreboding of his terrible danger and the agony I would feel if he were lost, again this feeling comes over me, that somehow, in some way, I must revenge the fate of these young people, people like Toni ... and Adrian, to whom the world of today offers such a cruel and frustrating fate.

Against the cruelty of Hart's youth, he resolved to try harder, to formulate that strengthened faith that would deliver the boy from the nihilism that threatened to ruin him.

*

Always the daily round to be dealt with. Rosamond brought Cecil Day Lewis to see Lehmann at Fieldhead; Leonard Woolf asked him to be his literary executor; the BBC, after much prevarication, offered him a job; there were the usual drinks parties, authors to be seen, and a farewell lunch with Harold Acton who was joining the R.A.F.

That April, Spender married the pianist Natasha Litvin; what was going through the minds of many of the congregation may be imagined. Plomer's view, 'He's mad', seems to have been a fair summary of general opinion. Lehmann noted 'Stephen sniggering about Tony [Hyndman, a guardsman boyfriend] subconsciously sabotaging it, Natasha very willowy and lyrical in white, rather too innocent for the situation I felt.' To help things along, Lehmann gave them a ten-volume edition of Schiller.

For him, there was 'lead in my heart.' It was as if Lehmann was giving himself up for a crucifixion in the stead of the young, a willing endurance of agony. There was a week at the end of May when stories about Hart had reached him from old friends (noted in the journals as 'W' and 'P', most probably Plomer and Dyer – Dyer subsequently apologised to Lehmann for any trouble he had caused). Much was expected of Hart as he had the potential of solving the problem that for ten years Lehmann had thought insoluble: how to find a perfect partner, a boy who understood the evolution of his ideas about art and life and politics, one who would be a complete support and give sexual gratification. It was settled in Lehmann's mind that Rassine would never be all this, but he had decided that Rassine knew how intensely he felt about him, accepting Lehmann's assurance that he found him precious in an entirely different way – Gordon Hamilton said that Lehmann was the rock on which Alyosha leaned.

Hart's place still had to be established. His first voyage into war filled Lehmann with horror, made worse because he could not imagine what the boy must be going through, not having been exposed to such dangers himself. There was the lack of news to be coped with, arrivals expected, reunions disappointed: it was a summer crucially unsettled by Hart's tantalising dithering at the edges of Lehmann's life. The more worldly of his readers could hardly have missed the implications in his 'Letter to a Friend at Sea' that appeared that autumn in *Folios of New Writing*, the outpouring of an older man for a youthful sailor. It was a discreet acclamation of Lehmann's adoration for some (to the public) unknown serviceman.

\*

The summer passed in crises of waiting, of expectations doomed to disappointment. These were the months of an elliptical poem, 'The Summer Story'. Puzzlingly, Lehmann notes in *I Am My Brother* that it evokes Austria, although it was 'transposed and blended with other elements to make a whole that is still mysterious even to myself'; a whole of 'inner coherence and truth' that was produced only after long labour. He had thought to make a play or short story of the idea: a young man's arrival eagerly expected by the inhabitants of a house by a lake.

> Great were our plans to greet this friend
> So long a legend to our love,
> And while we filled his room with flowers
> And sent for cakes and wine, we strove
>
> Each to recapture from the past
> A glance, a gesture that would bring
> His clear-eyed presence out of night:
> But it was hard remembering.

But the friend does not come. A cable arrives, telling them he will be delayed. One by one, other visitors to the house come and go

> Till I was left alone to meet
> (As I had always known must be)
> In the damp house, at summer's end,
> The dark Lieutenant from the sea.

The recognition of something ordained, fateful, is unmistakable here, as if the 'dark Lieutenant' had to be faced, and faced alone.

In reality, the possibility of divine union threatened by 'The Summer Story' was demolished by Hart's unpredictable temperament and his sometimes frightening losses of equilibrium. Lehmann understood his lover's need to get in touch with the rhythms of the life of men outside the privileged walled garden in which they both had grown up. He looked always for ways in which their lives might be linked and he was heartened when Hart told him that it was life, not tragedy, to which they both belonged. It gave Lehmann hope that something might yet come of a love that had to withstand so much:

I was only not strong enough to endure what happened, not wise enough to find the way to make you say Yes, Yes to the whole of life. It is for that that I have always asked your forgiveness ... the refusal to speak, to explain, to admit, caused misunderstanding and doubt and fear time after time. How long it took you to tell me even that you suffered from these neurotic compulsions: and how much easier it was the moment you had. I would not have been so entirely without fear in that moment of violence in Liverpool, if I hadn't known.

Ever ready to forgive, ever hopeful that Hart's refusals of opportunity could be turned about, that (like Lehmann) he might transform shame into gladness in a process of integration, Lehmann nevertheless wanted to know all that could be known about Hart. 'I have this unhappy knack of finding out most things that concern me sooner or later', he told him on 14 July, 'and this week I have come to hear much that has shaken me.'

\*

By the end of the month, the extent of Lehmann's depression became clear. When he picked up the telephone, he felt himself crumbling. Plomer saw the changes in him. They walked in Hyde Park and sat by the Serpentine, Plomer listening and solicitous. Hart was left in no doubt, either. Did he realise how his once energetic and fulfilled lover was breaking down in front of friends in sudden sobbing fits, that he could not concentrate or sleep, but would get up in the middle of the night to write letters to old friends telling them he never wished to see them again? The letters, presumably to those whom Lehmann considered had assisted in the deceit around Hart, were never, apparently, sent. Only a declaration of truth from Hart would convince him that they had a future together – but he was too easily convinced that he was essential to the boy's happiness.

Feverish bouts of malaria-like symptoms gripped him. In August he consulted a doctor who advised X-rays, but Lehmann knew his own diagnosis and struggled on alone. Sitting at Fieldhead under a drooping beech, in a moment of clarity the truth came to him again 'like a wine-glass ringing', that he would always love Hart no matter what happened, but that he must at the same time live in a tower of strength and secrecy. In such a way, he might yet keep what was so important to him in the present while protecting himself from what seemed to have been lost from the past.

'I've been very lucky in the friendships I've found, I think', he told himself, 'but things have turned out unhappily these last years. Tony so far beyond all sight and contact, who meant everything for so many years. And Christopher in America, changing in a way that's beyond my following.'

# 9

# Dark Lieutenants

Lehmann's published writings sometimes give the faintest pictures of those who were of crucial importance in his life. Reading *I Am My Brother*, the reader understands that Demetrios Capetanakis was indeed important to him, an associate with an interesting history and mind. It was in the autumn of 1940 that Lehmann met Capetanakis; Hart introduced them.

Capetanakis had come to England the previous year with a British Council scholarship, going to Cambridge where he was a pupil of Dadie Rylands at King's College. Born in Greece in 1912, Capetanakis had graduated in political science and economics at Athens University, and subsequently was Doctor of Philosophy at Heidelberg University. In Greece, he had published various philosophical studies with titles that suggested a fascination with how art was created, 'The Struggle of the Solitary Soul' and 'The Mythology of Beauty'. By the time he arrived in England he had only been studying the English language for a few months. Within three years, according to his close friend and admirer Panayotis Canellopoulos, he had transformed himself into an English poet with a mastery of language that seemed (and seems) astounding. As a poet, he was to become the darling of Edith Sitwell. He introduced a new generation to the poetry of such compatriots as Angelos Sikelianos, George Seferis and Odysseus Elytis.

It was not perhaps until the spring of 1941 that the two men came to know each other better. That April, Capetanakis came to dinner, and was persuaded to write something about Greek poetry and undertake some translations for *Penguin New Writing*. Talking of the poems, 'He grew enthusiastic about one of them, and said: "He has this vision of a world of heroic bodies, – a masculine world, of course…".' With this, the young man had made his own sexual preference clear. 'He is modest and charming,' Lehmann noted, 'as well as extremely gifted, and his melancholy devotion to Adrian touches me very deeply.' A few days later, Lehmann gave a party for him to meet Plomer.

By June, the sympathy between the two men was obvious, with Capetanakis assuring him how deeply devoted to Lehmann Hart was, with a 'greater strength of feeling than I know'. His role in Lehmann's life was, for the moment, to support Lehmann's belief in the goodness of the affair with Hart; but there was also Capetanakis's fascination with Lehmann's poems and *Evil Was Abroad*, 'works I have felt so lost', and his belief in Lehmann's future work: 'Yet another voice telling me to go back to poetry.'

In fact, in that leafy spring, cuckoos calling, the meadows full of buttercups, Capetanakis was becoming much more than simply another voice. He certainly said what Lehmann wanted to hear, but it was beginning to be a true meeting of mind and spirit. For Lehmann, it was the start of a new love and respect, at an intellectual level he had not experienced since his devotion (platonic as that had been) to Julian Bell. Truly, Capetanakis's intellectual abilities were far superior to Lehmann's, perhaps in itself one of the reasons why aspects of his personality so concerned Capetanakis. After reading Rosamond's novel *Invitation to the Waltz*, he thought he understood Lehmann more, 'but I also felt a little frightened of you'.

\*

In August Plomer brought J. R. (Joe) Ackerley for a visit, and with Ackerley Capetanakis struck up another friendship that would endure; he is mentioned in Capetanakis's final documents. Lehmann welcomed the chance to get closer to Ackerley, to see 'how out of the world he is: so many things I mentioned taking for granted he'd know about, rang no bell at first. I liked him better than ever, realising with what difficulty, what caution he gives himself.' Drinking wine, the four of them decided the only things that mattered in war were friendship and poetry.

Alone, Lehmann read Capetanakis his 'Prodigal Son' poem (published as 'The Summer Story'), and Capetanakis promised to show him letters he had received from Hart in which Lehmann was mentioned. There was never a time, at least early in their relationship, when Capetanakis did not support Hart's case or urge Lehmann to keep on with the affair. 'I am quite convinced, dear John,' he wrote in November 1941,

> ... that your friendship with Adrian is much stronger than all these powers of darkness which try to destroy it as if they were jealous of its light, solidity and beauty. I believe that a relationship which has its expression in the 'Letter to a Friend' and the poems cannot deviate and become the destructive power you are so frightened of; it *is* and it is bound to remain creative.

We cannot know how responsible Lehmann was for Capetanakis's development as an English poet. What may we take from his statement that 'My desire is now to create a work which will not only be mine, but yours too ... all I have created up to now was the work of both of us'? These are extraordinary words.

There is no reciprocation of feeling in Lehmann's journals: equally extraordinary. Where there might have been a great flowering of confidence and feeling there is a blankness. Is this surprising? Not if we see how Lehmann was basically unable to distinguish the degrees of intensity with which those in his life responded to him. It is largely through the letters of Barbara Cooper that we know much of what may have existed between them. Written after Capetanakis's death, these are moving documents, a testament to a depth of friendship that Lehmann does not come within worlds of expressing, or perhaps confessing to himself.

Some who knew Lehmann in later years assumed the relationship between him and Capetanakis was sexual, but this seems doubtful. It is not only that somewhere Lehmann must have had to draw the sexual, and emotional, line: his sexual life was already complicated by Rassine, Hart, Dyer and the various casual partners who came and went. There is certainly no evidence for believing it was. Capetanakis's feeling operated in another, less physical, sphere. Perhaps we need to think that what they felt for one another transcended the bodily, though there can be little doubt that Lehmann must have been attracted to the younger man who confessed to him 'away from you I am just nothing'.

Was it in part from this obscured passion that Capetanakis's poems, esoteric, accessible, other-worldy, humane, sprang? There would be no more than a handful of them, not enough to form a collection, but wonderfully concentrating the mind because of their sparse existence. From them, Leonard Cooper always remembered a line, 'They made a soup that was a great success'. This was from Capetanakis's first poem, 'Detective Story', which, according to Edith Sitwell, was 'really astounding. It has a force and concentration of tragedy, and a real fire and passion.' In sixteen lines, something remarkable had indeed been begun.

> The stranger left the house in the small hours;
> A neighbour heard his steps between two dreams;
> The body was discovered strewn with flowers;
> Their evenings were too passionate, it seems.
>
> They used to be together quite a lot;
> The friend was dressed in black, distinguished looking
> The porter said; his wife had always thought
> They were so nice and interested in cooking.
>
> And this was true perhaps. The other night
> They made a soup that was a great success;
> They drank some lager too and all was right,
> The talk, the kisses and at last the chess.
>
> 'It was great fun!' they said; yet their true love
> Throbbed in their breasts like pus that must be freed.
> The porter found the weapon and the glove,
> But only our despair can find the creed.

With this first poem bearing a quality that Lehmann knew was quite beyond anything he himself could achieve, he celebrated and tried to foster Capetanakis's genius. But, again, what was the texture of that friendship? Capetanakis was clear: 'I know that I am your friend, but I do not know if I am an artist. But since you expect me to become one, I shall try and I do hope that some day I shall be able to write something for you that will not disappoint you ... I am really much more interested in what you write than in my own writing.' And, for once, one does not question the sincerity of such a remark.

Capetanakis had a personality that must have entranced those who came to know him, one that apparently belonged to some other world. We have a picture of him from Panayotis Canellopoulos.

> He was the most discreet and self-effacing of persons. When he was present it was as if he was not there. And when he was not there you felt him quite close to you. He seemed something more than alive with his frail body, something more than robust with his delicate constitution, something more than dead in the sense that, even while still alive, he seemed already to have passed beyond his own life and death.

*

Certainly, Capetanakis stood by Lehmann throughout the terrible, long period of his love for Hart. Reading the journals for 1941 and 1942 one is confronted by page after page of the outpourings of a tremendously troubled writer and lover, by a chronicle of emotional instability that can only have its ending in pain. Lehmann, more and more, was being consumed by jealousy, insecurity and all the attendant problems of being passionately involved with a nineteen-year old with severe emotional and sexual problems. By summer 1941 Lehmann wrote:

> Sometimes the way he has made me suffer, the things he has done to me, rise up like a tidal wave and batter me down. I've found I still love him in spite of it all. I see now that the thing that tortures and tortures me is the fear that he may never come back to make it all right.

Surely, Lehmann thought, his letters to Hart made everything better between them. But there was always some new edge of disagreement, new revelations, as when Lehmann despaired at the 'ghastly psychological tangle he's in and his shame of it, the fantasies overwhelm him'.

Those fantasies were almost certainly sado-masochistic, and the depth of Hart's problems came as a shock to Lehmann. He went to see Hart's parents, and better understood why their son wanted to emancipate himself from them – years later, Basil Liddell Hart would tell Lehmann, 'You evidently have a penetrating grasp of his psychology.' A batch of letters confirms that Jessie

Liddell Hart had a respect for Lehmann, and that she kept in touch with him over several years, sometimes sending him letters her son had written to her, with her injunction that Lehmann should burn them (he didn't). She assured Lehmann how much she loved her son, and 'Please don't think that I have forgotten you or what you have done for me or mean to me.'

Meanwhile, throughout 1941, the journal continues, doom-laden: the relationship with Hart had 'slipped into a region I never wanted it to enter, because of Alexis Rassine'. Lehmann had told Hart of Rassine, explaining that he did not expect Hart to be exclusively his but felt all the time that Hart was caring more than he admitted, and was exasperated because he could not admit the extent of his sexual difficulties to Lehmann. Then there had been the fatal slip: joining the Navy without ever having discussed it with Lehmann (and another reason for having to spend long periods apart, the old problem that had always dogged Lehmann's relationships).

Watching Hart awake from sleep helped convince Lehmann that there was a deep-rooted mental imbalance, so long did it take Hart to make sense or piece reality together again. They went through old photographs and Hart's diary in which he had noted his first meeting with 'the Hogarth Press man'; they laughed, and drank champagne, 'and after that at last to sleep, with my outburst of sudden, quickly passing despair, and his cry, "After an evening like this, but you mustn't…" And all peaceful again.' Part of the attraction was to educate Hart, to urge him to become a writer, just as, at the same moment, Lehmann was urging Capetanakis to glory, and encouraging Dyer to extend his literary knowledge. With Hart, Lehmann also knew he had to be doctor and psychoanalyst, and felt he could fulfil these roles – the truth, of course, was that he was in as much need of both as Hart, probably more.

In summer 1941, when his passion for Hart was running high, Lehmann went to Edinburgh to see Rassine dance, to 'live for an evening entirely for Alyosha, and his world', watching him in *Les Sylphides* and 'The Blue Bird'. He stayed with Rassine in his digs, as he got into the habit of doing all over England, an experience he enjoyed. The old landlady somehow provided bacon and sausages for breakfast.

One evening, Rassine insisted on going through his old press-cuttings and photographs. Lehmann was tired. In the middle of the night, Rassine began to cry: 'There, I'm crying, I don't know why. Isn't it silly of me?' Looking back, it seems almost inevitable that they would always be part of one another's lives, they were united as much in pity as in love; but for now, Lehmann wondered

Why did he begin to weep? Was it that only? Or was it a fear, too, that he could never have a happy relationship because of his life as a dancer, with its endless movement and parting, its dedication? Or the thought of home so far away in wartime? I shall find it impossible to forget that moment. Or the moment on Sunday morning when, at the junction I saw the special carriage for the Anglo-Poles shunted on to a new train, and inside there he was talking with others of the company, laughing, eating his sandwiches: that isolated, glass bound carriage so mysterious to the loiterers on the platform, a symbol of his life.

In a week out, Rassine returned to London, where Lehmann tried to tell him at least something of his feelings for Hart, as well as how well he thought Rassine had coped with his 'adventures and rovings', to which Rassine replied, 'I'm not jealous, I don't understand jealousy.' It was just as well: the long pages of Lehmann's journals for 1941 and 1942 contain barely another mention of Rassine.

\*

Lehmann shifted his concern almost totally from Rassine to Hart. Suddenly, it was Hart who had been let down by the war, who was responsible for the 'sublime experience' Lehmann was undergoing, who needed so much to be healed as well as loved.

By early autumn, Hart had moved his books and clothes into Lehmann's Cambridge rooms. And then, as if on the roller-coaster Lehmann and Sikyr had ridden with such glee on the Prater, he was off on a switchback of emotion, all unimagined heights and unimaginable depths.

In September there was a blissful reunion in Liverpool followed by another terrible break-up, Lehmann 'blinded with tears, tortured with misery'. Perhaps, he thought, he had tried to say too much, cram too many words into what he knew was only one of their wartime glimpses of each other. He wept as he waited for Hart to come to him. Their meeting was an ecstasy, until, again, the wrong word was said and the edifice collapsed, making him realise how vulnerable he had become, how ill he was. It all had to be persisted with nonetheless: hadn't Hart's behaviour in Liverpool in itself been 'a demonstration, in a terrible twisted way, of love, – as perhaps my jealousy was to him'? Wasn't Hart's feeling for him obvious the next morning, 'desperately clinging and holding'?

There increasingly seemed no escape from the collision of their passions, and the damage was becoming clear to others. At Fieldhead, Lehmann broke down and gave Rosamond a garbled version of what was happening to him. She clearly understood the situation. It was unbearable when Hart went back to sea and news came through of attacks on a convoy; Lehmann was always braced for news of his death. He could not sleep when Hart was away, and could not sleep when he heard he had returned from sea. Too often, Hart delayed getting in touch when ashore – something that might have alerted a less besotted admirer.

Lehmann was encouraged in November – confident when Hart returned to Portsmouth that the worst between them was over – that a new, hopeful chapter had been started, only to be plunged two days later into 'disaster', 'misery and horror'. Still he thought 'there is something sublime in what happens to Adrian and me. I can't get rid of that feeling.'

That evening, they had guests. Hart had been drinking heavily, and felt ill. When they were alone, he asked 'Why do you look so stern, John?' Lehmann undressed him and put him to bed, tearing a nail deeply as he did so. Hart tried to kiss it. At last, he asked Lehmann to bed, 'And yet the same terrible pattern repeated itself almost at once.' Lehmann felt ashamed of the bad-tempered, violent things he said to Hart. 'We must find a formula,' Hart said. 'It's only because I love you I endure this abuse.' Lehmann had made up his mind they must part, but Hart insisted, 'There must be a time-limit to this separation. Nothing ever ends, John.'

Lehmann said he had given Hart everything, to which Hart replied 'I owe you a debt far greater than I can ever repay.' They both broke down, Lehmann begging forgiveness for what he had said in the heat of his agony. 'Not goodbye, John?' Hart asked in the morning, 'and at last I yielded to embrace him, as indeed I had been longing to all the time, but withholding the force of desperate yearning that was in me.' They promised to write, and again, as the door closed between them, Hart murmured 'Not goodbye, John?' No matter how intense the suffering, Hart remained 'my major personal problem that eats me like a cancer'. There were times when a solution seemed lucent and easily obtainable. Lehmann assured Hart that

> ... if you will only let me I can help you so much more. I shall not ask for anything more; only that you remember that the tiger's still inside me, and will work wonders if you can tame him one day; only that you should be without fear or doubt in speaking to me.

He exposed his own vulnerability as a young man, tried every tactic to rescue their future. Hadn't it been a Liddell Hart (Adrian's father) who decided that in war the best strategy was Indirect Approach, and couldn't the strategy be put to use for Hart's neurosis? 'When I see you,' Lehmann wrote, 'I will try to explain how I learnt to say Yes at last to so much I had tried to deny at your age, and turned shame into gladness, and began to integrate myself.' If only Hart, too, might be persuaded to say Yes, to allow the triumph of the blood as Lehmann had.

\*

Professionally and socially another life was going on alongside: the ups and downs of Lehmann's friendship with Dyer, *Penguin New Writing*, *Folios of New Writing*, the Hogarth Press, tiring of Auden's 'pulpit attitude' from the safety of America, introducing Rassine to Lord Berners, discussing the possibility of broadcasts with the BBC, just as there was defeat in Crete and Russia was attacked by Germany.

There was a little comfort in finding some sort of equilibrium with Spender; Lehmann wondered why it had not always been so. He suspected that Spender and he were drawn closer together by the war's continuance, but also felt more confidence in himself, and an indifference to much that had hurt his feelings in the past; not so, of course, as events would shortly prove. There was also the threat of the call-up, if and when and where. Meanwhile, Home Guard duty had to be done. He did a broadcast with Laurie Lee, and met Dylan Thomas at a pub, taking him back to Athenaeum Court to give him a cheque: Thomas was almost demented at the idea of getting some cash.

Whatever happened, it seemed little more than an interruption in the agonising over Hart. Always there was hopelessness at being apart and the promise of what would at last happen when Hart returned, 'H.M.S. Adrian, with sails rigged ... When two people love one another so much as we do, all these troubles are just plum crazy.' So much energy was used up in trying to solve the mysteries of Hart's life.

In January 1942 Lehmann was once more recording recent happenings in the relationship, moments that were 'complex and baffling, and might need volumes really to understand them'. When Hart confessed that when it came to his emotions 'I was left to find it all out by myself', Lehmann felt he might yet uncover the wonder of personal relationships to his troubled lover. At the same time, of course, he urged him to read more novels, essential if Hart was to become the writer Lehmann so wanted, needed, him to be

Lehmann was struck by how emancipated Rassine seemed in comparison, confirming in his mind the differences he had always perceived between 'the simpler peoples of Europe and the repressed, entangled English'. Rassine was not present when Hart was taken to meet Rosamond and Cecil Day Lewis, or at a party for him with Capetanakis, Sonia Brownell and other literary figures. Neither was Rassine taken to Fieldhead after Christmas as Hart was, piling up books in the library, walking by the river, travelling to Eton to stare at the bomb damage, and accompanying Lehmann to the Home Guard, never mind that Lehmann complained of Churchill's speeches and 'how they gripped one less and less, how more and more one resisted being forced to live in this brilliant schoolboy's world'.

*

All yet seemed as if it might be well when at the end of the year there was a point when the relationship reached a peak of contentment. 'It was wonderful, Adrian,' Lehmann wrote on 14 December. 'We went so far this time with so little fear: it was an entirely new experience.' And then, again, collapse. On 1 January 1942 Lehmann was writing:

... one must believe in the devil, such sudden and murderous strokes of evil coincidence and disaster ... I can note now that there seemed a compulsion in Adrian leading me on to violence ... and yet there was probably some strain of curious masochism in my own attitude as well; but there is truth too in what Adrian said later when trying to make all well, that 'at least there was the very opposite of indifference to you, John, in what I did'.

Some sort of interpretation must be made of this, the details of a scene that Lehmann knew must never again occur; 'indeed the violence of the event seemed to have killed something that perhaps had to be killed.' The thing that had to be killed was indeed violence, and we need look no further than *In the Purely Pagan Sense* for an understanding of it. Here, Hart appears as Rickie, with whom Marlowe has penetrative sex. In the morning, he notices purple marks on Rickie's buttocks. When they next meet, Rickie presents Marlowe with a black dog whip. Marlowe whips Rickie savagely, feeling a disturbing change overcome him. And though Rickie pretty speedily departs from the novel – there is no suggestion that he was the great torment and love of Marlowe's war years – Marlowe is left with a taste for flagellation, administering and receiving it.

Returning from Hart's rooms to Athenaeum Court, Lehmann was filled with 'nausea'. Hart tried to make all right, bringing Lehmann a great sheaf of daffodils as the hour of his departure by the night train grew nearer. They dined at the Café Royal, but there must have been the oppression of knowing the end was close. On 11 January, they lunched with Beatrix and went to see *Dumbo*. In February, Lehmann took a new flat, number 601, at Carrington House (Dyer helped him furnish it, and it was to serve as Lehmann's office, with Barbara Cooper installed in it during working hours), 'quiet, roomy and beautiful, where I can make a home for Adrian'. The likelihood of such a thing being possible was remote. Lehmann reflected that Hart's attitude to older men with strong personalities was that of a guileless spaniel: on 'one side a boy of 12, the other a grown man'.

The idyll of a nest at Carrington House was short-lived: there was only one weekend there, before Hart went back to Hove for another week at Lancing College where he was training. It was a weekend of tremendous happiness, and then

21.ii.42

There was a week-end that went wrong.

And a day that followed it at Brighton which had an almost ideal perfection, a unity of thought and feeling, in which we seemed able to say to one another more than ever.

Then came – out of a clear blue sky – bewildering chaos and the seeming, sudden, inexplicable triumph of the dark forces that have always struggled against our happiness:

What the future can be, I don't know. It cannot be like the past.

No more.

They should have been the final words, 'no more', but were not. A few weeks later, Lehmann was writing to Hart at Ambleside, having no idea where he might be or what his service designation was. What did Hart want done with his suit, which had come from the tailor?

In March, Hart was pleading that they restart their friendship. They met again, at least once, in April, an 'extremely unpleasant' occasion. The canker was still healthy. In October, Lehmann returned unopened a letter Hart had sent him months before. But the link was not broken even yet. They seem to have resumed correspondence towards Christmas 1943, Lehmann writing from 'Doodle-bug-land', telling Hart, by now a Sub. Lieutenant, that women thought of the new bombs as 'monster spermatozoa heading for them intent on super-rape'. Hart's enthusiasm for the sea had somewhat faded. 'How I agree with Dr Johnson' he told Lehmann, 'about no man going to sea who had the contrivance to go to gaol'.

Five years later, Hart is complaining that Lehmann offers him no moral support, support that would surely have been given at a distance. It was difficult for Hart to establish himself in a career. In 1945 he was an unsuccessful Liberal candidate for Blackpool South. He worked, at various times, for the United Nations and Foreign Office and in Germany. He tried his hand at journalism, working for the *Yorkshire Observer*, as political correspondent on the *Westminster Press*, and foreign editor of the Toronto *Saturday Night*. He wrote a novel that Lehmann turned down ('I think you have still to learn your job'). When in 1951, he joined the Foreign Legion and became Legionnaire Peter Brand, Hart gave instructions to his father that his self-chosen anonymity should be respected. He wanted no letters sent, and any letters in England kept unopened: 'If people think I am in prison, that can't be helped – and is, in a sense correct'. He had a temperament that he thought not British, and 'Not only do I deviate from normal practices – but I am not really at home with those, in the artistic and kindred worlds, who can accept this marginal situation and make certain concessions. It seems to me significant that almost all of my friends are foreigners ... or Englishmen who elect to live abroad.' Basil Liddell Hart told Lehmann that Adrian's presence in the Foreign Legion was 'a cause of embarrassment all round'.

Lehmann proved his enduring concern by writing to Hart in Indo-China in November 1951, urging his return. 'I was mad at you for throwing everything up;' he told Hart, 'now there's a chance to come back and start again, *please do* ... [the French authorities] poor things to give them their due, did not realise what a scorpion they were putting into their shirts when they accepted Leg. Brand. They didn't consult *me*. Once again let me say it, dearest Adrian: don't let a fatal pattern repeat itself yet again in your life, but be your wiser self and come home to where people love you.'

In the 1960s Hart was still one of the circle. There remained a sinister and menacing air about Hart that is evident in the rare photographs that have survived of him in later life. Violence seems to have been a natural component of his unpleasant personality. On a London bus in Trafalgar Square, he once punched a bus-conductress in the face. It seems likely that, much changed in its intensity, Hart's sexual relationship with Lehmann continued intermittently well into middle age.

Forty years after their love had begun, they were still in touch with one another. In 1980, Lehmann wrote to say that an invitation he had extended was 'still on, though 40 years is a longish time to wait for an answer. I have an idea we might come to mean quite a lot to one another'. A few letters later, Hart fades from the story. His significance does not. At the very end of his journal for 1942, there is a determination in Lehmann's last words.

Not again devotion heart and soul for one person, that is finished for as long as this war lasts; and however great the suffering and sense of catastrophe has been and may be on that score, I can and will remain free from now on of all narrowing and jealousy that such an intensity and devotion can bring in its train. No one can touch me now, or have power over me for ill, whatever I have lost. As long as civilian life is allowed me, I want to dedicate myself to making a positive centre, where one can nourish the belief in poetry and all that art means, and through them recover and maintain real values, real culture; and not only that, but also a positive belief in life in itself, through wit and imagination; I want to create a centre where one can at last say No to despair and nothingness. To live for that, for one's circle of friends, for the common human contact, to realise at last in full the great possibilities in this my work and position give me.

With which words, Lehmann closed his journal. It would be a year before he returned to it.

# 10

# Co-operation of the Penguins

It is easy to forget that *Penguin New Writing* had its origin in a political belief that, long before the end of the periodical's life, had become abhorrent not only to most of its readers but to Lehmann himself.

Early in 1938 Lehmann had written a series of articles about British writers for *International Literature*, a Moscow publication that blatantly expounded (as did Lehmann's contributions) Russian propaganda. By November 1938 the material had been reworked for a pamphlet, *New Writing in England*, produced in New York for the Critics Group Press and published in 1939. There could be no doubt of the imprint's philosophy: other titles included *Literature and Marxism*, Milton Brown's Marxist treatise on painting of the French Revolution, George Plekhanov's politically slanted critique *Art and Society*, Elie Siegmeister's thoughts on the corruption of contemporary music by a morally perverted economy *Music and Society*. There was also *Dialectics*, the Critics Group Press's literary and rhetorical journal, with its articles on 'André Gide vs. the USSR', 'Spanish Revolutions', and 'What is the Marxist Approach to Literature?'

Now, Lehmann's aim was to give a 'sketch map' of the current state of writing in England, and to indicate how its writers 'may all be viewed as related in one master-pattern'. He was conscious of writing at a crucial bend of time, and aware of the unpredictable fluidity art was subject to. Between 1935 and 1936 he had contributed notes on 'Some Revolutionary Trends in English Poetry' to *International Literature*, charting the development of a 'specifically intellectual-bourgeois revolt' which he now saw altered by accelerating events and the Spanish Civil War. As well as chapters on the Spanish conflict, *New Writing in England* discussed Isherwood and Berlin, the effect of 'the Man in the Street' (the Trespassers), 'Fantasy and Fable' (Edward Upward and Rex Warner), and 'Experiment in Drama'. Since writing his 1938 articles, the world had witnessed

the collapse of Austria and the dismemberment of Czechoslovakia, with the British Government's connivance and *against* the will of all progressive British opinion, have already dealt a blow at democratic morale the marks of which may already be traced ... but however these bruises work themselves out over the next few months or years, on a long view, on an optimistic and Marxist view, it seems impossible to doubt that a new phase in English literature is in sight, a new humanism in which original barriers of class and race among the writers, in so far as they affect their style and matter, will have all but disappeared.

It was *New Writing in England* as much as the series of on-going *New Writing* anthologies that alerted Allen Lane to the usefulness of what Lehmann was doing, although one of Lane's last achievements at the Bodley Head had been to instigate them. Lehmann's good fortune was to coincide with the tremendous success Lane was having with Penguin Books. At the coming of war, Lane was enormously helped by the generous paper allocation awarded to Penguin, based as it was on pre-war turnover figures of the publisher. His successes had included the Penguin Specials, begun in 1937, and, the same year, the birth of the non-fiction Pelican. It was in January 1940 that Lane commissioned a Pelican from Lehmann, *New Writing in Europe*, the manuscript completed that August.

Re-dressed from its Russian propaganda beginnings, the book was published in January 1941, but already by the previous May Lane's association with Lehmann was reinforced by the suggestion that a Penguin should be made of some of the best pieces that had appeared in the hardback *New Writing*. This first issue of *Penguin New Writing*, published in December, might have been the end of the matter, a paperback selection of Lehmann's finest titbits. Lehmann had already told Lane that two paperbacks might be made up of the already published material.

Lane told Lehmann that he wanted Penguin to have a monthly literary magazine. By October 1940 it was decided that Lehmann would be its editor and that (as from the second issue of January 1941) *Penguin New Writing* would also include new material. That same month, Lehmann signed a contract for six monthly numbers. And, at once, there was no doubt of its success. At 6d. a copy, the first issue sold out, after two printings, at 80,000 copies. The next two numbers settled at 55,000 each, an achievement that should be measured against *Horizon*'s sales which, throughout its long existence (almost exactly parallel with *Penguin New Writing*) never managed more than 8,000 for any issue. For Penguin, production was helped by the allocation of five tons of paper to each issue, the amount that was allowed the Hogarth Press for the whole of its annual output.

By the end of 1941, sales of *Penguin New Writing* levelled at 75,000, a figure that would be greatly increased in the immediate aftermath of war. Here was justification for Lehmann's original happiness that, with the co-operation of the Penguins, he could 'keep it alive for the future in the worst circumstances, and bring it at last to the enormous public it always should have had'. In October, when Lane had accepted his plan for the scheme, Lehmann perceived the development as

... something fated, and if it comes off will put me – and all we stand for – in an absolutely commanding position. And yet from time to time I ask myself: am I mad to try and plan something like this, a monthly magazine, as the savagery of the war increases?

Supply and demand made it imperative that he should. He was faced by a deluge of unsolicited manuscripts that poured in 'in a shady flood, with pompous, impertinent, tough-guy, pathetic, intelligently appreciative letters with them, but scarcely one in a hundred any good'. New writers must be looked for, known ones encouraged or deflected. By February, Lane was offering a London office, the services of a reader (this would be Rosamond), and more money for contributors. Sonia Brownell was brought in to give secretarial assistance, and pleased Lehmann by describing *Horizon*'s organisation as 'higgledy-piggledy'.

It was clear that Penguin and Lehmann were producing something that suited the public mood in a way that Connolly and *Horizon* were not. The hardback, expensive *New Writing* series had not reached beyond the middle and upper classes; now, Lane's factory made possible an entirely authentic popularity, making contact with the man on the Clapham omnibus who might pick up the latest issue in his local Woolworths.

There seemed almost a panic of desire for it. There were tales of units of soldiers scouring Wiltshire for copies. From Blackpool, Harold Acton reported that the Polish forces billeted there rushed to Boots to buy it. Adrian Liddell Hart's Petty Officer was about to use a piece from it for a signalling lesson when one of the cadets pointed out it would be useless, as he knew the piece by heart. Even the design of the British Army's battledress seemed to be in collusion: the outer pocket above the left knee was perfectly shaped to store a copy of the new magazine, and was sometimes known as 'the Penguin pocket'.

In the dark cast of its time, *Penguin New Writing* represented a real attempt to democratise literature. Art was being made common experience, something that was accessible, and valuable even in, or especially in, war. 'FOR THE FORCES', read a footnote in no. 5, 'Leave this book at a Post Office when you have read it, so that men and women in the services may enjoy it too.'

*

Lehmann was faced with a dilemma:

> ... the almost total failure up to date, in our generation, to relate the fragments in the new literature – in the novels, books of reportage, sketches, etc. – to a coherent whole conception. Perhaps we haven't really got one: what marxism offered we have only found inadequate. And a symptom perhaps is that there have been so few fiction *artists* in our time, writers who aim to make a completely self-contained world of their books; Henry Yorke [the novelist Henry Green] one of the very rare exceptions.

But the dilemma itself opened up possibilities that Lehmann would success-fully exploit for the rest of the magazine's existence. He was helped by the fact that the war favoured the anthology; it was often the short spurt that appealed to both writer and reader at a time when life was uncertain, disjointed. Suddenly, there was no guarantee that one would get through Balzac or Tolstoy or Dickens. Attention might happily be given, but came in short measures, stories, poems, a few pages of reminiscence, some paragraphs to amuse, or a brief documentation of real life.

Lehmann saw a lack of wholeness in what English writers were doing, and he seems to have followed a progress of his own devising, a progress discernible from the first *New Writing* of Spring 1936 up to the final *Penguin New Writing* of 1950. The detail of his intention underwent considerable alteration – shifts of emphasis and tone and content – but the line, basically, was held for fifteen years. Indeed, it is one of his greatest achievements that he was able to adapt the magazine to suit not only the tenor of contemporary feeling (and this changed tremendously throughout those years) but also his personal reaction to it.

Of course there were changes of gear, among them his repudiation of blissful solutions that Russia had once promised (already evident in his confession of the inadequacy of Marxism). One of his skills was to make such changes appear as natural development, made inevitable, forced on him by what the world was doing. He did not throw over the Trespassers. It was factors beyond his control that made them, by the beginning of the war, redundant.

Now, the Man in the Street, that untutored hopeful waiting below the Leaning Tower, was in uniform, and transformed by the fact; now, it was the wearing of uniform, army, navy, airforce, that united the men to whom Lehmann had for so long wanted to have duty and obligation. Uniform, too, when it was worn by the young writer, suggested a consolidation of a massive 'movement' the like of which the Trespassers, in peace-time, could never have dreamed of. It was indeed a time for what Patric Dickinson has called 'conscript prose in poetic uniform'.

What is perhaps most remarkable about the earliest of *Penguin New Writing* is the immediate sure-footedness of what Lehmann was doing. Despite the fact that no. 2 was mostly made up of the old plums, the tone of what was to come was almost instantly established. The importance of the recurring feature seemed particularly important when so much was transient. George Stonier, writing as 'Fanfarlo', started his accounts of 'Shaving Through the Blitz' with a wit that survives: his opening sentence, 'It was on the forty-seventh day of the new razor' could only raise recognising smiles among its readers. Plomer, writing as Robert Pagan, contributed 'a conversation with a Civil servant' – 'You Must Have Two Hats' – the first of his intelligent satires on war-time happenings. Lehmann persuaded Rosamond to write short stories for the new magazine, a distinguished collection that began with 'A Dream of Winter', and appeared intermittently throughout its run.

## 10. Co-operation of the Penguins

It was Coombes who wrote the first of the 'The Way We Live Now' articles, a feature that would carry some of the finest pieces the magazine had, commissioned from workers and soldiers (in other words, ex-Trespassers). For Coombes it was another chance to describe the subterranean life of the miner, for Willy Goldman, an expression – Orwellian in its directness – of how the Blitz was affecting the East End from which he came. Such strength of reportage was maintained at a high level throughout 'The Way We Live Now' – until its replacement by 'Report on Today' (in no. 13, at which time the magazine became a quarterly), an umbrella heading that embraced two or three pieces directly springing from an experience of war, from writers in uniform – another opportunity for new and ex-Trespassers. When war ended, this in turn was succeeded in no. 25 by 'The Living Moment'.

If the change of emphasis in documentary essays under the various headings was sometimes almost too subtle to detect, it still reflected Lehmann's understanding of the move away from extrovert reportage into something altogether more aesthetic and introverted – but this lay ahead, ready for when war was over. A heightened sensitivity to taste was also evident in the magazine's attitude to criticism. Spender, by now teaching in Devon, was commissioned to write a series, 'Books and the War'; the first of these was originally the only critical material the magazine published. By the end of the war, boldly, Lehmann had significantly increased the amount of criticism, a move that altered the purpose of *Penguin New Writing* and gave it another, in no way earnest, dimension. By no.13 'Books and the War' had become 'Book Front', with Spender still contributing an essay, but flanked by other writers. Lehmann himself began to write regularly for the paperbacks. 'A Reader's Notebook' was a series of six articles in which 'Jack Marlowe' (Lehmann) took the platform to air the concerns of an editor-writer.

Those wishing to revitalise Lehmann's reputation as an editor may turn eagerly to the jottings of Marlowe. Will Lehmann, under cover of his *nom de plume*, be dangerously provoking? Will literary heresy be done? Will he, with the coruscating wit that Connolly, when bothered, could summon, demolish and rain scorn on the pretensions and intrigues of the literati?

Alas, Jack Marlowe disappoints the highest hopes, and his prose remains resolutely earthbound (just as Marlowe's supposed autobiography, *In the Purely Pagan Sense*, would remain earthbound some thirty years later). We turn to the Forewords of *Penguin New Writing*, in the hope that it is here that Lehmann will light the imagination, will ignite the argument, will turn the memorable phrase. There are opportunities here as, issue by issue, Lehmann introduces his latest selection of writers, but Lehmann cannot turn them into gold, and there is the feeling that he is simply trying too hard.

Lehmann is that impresario who, having assembled a talented company, cannot resist appearing through the curtains and edging his way to the front of the stage before the entertainment commences. He tells us something that he

143

feels we should know. If we believe that the best of editors by definition should be invisible, made real only by the fact that they have made something possible, then Lehmann must be disqualified. If we take up his admission that he only half-believed in what he did, we may better understand the extremity of that effort, better appreciate how effortful his work as editor became.

The very fact that he had no reputation as a creative writer made it yet more necessary for him to bring himself forward bearing his statements on the health of the literary world, like the captain of a ship reporting to his passengers on what is happening in the engine room. Lehmann's basic skill as an editor, nowhere more evident than in the pages of *Penguin New Writing*, lay in discovering and bringing forward the right author at the right moment.

It was perhaps inevitable that it should be so, for he was the cynosure for English writers, the one person to whom the young literary aspirant would turn for reaction and, hopefully (and almost always) criticism, encouragement and, perhaps, publication. In this way Lehmann offered a public service, the idea of providing which would surely have appalled the more elitist Connolly.

The fact is that when young writers wanted to get their work into print, Lehmann was the obvious fountainhead to whom they turned. Connolly's inherent inability to offer this facility to the same extent may partly be explained by Connolly himself being such a good writer, while Lehmann was in the main inferior. There must be no doubt that Connolly would have rejected much of what Lehmann put into *Penguin New Writing* as second-rate and pedestrian (it may be so), and of course Connolly's *Horizon* was a very different beast.

Few writers would have known that their work had to pass the gimlet eye of Barbara Cooper before being offered up to Lehmann with her already pronounced opinion, but once Lehmann's support was won, it was exemplary. Once interested, he seemed full of care for contributions, even if work was rejected. And the richness of *Penguin New Writing* was made possible by the catholicity of Lehmann's interest; it is almost as if he was unable to differentiate between the mundane and the esoteric. Thus, the magazine presented a panorama of literature that *Horizon* did not attempt.

There was also the peculiar provenance of *Penguin New Writing*, suckled as it was on the many editions of the original *New Writing* that had gone before it, a history with which Connolly could not compete. Coming as it did out of the struggle for everything that had been struggled for before the war, *Penguin New Writing* emerged especially *for* the war; it needed the war to make it effective.

But let us consider the reputation of Connolly and Lehmann, Connolly eulogised and vividly celebrated in biography and anecdote, Lehmann overshadowed, become unpopular and unfashionable and not chic; so much that is positive and memorable in the one, so much that is negative and forgettable in the other. As a general statement, it may be true that Connolly has been overrated as much as Lehmann had been underrated. Connolly, undoubtedly, has been perceived as being more fun, of clinging ever so lightly to the underskirts of Bohemia; there is something handsomely disreputable about him, enough to be amusing but not dangerous. Fun is not a word one would associate with Lehmann, and his public manner inclined to the courtier-like and ministerial. It was Connolly who suggested that whenever Lehmann sat down to write he put on a formal suit.

Both men had a pronounced sense of their own importance, but Lehmann lacked the natural sense of humour of Connolly, the ability to find himself absurd. Lehmann's inability made it more possible for others to mock the absurdity they found in what they perceived as his pomposity, his sense of self-importance. And perhaps that lack of the absurd dimension is something else that shadows the work he collects throughout *Penguin New Writing*. But in that it only makes a stronger claim to be even more of its time; it is earnestness, not inventiveness, that is attempted. Perhaps, in wartime and the years that immediately followed it, that too was an advantage that led the magazine to its extraordinary success. But in the facts of its success lay the seeds of its own destruction and Lehmann's destruction.

*

In a world of Vera Lynn, of gas masks and rationing, of Lord Haw-Haw and, in the last years of the magazine, austerity, it would have been natural if *Penguin New Writing* had turned itself into something essentially inward-looking and insular. The war encouraged the discouragement of anything foreign; even speaking in foreign languages seemed a threat to national security. On gramophone records, opera singers of the period were forced to deliver coy English lyrics in place of what had been French or German. Those intemperate enough to be foreign in England at the beginning of the war found themselves questioned and under internment. Foreigners in films were depicted as stereotypes of the most obvious kind, not only Germans (in countless films that happily lapsed into the silliest propaganda) but any races unfortunate enough to speak in dubious accents.

What before the war had been the foolish foreigner became the untrustworthy foreigner, as England's ability to look beyond itself crumbled before the invading foes of cataclysmic change. In choosing to return to England at the beginning of the war, Lehmann had to endure the shrinking of attitude that pervaded its society.

The tragedy, perhaps the central tragedy of Lehmann's existence, is that he was a natural European whose career and life would have been very different had he stayed in Austria. Instead, the war cut off his European life, and there never seemed to be the opportunity (or the will) to take it up again. But Lehmann *was* a European, and steadfastly went on carrying the flag throughout the war years, even if it was a flag that had seemed less tattered during the early years of the original *New Writing*. When the war was done, England, rather than opening its arms to other influences, constricted even further, and the dimensions of Lehmann's world were irredeemably shrunk.

It was in these circumstances that Lehmann achieved the brilliance that was *Penguin New Writing*, and it is in these circumstances that we should imagine its conception, against the various whiffs of war on

> ... continual train-journeys accompanied by a suitcase full of manuscripts and proofs which I worked through; of frequent halts on the line during an alert, then progress in and out of King's Cross or Paddington sometimes being as slow as the game of Grandmother's Steps we used to play in front of the Pavilion at Fieldhead, sudden spurts while the Nazis weren't looking, dead stops when aerial eyes were upon us; sometimes dusk fell over the darkened train and reading had to be abandoned, and passengers in silent gloom reflected that their plans to arrive – or leave – before the evening blitz were going to be in vain; guns started to bark and the faraway thump of bombs changed, disagreeably, to the swish-swish-swish of a stick of them swooping down close by. Also I remember blissfully peaceful nights in Cambridge, where my secretary, Michael Nelson, would often join me, typewriter in hand; and of trips to the works where the Penguin was being printed, sometimes to find there had been a raid the night before and a tarpaulin was being hurriedly stretched over jagged holes in the roof under which the machining of the next number miraculously proceeded. And all the time the letters and manuscripts poured in, chests of drawers at Fieldhead were desperately requisitioned, old rowing vests, mountain-shoes, lederhosen and anti-fascist newspapers, maps of Prague and Vienna and A.A. itineraries of long-ago car trips across Europe flung out, to make room for the ever-increasing offerings of every day's post.

Forty years after the end of the war, Lehmann and Roy Fuller compiled an anthology from the faded leaves of *Penguin New Writing*. Lehmann wanted only the golden and silver names to reappear, the names of those whose reputations had survived and grown and gave credence to what he had done.

In this Lehmann was wrong. It is to others that *Penguin New Writing* belongs, to the voices that came up from the people and were in turn accepted by the people as the speakers of their time, to B. L. Coombes, dragging his heavy prose up from the coal-face, to the stories of Fred Urquhart, to the rough words of Jim Phelan, to so many names now forgotten but once made known. They eclipsed the contributions of the great and glorious, fitting time and circumstance to the limit of their talents. They gave substance to Lehmann's greatest achievement. They were born of his mission, Lehmann's almost dream-like integration of young writing and a world at once earthy, real and sexual.

# 11

# Penetrating that Room

Even as the misery of Lehmann's relationship with Adrian Liddell Hart faded, there was no lessening of the prodigious workload that had so long engulfed him. For a short time, long having been a contributor, he was literary editor of the *Tribune*, until turned out by Aneurin Bevan and George Strauss because (Lehmann said) they were uneasy about his politics. His work for the *Geographical Magazine* had taken a new turn in November 1940 when he was appointed advisory editor, to assist the editor Ivy Davison. This happy working relationship with Miss Davison, which only ended in 1945, suggests that Lehmann was not essentially a misogynist; but she was fond of dogs. Together, they broadened the content of the periodical so that its pages became unexpectedly hospitable to 'literary' writers and poets.

It was all part of the war effort, as was his continuing Home Guard work and his broadcasts for the BBC, some of them sheer propaganda for the German Service, talks on writers for the Overseas Service, and a series for the Austrian Service, the programmes always bearing the hope that his old friends in Vienna, most especially Sikyr, would hear his voice. This radio career had been reached only by a stony path. In July 1941 he had suggested to the BBC that he be employed to broadcast directly to Austria, and was turned down. In August he applied and was rejected for an Overseas News appointment, but at the beginning of 1942 he was asked to give two talks (on the Caucasus and Georgia), and the following summer George Orwell recommended that he did a book talk to China.

While the shadow of the call-up was always there – and Lehmann was startled to be told by Connolly that he was largely responsible for his deferment – he did his utmost to serve. In the months immediately before war, he was offering part-time assistance to the Foreign Office in the event of the expected emergency: 'I have no political axe to grind, my strongest feelings in the present conflict being for the freeing of the Austrians from Nazi control and the maintenance of internationalism on the Danube.' The offer was rejected (his homosexuality was undoubtedly against him) and he turned his attention instead to the more welcoming Ministry of Information. It looked for a while as if he might be employed to facilitate relationships with Rumania, but in 1940 he suggested to the MOI 'a cultural-propaganda centre' in Russia, his proposal stimulated by the editor of *International Literature*, Timofei Rokotov, who had begged Lehmann for information on the English literary scene for dissemination in the Soviet Union.

It was fortuitous for Lehmann that Archibald Clark-Kerr, then British Ambassador at Moscow, was sympathetic to his cause (and to homosexual writers, already having made friends of Isherwood and Auden), and had already urged the Russian department of the MOI to make use of Lehmann's expertise. Soon, Lehmann was organising the shipping-out of books about ballet, art, documentary films to Russia, 'careful to emphasise the national and progressive tradition ... without falling into any party political nettlebeds'. He wanted to do more. In October 1941 he applied unsuccessfully to the Intelligence Department of the Admiralty's Naval Staff; it was to be the MOI that made use of him. His duties included writing a monthly 5,000 words on English literature for Rokotov's *International Literature*, and responding to his sometimes desperate cables: who were Henry Green, Laurie Lee, Walter Allen, William Plomer? When *International Literature* ceased publication, Lehmann switched his writing to *Britanski Soyuznik*, a British propaganda newspaper published in Russia. Through it all, he was encouraged by his friendship, unexpected and unlikely, with Clark-Kerr, a pipe-smoking Scot who seemed to Lehmann always to be struggling against the timidity of the Foreign Office.

Another ally was the politician Panayotis Canellopoulos – 'his pale and ardent face seemed suffused with a sacred inspiration as he spoke' – who had the added recommendation of having been Capetanakis's tutor at Athens. Canellopoulos was important in bringing the Greek problem so much closer to Lehmann, and the men met often, sometimes in the company of Capetanakis. With Hart removed from the picture, there was the beginning of what seems to have been a more settled period in Lehmann's friendship with Capetanakis, and this was a period when his attitude to Rassine, too, had consolidated.

Lehmann felt his intense involvement with what had been happening to Isherwood, and Auden, fading: how could it compare with his feelings for Rassine and Capetanakis, and all they had done for him during the years of war? One evening at dinner, 'in sudden clear light', Lehmann understood how Alyosha felt about their friendship.

> He spoke of how few real friends one ever has, who think for one, who want the best one can do (even S. [Spender] only thinks of himself I'm sure, he said) ... but of course to him, as he loved me, nothing else could come first, – except that I should devote myself to the work best for me, my poems and novels, not always the work of presenting and forming other people. It is a thing I can never forget, the inevitable way he said it.

Thoughts of Sikyr still obtruded, of course, but Lehmann knew Sikyr belonged to a world to which Lehmann would never properly be able to return. It seemed strange that for so long he had refused to see happiness where it existed;

in Rassine, 'it had grown, it was there, in all its completeness, a perfectly expanded flower'.

\*

England demanded so much, and with the new vigour and confidence Lehmann had discovered since Hart, he found himself even more at the centre of literary activity than before. War did nothing to stop the social round: lunch with Joe Ackerley, E. M. Forster and Plomer at the Istanbul restaurant; his first meeting (taken by Capetanakis) with Edith Sitwell – 'only the forehead disappointed me a little'; Eddy Sackville-West and Quentin Bell came in for drinks; Spender and Roger Senhouse came for lunch; he listened to Kingsley Martin and his cohorts at *New Statesman* lunches; met Harold Nicolson ('the stuffing has gone out of him now') at Sybil Colefax's with V. S. Pritchett. Tiring of such distinguished company, he made forays to old and new haunts to meet sailors, airmen, soldiers, in the Bunch of Grapes, the Fitzroy, the Windsor. Then, a dinner party at Emerald Cunard's with Duff Cooper and Diana Cooper, when he was almost in awe of this close acquaintance with what he called the 'rooling clawss', coming away with 'a fascination for their immense assurance and underlying flexibility, their obstinate and even petty narrowness of view about Beveridge'.

In April 1943, a charity poetry reading organised by Osbert Sitwell and given before the Queen and the two Princesses gave him the opportunity to paint thumb-nail sketches of some of those attending. Here was Edmund Blunden ('a startled ferret on its hind legs'), Walter De La Mare ('a wizened gnome king'), Edith Sitwell, looking like a Roman emperor and wearing a green laurel-wreath hat, and the editor of the *Times Literary Supplement*, 'that fat little toad' D. L. Murray. Lady Dorothy Wellesley turned up drunk and was declared unfit to appear before the royal party. Reeling about, she cried 'And it was the chance of my life!' Both Colefax and Cunard were present, the latter afterwards dancing along Bond Street with Duff Cooper saying, 'Leslie, recite me some Ronsard – you do it so beautifully!' Lehmann went on to Colefax's dinner party that evening at the Dorchester, where Violet Hammersley, 'giving one of her most finished and thrilling performances in the leading role of V. H.', and Connolly, were fellow guests.

Writing of Connolly in his autobiographies Lehmann suggests that what existed between them was nothing more than healthy competitiveness. Lehmann's journals suggest otherwise. Hammersley's verdict, at the Dorchester, was that Connolly had been unsmiling and pompous. Lehmann was ready to agree about 'Scallywag Connolly', whom he saw as representative of the Old Guard of English writing, one of the

... old Mandarins – and Cyril, Raymond [Mortimer], Eddie Sackville-West, Harold Nicolson have become that – how they cling together, with a dread anxiety lest anyone whose tenure is not absolutely 'correct' should get into their palace gardens, worst of all should threaten their occupation of it ... And it occurred to me: perhaps they are on guard against me too, perhaps I shall always have them to battle with, however friendly our relations may be in human terms.

With Connolly, perhaps, most of all. After the Colefax party, Capetanakis overheard Connolly maliciously relating how everything that Lehmann had said to him that evening had been a calculated insult. Lehmann was convinced that in Connolly guilt and envy had risen 'to an almost pathological point'. It was a good example of what Lehmann was finding increasingly repulsive, 'the insincerity, the pettiness and envy in the literary world, more enclosed than ever owing to the war and the draining off of the young from London ... at times so disagreeable, so stifling that one wonders how much longer one can exist in the atmosphere'.

Spender seemed obsessively egotistic, a deadly bore with his tedious expositions on the National Fire Service in which he served, and when that failed, a deadly bore about his personal problems. A capacity to bore might be forgiven, but betrayal never. When it was published in 1942, Spender praised Lehmann's little collection, *Forty Poems*, to his face, and then damned it with faint praise in the *New Statesman*. Capetanakis assured Lehmann it was mere jealousy. Somewhat more dramatically, Lehmann concluded that Spender's 'utter lack of a conception of reciprocity in friendship seems to me sometimes almost to approach insanity'.

Lehmann might have been forgiven for thinking he was the subject of a literary conspiracy, for Connolly too made unpleasant noises about *Forty Poems* in the *Observer*. Plomer said 'If I were you, I think I should suffer from real persecution mania.' Alas, none of the critics threw their hats into the air over the book, in which only the final sixteen pieces had not previously been collected. Richard Church saw the work as representing Lehmann's response to the last decade, reflecting 'instantly the great issues of these history-tumbling years ... He has to listen to new voices, such as those of the Russian workers in their new world', while *Time and Tide* thought the poet 'seems to have squeezed all emotion out of the poems and left only the shape, like a pressed flower'.

The new verses were mostly 'Poems before War 1934-39', including 'A Sleeping Giant', set in a workers' tenement house in Vienna on the anniversary of the February uprising, and 'His Hands', recalled from a visit to Zernograd in 1934, about an engineer called Vanya working in a 'new town of grain and tractors' at his machine 'In whose blood-throb he feels his hands / Moving over the responsive iron / Move with a thousand others out of dark.' 'We Remember' celebrated the hope instilled by the exiled *Schutzbündlers* in the Moscow of 1934, blue-shirted and young, marching through streets filled with music and everywhere the colour red. There was a 'Song of the Austrians in Dachau', adapted from the German of Georg Anders. And, finally, five poems written in wartime, the most interesting of them 'The Summer Story', the piece that told a little of Lehmann's obsession with his 'dark lieutenant from the sea'.

*

The gap between Lehmann's manifesto of what he *might* write and what he was *able* to write seemed as wide as ever, perhaps because to some extent he was constricted by a feeling that his poetry must be made to work in a way that made it relevant to his fellow men.

In this way, poetry had become a sort of duty, it could not be obscured, it had to speak of reality, the world reflected in it gave it its potency. And how chastening it must have been to him to be forever in the eye of the storm, at the absolute centre of interest for so many young writers. 'To all these boys,' he wrote, 'I can, I believe, play a special role: I can see in each case the person they want me to be, and can, so I hope, make myself into that person in some degree for them'.

When Lehmann consulted a doctor in Shepherd Market about a poisoned hand, the old man was astonished to learn that he was the son of R. C. Lehmann.

It made me think again what a legend my Father had been, and how that legend was dying out as those who had known him died off: soon it won't be possible any more to reconstruct it, and perhaps I shall never know what it really was. R. C. L., in the strict and most concentrated sense of the word, was a failure: his poetry, which early on (or so it has always seemed to me) showed signs of high promise in a certain genre, dropped into easy grooves, just as ambition seemed to desert him after the high promise of his early days in his public political career. And yet, in another sense, on another plane, he was an unique success. There is an inspiration and a warning for me in this.

Something to inherit, too, through Rudie's easy attachment to sentiment, which of course could never quite become Lehmann's quality.

What Rudie had put into his work somehow, in his son, was transmuted into a striving belief in humanism. He exposed what Rudie had believed but never wholly been able to express – an importance of being, of equality. Rudie, like all writers, was stuck at the gate of his capability, and it was for his son to make possible what his father had found impossible. If we see Lehmann's poetry as in part a tribute to the father he felt he had lost too early, it is suddenly revealed almost as glamorous in its generosity of spirit. Its worth is in its feeling, not its quality. No matter that too often it seems stunted, half-born, clumsy in construction and expression, devoid of a deeper meaning waiting to be translated. No matter, for it is meant.

We must see that the passion Lehmann had for poetry was so often diverted into the passion he felt for the poetry of others. It is this that helped make him such a superb editor. And that passion always wanted new channels: just as *New Writing* was to become *Folios of New Writing* and *New Writing and Daylight* and *Penguin New Writing* and, briefly, *Orpheus*. In May 1943 he was hoping that when the war ended he might begin a periodical 'where *we*, that is people who put art and literature first but have the interests of the whole man, can discuss history and historical books and foreign affairs as well as literature and aesthetic-philosophical questions'. He discussed the foundation of such a magazine with Capetanakis and (when he was in favour) Spender. Always, there was the encouragement and strength he found in the young writers and poets with whom he struck up what were really friendships in the age of the airgraph. The time and trouble he took to nurture them cannot be forgotten.

Years later, the poet Roy Fuller praised Lehmann's 'ceaseless, energetic, discriminating, on the ball, selfless work for our art. But for you we would not have written so well ... To all of us who depended on you – and what a number and diversity there were! – this is a record others cannot properly understand.' We must try to understand it now, though the scope of what Lehmann was doing is almost unmanageable, and any attempt to summarise it can only be diminishing: we can sympathise with Fuller being 'moved by the astonishing panorama of you, dear friend'. With encouragement came criticism, often fierce; he certainly never seems to have been able to look so severely on his own work as he did on that of others.

Among the many others was a young poet, Alan Ross, twenty years old when Lehmann first met him. In the Navy, Ross had already seen action in the Fleet Air Arm and been in the terrifying Arctic convoys. He was not only a keen propagandist for *Penguin New Writing*, his letters also 'conjured up pictures of devotion to literature and the idea of an *avant-garde* under the most impossible circumstances'. Ross was 'a boy whose natural charm, spontaneity and intelligence are clouded by I don't know what mildew of youth'.

The first poems sent in 1941 by a Highland Scots, Hamish Henderson, were rejected, but Lehmann, who always urged promising writers (even when he turned their work down) to keep in touch and send him new poems, became excited by the quality of the poetry Henderson wrote after his time in Alamein and the desert war. He was attracted by Henderson's obvious patriotism in pieces such as 'Fragment of an Elegy', written from his experiences with the 51st Highland Division in Italy, Sicily and North Africa. For Lehmann, of course, this was another way of being one of the men at the Front, even if, as Henderson told Lehmann from the Anzio beachhead, it was 'not as fucking awful as you might think'.

Lehmann had met David Gascoyne before the war in Paris, where Gascoyne lived for many years, but in September 1939 they were having lunch in England, Gascoyne 'looking longer and more like an agreeable, soft prehistoric reptilian monster than ever'. Lehmann was fascinated when Gascoyne declared that the war was nothing but a surface manifestation of something no one was conscious of: what he called 'an experience of the void'.

The brief snatches we have of Lehmann's relationship with Gascoyne tell us something of his attitude to the young writers he gathered. Faithfulness, on Lehmann's part, was guaranteed, and would usually carry through the years. After the war, he was largely responsible for Gascoyne being given a grant by the Royal Literary Fund, and even suggested to the appropriate authorities that Gascoyne would be an outstanding Poet Laureate (in the sense that he was an outstanding poet, he might indeed). In April 1941 he took Gascoyne to dinner at the White Tower, where he warmed him out of his 'fluttering anxious misery': 'I like him, and always have a fondness for him, but feel he has a dangerous un-human indifference at the bottom of his heart.'

\*

'I believe in you and in your love, that is something great and must create something great' Capetanakis had assured Lehmann in November 1941. But now he no longer was the voice of reason between Lehmann and his sailor. No longer distracted by the presence of a departed lover, his belief in Lehmann's being had become unalterably personal. In March 1942 Capetanakis, then working at the Greek government's Ministry of Information in Park Lane, had a complete collapse brought on by a self-confessed 'destructive passion which … is still at work in myself, decomposing my soul and degrading my life.' He was diagnosed as having leukaemia. Now, he yearned for a mystic understanding, and luxuriated in the preparation for a sleep from which he hoped he would not wake. 'I want you to understand why my attitude towards you and Adrian has changed a little since last week,' he wrote,

> My new contact with this night reminded me that one must never be too categorical with the things of the world. Everything is changing in it. We have the right not only to fear the worst, but also hope the best.

By some sublime twist, the best was revealed in his passion for the goodness in Lehmann. 'You are life to me,' he insisted. 'The mere fact that you exist is already a miracle to me.' At an evening of ballet, he had suddenly been convinced by a new sense of fulfilment, a confidence of complete happiness with Lehmann at his side. His will made it possible for Capetanakis to live again.

Later in 1942 Capetanakis returned to work. But his health failed that autumn and, sent to Devon to recover, he endured frequent nightmares. He seems to have been mortally ill in Westminster Hospital in January 1943. It was now, Panayotis Canellopoulos saw, that his friend decided he would live again. Now, too, he may have told Lehmann

You saved my life, or rather you gave me a new life, yesterday, John. To lose you, to lose my belief in you and our friendship would have been my end. But you could not have been more wonderful. It is such a relief to be able to write to you freely, as I do now, full of the faith which only can give a meaning to our life. My desire is now to create a work which will not only be mine, but yours too. You saw that as long as you keep me away from you I cannot create anything, – all I have created up to now was the work of both of us ... don't keep me away from you, because away from you I am just nothing.

Canellopoulos wrote a sonnet for Capetanakis in which he described both love and hate as nothing but shadows; when Capetanakis heard it, he 'triumphed, but I could not help feeling sad myself'.

There was one more happy phase, when Capetanakis moved to Manor Farm, headquarters of the Friends Ambulance Unit in Birmingham, where young Quakers were trained for the work that awaited them in his beloved Greece. He impressed Dame Elizabeth Cadbury who, learning he was writing an essay on the English poets, gave him a room in her house to work in. It was for Lehmann that Capetanakis wanted to write something that would satisfy everything he demanded and, for that brief moment, it seemed there might yet be time and health for it. When he returned to London, the illness savagely returned. Desperately ill as he was, he only got a hospital bed when he staged a collapse at his flat in Prince of Wales Terrace.

Early in 1944 Capetanakis was admitted to a general ward at Westminster Hospital. Weak, barely able to read or write, he watched the events unfolding around his death with a brilliant fortitude. 'I am experiencing the most *fantastic* things which I must use later on,' he told Lehmann.

He had no doubt that death was here. When the night nurse asked him how he felt he replied, 'A little better', but she moved away and asked the nurse in charge 'Is he really better?' and the woman shook her head. A blood-transfusion was organised. Because the doctors could not penetrate his veins the skin above them had to be removed. The anaesthetic was ineffective; Capetanakis 'had to suffer pains I cannot describe'. In what may have been his final letter to Lehmann, Capetanakis wrote 'Yes, we can do lots of things together and we shall be very happy if I get well.'

Capetanakis died in the afternoon of 9 March, at 4.15 p.m. After a funeral at the Greek Cathedral in Bayswater he was interred in the Greek enclosure at West Norwood, in Grave 39710. His brother, Dr John Capetanakis, was anxious that his mother, in ill-health, should not learn of her son's death. A scheme was devised whereby he wrote letters as if from Demetrios, and had them posted from America, where Demetrios was supposed to be.

It may have been at this time that the letter Capetanakis had written in March 1942, when he might have died, came into Lehmann's hands. On its envelope is the pencilled instruction 'If I die to be given to J. Lehmann Esq'. 'I must thank you once more for all you have done for me,' he wrote,

> Our friendship is really something achieved. That helps me to leave life without regret: I can use a symbol to express something I feel: It will help me to rest for ever undisturbed. But if my lot is rest, yours must be life. You must have a long, intense and creative life: I believe in you and your work. You are suffering now, but that will help you in the future. I also hope that my death will help you. I want it to be a present for you, as it is for me.

Canellopoulos recognised that for Capetanakis 'it was life that expressed Death. His optimism was too great for him to be able to content himself with what others call life ... my friend knew very well that clear vision has little to do with light. It is not in light, it is rather in darkness that lucidity is born.' What could death do but confirm the truth of those perceptions?

The godliness that had surrounded him in life canonised his passing. There was sacrifice and martyrdom in it all. Edith Sitwell mourned the taking of his being 'destined to be eternally young ... he did not remain a thing apart from the element he explored. He *was* the element itself.' Of his poems yet unwritten, she could not bring herself to speak, so aware was she of potential greatness working through into them.

Barbara Cooper, typing the last of his poems, 'Lazarus', experienced a complete black-out from its terrifying impact, perhaps affected by its prescience of the void. 'This knock means death,' Capetanakis began, ending

> And now I hear the knock I heard before,
> And strive to make up for the holy time,
> But I cannot remember, and the door
> Creaks letting in my unambiguous crime.

Barbara never forgot him. She remembered a summer evening when she met him by chance in Kensington Gardens, the swans statue-like across the Round Pond, bare-legged children playing in the grass, and him smiling, a faded red volume of Dostoevsky in his hands. One damp, New Year's Day he called 'Happy New Year' to her in Berkeley Square. Once they bumped into one another in Shepherd's Market and he walked with her to Piccadilly Circus, talking of music. Her first memory of him had been his eyes, deep velveted brown, suggesting that personality with its 'mysterious reserves of power and intensity and a twist towards pain', emphasising the spirit of him, religious, profound, Olympian. The last time she met him he was sitting in Lehmann's flat, a hand hanging by his side as if he had no strength to lift it, in his face the pallor of death. She went out of the room and made a cup of tea for him.

There is no journal that covers Capetanakis's last months: by the time Lehmann's memoirs begin again, there is already an altering distance from the tragedy itself. Two years before, he had told Lehmann

You know that my friendship for you is more than friendship, more than love – it is religion. I am afraid that in everything that concerns you I lose all my sense of humour. But – I am sure of that – real life begins where the sense of humour weakens.

How to measure the intensity of those words, the utter, serious intention that moved their relationship into religion? Capetanakis beckons Lehmann to a higher appreciation of everything, revealing celestial and immortally meaningful solutions; the inevitability of his going turns so many of his words into a benediction. Something in Capetanakis seems almost to have been leading towards that early end, always with the awareness of

> The ageless ambiguity of things
> Which makes our life mean death, our love be hate.
> My blood that streams across the bedroom sings
> 'I am my brother opening the gate'.

Capetanakis's mother long outlived him and was at last told of his death. In the autumn of 1956 she and her son John came to England to visit Lehmann and to see the grave. Barbara Cooper told Lehmann that John Capetanakis's parting words to her were 'Those whom my brother loved he loved very deeply'; she told Lehmann 'I knew the message was meant for you.' On each anniversary of the death Barbara wrote to Lehmann. 'You know that I remember him constantly,' she said in 1948, 'that I love and admire you both, and that I feel deeply for your unhealed grief ... I can only tell you from my heart that nothing I have seen or known in life has ever moved me more deeply, or seemed to me as real as the relationship between you and Demetrios. It is one of the positive and beautiful things that are the only answers to despair and no-meaning.'

With Lehmann, Capetanakis had shared dealings with the unanswerable expressions of philosophical anxiety. He looked to Lehmann's attempt to define the finding of an absolute knowledge where

> To penetrate that room is my desire,
> The extreme attic of the mind, that lies
> Just beyond that last bend in the corridor.
> Writing I do it. Phrases, poems are keys.
> Loving's another way (but not so sure).

There was sureness for Lehmann after Capetanakis's death, an event that was

... so terrible for me – not only because he was so dear to me as a friend and his suffering was so horribly painful, his own sense of waste and loss but also because, more selfishly, I had grown so dependent on his affection, belief in me, collaboration and perfect perceptiveness – that I was dazed by it, as if part of my mind had gone unconscious, as if something in one refused to allow me to think what life would be without him. And yet it is as if his relationship towards me had secreted some honey in me, on which I can feed, feeling him as living and encouraging in a timeless memory, to put against the jealousies and coldnesses of those one had hoped would be friends but are not; as if [it] were possible still to work and create within his love, within that belief in myself which he restored to me.

\*

Rosamond's friendship only disappointed. Lehmann felt for her, worried that her relationship with her lover, Cecil Day Lewis, was souring. At Aldworth, he walked with her through woods (an expedition that inspired his poem 'The Sphere of Glass'). She was writing *The Ballad and the Source*. A 'running sore' had developed between them over her association with the periodical *Orion*. It seemed there was nobody that Lehmann could turn to. In Rassine he felt the difference set up by their ages and Rassine's lack of intellect, for he would never replace Capetanakis in that way.

As Lehmann recovered from the death of Capetanakis, and seemed to have accepted that his life with Rassine had become inevitable, there was no shortage of other relationships. There was nineteen-year-old Bobbie who asked in March 1944 'Do you write any crime or exotic love affair stories?' At their last meeting, Bobbie had been glad to 'clear up any mistakes or rather misunderstandings'. 'George' from Blackpool reminded Lehmann twenty years later how they used to drink together at the Athenaeum: to jog Lehmann's memory, he added 'You may remember I crack a good whip.' And could Lehmann send him £50? 'Ben' wrote from the Royal Naval Barracks at Chatham, about more misunderstandings 'and as that is the case well I would like to clear it all up,' he wrote in April 1945, 'so as we may be able to see in a different light ... So you have got that person living with you now, well I am sorry to hear that, but still I suppose that it was unavoidable, it is a pity though ... I have still a great feeling for you.'

An Irish guard called John waited at the Bag of Nails but didn't see Lehmann: 'Still at the same old job?' John asked. Five years later he was still in touch, wanting money as well as friendship. David wrote from Plymouth, 'extremely gay and I should think very you. Wonderful chickens and all waiting to be plucked!!! However I'm sure you would frighten them, so big, so massive, so awe-inspiring. Yes that's what I think of you.' David was still seeing Lehmann in 1949, 'enchanting with perhaps a little the pleasure of you in me and around me'. He was another to whom Lehmann gave financial help.

As always, any crises in Lehmann's personal life were matched by the continuous agonising over what his future in literature should be. He was writing verse again, and in December 1944 the Hogarth Press published his pamphlet *The Sphere of Glass and Other Poems*, pieces 'collected for Christmas 1944'. There were eleven poems, their prevalent tone one of regret for something lost, whether, as in the title poem, the relationship with Rosamond, or in 'A Death in Hospital' (Capetanakis's, of course). 'At a Time of Death', specifically written for J. Drummond Allison who had been killed in Italy, might as well have stood for the deaths of all the unknown men whose loss he mourned, while 'The House' was a backward glance at Fieldhead, abandoned as nature went on all around it. 'The Ballad of Jack at the World's End' tells of a young sailor who pours out his war-agony in a bar, but while Lehmann's integrity is obvious, he cannot make the piece work, even when the poem switches at its end to fantasy, and the London night is filled with the cries of drowning airmen. Rosamond was appalled by it; 'it shocks me,' wrote George Stonier in the *New Statesman*, 'by its chinking vulgarity'. It was dispiriting stuff. The *Listener* kindly noted 'a charming lilt, deftly registered in a minor key', but the *Tribune*'s critic wondered 'what Mr Lehmann would think if these poems were sent in to him?'

*

Lehmann had worked long enough at a philosophy to get him through the war; what was needed now was the philosophy to approach the peace. In the last days of Hitlerism, he felt he was living through an adventure beyond anything Rider Haggard or John Buchan had invented. Every day brought new accounts of the concentration camps at last being relieved by Allied troops. He saw that the conditions of evil had flourished in a society that had welcomed

> ... the death or murder of the imagination, the atrophy of the faculty of considering others as oneself ... There is only one seed, agent, impulse of revolution, renewal, in human society, and it has always been the same – the idea – the deep instinctive belief, for it can never be proved by reason – that another man is as good as yourself, that all men are born under God's equal love – this is the idea that is perpetually renewing open societies, and has always in the end broken up hierarchical and closed societies.

An age was passing, changes marked by sometimes grinding gears. On 6 May 1945 Auden, in his American officer's uniform, knocked at Lehmann's door. He had forgotten how egotistical, how impersonal Auden was. Now, this 'great Huck Finn', this 'Uncle Sam Auden', assured Lehmann that Britain was lucky to have emerged from the war at all, that its power and empire were over. He delivered a lecture on the superiority of American civilisation.

## 11. Penetrating that Room

Lehmann, of course, was offended, and pleased when Spender shared his disapproval. If he had ever had fondness for the returning Auden, it had perished; he was 'disappointed, feeling that the immense development of the intellectual machinery has not compensated for what seemed to me the drying up of that juice, or sap, that came from his intensely English roots'. He might, of course, have said the same of Isherwood, but could never do so.

Now, the world he knew was shifting swiftly into another age. On the evening of the first VJ Day, Lehmann and Rassine walked to Piccadilly. They were staggered at its light, shocking and beautiful in its brilliance. They longed for music and bands, but there were none. It did not matter. Sailors gave long kisses to girls, others climbed lamp-posts below the raw, half-moon. They walked past the Athenaeum, its portico surmounted by flaming torches, into the Mall. Everywhere were crowds, turned towards the illuminated façade of Buckingham Palace. Rassine was fascinated to see the dancing in the streets. Together, they passed through the gates into the park.

As they walked on, they saw lovers beneath the trees look up as fireworks burst overhead.

# Part III

# GILDED NUTS

# 12

# Ends and Beginnings

Ends and beginnings: it is almost as if, with an end of war, Lehmann simply turned his back on so much of what had been before. And if there must be a symbolic event that marks this change, it was his decision to leave Carrington House for an elegant town house in South Kensington, 31 Egerton Crescent. The contract was signed in August 1945 (£1,100 for the freehold and an annual rent of £200), and Ernest Freud was brought in as advising architect.

For Lehmann, Egerton Crescent seemed the fruit born of his hard-working war years, a proper centre at last for 'the pictures, the books, the furniture that will be inside it, the place for study and for entertainment of friends'. It was to be much more, a literary salon of which Lehmann was the natural host, whether at his annual 'laburnum' parties, when great armfuls of the stuff would be brought up from the country, or at parties given for visiting writers or artists, or to celebrate the publication of a new book. Very soon, no. 31 would come to have its important purpose in Lehmann's life, but from the beginning it established the post-war persona that Lehmann seems so easily to have slipped into: the once fervid communist who now saw himself at the very centre of the predominantly conservative literary establishment. Shards of the old Lehmann might still be recognised, but this was a new man, one who had shaken off so much of the moral responsibility that had worked within him in earlier years.

The past was being cut adrift in other ways. Perhaps the war was partly to blame for the selling of Fieldhead in 1947 for £12,000, but ever since Rudie's death there had been something unwieldy about the great house and garden; they, too, seemed to have lost whatever purpose they had once had. The family life it had nurtured had for so long been fractured, altered again during the war when the Red Cross used it as a hospital, and when peace came it was unthinkable to Alice that she could any longer share her home with an institution. Now, the Women's Voluntary Service wanted to keep Fieldhead as a residential home for the elderly. Alice was increasingly immobile, and could no longer afford to keep Fieldhead as a private establishment. A new house was found, near Beaconsfield, and christened Little Fieldhead.

Fieldhead, of course, had always been proof enough that Lehmann's socialism was ultimately little more than well-intentioned. Leaving it behind might have seemed just, a proper acknowledgement that the honeyed days of privilege were over, but Lehmann was ever conscious of being 'one of a generation that was accustomed to being called in the morning, have clothes looked after, go down

to an already swept and polished house, have meals made ready and served ...
and can never absolutely accustom myself without nostalgia to the new world
we live in now, whatever righting of the scales we may find in it'. The pain of
parting from his childhood home was a moment at once inevitable and unbearably final.

The boy standing amid the debris of broken glass, the warm deep musk of
bonfire around him, holding in his hand the too ripe nectarine, hearing from the
river, beyond the walls that divide water from house, the tunes that float into
the distance.

Now the desolation is understood. In middle age, the boy grown into a man
wanders across the grounds for the last time, enters the green darkness of the
boathouse, sees the sad hummocks that are the burial places of long dead dogs,
finds Goodman the gardener and listens, a final time, to his stories of the past.

> The secret is in the figure
> And the figure is not there until the end
> And the secret is different for every one of us.
> The spell of love that haunts this place
> Haunts all our lives and deaths
> Under the shadow of one will, one dream;
> But no exchange of memories
> No questioning of you or you
> If I could trace you as you are today,
> Can tell me where the children are for me,
> What they alone can whisper,
> Though all were changed and blessed
> By the urn and the river
> Can tell what I have lost
> What is absolute from time for their revealing.

It was now for Egerton Crescent to become the ideal, the perfect setting for
the gilded creatures who moved through its rooms. When Edith Sitwell came
for tea at No. 31 (she often did), it seemed that the library might have been
expressly designed for her to sit in. The room framed her, 'a sombre spirit of
prophecy and poetry ... a mask of a suffering and tragic spirit', with its green
and gold light, with the green of the trees beyond its windows and the light
thrown back into the chandelier, the light – red, orange, gold – on the spines of
books, and the Venetian light of the Guardi over the mantelpiece.

In this house, Lehmann was at last omnipotent, managing with ease to be the
natural patron; and that, as James Michie has remarked 'involved some patron-
ising'. Here they came to be entertained: Thornton Wilder, Carson McCullers,
the Sitwells, William Chappell, E. M. Forster, John Gielgud, Paul Bowles,
Elizabeth Bowen, writers, artists, playwrights, actors, dancers. For many a young

writer the atmosphere of Egerton Crescent was heady. David Hughes recalls once sitting on a sofa between Forster and Edith Sitwell. When Louis MacNeice stubbed out his cigarette, Hughes quietly pocketed the butt. After Lehmann's death, a woman who lived across the street from no. 31 recalled how she used to watch entranced as the great and good of the literary world made their way to Lehmann's door. It was a salon, a place of pilgrimage, for those who worked, with what seemed consistent and almost incestuous zeal, for literature, seeing themselves (according to Hughes) as 'a huge, immovable, incontrovertible part of the culture'. No. 31 was soon to be a place of work too.

\*

The house immediately became a home for Rassine, whose career had flourished during the war. A permanent home must have seemed a luxury, even if it was a room at the top of the house – Lehmann's visitors were usually aware, sometimes vaguely, of there being a dancer who lived in the attic. In 1941 Ninette de Valois had invited Hamilton and Rassine to join the Sadlers Wells Ballet. Hamilton had accepted, but Rassine, wanting to work out his contract with the Anglo-Poles, had not. It was only when the company was subjected to a too punishing schedule that Rassine became a dancer with the Sadlers Wells in February 1942. Rassine was blessed and scarred by this wartime success: blessed because to an extent his opportunity with de Valois came about through the loss of so many leading dancers to the services; scarred because the reputation he would make would always be seen as having been made in the gap between two generations of dancers. He was at the summit of his profession before a new virility, agility and athleticism in male dancers suddenly made his style unfashionable.

No sooner had Lehmann joined Sadlers Wells than he was at the centre of it, understudying Robert Helpmann in *Hamlet*, and Helpmann worked out much of the role on him. Before the end of the year he had created the Dove in another Helpmann ballet, *The Birds*, partnering the 15-year-old Beryl Grey. Rassine's relationship with Helpmann had no rivalry in it, for their personalities were very different; anyway, the work was so hard that dancers who often appeared together did not get to know one another well. In March, de Valois told Rassine he would share *Les Sylphides* and 'The Blue Bird' with John Hart; to Rassine, the roles were 'like a scurge'. Seasons at the company's London home, the New Theatre, meant that he and Lehmann saw each other regularly, but there would still be long tours, still long searches in a strange city's blackout to find some digs for the week, still letters written in badly heated dressing-rooms to Lehmann from 'Your loving Hunky'. He spent Christmas 1942 at the Royal Station, York, with Margot Fonteyn, Constant Lambert, Helpmann and Hamilton.

By the end of the war Rassine had consolidated his reputation as a *danseur noble*, marking several roles as his own, among them Franz in *Coppélia*, the Bluebird in *The Sleeping Beauty* and Albrecht in *Giselle*. In the Bliss-Ashton

*Miracle in the Gorbals* he and Moira Shearer created the roles of the Lovers; in the 1944-5 season Tamara Karsavina worked with Rassine and Fonteyn on a revival of *Le Spectre de la Rose*, one of many occasions on which the pair danced together. In early 1945, Sadlers Wells undertook an overseas tour for ENSA. In Brussels, he and Fonteyn shivered through performances of *Les Sylphides*, 'like dancing in an ice box'. But with the end of the war, he was billed only second to Helpmann. 'I think it's very fair,' he told Lehmann. 'I'm very pleased that Michael Somes and [Harold] Turner are coming back as it will relieve me of so much over work ... Donald [Albery, the company's manager] said that Ninette will always give me first place as regards roles etc. go, as she regards me still the best dancer despite the two new arrivals. I must say I can't wait for competition now.' In fact, the great post-war tours of America undertaken by the Sadlers Wells were probably the highlight of Rassine's career.

From the end of the war, Rassine was accompanied on many of his tours by Carlotta (Lottie), a golden spaniel, who seems to have made one of her first appearances in his dressing room at the New Theatre, London, after which she ran away and was almost lost in Hyde Park. But she returned, becoming a true theatre dog, exploring England with Rassine, happy to sleep in the overhead luggage rack of a railway carriage. It was Rassine who discovered that Carlotta could sing and was easily tempted to give recitals at social gatherings, her vocal talent endearing her to a wide circle of famous admirers. Edith Sitwell suggested that excerpts from *Wozzeck* would suit Carlotta's dramatic style, only to be contradicted by Osbert who insisted that she was a natural *Lucia de Lammermoor*. Most unprofessionally, Carlotta was as fond of jumping into the Serpentine, or the Thames at Fieldhead, or the lake at Three Bridges, as she was of giving public performances; but she was so often persuaded, like the female singers of an earlier age (the wonderful Liza Lehmann among them), to sing after dinner at Egerton Crescent. Lehmann adored Carlotta more than any other dog he had known. In her could be realised untroubled, uncomplicated love, constancy, dependence. She was of inestimable importance in his life. He wrote that, when alone with Rassine, she was the third person always there with them; the child, of course, that they had never had.

\*

Somewhere between the idyll of Fieldhead and the life that went on beyond its garden, the links of future promise had been broken. Only Helen seems to have achieved emotional contentment, emerging from the war with her personal happiness intact. This was not merely a stroke of fortune. From the start, Helen stood apart from the Lehmann trio. She wanted and took no part in the almost Sitwellian desire to achieve not only as an individual but, in the public consciousness, as one of the Lehmanns.

Lehmann expressed regret that, when he, Beatrix and Rosamond posed for group photographs as the siblings achieving great things in literature and the drama, Helen was absent. He may have been deluding himself. If his regret was not disingenuous, it is inaccurate; Helen had never aspired to be part of the questing, ambitious Lehmann machine for which Rosamond did such sterling work in the boiler room. Rosamond had brought off an amazing trick so long before, establishing herself not only as a novelist of celebrity but, even rarer, as a creature of high glamour. Attempts to glamorise Beatrix were, over the years, amusing but disappointing; her extraordinary qualities needed no tricks of false enhancement, and resisted them.

Helen was simply above, beyond, outside it all. Sensibly, we might think, she had escaped into real life with a husband who perhaps mostly distinguished himself by becoming the centre of her devotion. Her relations with her brother seem to have been good, unclouded as they were by the dreadful impediments that existed between him and Rosamond.

Certainly, Lehmann always regarded Helen, not himself, as the head of the family. In her quiet way, she was no less distinguished than her siblings. Early in the war she laboured in a smoke bomb factory, and then worked for the FANY as a driver until the end of the war, when she served in Wiltshire as a county officer for the St. John Ambulance Brigade. She subsequently made her own acknowledgement of the Lehmann dynasty by working for her fellows, for in 1948 she joined the staff of the Society of Authors, becoming Secretary of the Radiowriters Association. Her professional life was thus a reflection of the work done by her uncle, H. P. Davis, that 'Father of Broadcasting' and Vice-President of the Westinghouse.

From under the shadow of war, too, comes Rosamond, damaged by relationships, with unhappiness that would be remembered in later years with her brother. She had always been interested in his sexual life. 'It fills me with mingled alarms and pleasure to hear you are in love,' she wrote from Ipsden in February 1940, and 'alarms and pleasure' might stand as an indication of her attitude to his life. When Capetanakis died, she asked Lehmann precisely what their relationship had been. She was always curious to know what he was doing and with whom.

Perhaps the greatest satisfaction of her life was her children, Sally and Hugo, for both of whom Lehmann had a genuine affection. In 1944, Rosamond's marriage with their father, Wogan Philipps, was dissolved. Concealed to the public gaze was the fact that the marriage had collapsed before the war, and that in 1941 she and the married Cecil Day Lewis had become lovers.

By the end of the war, when Rosamond discussed with Lehmann her relationship with Day Lewis, Lehmann 'got the impression that the passion was turning sour because of the enormous tension the whole situation had put him under for so long. She also revealed, what I had not realised, that earlier on Cecil had had a Greek streak.' In February 1950 Helen told her brother that Rosamond's affair was over: 'another fearful landmark in her life'.

Lehmann had always enjoyed a good professional relationship with Day Lewis, who seemed 'like a Victorian clergyman whose inner peace had been forever destroyed by the publications of Darwin', but he was alarmed at this new crisis for Rosamond:

> She cannot believe that any one could fall out of love with her, or feel that the possessiveness was too overwhelming: she is having to pretend that Cecil is out of his mind and can be restored by psychiatrists (of all people!) and an alliance of two noble women determined to rescue and stand by him – Rosamond and Cecil's wife (of all alliances!) It is tragic to see her feeding so recklessly on illusions, and about to make herself iller still.

For the moment, it seemed that the collapse might bring a new understanding and closeness with her brother. Lehmann was sympathetic when they met in April at Egerton Crescent. She 'burst into a long and painful tirade about Cecil ... it was so wretched to see her unaware that all she was doing was to prove how deep the barb still stuck in her heart'. Learning that Day Lewis had begun a new relationship with the actress Jill Balcon considerably puzzled Edith Sitwell, who told Lehmann 'After all, one *cannot* be called Jill.'

For Beatrix, peace brought no new promise of enduring personal or professional happiness. Throughout the 1930s, she felt success had eluded her, despite a list of notable roles and a long relationship with the director Berthold Viertel who directed the first film in which she appeared, a marvellously performed adaptation of Jerome K. Jerome's religioso drama *The Passing of the Third Floor Back*. Her performance as a sardonic, sharply sophisticated spinster is early evidence of her highly individual qualities as an actress. There is something eerie, almost, in the precision, the intelligence, of what she does on screen. In the theatre, such intelligence was too often unwelcome, and Beatrix could be a forbidding and arresting presence. Too many of the parts she was offered were in 'horrible and useless, arty plays ... like a baby dribbling', 'cheap, stinking'.

By 1939, Beatrix was being asked to play women of sixty. 'I'd rather go to Russia,' she told Lehmann, for she was a vociferous, active and card-carrying communist, staunchly proud of a political allegiance that did her no favours within the theatrical establishment. There had also been two novels written at the beginning of the 1930s, but to call them even promising would be generous; as a novelist, it was obvious that Beatrix did not matter. Achievement was important to her, but too often she missed the final step to real success.

What is clear from the many references that occur in his journals is that Lehmann was anxious for Beatrix's welfare and happiness. Rosamond had a Queen Victoria-like attitude to Beatrix's sexuality, simply believing it did not exist. One may imagine that for Binkie Beaumont, that impishly named but ruthlessly influential West End impresario, the thought of an outspoken sexually ambiguous communist was just a little too much. Beatrix had once been engaged to Ralph Richardson, who made her laugh. When he took her and her dog up in his aeroplane, he put out his hand to indicate when he was turning left or right. Asked why she had broken off her engagement to him, she explained, 'You can't have sex and laugh.' She became pregnant by another actor, and was told she was expecting twins. Beatrix would have loved to have had children, but Rosamond insisted that she have an abortion, for which the father refused to pay.

Lesbians were attracted to her. A noted lesbian actress, Mary Morris, was for a time her understudy, and nursed a passion for her. Beatrix's young secretary became obsessed with her and broke off her engagement. On returning home one evening, Beatrix found the girl hanging from the ceiling, having staged an attempt to kill herself. Lehmann, of course, was no less anxious for Rosamond, but the impediment between them could not weaken.

*

Ends and beginnings. Despite the fact that Leonard Woolf's relationship with Lehmann had been relatively trouble-free for the two years following Virginia's death, the tensions between them had once again become intolerable. A vituperative correspondence ensued, aggravated by the difficulties that arose with Woolf leaving so much of the running of the business to Lehmann.

For a while they seemed bound together by a single energy, pushed forward by the need to publish the mass of unpublished material Virginia had left. There was, too, an eagerness to compile a selection of the finest of the Hogarth Poets to celebrate their twenty-fifth anniversary. These schemes alone might have helped to unite what Woolf described as 'two prickly people', but there was too much else waiting to trip up their partnership. By October 1943 the cracks were gaping, with Woolf suggesting weekly meetings at which he and Lehmann might discuss the Press's business, '*before* decisions are made by you'. Lehmann agreed; it might stop Woolf sending him 'tart little flimsies'.

Woolf tried to put Lehmann in his place: it was the duty of the General Manager to carry out the directions decided by the partners. Lehmann dismissed this. 'I cannot agree that my job as general manager is merely to carry out directions. You put an entirely new interpretation on it, which astonishes me.' Three days later, Lehmann poured out the feelings that for so long had been festering. 'I scarcely trust myself to put into words what I feel about the way you have handled our relationship in the Press during the present year,' he told Woolf.

I feel you are badly out of touch and your interventions either (and increasingly) irrelevant or petulant. As you clearly have ceased to trust me, and never ask my advice – as I have been the one in charge during the last three years of rapid changes and complex difficulties there are things I am

169

in a much better position to judge than you – but only issue orders, or make categorical demands, I frankly despair for the future.

Woolf's response was that over the past year Lehmann's attitude and language had been 'absolutely inexplicable'. He had been met with the 'grossest rudeness. In no other of my many business relations am I consistently told that I am senile, out of touch, irrelevant and petulant.' Furthermore,

> The moment I express an opinion of any sort or kind about anything, you say I am not 'trusting' you or that I am 'giving orders' or making categorical demands. No partner has ever given another partner a freer hand than I did to you or treated him with more consideration. Instead of showing some appreciation of the fact, you have in the past 12 months shown more and more resentment of my having any say in anything connected with the PRESS, twisting every remark of mine into 'interference' or 'orders' and treating me with a rudeness such as I have never experienced from any one with whom I have had relations before. I ignored it for months, for I know your irritable nature, but when you use this method to deny me any say of any sort or kind in the Press, you are creating an impossible situation ... I am prepared to put up with a great deal of rudeness and ill-temper from you as I have done in the past, for I knew that I should have to ... I turn to you as a friend and beseech you to think again, read over our correspondence of the past years (as I have done) impartially, and don't push us into a totally unnecessary position of hopeless difficulty and unending trouble. Nothing but trouble and evil will result from it for both of us.

One of the essential disputes between Woolf and Lehmann concerned which of them was the arbiter; which had the right to force a book on to the Hogarth list, or reject it, in face of the opposition of the other. There had often been 'give and take' (the business would have been impossible to run without it) and at many points either man was willing to give way to the other.

There is evidence that Woolf was ready enough to submit to Lehmann's opinion. Woolf was prepared to accept Victoria Sackville-West's novel *Grand Canyon*, although he thought it a poor book, but was persuaded by Lehmann's insistence that its argument, dealing with Hitler's conquest of the world, was 'profoundly defeatist'; Sackville-West, one of the Press's most steadfast authors, never published with them again. Woolf was enthusiastic over a manuscript submitted by Harold Laski. 'I am horrified to be the publisher of such pernicious and boring nonsense,' Lehmann protested, 'which seems to me to be nothing but a chain of slipshod deductions from faulty premises, but as you are keen on it I will not stand in the way.' Woolf rejected the book.

In the summer of 1943, however, there was a serious disagreement about a new collection of poetry by Terence Tiller, whose career Lehmann had promoted; there must have seemed little doubt in Lehmann's mind that the Hogarth Press would as a matter of course take on *The Inward Animal*. Woolf would have none of it. Tiller's work was 'unintelligible ... rather feeble and dreary stuff'; it would simply be a waste of paper to publish it.

Tiller was merely another factor in the breakdown between Woolf and Lehmann, caused by irreconcilable differences. Woolf subsequently claimed that a real reason for the collapse was that Lehmann wanted to expand the firm and Woolf did not. By Lehmann's admission, by the summer of 1945 he had already made up his mind to quit the Press, but gave no hint of his intention to Woolf until (an echo of his sudden departure years earlier) he wrote to Woolf in January 1946 terminating their partnership. Woolf's intention was to buy Lehmann out, but through a happy arrangement with Ian Parsons, Lehmann's share was bought by Chatto and Windus, with whom the Press now began a long association. There is surely a lurking shadow here. Lehmann's second defection from the Hogarth Press was essential if he was to set up his own imprint. It is only a marvel that his autocratic nature had survived the Press for so long.

There was some satisfaction for Woolf, of the 'I told you so' variety, when Lehmann's career as a publisher subsequently foundered, an opportunity for Woolf to damn with faint praise, listing reasons why Lehmann might well have made a good publisher. Lehmann

> ... takes life and himself much too seriously, never having learned that nothing, including 'I', *sub specie aeternitatis*, and he is much too certain that he is right and the other fellow (even Leonard Woolf) is wrong – a dangerous generalisation.

There is something amusing in Woolf's condemnation of Lehmann taking himself too seriously (Woolf, after all, was hardly the Sid Field of publishing), but it is preferable to his denouncing Lehmann as an egomaniac (he did so in his autobiography, but Lehmann insisted that the word be struck out of the manuscript). Lehmann's tremendous energy and ambition had, from the beginning, been frustrated by so much that seemed to hold him back from reaching a full potential, held back by those who kept financial, and therefore intellectual, control. The sourness of his relations with the Woolfs seems to have evaporated over the years, but Brian McColgan remembers Lehmann telling him that he had come to realise that they had only wanted his money.

\*

Cut free from the Hogarth Press, Lehmann could at last dedicate himself to his own publishing house, John Lehmann Ltd., which in a particularly difficult period for publishing was to be another outstanding achievement.

During the war, a blissful state had existed in which it was reasonably easy to sell anything that got into print, regardless, it seemed, of subject matter or quality, so hungry was the public need for diversion. The major problem lay in the continuing paper shortage, and supplies of paper were strictly controlled by a system of allocation.

The answer, in Lehmann's case, was Purnell and Co., a vast enterprise (compared to any Lehmann had so far had dealings with) with its unscrupulous chairman, Wilfred Harvey, flanked by his son Eric (also the manager of Macdonald, which Purnell controlled). Purnell offered more paper than Lehmann might have hoped for, and an agreement was reached, intolerable as it was to Lehmann, that Purnell would retain 51 per cent control, with Lehmann having complete editorial sway.

For a brief respite Lehmann enjoyed a real and complete independence, if not free of Purnell as a provider of paper, and financial support from the family, from which Rosamond was appointed as fellow-director. The firm would operate from the basement of Egerton Crescent, with Barbara Cooper, Anne Court-neidge (sister of the ebullient Cicely), the business manager and poet Clive (John) Hall, and Michael Swan as the office staff. Cecil Day Lewis, who was to have worked as a full-time reader, vanished when the deal with Purnell fell through. In charge of design, assisted by Swan, was the artist Keith Vaughan. And Barbara's slush pile was guarded by the office tabby, Boakie, said to be able to detect a manuscript that made any allusion to fish.

No. 31 was a place of industry over which Barbara ruled when Lehmann was away. 'I miss you very much,' she told him in the summer of 1949. 'There isn't anyone to tell things to or laugh over things with'. She had to fend off unwanted authors, such as a fearful woman who wrote 'whimsy stories. She said to me, "I must have my little fairies!"' In Lehmann's absence, Barbara felt a midsummer drowsiness overcome the house. She worked selflessly through any illness, collapsing because of sickness and diarrhoea and having to be laid out in the spare room while Rassine brought her a cup of tea. It was a consolation that, during one of Lehmann's absences, Edith Sitwell was 'very quiet'. Meanwhile, 'I long for mid-July, and cross off the days in my calendar, as I used to do at school towards the end of term.' There was much talk of the tadpoles that Rassine had brought into the office.

Like other editors before and since, much of Lehmann's success in publishing seemed dependent on taking 'his' writers from the Hogarth: the Press's loss must be the new imprint's gain. Laurie Lee and Roy Fuller willingly defected with Lehmann; Henry Yorke and William Sansom, pleading contractual obligation, did not. But the net was spread wider. There were the many young writers he had encouraged through the various guises of *New Writing*, among these the poet Hamish Henderson, Frank Sargeson (at the head of the New Zealand writers) and John Sommerfield. From America, there was Saul Bellow's *Dangling Man*, which Woolf had turned down. Wider still: Ivan Bunin, George Seferis, André Chamson, and the many other foreign authors whose work would appear in

Lehmann's Modern European Library. As well as this generous representation of contemporary writing, there would be the revival of classics for The Chiltern Library.

In the autumn of 1946 the first books appeared. 'A recklessly audacious offensive it seems to me now, as all the books were literary, most of them high-brow or near-high-brow.' John Lehmann Ltd. burst into life, ready-formed, at a peak as it was born. It was an assumption of grandeur that signalled a reversal from what had been. The utilitarianism of the war was over, even though it lingered in rationing and a dullness that fogged everything, and Lehmann was sweeping it aside.

Belief had to be altered. This is no longer the Lehmann who offered B. L. Coombes and the Trespassers a platform for their proletariat prose, who urged the need for the common voice, who saw the validity of art proved only when man could speak to man with one voice, slicing through privilege and education and the accumulated wisdom of literature.

This is Lehmann giving an imprimatur to the accepted, the committed, the qualified, the unquestionably literate. It is literature as luxuriance that Lehmann now represents. Of course throughout the many lists the house produced in its life there is much that was modern and innovative, but there was never a question about it: John Lehmann Ltd. existed to make writing beautiful, it beautified the art of reading, it sanctified what it promoted by bathing it in beauty; it made of itself a beauty that perhaps has never quite, in the literary sphere, been achieved since. Society was seen to have nothing so important as its literature, which now became almost a reserved profession.

The stolidity of such a theory was leavened by the work of the artists that Lehmann made an integral part of the firm; indeed, here was a true collaboration between publisher and artist, in which the physical beauty of the book was of paramount importance. The importance of such work to the careers of such as Keith Vaughan, John Minton, Philippe Jullian, Robert Medley, Michael Ayrton, Edward Burra and Leonard Rosoman should not be overlooked. Lehmann's commitment helped them towards a genuine popularity, which he had done so much to promote through the pages of *Penguin New Writing*, where he was an unfailing champion not only of the school that came to be known as the Neo-Romantics, but of modern art from all over the world. For Lehmann, Vaughan's spine designs showed something near genius; they made it possible for even the shelved book to be attractive.

In this marrying of artistic perfection to the printed page Lehmann remains the exemplary example. The importance of his artists of course came directly from his personal, highly emotional, thoroughly unintellectual, response to visual art, particularly that which displayed homoeroticism. There is no question that Lehmann enjoyed and employed heterosexual artists, but his predilection (not practised, but organic) was for the work of the homosexual artist, for art that had about it a homoeroticism.

Peter Burton, the sterling publisher of so much homosexual literature, has pointed out that John Lehmann Ltd. was in effect a homosexual publishing house. The lists are of course full of heterosexual contradictions to such a theory, but there is a distinct sense in which, in catering to his own preferences, Lehmann introduced the emphasis. He was simply more interested in the lives and fortunes of homosexuals, in their difficulties and dramatic dealings with society. We see it in his passionate interest in the destinies of Keith Vaughan and John Minton, seeing in their lives the need to match professional and personal lusts, problems he himself faced all his life. The writer or painter returning after a hard day at desk or easel to the welcoming arms of a wife did not fascinate him. Where women existed in the lives of the men he admired, Lehmann was not above simply ignoring their existence. The boundaries of his taste were set.

In this new age, when Lehmann seemed obsessed with a new cleanliness of line, *New Writing and Daylight*, born out of need, did not belong. *New Writing and Daylight* had been born of *Daylight*, the work of English and Czech forces, led by Jiri Mucha; it had no purpose in a country that had once been at war, and made its final appearance in 1946, even as *Penguin New Writing* was still enjoying a soaring success.

The replacement to *New Writing and Daylight*, *Orpheus*, came out two years later under the Lehmann imprint, its first edition designed throughout by Vaughan. Its elegance was typical of the post-war Lehmann. Subtitled 'A Symposium of the Arts', *Orpheus* was another attempt to create a meeting place of culture, of writing, prose and poetry, painting and theatre. Here is Peter Brook on 'Style in Shakespeare production', the director Norman Marshall as 'A Producer in Search of a Play', Harold Acton on 'Modern Painting in Mexico', John Fleming on the Italian artist Renzo Vespignani (an excuse for Lehmann to publish a photograph of the swarthy painter attractively languishing), Lehmann's essay on Yeats, 'The Man Who Learnt to Walk Naked', Osbert Sitwell on Arnold Bennett, Rex Warner on Seferis, Edith Sitwell on the making of a poem, and poetry by Sitwell, Tiller, Day Lewis and Odysseus Elytis, the whole enhanced by Vaughan's exemplary design.

Even now, in his new aesthetic disguise, Lehmann was expounding beliefs that seemed not so very different to those that had inspired earlier anthologies. 'The deep need today,' his foreword noted, 'is to assert the lyrical and imaginative spirit against materialism and the pseudo-sciences; this is not new, for it is precisely what Shelley and other great creative minds of his time were proclaiming one hundred and fifty years ago, but it is even more urgent in our own lives upon which the same dangers can act so much more frightfully and more swiftly. Nor is it new that it should be equally urgent to assert the rights and dignity of the individual human being against the pretensions of the state; it is one of the oldest of wars.' Forever, 'the poet is the creator, and the word of the poet is the mainspring of history'.

In the foreword to *Orpheus*'s second edition, published in 1949 and designed by Minton, Lehmann made much of an attack launched on the first edition by the communist periodical *Soviet Literature*. *Orpheus*, it said, was artificial, reactionary, useless, epigonic, decadent, stale, a hopeless void, a collection (and what a wonderful phrase) of 'gilded nuts'; it avoided anything like real life: 'Everything that is real, that is genuinely progressive in art is studiously avoided by *Orpheus*, which evidently is afraid of contact with actual life. Separated from the people, from the urgent social problems of the day, these decadent poets and artists produce artificial, phantom, reactionary works.' Lehmann balked at this, to the extent even of claiming that Sitwell's airy poem, 'Song', dealt with those very same 'urgent social problems'; a nice conceit, but founded in a philosophy that saw all in terms of absolute aestheticism. The truth was now that the communist 'view of art – and of life – is so appalling to anyone nourished in the traditions of the West … that all we can want is to turn our backs – and let them keep it'.

In the new climate, however, *Orpheus* could not find a sufficient readership for it to last beyond its second appearance. Its commercial failure was a presage of some of the difficulties Lehmann was facing as an independent publisher – failure when critical welcome was generous. An allegiance with Purnell seemed imperative by mid-1947 if he wished to survive. An agreement that Purnell had tried to force through the previous year now went through, with Purnell providing funds that allowed Lehmann to pay off the money his family had invested. Lehmann was now in effect a salaried employee of Purnell, with Rosamond reduced to the position of the firm's reader.

At least the future looked more secure with this backing in place, and Lehmann began a perilously ambitious programme of expanding the firm's output, introducing The Holiday Library (prestigious reprints of novels and biography) and The Library of Art and Travel. It was a sign of the huge confidence he felt he commanded, though, even as it was happening, he fleetingly wondered if within it lay the seeds of eventual failure. Yet, failure seemed unthinkable, placed as he was at the centre of so much: writing, the publication of periodicals, the publishing of books, artists, and (through Rassine) the world of dance. He was playing 'the impresario of the moment … bringing the rabbits out of the hat'.

\*

All through the years of Vienna Lehmann had longed for a cottage where Sikyr and he might live together, and when Vienna was part of the past he longed for a cottage in England, a home where he might rediscover something of the delight Fieldhead had instilled in him. In 1949, he found it, for a freehold of £4,500. The Forge, Worth Park Drive, at Three Bridges near Crawley, had been newly converted from a farm building into a whitewashed cottage with three bed-rooms, two reception rooms, bathroom and kitchen. Unexpectedly rural in an urban area, The Forge had a well-guarded secret – extensive 'secluded rural grounds' with wooded walks, and a private lake of almost three quarters of an acre 'in beautiful sylvan setting'. Rassine surrendered an insurance policy to purchase it.

The Forge became Lake Cottage, a diminutive Fieldhead where Lehmann and Rassine's life came together. While their existences in London seemed to most observers to be quite separate, they were united by Lake Cottage, where they spent their weekends, though they would not travel down together. Rassine, when he was not working, would go ahead, and Lehmann would follow by car. Rassine had his own small bedroom at the front of the cottage, while Lehmann's bedroom also served as a study, looking out over the lake: it was the room in which so many of his boyfriends were taken before being sent to the spare bedroom at the rear of the property.

Beatrix hated the place. Alan Ross remembers it as deadly, returning from visits bitten by mosquitoes that gathered over the lake. Plomer could not bring himself to call it a lake ('It's a *pond*,' he would tell friends, and it *is* indeed a pond) and addressed his letters to Pond Cottage. But for Lehmann it was the realisation of a dream, and revived his interest in the natural world. Rassine's passion for gardening had full play, the raising of seedlings in the little greenhouse, the planting of potatoes and tomatoes, the clearing of land between the water's bank and 'Lottie's Meadow' for the landing stage that Lehmann was planning, the cropping of blackberries, and the superintending of landscaping by a local firm. The home-grown produce no doubt appeared at the dismal meals that Lehmann was likely to serve there; one friend recalls a tea that was 'decidedly off'.

One visitor who might be found mowing the lawn was Eric Oliver, the boyfriend of the writer Denton Welch, whom Lehmann had met after Welch's death. How much of a welcome assistance Oliver was to Rassine is questionable, but Oliver was confident enough in Lehmann's friendship to give over to his safe-keeping several of Welch's prized possessions. Increasingly, Lake Cottage would prove a necessary retreat from the troubles that crowded in peacetime. But there were prices to be paid. The regeneration of animal life delighted Lehmann and stirred in him the primeval adoration of the natural world instilled by Fieldhead; the death of animals profoundly shook him. Lake Cottage exposed him once again to the cruelties of loss, and for days he would be in the state of highest anxiety about the death of a tortoise, or the marauding of a birds' nest, or the disappearance of young moorhens.

In 1949 Lehmann had noted the steady progress made in John Lehmann Ltd., 'the consolidation of its position, the enhancement of its prestige, the envy that the rapid growth of [the] list of young authors aroused in the breasts of some of his colleagues and rivals … nothing succeeds like success', but by the start of 1950 his accountants told him that despite improved sales the imprint was losing money.

## 12. Ends and Beginnings

The boom years for literature seemed distant, and the small literary magazine was disappearing from the bookstalls. The final issue of *Horizon*, Lehmann's most troublesome but trailing rival, limped on to the bookstalls in January 1950. In October, Connolly had told Lehmann he intended to close it down for a year 'partly because of the dearth of good material, partly *to give Cyril* a rest. The latter struck me as one of the most outstanding remarks of the year.' When it was clear that Connolly was in fact abandoning *Horizon*, Lehmann was nagged by a feeling that he should take it over.

It was a relief to be in Paris in early December for three days of meetings and business. He paid a last visit to a grey-faced, breathless André Gide. They spoke of friends in England, of Rilke, and of *De Profundis*. Gide recalled how he had once witnessed a terrible row between Oscar Wilde and Bosie which had left Wilde white and shaking. 'Everyone imagines I am in the midst of joy and careless happiness,' Wilde told him, 'and you see what has just happened – it happens all the time.' Among others, Lehmann met Truman Capote, 'more doll-like' than at their previous meeting, 'more perhaps like the small boy who seduced the headmaster – the small boy who had wizened without growing – very malicious with a bad word for everyone … he departed miaowing into the night'. Back in England, Connolly visited Lehmann, making another attempt to get him to take over *Horizon*. He was particularly malicious about Sonia Brownell who in October had married the dying George Orwell. 'She'll die young, of course,' said Connolly, 'very suddenly.' He had a shilling to get home with.

The end of *Penguin New Writing* was not far behind. Its decline had been obvious since the war's end. Its left-wing idealism (and Lehmann's) had weakened against a background of a Welfare State. One of its main purposes, the cohesion through literature at a time of spiritual and intellectual tension, had been achieved, and the purposes that might replace it were unclear. The format had shifted, the contents been juggled, but its life was worn. There had always been problems about the regularity of its appearance. In the spring of 1948, Penguin cut it to three issues a year, largely as a result of the significant drop in sales since the high selling days immediately after the war; the first peacetime edition was of 100,000 copies, a number that by 1949 had been reduced to the still creditable 40,000.

Lehmann knew the magazine was slipping, partly because he could not devote the energy and time needed to keep it sharp and at the edge of its culture. Still, the wheels of the day-to-day business were turning, as when the writer Elizabeth Berridge submitted two short stories in late 1949. Across the top of Berridge's accompanying letter, Barbara writes

> I don't think her style is particularly distinguished, but this story of an ageing vicar and his wife whose lives are complicated by the vicar's increasing deafness is human and touching, and the relationship between

them is not without subtlety. Also the vicarage atmosphere is rather well done.

The letter is passed to Lehmann, who writes at the foot of it

*I don't think much of this*: write her a very kind letter saying I've been overwhelmed with work, not very well; liked *The Lie* particularly, but – under circumstances of PNW move, felt no room, etc.

Lehmann passes the letter back to Barbara, who writes the requested 'very kind letter'

Dear Miss Berridge
I am so sorry to have been rather a long time in writing to you about your stories, but, as I believe Miss Cooper has told you, I have been unwell and overwhelmed with work since my return from France. I read them both with great interest, and liked *The Lie* particularly, but there is such exceptionally heavy pressure on my restricted space just now, and I still have a long waiting list for future numbers ...

And, having offered Miss Berridge and her husband Christmas greetings, Barbara passes the letter she has written to Lehmann for signing. Miss Berridge is satisfied, at least, that Lehmann has taken the trouble to write a charming letter, little suspecting that it was written by the Amazon Queen of Lehmann's Slush Pile.

In part, Lehmann's disinclination to take Berridge's offerings was because of the increasingly unstable nature of *Penguin New Writing*. It was obvious that Penguin was losing interest as well as money, and he turned to Wilfred Harvey for support, which was not forthcoming. On 26 April 1950 Lane informed Lehmann that issue no. 40 would be the last. For Lehmann, it was as much a relief as a disappointment.

It was not until July that the story broke in the press, and in its wake was a great outpouring of regret and praise for what Lehmann had achieved. Tears, of course, from Barbara. Spender seemed genuinely to want to collaborate with him on a new venture, essentially Anglo-American, but nothing came of it. We can see now that it was right that *Penguin New Writing* should die a natural death. In ending when it did, it remains forever linked with the whole fervour of war, of struggle and endeavour through the blitz, of making do, of carrying on in spite of Hitler, of the strength and power of word over violence and despot.

For months after its final appearance, he was searching for ways in which it might be brought back to life, plagued by a doubt that 'I had run my race'. At last, another corner of his life had been cleared, a space created in which he might yet become the creative writer he wanted to be.

> If I ever write a novel again, it must have as a basic theme running through it my passionate belief in – what has turned me from a revolutionary sympathiser to almost a conservative – what gives focus and centre to life: what maintains standards and principles of judgement, behaviour, taste, learning in the flux, the aimless seeming drift and transformation scene of life – what makes a radiating point for art and love – and a great country house, as Yeats knew, could be as important as a great theatre or a great magazine ...

*

It was in 1951 that James Stern sent Miles Huddleston, a twenty-one-year old in search of a publishing career, to meet Lehmann. An avid and intelligent reader, Huddleston was not the product of any university, having left school at seventeen and worked for four years as a cowboy on his uncle's *estancia* in Argentina, and, briefly, in the Royal Armoured Corps.

Even for a young ex-cowboy, meeting Lehmann proved 'an awesome experience. In those days he smoked fat, rounded Turkish cigarettes especially made for him by his wine merchant, and these he puffed from a long cigarette holder clamped at the corner of his mouth between strong even teeth. It was as if he knew the effect his physical presence had on others, because he was quick to put one at one's ease.' They warmed to one another.

To Lehmann, Huddleston was almost a boy alone, whose father had been lost at Dunkirk, who lived now with his sister. Huddleston noticed the endearing habit Lehmann had of repeating one's last phrase, as if relishing it and letting it linger on the air. Soon, he had become 'Dear Boy' and, more disconcertingly, 'Honey', which must have proved puzzling to the heterosexual Huddleston. Many young hopefuls beat a path to Lehmann's door, but Huddleston's qualities seemed out of the ordinary, and Lehmann at once became his 'English tutor and literary mentor, providing a reading list which became the basis of my literary tastes'.

In August, Huddleston was at Lake Cottage for a weekend, during which Lehmann's first impressions were confirmed: 'My liking for the boy increases, he is the most sympathetic and undemanding of companions, immensely interested in all literary things, and seems genuinely fond of me in spite of his admission that he makes no friends – and lives in a kind of negative, withdrawn chill of his own.' Lehmann recorded that Huddleston had reacted with 'considerable coolness and charm' to what Lehmann had told him of himself, but failed to record everything that happened that evening. Huddleston remembers that

Lehmann kissed him on the lips and, realising how startled Huddleston was by it, immediately drew back from him.

It was Lehmann's only attempt to seduce him, and did nothing to impair the quality of a friendship that would last for 36 years. Eventually, Huddleston boarded for a time at the house next to Lehmann's at Egerton Crescent, owned by a cousin of Connolly's, Dorothy Russell. Russell had 'a wonderful old queer butler' who used to talk over the fence to Rassine. Rassine himself, he recalls, seemed 'very lonely', often glimpsed as he walked through Kensington, a beret clamped over his ears. It was thus, as a sort of shadow, that beloved Alyosha drifted into the consciousness of so many.

Rudolph Chambers Lehmann (courtesy Martin Taylor)

Rudolph Lehmann and Alice Davis (courtesy Martin Taylor)

Fieldhead (University of Princeton)

John Lehmann in boating dress
(University of Princeton)

Julian Bell and Lehmann punting
(courtesy anonymous)

Michael Redgrave (courtesy Martin Taylor)

Julian Bell (courtesy anonymous)

Lehmann and Virginia Woolf at Rodmell
(courtesy Paul Blanc)

Lehmann and Leonard Woolf at Rodmell
(courtesy Paul Blanc

Toni Sikyr (courtesy
Martin Taylor)

Lehmann's Invalidenstrasse flat
(University of Princeton)

W. H. Auden, Stephen Spender and Christopher Isherwood (University of Princeton)

Alexis Rassine about 1940

Alexis Rassine in *Le Spectre de la Rose*

'Bobbie', a lover (courtesy Martin Taylor)     Adrian Liddell Hart (University of Princeton)

The Lehmann dynasty: Beatrix, Rosamond, and John Lehmann (University of Princeton)

Beatrix Lehmann

Demetrios Capetanakis.
(University of Princeton)

Rosamond Lehmann

Lehmann at 31 Egerton Crescent.
(courtesy Martin Taylor)

31 Egerton Crescent (author)

Lettice and Barbara Cooper
at a wedding
(courtesy Leo Cooper)

Lake Cottage (courtesy Jean Watson)

Lehmann with Carlotta (courtesy Jean Watson)

Penguin New Writing (author)

Jeremy Kingston (courtesy Jeremy Kingston)

Alexis Rassine at Lake Cottage
(courtesy anonymous)

Colin Spencer (courtesy Colin Spencer)

Jeremy Kingston, right, and
Lehmann in Austria
(courtesy Jeremy Kingston)

Beatrix with Carlotta (courtesy Martin Taylor)

Rassine and Marina Svetlova

Adrian Liddell Hart, left, and Douglas Stoker, far right (courtesy Bruce Cruickshank)

85 Cornwall Gardens (author)

Douglas Stoker (courtesy
Bruce Cruickshank)

Lehmann with Angus Wilson, far left, in Russia (courtesy Tony Garrett)

Frank Oatman by Lehmann in 1971 (courtesy Frank Oatman)

Lehmann, far right, with Christopher Isherwood and Douglas Stoker (courtesy Brian McColgan)

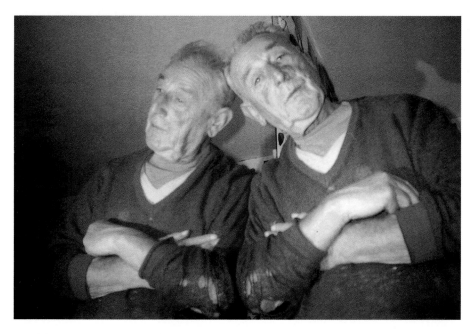

Eric Oliver (courtesy Martin Taylor)

Pamela Foster (courtesy
Pamela Foster)

John Lehmann, 1971
(courtesy Frank Oatman)

# 13

# Looking for Ganymede

In the summer of 1952 a young actor studying at the Central School of Speech and Drama wrote to Lehmann 'I have only known you such a short time and yet it seems like we always belonged together, I am sure it was written in the stars.' Thin, with a starved pretty look about him and wavy swept-back hair, the twenty-four-year old actor, christened by Lehmann 'The Faun', had the features, according to a Clacton landlady, of the young Ivor Novello. There had been an instant attraction, and Lehmann swept The Faun up in a burst of attention and meetings. For The Faun it was the sudden access to a society he might never have broken into. 'Oh darling,' he told Lehmann, 'I do feel good, it's like the beginning of an epoch.' For Lehmann the beacon had been lit 'after my shot in the dark, something that was as if it had always been meant, as if we'd always known one another in the deepest sense, but had just been waiting to start'.

The same words, of course, Lehmann had once used about falling in love with Rassine; there was at least still a belief in old delusions. The Faun was a guest at the cottage, taken to the Old Vic and to a John Cranko ballet at John Piper's Kenton Theatre after which The Faun's excitement 'boiled right over on the night journey home, and aided by a bottle of champagne caused an upset only healed in the morning'. There was another quick test when The Faun became seriously ill and was taken into St. Mary's Hospital where Lehmann visited him, awkward to be at his new lover's bedside in the presence of other friends. When The Faun made a speedy recovery, his place in the fabric of Lehmann's life was established. It was a presence that posed an immediate threat to his future with Rassine who 'has always been so extremely intransigent and unadaptable in his attitude'.

Lehmann knew his own position. He wanted to prevent a final parting from Rassine despite the poisoning unhappiness between them, while not giving up the sexual and romantic bliss he was finding in The Faun. The weekend before The Faun arrived at the cottage for a two-day recuperation, Rassine, deeply wounded, railed against Lehmann's behaviour, threatening to quit Lehmann's life altogether. Two days of tearful recrimination and argument were followed by a Sunday of perfect contentment when they planned the garden and enjoyed each other's company until, that evening, Rassine again broke down and spoke of walking away. 'I pleaded with him not to do that,' Lehmann wrote.

I hated to make him unhappy, but I had the memory of what seemed to me the increasing bitterness and unsatisfactoriness of our relationship over the past two years or more, the conviction I had come to that the design of it needed at least to be changed. It was so clear he'd taken me for granted for so long, he'd never thought it would happen; but in spite of all my pleas it had to be black or white.

He told himself that Rassine's attitude had nothing to do with the introduction of The Faun. Neither had it in Lehmann's mind. The problem was fundamentally how Rassine and he might co-exist, how that tortured, misunderstood nagging at what was essentially a destined bond between them might be eased.

In August The Faun was taken for a weekend in Paris, wonderful because 'the harmony was so perfect and [The Faun's] love so extraordinary, so passionate and cloudless. And yet there *was* a cloud for me: how could there not be for anyone of my age and life?' We can look to the journals for a definitive statement of Lehmann's intention, with his wishing

> I could get past the blank-wall determination of Alexis to break completely, which – and I see it – will only cause pain to everyone ... It is thus that a new, happy relationship might be built up between Alexis and me, as he seems to believe and desperately want; but I cannot, ever, endure again the cruel, hostile, nagging element without sympathy or understanding that poisoned so much in the past – I cannot create in it and I cannot live my life as a social being in it; though I know too well there was the other side, the fanatical instinctive devotion, more like blood-relationship than love, the passion for the household, the cottage, the garden, the natural turning to me in difficulties and problems, the bouts of astonishing generosity; but again I stub my toe against the narrow hostility to friends, the increasing fallowness of the mind, the Sadler [*sic*] Wells affectations of femininity that I can no longer endure except as party gaiety: all the things from which [The Faun] will deliver me.

\*

At the beginning of September Lehmann returned to Vienna for the first time in five years to find the city slowly repairing itself, but still poor and broken. He arrived on a perfect late summer's day, with sheets of golden light falling across everything he saw, conscious that this had been the light he had seen twenty years ago, almost to the day, when he had first come to live in Vienna. The looks of the girls and the boys in their lederhosen with their honey-coloured legs and dusty gold hair were the same, and Lehmann was in a state of wonder, 'how much I'd had to learn and change, how much they'd changed, how many earthquakes and tornadoes of history had left their mark on all of us, on Vienna's body'.

Sikyr and Gretl, both grown stouter, greeted him. There could have been no more palpable reminder of what Lehmann's world had once been and what it might have been. Sikyr's five-year-old son, Peter, was excited at his arrival. Sikyr suggested that Lehmann might want to come back to his old flat in the Invalidenstrasse, but 'I suddenly realised how I never could or would, how all that was past, past ... and some of the boys who used to come there killed or vanished beyond trace and nearly everyone else sunken in the foxholes of their own married lives'. Lehmann noticed some old possessions of his in their flat: a few volumes of *New Writing*, a travelling clock, a tray. He listened as Sikyr told him of his mother's and brother's death and of his fears for Vienna's future; the war had taken so much.

He walked to the Prater one evening, hearing it had been reopened, but the experience was horrible. He was almost alone there, unable to find any of the familiar restaurants, and none of the remembered walks; only the scars of finished battles dominated. He looked for old boyfriends, but could find none. On the 7th he drove into the Styrian mountains, to Mariazell, exulting in the 'climbing pine-forests, the dark, dark green and then the sudden brilliant green of an alpine meadow (the saffrons out in most of them) with an isolated farm and stooks standing like hooded men on a small piece of cultivated land, the hollow echoes, the bursts of travelling sunshine among the clouds, the sudden naked rock-faces and waterfalls'. Mariazell itself was full of trippery booths and in the cathedral he was appalled at the tinsel flummery of the 'miracle-working' Holy Mother and Son dolls, and astounded at the beauty of the high altar.

As a farewell to the city, he and Sikyr and Gretl went to Grinzing for an 'old Viennese' night of *heuriger* wine and song. They sat under the rain and drank sharp, new white wine as the musicians serenaded their table, bringing back sometimes almost unbearable memories for him. He was caught by the unique quality of the Viennese, the ability to be unsophisticated and civilised, poetic and ribald, fresh and traditional and all this, he realised, 'in a war-shattered city without any future'.

*

Throughout the 1950s, the troubles between Rosamond and Lehmann deepened, almost certainly aggravated by Rosamond's break with Cecil Day Lewis in 1950. So disturbed was she by this event that she told her brother she did not wish to see him because of what he represented: 'I don't know,' Lehmann told her, ' what it can be that I "represent" that could have daunted you.' In part, Rosamond's dissatisfaction with Lehmann was because he would not agree that Day Lewis's behaviour towards her had been psychotic. She asked to be relieved of her work for John Lehmann Ltd. unless a harmony could be restored.

A miserable, unnecessary and unexpected deterioration of their affairs came in the summer of 1951 when Guy Burgess and Donald Maclean fled England for Moscow. Rosamond told Lehmann that during the war she had suspected Burgess of being a Soviet agent and, with hindsight, was convinced of the fact. Patriotically, she went to MI5 to tell all she knew. Lehmann committed the grave solecism of writing to Spender, then in Italy, with the news that 'I was in touch yesterday with someone whom you know very well, who told me she'd worried for *years* about Guy, owing to a piece of information that came her way during the war; and now that all the pieces fitted together, she was absolutely sure.'

Spender, unbelievably, showed Lehmann's letter to the *Daily Express*. Reporters duly arrived at Egerton Crescent, bearing, to Lehmann's consternation, a copy of the letter he had sent to Spender, and demanding to know the identity of the Mystery Woman (which of course he would not divulge). Rosamond felt doubly betrayed: by Lehmann, having considered any correspondence between them to be confidential, and by the untrustworthy Spender, whose thoughtless action had caused such embarrassment to her, and to Beatrix, who was also hounded by the press.

Meanwhile, the *Daily Express* headline, DIPLOMATS – THE SECRET, preceded a photographed reproduction of parts of Lehmann's letter, a breach of copyright that cost the newspaper 100 guineas (which Lehmann donated to the Royal Literary Fund) and a printed apology. With his instigation of legal action against the press, the persecution of his sisters ceased: 'It had become extremely painful, because Rosamond was in the end becoming extremely nervous and tragic about it and inclined to blame me' (not, it must be said, without reason).

The silliness of Spender's action seemed almost to paralyse Lehmann's invective. He did confide to his journal that Spender had committed 'a breach of trust almost approaching lunacy and unparalleled in the dealings of gentlemen'. Spender had rather implicated Lehmann in the affair, somehow making Lehmann identifiable with the discreditable doings of Burgess and Maclean; it was not the behaviour of a friend. The affair subsided as quickly as it had flared, but one suspects that Lehmann rather enjoyed the sympathetic disapproval of Spender that he encountered everywhere through the ensuing weeks. Spender had disgraced himself publicly and proved Lehmann's point: the tut-tutting was music to his ears.

More lasting was Rosamond's reluctance to let the matter drop. Whenever she enters the frame she comes bearing the furniture of the past, old disagreements, unhealed sores. A year after the Burgess débâcle, she was still groaning about Lehmann having caused such an upheaval. In June 1952 he told her

> I am hypersensitive, I know, to a slight or suspicion of disloyalty from those who can count on my loyalty, but the underlying tension of my nerves this year must really, I feel, be put down to overwork, acute worries and despair.

While aware that Rosamond held him partly responsible, he found her attitude 'difficult to credit. It remains incomprehensible to me, and I think always will.' He went on to complain that on her visits to Lake Cottage she never helped with the washing-up.

We cannot know what other causes of resentment and distrust between brother and sister remain obscured. We do know that in March 1958, on a day of terrible weather, Lehmann was driving Rosamond in his car. The road conditions were hazardous. Rosamond pressed him to take a shorter route to their destination. Lehmann would not take it. He shouted at her, and Rosamond attacked him, punching him in the head. It was an action that left Rosamond almost as shaken and distressed as Lehmann. She confessed

> Shock, shame, humiliation to the uttermost ... I hit out blindly, as in a nightmare, to stop the torrent of rage and cruel abuse that you unloosed on me – No doubt you will say that I provoked you, and in so far as I was trying to press you to listen to me and take a shorter route I did provoke you ... The nightmare feeling keeps recurring when I remember what poured out from your subconscious – A very far back, deep-rooted panic and horror rose up in me when you were shouting: it wasn't [illegible] you shouting at me; it was Daddy shouting at Mother, which is one of the deepest traumatic memories of my childhood. Perhaps you never witnessed it, but I did, more than once. I am always sad nowadays about our relationship, and I am sure you are too. I do love you very much, and think that you love me ... I feel that you disapprove and judge without trying to understand.

There can be no doubt of the violence of the moment they now had to negotiate. Forty years later, the pain is palpable. Attempting to define at least some of their difficulties, Lehmann told Rosamond

> You do not like to be crossed or thwarted in any way, nor perhaps do I, but sometimes even for me to hold a different opinion about a book or a play seems enough to set the alarm bells ringing in you that drown reason ... Flatterers do not really love the people they flatter, and I cannot be just a flatterer to you ... I shall try and *get past* your assault on me in the car. But I can't yet, because it was the most horrible and frightening thing that has ever happened to me. I felt dazed for twenty four hours, then very ill; then pulled myself together to deal with all that had to be dealt with, but went down like a stone at the weekend with a high temperature ... I'm afraid I'm sure we ought not to meet at all for a while. Try and let time do its work, because if you made another scene with me now I should go out of my mind. Don't answer this: I shall burn any letter that comes: I have to go on with my life.

185

Their friendship could not end, but neither could they find a plane on which they co-existed in the harmony of their Fieldhead childhood. On one occasion, Rosamond and Sally were to lunch with Lehmann at the Brompton Grill. They arrived at Egerton Crescent, Rosamond in a 'disastrous' mood. Lehmann had asked her to write a book review, and she began complaining ('the old, old complaint') about having to write for him. She flounced out of the house and made a scene in the Crescent.

Lehmann 'sank to the bottom of a pit of despair in the process, and felt sick for the rest of the day'. He saw Rosamond as a pathetic figure, one who was 'incapable of grasping who really loves her and cherishes all that is wonderful in her, but seems to prefer the flatterers, the superficial and shallow social gad-abouts, and less and less to base her judgements and enthusiasms on a perspective – only on the emotion created by the insincere illusion of the moment'. For the rest of their lives, the mutual disappointment would not weaken and the loss of Rosamond's support and unquestioning love and admiration was a central tragedy in Lehmann's life. The pity of it all was made worse by the fact that he desperately needed her love, and could not express his own deep-rooted feeling for her. Thus constrained, how could their love not erupt in violence?

*

The expected blow to John Lehmann Ltd. fell in November 1952 when Wilfred Harvey rejected Lehmann's offer (financially supported by Robert Maxwell) to buy back the firm. The waves felt by Purnell's decision were so considerable that it is difficult for us today to appreciate them; to understand how the collapse of a relatively small publishing house could have the impact it had almost fifty years ago. On the day of its official announcement, the news made the front page of the *Evening Standard*.

Two weeks later Rose Macaulay organised a letter to *The Times* signed by, among others, A. J. Ayer, Graham Greene, Harold Nicolson, Arthur Koestler, Spender and Angus Wilson, which claimed 'There can be few people of literary interests who, during the last fifteen years, have not often been grateful to Mr Lehmann for the breadth and fervour of his enthusiasms.' They praised the patronage he had worked, particularly in France, Italy, Greece and Czechoslovakia, and his promotion of the painters who would also regret 'the departure of one who has chosen to neglect his own considerable gifts as a writer in order to devote himself, unselfishly and unsparingly, to furthering the gifts of others'.

Lehmann told the *News Chronicle* that he had, effectively, been fired by Purnell, and that his connection with his imprint would end on 31 December. His mood was one of melancholy regret for what had been achieved and thrown away. In a warning note for *The Bookseller* he told of the difficulties any small publisher would face in the uncertain future. 'The small people will get hurt, badly,' he wrote.

> That the big people seem to fear the same hurts, which to them can be no more than the pinpricks Gulliver received in Lilliput, is a symptom of our age and a matter more for sorrow and bewilderment than for anger.

Sorrow, bewilderment, anger: all were felt by those involved when Lehmann put his 'Operaton Scuttle' into action, conscious of his responsibilities to himself, to his authors and staff. Barbara Cooper needed all her resilience. She was completely demoralised by the event, sitting at her desk 'like a dripping sponge, never squeezed dry', all the time vowing to remain loyal to Lehmann, who saw her devotion as something of a hopeless responsibility. When she went to have tea with Rosamond she was still weeping.

There were more positive elements to the affair. Maxwell seemed about to offer him the job of running the British Book Centre in New York. There was a supportive leader in the *Times Literary Supplement*, offers from publishers, shoals of letters

> ... so full of warmth, admiration and sympathy I feel I don't deserve or could believe would pour out so spontaneously, it is as if I were watching myself dying a death, and were living some kind of posthumous existence.

As Lehmann moved away from the concern that had dominated him since 1946 he took stock of what he considered had been most satisfying to him. From America he had brought Paul Bowles's *The Sheltering Sky*, Merle Miller, Saul Bellow's *The Dangling Man*, Tennessee Williams and John Powers. He published Gore Vidal's homosexual novel, *The City and the Pillar*, waging a friendly battle with Vidal over delicate passages in the manuscript that might offend the timidity of Lehmann's printers.

From Europe he had brought Sartre's *Diary of Antoine Roquentin*, Bunin's *Dark Avenues*, Kazantzakis's *Alexis Zorba* (memorably renamed *Zorba the Greek* by Lehmann), and Malraux's *The Walnut Trees of Altenburg* onto The Modern European Library list. He had begun the reprint of classics in The Chiltern Library and introduced new travel writing in the Library of Art and Travel series. He commissioned Alan Ross and John Minton to create a book about Corsica, *Time was Away*. He revived interest in Stendhal by publishing the unfinished novel *Lucien Leuwen* for the first time in English, and bringing out an edition of Stendhal letters. He began a series of the Balzac 'Vautrin' novels. In these ventures, the work of trusted translators was of paramount importance, and there could be confidence in Kathleen Raine, in H. L. R. Edwards, in Norman Cameron and the whole school of them.

Rosamond's keenness for Mrs Gaskell was reason enough for the reprinting of her best work. There had been the elegant *Orpheus*, and the decorations on page and jacket of Burra, Ayrton, Medley, Biro, Jullian and, above all, Vaughan and Minton. It was Lehmann who was largely responsible for beginning the vogue enjoyed by the work of Denton Welch, publishing (after Welch's death) the autobiographical novel *A Voice Through the Clouds* and a volume of short stories, *A Last Sheaf*. Julia Strachey recommended a thoroughly badly typed manuscript about cookery that, unsolicited, had found its way to the office. John Minton was commissioned to decorate this outstanding piece of writing, Elizabeth David's *A Book of Mediterranean Food*; the quality of its production, born of Lehmann's new aestheticism, remains a brilliant example of the Lehmann imprint, of the marriage of visual art and word. He published the work of Phyllis Primrose-Pechey, better known as Fanny Cradock and then writing as Frances Dale. He published Laurie Lee, and encouraged him to write an autobiography, which became *Cider with Rosie*. Although it appeared long after Lehmann's career as a publisher was over, Lee told him 'This is really your book and you are responsible for it.'

A catalogue of commissioned biographies accentuated the literary emphasis of the imprint: scholarly and fresh evaluations of Lehmann's revered Rilke, Tolstoy, Dostoevsky, Chekhov and Melville. And poetry gathered from the world, and Norman Marshall's *The Other Theatre*, Eric Walter White's *Stravinsky*, and *Studies in Ballet*, written and illustrated by William Chappell, and adventure stories for boys. Even today, when one takes up a book published by Lehmann, there is added to the sense of holding a precious object, so obviously cared for in its creation, that sense of its being merely the part of a whole, the surround of taste and flair and purpose. Who in British publishing has since claimed the crown?

The last days before Christmas were spent in packing and tearing up so much of the paraphernalia of John Lehmann Ltd., Barbara crying as she and the girls marked everything in the office before it was handed back to Purnell, labelling the table 'table' and the floor 'floor'. By lunchtime on Christmas Eve everyone had gone except Lehmann and Barbara, and at the end he got into his car, laden with belongings and Barbara, tear-stained, waved him off.

For Lehmann, it was not altogether an unhappy time. He went with the family to see Rassine and Nadia Nerina dance in *Sylvia* and afterwards gave a supper party at No 31; he was made Chairman of the British Council Publications Panel; Christopher Hassall and George Hamilton read his poetry at the Royal Society of Literature. On the night after Barbara had waved him away from John Lehmann Ltd. he listened in the library with Rassine and Nerina to records of *Madam Butterfly*. Beyond the end of the year was the thought of what The Faun might mean in the new:

> I have never, I believe, known anything like this: the tender gentleness and gaiety, the sympathy, admiration and love; the passion, and the ease of

companionship; the image of fawn [*sic*] and renaissance page and youthful
St. Sebastian.

The official crowning of Lehmann's achievement as a publisher was the lunch
given in his honour at the Trocadero on 14 January at which T. S. Eliot proposed
the toast. The idea had come from Henry Yorke who kept muttering to his guest
that it was the first time a group of distinguished authors had made such a
gesture to one of their circle since Coleridge had organised a dinner for Leigh
Hunt on his release from prison. Connolly was so taken with the occasion
(which cannot have been a particularly easy one for him to countenance) and
the opportunity for malicious talk it presented, that he suggested the formation
of a monthly lunching club.

It is unlikely that a more impressive gathering of writers could ever again have
been managed: what we must remember is that they came in homage and
admiration for what Lehmann had done. One can only list them: Yorke, of
course, and Rosamond, Joe Ackerley, Walter Allen, Noel Annan, A. J. Ayer,
E. M. Forster, Roy Fuller, John Hayward, Arthur Koestler, Laurie Lee, Rose
Macaulay, Louis MacNeice, Raymond Mortimer, P. H. Newby, William Plomer,
Anthony Powell, V. S. Pritchett, Alan Ross, William Sansom, Stephen Spender,
James Stern, Philip Toynbee, Rex Warner. When the day came he was too tense
to properly enjoy it but it was, as he had written, 'as if I were watching myself
dying a death'.

The guests seem to have reacted to the occasion in the way those who knew
Lehmann tended to react: with respect, but a feeling, too, of slight absurdity.
Alan Ross describes how Lehmann's headmasterish manner rather encouraged
the telling of tales about him when he was not present; like little boys let out of
school, his friends felt at last free to let themselves go. Lehmann's speech at the
Trocadero does not seem to have been particularly original or witty. One
wonders if he appreciated the tribute that had been paid him. Connolly complained about the dreadful food. It was one of the last acts of kindness that would
be done to Lehmann by those to whom he had given himself.

*

Lehmann was 'amused at the grand, grown-up tone' of the letter seventeen-year-
old David Hughes from Wimbledon wrote, introducing himself, in October
1947. An admirer of *Penguin New Writing*, Hughes offered two poems that were
not accepted despite 'definite gifts'; but an invitation to Egerton Crescent was
extended. His first impression of Lehmann was of a monumental presence, of
something carved out of stone despite the animations, and 'there was an
enormous narrowing of the eyes, with a need to desire and seduce'.

In 1949 Hughes joined the Royal Air Force, rising to Pilot Officer, and went
on to Oxford, where he became president of the Writers' Club and editor of *Isis*.

Intensely handsome, Hughes had tactfully to deflect Lehmann's insistent proposals that their friendship should be more than platonic. In early 1950 it
seemed uncertain how their friendship would progress. There was at least no
doubt from Hughes, who straightforwardly admitted that he felt ill at ease in
Lehmann's company.

> I've a strange feeling I could never become intimate with you, John. I'm
> never completely at ease in your society, never fully at home. There always
> seems to be something in the way. The nearest I ever got to you, I felt, was
> in the kitchen at the cottage, but even then I felt your world was something
> I could never properly come to know ... there is a lapse in my knowledge
> of your life which makes the friendship vague and unreal. Maybe it's just
> different from my other relationships in that I'm not in control of it, can't
> dictate its course, organise it. There's a clash somewhere – so I don't like
> it altogether, I'm sorry for it.

It was Hughes who not only suggested to Lehmann that the moment was ripe
for a literary magazine 'of the air', but also so interested P. H. Newby of the BBC
in the idea that in September 1951 Newby offered the programme to Lehmann.
Lehmann was immediately enthused with being at the beginning of something
that might be 'big and revolutionary'. Hughes arranged that Lehmann would
visit Oxford to meet those, almost all unknown, authors and poets whom
Hughes thought might provide a nucleus of talent for 'OUR radio programme!',
though he was unhappy that Newby had not kept him well informed, 'rather
like keeping a father in the dark about his child'.

Lehmann, meanwhile, seems to have been happy to play the single parent;
there would be no reflection of glory from *New Soundings* for Hughes, without
whom it would not have happened. First heard on the Third Programme on 9
January 1952, this aural literary periodical sought to reverberate with 'new
soundings that are being made, new ideas stirred into life and old arguments
brought up to date', the whole being selected, edited and linked on air by
Lehmann.

In his spoken introduction to the first broadcast Lehmann established what
seems to have been a thread of regret, of melancholic reflection on what had
been lost from writing and what needed so desperately to be recaptured, that
ran through the editions that followed. At this point his sentiments were
particularly valid since at its inception the series of forty-five minute programmes was supposed to limit itself to English literature, and there was truth
in Lehmann's theory that it had been struck by 'Bud Blast', cutting back young
talent before it adequately flowered, and leaving behind it a trail of unfulfilled
promise.

One of his hopes for *New Soundings* was that it would stir the new, exciting
writers from their burrows, but there was a willingness, too, to follow where

*Penguin New Writing* had already been. The first edition introduced Elizabeth Jennings, James Michie and Lynette Roberts – young poets all – as well as a long ballad by Vernon Watkins, a prisoner-of-war story by a Leading Electrical Mechanic Wilde (a real whiff of *Penguin New Writing* here) and, giving advice to young writers, Tom Hopkinson. Henry Yorke, looking debauched and hardly able to keep his mind on what he was doing, read from his work, but, despite being left nervously exhausted, Lehmann felt he had pulled the programme off successfully.

There was no doubt of it. In February Harman Grisewood, Director of the Third Programme, confirmed the impact the magazine had made by extending its allocation to sixty minutes, and by letting in American and foreign writers, thus freeing Lehmann's hand tremendously. Lehmann barely rested in strenuous attempts to make the concept vital, meaningful and accessible. He was constantly occupied with balancing prose against poetry, imaginative writing against critical evaluation, with creating a seamless effect of one intellectual process working itself out with the listener. His statements of intent were adventurous: to 'rescue creative writing in a dying-off of literary magazines that threatened to become a total extinction'. In effect, he was working towards a substitute for the printed page. He exercised a tenacious control over standards, just as he had when print had been the medium, for – how could it have been otherwise? – he saw the material textually as well as having to consider it as being broadcast. He said that 'a good radio programme should be available in print as a whole'.

In his melding of the old and new, known and hopeful, Lehmann perhaps faced a struggle with finding an individual voice by which *New Soundings* might be identified. It seemed made up of elements that might have been more comfortable in a printed periodical where the reader might at least exercise some serendipity. Some of the Oxford protégés were in place, including Jennings, Simon Broadbent and James Price; among others at the early stages of their careers were Thom Gunn, Hugo Charteris, John Wain and Charles Causley. For the heavyweights, Lehmann brought in Isherwood (on contemporary American writers), John Betjeman (reading his 'Song of a Night-Club Proprietor'), Mac-Neice, Plomer, Lee and Edith Sitwell. There was a tendency for the programme to go Grecian, because of Lehmann's belief that so much that was good in modern writing had Greek beginnings. Translations of Elytis and Sikelianos were surrounded with poems on Greek themes by Francis King, John Heath-Stubbs and Lawrence Durrell, with Capetanakis's essay on *The Tempest* brought in for good measure.

The concentration on style and language that permeated Lehmann's approach showed his obvious preference for them over content. The subject matter of what was written about was obviously less important than the manner in which it was expressed, although the thesis was never announced. It is no surprise that for one of the spoken introductions he invoked Keats's cry to Benjamin Bailey, 'O for a life of Sensations rather than of Thoughts.'

All this was reflected from what had been rather than from what might be expected of the future. When Lehmann spoke of writing having 'reached a kind of doldrums, a kind of sargasso sea of becalmment'. he was reiterating the difficulties of progress rather than pointing the mast in new directions. Lehmann was clearly handicapped by the quality of material that was submitted for the broadcasts, a principal problem being that writers simply could not adapt to using so small a capsule as four or five minutes on air allowed. Short stories, a genre that Lehmann had always had an intense belief in, suffered particularly. There were other hurdles: the difficulties of excerpting a new novel or work in progress; delivering effective critiques that did not deteriorate into shorthand; how to integrate sometimes obtuse poetry without adopting a tutoring or condescending stance. He overcame each as best he could, while trying to solve 'the problem of defining an attitude, or discovering the symbols of a philosophy', always emboldened in the faith that 'there never was a time, a challenge to which art, poetry, could not find an answer'. The critical reaction to *New Soundings* was good, the BBC was pleased, and Lehmann's reputation as an editor of taste and fine judgement was vindicated.

*

It came as a complete surprise when, after the fourth broadcast, Newby informed him that the magazine was so successful that it would be extended beyond a year's run, at which point a new editor would be introduced. Lehmann, in effect, faced another dismissal. From Lehmann, there was anger, from Hughes, only another kind of disappointment, for 'I always thought it a pity that the venture was surrounded with such trickery and discourtesy: all this sounds bitter, but it is something I can't forget.' The knowledge that the game, again, was up, clouded the remaining broadcasts. Recording the tenth edition, Lehmann was full of anxieties, hardly knowing how he had got it together.

A few days before the final programme, John Morris (who had replaced Grisewood) and Mary Somerville seemed to offer a hope that *New Soundings* would one day return. His understandable distrust as to what might happen had its misogynistic focus in Somerville, in whose face he detected 'that mixture of a woman's response, a woman's frustration, and a need for power'. Matters were hardly helped when Newby congratulated Lehmann on the exciting nature of the final edition: Lehmann's feeling for Newby hardened to a positive dislike.

Only a month later, *New Soundings* was replaced by *First Reading*, edited and introduced by John Wain, the BBC's literary changeling. If Lehmann had been asked to organise a wake, it seemed now that Wain was asked to officiate at a christening. Wain, of course, had been one of Lehmann's gallery, his poetry heard in *New Soundings* and, ironically, his had been the last piece, an essay, 'Ambiguous Gifts', on William Empson, ever to have appeared in the pages of *Penguin New Writing*. Wain was the newest of brooms, declaring the inauguration of a new Elizabethan age of writers brought together in a spirit of consolidation after an interregnum of experimentation. The promise was clear: 'the decks are going to be cleared and a special effort made'.

Overblown and indefinite – and sounding a little like a determination to smarten things up at the local Women's Institute – Wain's proclamation was not universally welcomed. In the *New Statesman* Hugh Massingham deplored Lehmann's removal, provoking Wain to revise his manifesto, now insisting that he would attract writing that 'invoked discipline and detachment rather than luxuriance and emotionality'; romanticism, it appears, had had its day. For the first *First Reading*, Kingsley Amis read from a yet unfinished *Lucky Jim*, there was poetry from Dannie Abse and Philip Larkin, and anything that smacked of the old guard was resisted.

In the linking of Wain and Amis, strongly suggested by Wain's initial broadcast, there was the germ for the 'Movement', that group of writers so defined in the pages of the *Spectator* in 1954 by J. D. Scott – for no better reason, apparently, than that the circulation of the paper was falling and a little controversy needed to be provoked. It gave a name to the division of seventeen years that lay between Lehmann and Wain, or perhaps, as Philip Oakes wrote in 1956, it simply drew attention to the opposing armies in English writing; crudely, the likes of Wain and Amis united against the likes of Lehmann and Spender. It did not escape Lehmann that many of those who claimed membership of the 'Movement' were those he had once encouraged and published, bearing out Peter Burton's words that 'people are always resentful of those who have helped them'.

Perhaps Lehmann's only mistake with *New Soundings* was to be caught on the cusp of alteration. Wain's first novel *Hurry on Down*, published in October 1953, had as its anti-hero the lower-middle-class Charles Lumley who embarks on a frenzied catalogue of occupations after leaving university. In its deliberate try for modernity, this marked a way for other fiction, most immediately *Lucky Jim* (1954), whose hero Jim Dixon is not only provincial but articulate, young and angry. The 'school' established by these novels, along with others that flooded the market in the mid-fifties, is essentially artificial, but defines the shift that was taking hold. Walter Allen, whose *All in a Lifetime* (1959) might be thought to be another novel along the same line, with its working class ethos, its strong provincialism and its keen eye on the rise of socialism, had as long ago as the 1930s written three potent novels about Birmingham working-class life.

The 'Movement' was as much a label for what had been for some years quietly apparent in writing, as much as the recognition of something hitherto unknown. It seemed at times as if the popularity of modern British novels that appeared in Penguin editions was enough to constitute a movement, if not *the* 'Movement'. In the theatre, young and angry was also a newly acceptable currency. Indeed, change was perhaps more perceptible in drama than in literature. Almost overnight, the plays of Rattigan, Eliot, the statuesque gentleness of N. C.

Hunter, the supposed grace of Christopher Fry, the deliberate well-made qualities of a Graham Greene three-act drama, were redundant. John Osborne's *Look
Back in Anger* (1956) had Jimmy Porter – the angriest of all the angry and young
– and cleared the way for the plays of Arnold Wesker, of Bernard Kops, of
Shelagh Delaney. The perception of art as 'kitchen-sink' happened to be applied
to drama, but might just as well have been attached to literature. There was
undeniable kitchen-sinkiness, by the late 1950s, in John Braine's *Room at the
Top*, in Alan Sillitoe's *Saturday Night and Sunday Morning* and *The Loneliness
of the Long Distance Runner*.

The dawning of this supposed new age brought with it something else, a
sexuality that had previously been underdone: perhaps it would be true to say
that where literature had once been predominantly asexual or homosexual in
tone, its popularity was now shifting to the heterosexual, only one of the prices
paid in British writing for the new gritty realism. No matter that so many of the
careers of novelists and dramatists fizzled into nothingness, or that by the time
Osborne wrote *The World of Paul Slickey* in 1959 he could come up with nothing
more than a pale drizzle of shambolic invective, or that Braine and Delaney and
Kops never repeated their first successes: they had all had a hand in proving that
content, surely, was as important as style, and sometimes had precedence over it.

The gap between these developments and the tenet Lehmann had promul-
gated throughout his life seems, even in so brief a consideration, unbridgeable,
and though the gap between *New Soundings* and *First Reading* is arbitrary, it
nevertheless marks, at the eve of a revolution of sorts in English writing, the
passing of power from the mandarin to the tyro. And this was, for Lehmann, a
very public dismissal. Despite his disingenuous extension of good wishes to Wain
in *The Ample Proposition*, Lehmann rejected his successor's efforts, denouncing
in the *New Statesman* Wain's preferred provincialism, and confiding to his
journal his repulsion at 'the pretentiousness, the third-ratedness, the nonsense
talked about "consolidation", and then the third-rate mix of poets who get
published in such once respectable papers as "The Listener" ... Should I rejoice
then, or feel fury that J [John] M [Morris] prefers them to mine?' Only when
the furore had quietened did Lehmann meet Wain face-to-face for the first time,
in November 1954, finding him engaging and interesting but 'very hysterical and
alarming ... His conceit will ruin him in the end, however.'

*

For respite Lehmann travelled in April 1953 to the Mediterranean, taking The
Faun with him on the first stage of the journey. They moved from Rome to
Amalfi where they coincided with the great Good Friday procession bearing its
black crucifix. They were rowed out to the Emerald Grotto, and on Easter
Sunday walked on the mountain road above a bottle-green sea to Ravello. The
Faun was the ideal companion, with a chameleon's talent for making his mood

right for the moment; in the evenings they read poetry together. Importantly, due to his happiness with The Faun and the freedom he had regained, his poetry was again being warmed to life. One can feel its beginning in 'Sunrise: Amalfi'.

> Yes, it can really happen. Wait. Believe.
> Always and everywhere is place and time.
> An angel leaning by the garden pool
> Looks up, to give the long forgotten sign.
> The hand will touch what hope could not conceive,
> The poet wake to find the fragments rhyme.

Lehmann began 'to rise like a piece of grass long crushed under a heavy stone: words and phrases of poems did indeed begin to move in my mind: perhaps the old power, tiny but with its ever potent spell over my life, was not dead, merely sleeping'. On Easter Monday they were driven to Paestum, but its temples and ruins were almost buried by the Italian bank holiday that was in full play there. At the end of a week, they returned to Rome, from where The Faun departed for England on 10 April, Lehmann bemoaning the loss of 'the sensitiveness, the sweetness, the intelligence, the devotion – it is something I have never known'.

Alone, Lehmann went on to Athens, meeting Maurice Bowra and Isaiah Berlin there, and the poets Odysseus Elytis and George Katzimbalis, who complained of feeling old, fat and castrated. From Athens he went to Nicosia and from Nicosia to Platres with its Homeric shepherds and ghostly poplars, its flocks of house-martins, Byzantine churches, marigolds, judas trees, cornfields, goat-bells and, one afternoon, a blond haired Air Force boy leaning from a truck on a mountain road, asking the way to Paphos and inspiring a poem, 'Out of Time', in which the lost splendours of Cyprus's past are echoed through the meeting with the handsome soldier.

> The Air Force boy has vanished with his chore
> Into the burning hills.
>
> Hot on my throat, hot on the bones and stones
> Under the flowers above the shore.

For Lehmann, place and moment were perfectly aligned. As in 'Greek Landscape with Figures', they brought out his old simplistic but passionate reactions to natural beauty, to a lost classicism.

> I watched the peasants working there, who seemed
> Tough like the olive trunks, determined too
> To grip the earth with deep
> Unflinching will not to be dispossessed.

Quarrelsome, heroic, fruitful in their season
As when the bull roared and the temples rang:
Equally proud against
The rage of history, the whirling globe.

Then, with Maurice Cardiff from the British Council collecting him in a car, he saw Curium with its temple of Apollo, and then on to Old Paphos, reached between fields of corn and poppies, convolvulus and gladiolus, olive and carob, and to the bay (reminding him of Freshwater Bay) where Aphrodite was said to have been born, and so on to the Dome Hotel at Kyrenia, 'a sort of Buxton-cum-Cheltenham', with its doddering tourists and old ladies who seemed to be held together by pins. He found an equable companion in Lawrence Durrell who talked endlessly and took him to St. Hilarion and Bellapais, above whose abbey perched a small house Durrell had bought. Lehmann wanted to end Durrell's exile; he wanted him to write something that would break the barrier for him and return to live in England.

Wherever Lehmann went, little boys acted as guides. On 28 April he went on to Salamis with its remains of half excavated temples, broken columns, collapsing pillars, and everywhere abandoned shards of stone and marble; the feeling for a lost civilisation was overwhelming. Famagusta, its walls festooned with hibiscus, wisteria and bougainvillaea, had more compliant hospitality and a hotel on the beach, close by a busy bay for fishing and bathing, and beyond it a rest camp for servicemen on leave from Suez. At night, the painter Valentinos Charalambous showed Lehmann Famagusta's nightlife: sailors who winked at him in Pop's Bar, whores and boys getting drunk in the Spitfire Bar.

On 1 May he travelled with Charalambous to his family's pottery on the Salamis road, a visit celebrated in another poem, 'The Hidden Barn'. Understanding family conflicts, and the wish of the son against the wish of the father, he was sympathetic to the painter's need to produce more modern, sophisticated pieces rather than carry on producing pottery that conformed to all the classical needs, and, as always, he was intrigued by the knowledge and skill of the craftsmanship involved.

Bathing in front of his hotel Lehmann was suffused with a sense of well-being, a renewed identity with nature itself, which reached its apex when he bathed at Dhavos, an experience that seemed mystical, an absolute union with peace and, thus, the making of poetry.

The allure of an ideal retirement floated in his mind, but he knew, even then, it could not be. When he visited a monastery among Famagusta's rocks, a place that supposedly guarded a fragment of the very cross that Christ had died on, the food in his hands was snatched away by the starved old abbot who ruled there. A young man came out, looking wild, thin. And so to Nicosia, where he lectured at the British Institute about Capetanakis. Did he, that evening, read Capetanakis's 'Return', with its peculiarly apt expression and attitude?

> The traveller returned with empty eyes.
> 'That is not you!' wept the forsaken friend.
> 'You promised me the fire that never dies,
> And what you bring can only be the end.'

*

The last of the Lehmann periodicals, the *London Magazine*, began in January 1954. Its financier, Cecil King, had expected a highbrow readership with a circulation of 2,500, 'and now,' he told Lehmann early in its life, 'all we've got is another popular success'. Not without reason did Lehmann suspect his benefactor was guiltily making sacrifices at the altar of culture, giving succour to a paper that was the antithesis of King's business interests, and his ownership of the *Daily Mirror*. The two men had been brought together in September 1952 by another man of letters, John Hayward, to discuss the possibility of a new literary magazine, but it was only in the Coronation frenzy of June 1953 that they met again, and firm plans began to be made. Lehmann drew up estimates and produced a dummy edition. They discussed the setting up of an Editorial Board. Two names Lehmann put forward, Plomer and Warner, met with blank stares from King, who had heard of neither, and he pooh-poohed the idea of any Sitwell being involved (a slightly bad omen, Lehmann thought) but he accepted Plomer and Warner, and Lehmann's other proposals, Hayward, Elizabeth Bowen and C. V. Wedgwood.

King was keen that Lehmann should have at his side a younger assistant male editor (an idea that Lehmann was unlikely to resist), a post for which David Hughes seemed ideal. For months before the launch, Lehmann was coaxing contributions from established writers and doing his best to discover the unknown. In September he motored with Carlotta to Rustington, near Worthing, where Plomer lived in bungalow-land with his partner Charles. Lehmann was puzzled and anxious to see Plomer in such surroundings, in a home that seemed so poor, where the coffee cups did not match, where he could see no sign of any books. He and Plomer, looking old, walked by the sea.

Then it was off to Elizabeth Bowen at Bowen's Court 'in the deep green rural make believe of the Irish countryside', where he was bowled over by her endless enthusiasm and her driving always on the wrong side of the road. In October he was in Paris, wanting to strengthen the French contribution to the new periodical. From one young author, Pierre Gascar, he took the story 'The Animals' for the first issue, and from Felicien Marceau 'The Armistice in Vienna' for the second. He was reunited with Dionys Mascolo, the poet Pierre Emmanuel, Marguerite Caetani, Marguerite Duras and Marie-Laure de Noailles. At the table of de Noailles he met a handsome young American composer, Ned Rorem, who subsequently set some of Capetanakis's poems to music. Rorem enjoyed Lehmann's platonic friendship, though Lehmann wanted more. Two years later, meeting him again, Lehmann was overcome by 'an evening on the tiles with a chausseur alpine beret (his) in my coat pocket and a sudden ache of nostalgia for what can't or won't be ... I am fascinated by his beauty.'

It was decided that the magazine's office would be at Egerton Crescent, and in late autumn work began. Since Hughes's appointment, Barbara had been at her most exasperating, in a state of resentment and jealousy (according to Lehmann) at having been overlooked. In June she had told him that 'I could not, at my age and with my twelve years of editorial experience behind me, work under a boy (or a girl, for that matter) in the twenties, or take any instructions from him.' Would Lehmann be able to offer her full-time work? She could not go on indefinitely at £3 a week, and her savings were draining away. She wanted some sort of title, 'a face saver'.

> I want to make it quite clear that it is not only disappointed ambition that has made your announcement such a blow to me: the worst of my distress is that I fear that in the future you will naturally discuss all the MSS. with the assistant editor, and I shall no longer have the fun and satisfaction of this side of the work. You will see, I am sure John, that I *cannot* spend the remaining years of my life just weeding out MSS., packing parcels, sending back contributions, etc., without the close co-operation with you on the literary side that made all such drudgery worth while before.

Lehmann was exercised by feeling that 'her judgement is extremely unreliable about fiction, [she] has the absurdest blind spots where cats, Freud and America are involved, and no flair for the kind of thing that will "sell" at all ... this is all tragic, because her gifts are many, and she has been of immense help to me'. It is to Lehmann's credit that the magazine eventually listed Barbara and Hughes as 'Editorial Assistants'.

The path to publication was clear. Lehmann seems to have been largely responsible for the extraordinary success the magazine had in attracting advertisers. Chatto and Windus would act as distributor. Eliot would write an introductory piece for the first issue. Connolly brought Barbara Skelton to lunch. Looking round at the library he said, 'Well, you've been able to keep all this.' Connolly promised to write a series of literary pastiche, but never did. From the ranks of *New Soundings*, Elizabeth Jennings, Thom Gunn and Hugo Charteris were brought in for the first number.

King agreed that the magazine should be monthly if it was to make its impact. He agreed that it should be in the main for creative writing, English, American and continental, but would not hear of it embracing other forms, the theatre, music or the visual arts; at once, the *London Magazine* was more restricted than the latter-day *Penguin New Writing* had been.

How conscious Lehmann was of jumping through all the old hoops, we cannot know. As always, he had to look over his shoulder at the activities of Spender, who in September 1953 became editor of *Encounter*, a periodical published by the anti-Communist Congress for Cultural Freedom. King was alarmed when *Encounter* beat the still gestating *London Magazine* to the bookstalls, but Lehmann placated him.

At the first lunch of the Editorial Board in no. 31's newly decorated red and gold dining-room, everyone was united in a happy condemnation of Spender's latest venture. The Editorial Board listened and discussed, but it was soon clear that 'the real point of these gatherings is just to have stimulating and amusing parties, the serious work being done by individual contacts afterwards'. Barbara and Hughes might be asked in for coffee and port afterwards.

All seemed calm, but there were already problems with Hayward who 'thinks of everything ... in the literary world, in terms of intrigue and influence' and who was 'totally unscrupulous about the way he damns people he wants to eliminate or score off', behaviour that Lehmann excused to others as in part caused by Hayward's muscular dystrophy. Their relationship was further strained when Lehmann was asked to succeed Eliot as President of the British Alliance Française. Hayward told him that if he accepted he would resign, a threat that did not prevent Lehmann becoming the organisation's President from 1955 to 1963, even if he had tried to wriggle out of it. Hayward subsequently attacked Lehmann for not making his Editorials more violent.

The old energy was made available to the making of the new periodical, but at what cost? Once again Lehmann was expected to make the noises of setting a new style, to reinvent reasons and philosophies. Once again, there was the need to bring himself, his staff, his Board, his readership, to a pitch of excitement at what, constantly, lay ahead.

There is a slight lack of conviction, by the time we come to the *London Magazine*, made more distinct by our knowing what Lehmann had admitted to himself years before: he only half-believed in what he was doing. In the achievement of everything that King promised, Lehmann must have suspected the canker that would destroy him again; why should it succeed when everything that had gone before had been snatched from his hands?

*

By the mid-1950s it was obvious that Lehmann was not going to make the impression he had wanted as a creative writer, no matter how satisfactory his autobiographical writing. His poetry had dried up to the extent that his 1951 collection, *The Age of the Dragon*, was a monster of Frankenstein made up mostly of poems from earlier volumes, one of the notable exceptions being the verse drama 'The House'. Richard Eberhart considered the poems were simply not peculiar enough, that 'his intellectual *a priori* specifications for poetry ... quelled whatever might be wild, odd and free within him ... He has not invented a new language or way of saying things, some inescapable idiom of his own.' Noting that the war and political disillusionment had had its effect on his style, the *Listener* thought the later verse 'still about objects and events but it frequently finds its inspiration in dreams, the inexplicitness of life, deep self-searchings'; Lehmann's 'political doubts make, by and large, better poems than his earlier certainties'.

The following year a collection of essays, many of them from *New Writing*, appeared as *The Open Night*, pieces on some of those whose work had been so relevant to him, among them Capetanakis, Yeats and Woolf. All of them, even Proust and Joyce, Lehmann saw as poets, even if working through prose. English history and civilization was inconceivable without the centuries of poetry that accompanied it. 'Poets, one might say, are the lobes of balance we cannot do without in times of violent transformation and uncertainty, when old creeds are broken up and new false creeds eagerly grasped, are leading men into their hidden traps of despair'; it was the poetic imagination that alone could heal the split between knowledge and morality.

In poetry, it seemed he might be better remembered as a commentator and facilitator than a creator. It was as an editor that he had constructed his reputation. Why then did he awake in early January 'with that curious feeling of distaste, of spleen that has haunted me almost continuously since Christmas: perhaps the result of my chill – perhaps the strange usual exhaustion of an almost spiritual battle against the death of the year – perhaps also the bored bewilderment that overcame me after producing New Writing No. 1 – "Why on earth – and how – did I do this?"'

*

Lehmann brought what freshness he could to the guiding theories he adopted for the magazine. The cardinal importance of which books to review, the use of good critics not being used elsewhere; the introduction of young reviewers 'bearing in mind my firm conviction that first-class criticism is fundamentally a matter of experience, reflection and discrimination'; the relevance of craftsmen criticising the work of fellow craftsmen, 'what George Barker thinks of Vernon Watkins is essentially valuable'. Space for all poetry, regardless of school or age, 'to discriminate in *new* poetry (I feel I was recently becoming too kind to too many beginners)' and to look for 'transformers', 'where poetry, wit, fantasy, new use of language, flowers with especial freedom'. With Plomer's urging, he also looked to the magazine to include memoirs and personal recollections, essays on 'Coming to London' that were collected and published in book form in 1957.

Of course, the birth of *London Magazine* was a sort of miracle, and there was no shortage of praise for what Lehmann had done, but 'I also know that those who say the London Magazine proves we are in a literary doldrum in England have a little too much of truth with them to make me feel contented.'

All too soon King's support began to fade. Lehmann felt he had been expected to come up with something that would equal the appeal of the *Reader's Digest*, though he felt his enemy was the core of people that surrounded King rather than King himself. Lehmann was told that support might only be forthcoming until mid-1956, 'a nasty disappointment that makes planning difficult ...and that with a print order of over 10,000 still! ... after some days, my reaction was one of fuck-all'.

Alongside, the troubles with Hayward continued, Lehmann conscious of his 'obsession with the idea that nothing, either thought or action, goes on unless he initiates it, his mania to control and dominate'. Some would have attributed the need to dominate and control to Lehmann himself, businessmen and writers and lovers among them. The pattern repeats itself too often, as the ability to remain in control falls away from him. The Faun, too, that classical creature of perfection to Lehmann, became an increasingly remote figure, receding to the margins of Lehmann's life, before vanishing from it.

# 14

# Thinking Poet, Writing Editor

The writer and artist Colin Spencer was working as secretary to a Canon Hood when John Betjeman, a friend of Hood's, introduced him to Lehmann. When Spencer first visited Egerton Crescent in April 1955 'it was the most amazing shock. His eyes were this incredible blue. He wore a blue pullover of exactly the same shade, and there was this Nordic giant bearing down on me.' Though the relationship was sexual, Spencer never considered himself as anything so positive as Lehmann's boyfriend.

> John was the most egocentric lover I've ever been with. The only thing he was interested in was screwing, and I wasn't interested. He used to refer to my arse as being locked and sewn up. I hated to have sex with him; the sex was ghastly. I discovered there was a mean, sadistic streak in there. Once you got away from the urbane, literary person, underneath there was someone who had not got a clue how to have human relationships. Somewhere the emotional growth had stopped very early on, because he didn't have the beginnings of understanding. He was frightened of emotionally committing himself to anybody.

Lehmann never mentioned Rassine to Spencer, and the information he divulged about previous lovers was usually derogatory. Spencer was ill at ease with the atmosphere at Egerton Crescent, and his lover's coldness. After sleeping with Lehmann he had to move into the bedroom next door so that when Screwie (Mrs Crewe, Lehmann's housekeeper) brought up breakfast in the morning all would seem proper. Lehmann christened Spencer 'Cold, Callous Colin'.

That August, Lehmann called on Spencer at East Croydon where he lived with his mother. When Lehmann went to answer a call of nature, Spencer told her 'You've got the cornerstone of modern English literature pissing in your lavatory.' 'Do you always talk to your mother like that?' Lehmann asked. 'Yes' replied Spencer.

In October, Lehmann employed him for some office work, and there is no doubt that he taught Spencer much about writing and how to stop doing it 'like a champagne bottle fizzing all over the place'. But any possibility that their relationship would flower petered out in June 1956 when Spencer told Hood that he was having a sexual relationship with Lehmann. Hood, himself attracted to Spencer, denounced Lehmann as a dark influence and demanded that Spencer write Lehmann a letter breaking off all connection; he almost dictated it there and then, and sent Spencer off to post it. Spencer went directly to Lehmann, with whom he was spending that night, and told him what Hood had made him do, and of the letter that would be arriving by post the following morning. Spencer's sense of humour was not appreciated by Lehmann, who was appalled that his sexual activities had been betrayed to a clergyman.

For Spencer, there was to be no fondness in his memory of Lehmann. Over forty years later he remembers Lehmann as 'such a monster ... Power is the key to his character. He had to dominate and exploit and the more sadistic it was the more delight – psychologically, I mean, though he did like to do a little whipping of bottoms for those who were happy about it.' He recalls an incident when a friend of Lehmann's was expected to have sex with him one evening. The boy explained that he could not, as he was meeting somebody. 'First come, first served,' said Lehmann, unbuttoned his flies and pushed the boy's head down.

In the background of Lehmann's relationship with Spencer hides another, more surprising, relationship. Almost lost among the countless homosexual affairs of *In the Purely Pagan Sense* is Jack Marlowe's heterosexual affair with the coyly titled Mme. La Vicomtesse de B–, soon to be better known to him as Oriane. A friend to the French Ambassador and his wife, Oriane invites Marlowe to her house on the French Riviera, where she successfully seduces him. There is something masculine in her personality. She dresses as a sailor in his presence. Not an intellectual, she is nevertheless a collector of intellectuals, and professes an intense interest in Marlowe's writing. He reads poetry to her. After some rather obvious flirtation, she slips a note under his door for him to join her downstairs. They make love, but she is soon madly jealous at his persistent interest in men, and the relationship dwindles amid violent quarrels. All this, of course, is meant to confuse, for Lehmann's female lover was the wife of René Massigli, the French Ambassador to Great Britain.

Massigli had brought his wife Odette to London to begin their reign at the French Embassy in 1944. He had married Odette Boissier in 1932, and it was to a great extent her highly accomplished social skill that had helped him to so glittering a career. Lehmann had always admired her, her genuine glamour at a time when too much in England was dowdy, her receptivity of spirit. At a party of Sybil Colefax's in July 1950 (the hostess was all 'matchsticks and old wool') Odette and he decided to team up to go together that evening to a party of Beverley Nichols, to which only men and unattached women (what in a more modern vocabulary might be described as fag-hags) had been invited. Odette 'proved herself at the same time even more attractive than I had always thought her, so lively, so slyly perceptive – and told me of her own unhappiness, her inferiority-complex in intellectual circles, and how she had never bargained for the grand diplomatic life'.

Lehmann's relationship with Odette changed only after the Massiglis had left the Embassy in 1955. She invited Lehmann to stay with her at her home in Oletta, Corsica, in April 1956. Odette's husband was not present and Lehmann was bewitched by her. He wrote of her emerging from her Jaguar, 'staggering' in English tweed cut by Dior, a pale blue scarf at her neck, but no hat, her hair dark and bobbed, her manner imperious, commandeering, as she bestowed royal smiles on those they met.

At Oletta they wandered through the afternoon over hills above the sea, talking of the need for peaceful relationships, the tensions and comforts of marriage and children, and loneliness. Her reputation as the lover of other men was, she told him, exaggerated. She had wanted to divorce her husband immediately after their honeymoon, and only stayed with him because he had threatened to kill himself if she left, a threat that was repeated whenever his appointment to a new post might have been overshadowed by her desertion. The strain of emotional and professional commitment had resulted in Odette having a severe breakdown. Taken off the Golden Arrow on a stretcher, she had spent six months unconscious in a psychiatric hospital. Lehmann did what he could to stimulate her confidence 'and she has to be soothed, though there is some violence in it'. 'What more can one say?' she asked him. 'We just clicked, the moment we met, and everything that has happened since had to be.'

The next day, Lehmann recorded 'Last night Odette very tempestuous, and needs handling like a wild horse. Didn't get to my own bed until 3.45 a.m.' They spent a day at Fomali and took a boat out to a sandy cove where they lay in the sun together. He told her he had been obliged to rebuild his career four times since the war. 'Perhaps that means you ought to write now,' she told him. He christened her Penthesilea (after the Queen of the Amazons) and she gave him a watch with the name engraved on it. He detected something masculine in the way she talked of going sailing by herself 'with undiscovered shores ahead of you' and teased her by telling her she had always wanted to be a boy. 'Perhaps,' he thought, 'all this is a case of the homme-femme and the femme-homme who dovetail perfectly into one another.' Lehmann later told Thomas Urquhart-Laird how Odette had come to his room at night in her sailor's dress and whipped him.

Rassine, meanwhile, was being 'his other self to me: amusing, sympathetic, tender, understanding'. He must have been perplexed and anxious about this latest, unexpected twist to Lehmann's sexual life – as was Lehmann himself. This was an achievement; it was clear that Odette had fallen passionately in love with Lehmann, and wanted their relationship to continue as a strongly emotional and sexual one. Letters from Odette to Lehmann, addressed to 'Jupiter, ducky', written from the Avenue D'Orsay in Paris, urged him to live with her in Corsica, even though she must have been aware of his promiscuous homosexuality. The transparent difficulties this set up must have played some part in the physical arguments that often broke out between them, themselves so typical in Lehmann's dealings with male lovers.

There seemed no hope that Odette would bring the relationship to an end; it was left to Lehmann to do so. He told her of the dark wood he found himself in, realising

> ... even more painfully than before the disparity that still exists between what you feel for me and what I feel for you. I adore you, I admire you, I love you, I was carried willingly into all we explored together in Corsica; but there's a difference between loving and being in love with someone, a difference that can bring great danger and unhappiness ... It is this hidden disparity, I am sure, that has been the cause of all the violence that has exploded again and again at the end of our evenings together ... I don't like saying all this to you, dearest, but it would I believe be cowardly of me if I didn't. And if I could foresee the time when our being together would *not* bring you unhappiness, I would be happier than I can say; but I do not.

We cannot know quite what Odette made of that extraordinary final statement, or precisely what Lehmann may have meant by it, even if it suggests that she had merely to say the mist had lifted for him to move to Corsica. It hardly seems genuine, when what Lehmann surely longed for was a passing of the crisis, and pass it did.

\*

In fact, it was another year of various crises through which Lehmann had to wade. At least one of them had to be faced with Rassine: the death of Carlotta, on the afternoon of 11 April 1956. She had been ill for a year, for much of which Lehmann willed her to survive until Rassine returned from a lengthy tour of South Africa. A new vet had been summoned, and he seemed to work a sort of miracle, but there was a week at Egerton Crescent when she quickly deteriorated. Lehmann was frightened and distressed by her obvious failing. At 3.30 p.m. 'she unexpectedly asked, putting her paws up, to be lifted into her favourite armchair where she had not been for some time; then a few minutes later looked round at me, resting her chin on the arm in her sweet way which recalled all the past'. He knew she was dying, and called to Rassine to come downstairs. Her end was so gentle and natural that they could not believe she had died. The next day they took her to the cottage and buried her in a grave in the glade where white bluebells grew, on the further side of the lake. Alone with Rassine, Lehmann realised she had always been the 'third person'.

It seemed to have marked some sort of turning point, some realisation of what their togetherness meant. In the weeks that followed, as spring burst through into summer, 'Alex has been at his happiest; not worrying too much about career plans ... and gentler, in greater harmony with me, a change that seems to have started with Lottie's death.' What all those who shared Lehmann's bed in the years ahead could not realise was that Carlotta was proof of the unbreakable bonds that existed between him and, as Gore Vidal has described him, 'a ballet dancer called Alexis Racine [*sic*], an uncommonly plain, uncommonly effeminate man'.

Carlotta's death exposed Lehmann and Rassine as dependent on one another, forever linked by years of shared fortune and, increasingly, misfortune. Every proper feeling in Lehmann seemed coherent and satisfied by Carlotta, and we delude ourselves if we do not believe the regret Lehmann heaped on himself now. He wrote, 'I should have been a happier person if I had devoted myself to quiet work with her beside me – all the time.' Here was another acknowledgement that his life had always been too fragmented, too spent apart from where he mattered, and where others mattered to him. How could the men who came later know any of this, or begin to impinge on his life as Rassine had?

The wider world could better understand the loss of Lehmann's mother. In August she had a cyst removed at High Wycombe Hospital; a second operation followed on 5 September. The family gathered. Violet Hammersley dashed from the Isle of Wight to see her, a last act of friendship that moved Alice very much.

On 7 September Lehmann was with her, taking her the sweetest smelling red roses he could find. She had always said they awakened her sense of natural beauty more strongly than any other flower. He went out to buy her fruit and grapefruit juice. They talked of American politics, which had always fascinated her. He asked if she was in discomfort. 'Yes, I'm afraid I am, darling,' she said. 'I'm old, and I can't stand much more.' She lapsed into a coma. Rosamond, Helen and Beatrix took turns with him to sit with her through the night. With Rosamond he went back to Little Fieldhead early the next morning to wash and eat, but they had barely arrived when Helen telephoned with the news that Alice had died.

> It has all happened so suddenly, so much sooner than I expected, something I have dreaded all my life, the loss of someone I knew was always following everything I did with sympathy and love, to whom I could always turn, that I can hardly believe it. I feel much older; a new period begins in my life, when I am so strangely relieved of all financial problems for years, and at the same time am alone in an irreparable way, I don't understand it yet.

Little Fieldhead was left to Lehmann and sold in November. Alice had always supported him financially, investing her belief in him with substantial sums of money. Now, her death brought with it a new financial confidence, the feeling of being well-to-do, 'my own master in everything'. It was an inheritance confident in the belief that Alice had inspired 'more love and devotion in her children in her last years than ever before'.

There was only one smarting disappointment. Before her death, Alice had made Rosamond promise that she would never quarrel with her brother. It was a forlorn wish, for on the night of Alice's death Rosamond stayed with Lehmann at Beaconsfield and 'succeeded in wounding me deeply by an incredible failure of tact and imagination'. But he felt the lack of support from all his sisters – for all of whom he had a tremendous affection. Whatever financial benefits Alice's death brought him, it could not guarantee the family love he so craved. It may be that such love had to be looked for elsewhere, that his acceptance as an attractive and valuable person had to be proved without ceasing. Thus, perhaps, we bring into sharper focus the string of emotional attachments that were to distinguish the second half of the 1950s as particularly active for Lehmann.

\*

On 18 July 1956 a struggling playwright, keeping himself by selling Good Housekeeping cookery books, working in a theatre box-office, as a sculpture model at the Royal Academy and, at nights, in an espresso bar, visited Egerton Crescent for the first time. It was from him that Lehmann first learnt the homosexual connotation of the word 'bent'. Throughout the evening the young man became 'Dear Boy' and 'Ducky' and, eventually, was christened 'Chunky Ganymede'. Above Lehmann's bed, Chunky Ganymede saw a portrait of Alice as a young woman, a positioning that Lehmann maintained had no Freudian significance. Elsewhere there hung on the walls Duncan Grants, John Mintons, and a Cecil Beaton drawing of sailors. Lehmann said

> 'This is my test. Which one do you like best?' I chose the sailor whose mouth was covered by his hand – I'd like to see the mouth. His was another. 'My really perverse friends choose this' – pointing to a sinister figure in the background.

Jeremy Kingston was twenty-three. By the end of the month Lehmann was ecstatically recording 'Jeremy's explosion of extraordinary passion, that rings true all through ... and then, in the car, with his arm over my shoulder "I think it's natural, don't you, to want someone to unburden oneself to, I mean it helps to clear it all up, doesn't it?" ' By the autumn Kingston had been taken on as editorial assistant at the *London Magazine*, typing and filing letters: he went on to type several of Lehmann's books.

Kingston appeared the epitome of a perfect companion: the young man who would prove the idyllic secretary-lover; the boy with aspirations to a literary life; the young man learning at Lehmann's feet. It was never an easy role for the novice expected to play it. Always there was in the background the scowling presence of Rassine – Lehmann's consoling 'Oh, you don't need to worry about Alexis' was hardly reassuring. The affair had to be kept secret from the office staff, and there was the usual ritual, after sleeping with Lehmann, of having to move next door so that Screwie would not be suspicious in the morning.

There is no doubt that Lehmann was deeply in love with Kingston: 'I feel his deep affection a wonderful surprise gift to me, coming out of the blue as it seemed to.' Although their affair lasted no more than a year, their friendship mattered and endured, and they would remain intermittent lovers almost up to Lehmann's death. It was Kingston who educated Lehmann to appreciate the torsos in *Physique Pictorial*, to which the photographer Royale contributed studies. One day when Kingston called, Lehmann opened the door to him dressed only in lederhosen and a sheet of white cardboard on which he had written 'I am a Royale fantasy figure'.

Together, they travelled to Paris in the autumn of 1956, to Brussels in the spring of 1957 and, in June, to Austria and Vienna – a time of consolidation and maturity, lightened by their invention of 'Spender Spies' who tracked their every move, and a Baroness Gugulhupf, whose startling and amoral adventures followed them everywhere. The Baroness's arch-enemy, Kurt Von Steiermark, had sired five sons, the Mortadella boys, of startling beauty. There were fantasies, too, of naughty cabin boys being disciplined by brawny sea captains. For Lehmann there may have been the satisfaction that at last he had his own fictional world to rival Isherwood and Edward Upward's 'Mortmere' stories, but it seems likely that the Baroness and her retinue were born of the machinations around Lehmann's relationship with Kingston. By a diffuse arrangement, Kingston sent postcards to the office posted by a friend from Toulouse to allay any gossip that he and Lehmann might be holidaying together. It is unlikely that anyone at Egerton Crescent was fooled; Barbara, marking the days on her calendar against Lehmann's return, almost certainly was not.

In Vienna, Kingston was introduced to Sikyr, who remembered so much of his life with Lehmann, things of which, Lehmann realised sadly, he could himself recall little. Kingston suggested that Lehmann had been more important in Sikyr's life than Sikyr had been in Lehmann's. They stayed on the Attersee, a particularly evocative place for Lehmann, at a little hotel south of Zel, the same hotel to which he had come with Sikyr in 1935, perhaps even the same room. 'I am not merely Jeremy that you have known since 1956,' Kingston told him. 'I am also all the people you have ever known since 1932, and loved.'

Kingston proved the ideal partner who could co-exist beside Rassine, one with enough sympathy and kindness, and with a keen intelligence. At Christmas, Lehmann had bought Kingston a donkey jacket (Kingston gave him a pair of Harrods' cuff links). Walking back from the shop, Kingston looked at Lehmann in his blue overcoat, its collar upturned, his white hair and head, smiling, slightly held to one side, seeing for the moment 'a genial and elderly child'.

Being the intimate of a distinguished man of letters might have overwhelmed a more impressionable young man, but Kingston held up against the barrage of stories that Lehmann launched on him, the accumulated wisdom, the *bons mots*. Lehmann railed against 'all right' being spelt 'alright'. 'I've been fighting "alright" for twenty-five years,' he told Kingston. ' "Alright" will come into English literature over my dead body.' 'Fowler,' began Kingston. 'Rubbish' said Lehmann. 'Fowler,' Kingston insisted, 'declares that language is a living thing and absorbs ...' 'A reed blown by every Atlantic wind,' said Lehmann. Naturally, Kingston was expected to take on a dislike of Spender, 'that Shelley of the Depression', and was told how in the 1930s Lehmann and Isherwood had once considered murdering him. 'We had decided on *poison*, I think,' said Lehmann, smiling, 'and who is to say that we would not have been right?' Hilariously, he described Spender as having 'the mouth of a spider-eating orchid'.

\*

It is through Kingston, and the other ambitious young men who passed into the secreted world of the *London Magazine* office that we have some feeling for the place. Perhaps a plate of the preferred biscuits, sold as 'Arab Delights' (they had dates in them) but known in the office as 'Paul Bowles's Biscuits' has just been brought in. If it is noon, Lehmann is pouring out his usual whisky and ginger ale at the marble table in his room. Kingston is sitting at his desk, typing. Barbara sits at her desk, her special cushion beneath her, for she suffers from piles. She is perusing manuscripts, discarding some, passing others to Lehmann. He looks up from the page he is reading. 'Would you say that a harpsichord has deathless folds?' he asks. There is some tittering. 'You shouldn't laugh,' Kingston says. 'It's a daring image.' 'And I shouldn't blind myself to experimental work?' asks Lehmann. Barbara wants more clarification. What, she wants to know, does the author *mean*? 'He's writing about a sonata by Couperin,' Lehmann tells her. 'Deep within it, you'll be glad to know, glow the floral scars of wounded music and deceit. Rubbish!'

There is a flavour here of the closed climate of the *London Magazine*. James Michie, a member of the magazine's Advisory Board, earning no honorarium but expected to discover promising new writers, considered that Lehmann ran it 'quite rightly, as a monarchy rather than an oligarchy, but he could at least have made a pretence of there being other hands at the helm'.

David Hughes was one of the assistants who had to set up the office for the lunch parties held there, at which German champagne was served. Barbara and the staff would erect a screen across the room, behind which they worked while the party progressed. Hughes recalls the false geniality at such gatherings, 'full of guttural laughter and laughter that sometimes came too early. They seemed to give themselves the idea that they were frightfully amusing.'

Rosamond, of course, was frequently present at the lunch parties. Michie, remembering her as 'a person who wished to be treated as what she deemed herself to be', found her *grande-dame* demeanour wearisome. To Alan Ross, she seemed 'like a great meringue. One felt one could have put one's finger right through her.' Kingston recorded her departure from such a congregation in revealing detail.

> She kissed John at one end of an ellipse stretching from John to the door. And took a long time to move to the other end of the ellipse, clung to the door, *held* the door, that is, and leant away from it, said Goodbye to us all generally, then individually, then generally, went out, leant back, said Goodbye, and as I followed John Holloway and her down the stairs she smiled back talking vaguely of the fog with an expression that suggested her worry that she had not properly yet said Goodbye.

Barbara, secreted behind the screen, no doubt assumed her sentinel role when the last guest was gone and the screen folded away. Hughes saw in her greeting the art of being both off-putting and welcoming. There could be difficulties in the male environment. Once, after a few minutes absence from the office, she returned with her skirt tucked into her knickers. 'What is the meaning of this, Barbara?' Lehmann roared. Barbara was at a loss to know what he was talking about. 'Kindly leave the room at once and adjust your clothing,' Lehmann boomed. Suddenly conscious that she had inaccurately left the lavatory, Barbara plucked up her handbag and rushed from the office in tears.

Telephone calls were possible intrusions; the telephone was allowed to ring three times before Barbara and John picked it up simultaneously. Those wishing to speak to Lehmann would be told she was putting them through, but a long silence from Lehmann was her sign that he did not wish to speak to the caller. Hughes recalls the self-consciousness that overcame him when girlfriends rang him, for he knew Lehmann was listening in, and only relaxed when Lehmann became bored with what he heard and replaced his receiver with a tell-tale click. Access to the petty cash was strictly controlled, though not enough to prevent one of Lehmann's assistants from doing some minor embezzling. Once, when the milkman called, Barbara told Lehmann that, for the first time in years, he had cream cakes for sale. 'I think I could stand a round of them,' he told her.

Behind the minutiae of office life, one feels that, throughout his time at the *London Magazine*, Lehmann was doing little more than treading water. Hughes noticed, at its very beginning, the telling flaw. He felt that in asking T. S. Eliot to write the Foreword to the first issue Lehmann had set the wrong tone: 'it didn't give the magazine authority, it gave it pomposity'. Perhaps, after the industry and innovation of the *New Writing* years, such regression was not unexpected, but Hughes felt Lehmann was by now identifying with literature as 'a huge, immovable, incontrovertible part of culture; there was nothing progressive about it'. There was something, too, in the magazine's appearance and style that stopped anything startling happening: 'somehow the look of the page deadened a poem by Adrian Mitchell'. He no longer had his pulse on the changes that were taking root in literature.

Lehmann's journals for the period, too, are strewn with the conviction that the game is over, and Kingston tried to persuade him to give himself up to his own writing. Such a course might have been simpler than ploughing on with the *London Magazine*. By June 1955 the print run was around 10,500, a dramatic reduction from the 30,500 of the first issue (though only 23,500 had been sold). Sales were now hovering around 9 –10,000 copies. Gliding through Oxford Street in Cecil King's Rolls-Royce, Lehmann considered that King 'has no other criterion except circulation at all; in fact his standard of values is entirely vulgar, corrupted as he is by his appalling success'. What other criteria did Lehmann expect of a tycoon – indeed, '*The* Tycoon' as he called King? King had expected sales to settle at a higher figure after the expected drop from its initial reception, but he thought the content too safe, too placid. Too often the content did not aggravate discussion; Lehmann needed 'a young assistant of heavier calibre … to set the younger highbrows arguing more often'.

In this lack of controversy, Lehmann considered himself a victim rather than a perpetrator. As he told Lionel Fielden,

> … there is not nearly so much creative ferment as twenty years ago, even as ten years ago. One of the hopes of *The London Magazine* is that its very existence will in the end stir it up a bit. I have had to fill up gaps I am well aware of with stories from other countries … I am nevertheless certain I have published some excellent poems and stories by English writers as well as excellent critical studies and literary reminiscences.

He wished he had never begun the magazine when 'the creative impulse in literature was at a low ebb'; but it was 'something that had to be created because no one else was doing anything about it' even if the result was likely to be far below what he had achieved with *New Writing*. He was constantly looking for ways in which the magazine might survive King's withdrawal, while trying to inject each number with strength and stimulus.

In September 1955 Hughes told Lehmann that he was leaving. It was a blow, if not altogether unexpected; he felt Hughes had been growing passive towards the magazine, though he had stayed 'sweet-tempered and able … I have had the further feeling of him drawing away from me; and though I think he has had grim psychological struggles in his relations with his family, it has made me unhappy to sever a relationship that has failed.' Hughes was replaced by another young hopeful, Martin Seymour-Smith, but would remain a loyal friend to Lehmann.

\*

The publication in September of Lehmann's first volume of autobiography, *The Whispering Gallery*, was a welcome sign of hope in a troubled year. Its success was tremendous. Suddenly, at the age of forty-eight, it seemed that a reputation through the power of his own writing was within his grasp.

The first printing sold out in three days and for once there was a majority of praise from the critics. G. S. Fraser in the *Observer* predicted it would stand as 'a classical document for historians of the 1930's'. For Guy Ramsey in the *Daily Telegraph* 'It is the poet who thinks, the editor who writes: a lucky combination.' Rose Macaulay found in it 'intellectual ardour, zest in taking hold of life at many points, and a generous humanity', while Spender rather tortuously warned that 'The discerning reader may feel that what Mr Lehmann has to explore in himself is the core of a very deep loyalty to his friends, under the surface of his public career.' An especial pleasure was Connolly's eulogy in the *Sunday Times*, his old rival's appreciation of 'the bland, sane, cultivated intellectual but also the desperate, wayward and even ferocious sensibility of the author – and there, on the jacket, is the face I have grown up with, still kind and wise, if not seraphic, still with that hawk-like downward pounce – as of a man who has just received 860 francs for his pound'.

In fact, it was at the surface of Lehmann's public career that the book remained fixed, bereft as it was of any indication of an emotional dimension. There was the feeling for plants, for animals, for books, and friendship, as if all this would be enough for a life. Those wanting to know more had to read between the lines. Despite this, the accolades heaped on *The Whispering Gallery* were justified, for it is for many of its pages a finely shaped and controlled piece of lyrical writing, evoking, with what may sometimes seem unfashionable pedantry, images of beauty that halt the reader. The first hundred pages, dealing with his childhood and the magical properties of Fieldhead, the island of which Rudie had been the Prospero, are among the finest Lehmann was to write, done with a skill that still has a power to move the spirit.

The book's welcome clearly held out a promise of subsequent autobiographical volumes. At the *London Magazine*, Lehmann's plan was that Seymour-Smith and Thom Gunn, the poet whose talents had been spotted and very much nurtured by Lehmann, would effectively take over the running of the business, allowing Lehmann more time for his creative writing. So many plans seemed half-hearted, and Lehmann was anyway haunted by a suspicion that there was no longer a receptive middle-class readership 'who really care for literature as literature and part of life, for the creative imagination first wherever it comes from; that is where the action of the London Magazine should be, that is what I want always as before to stand for – and yet I feel sometimes as if I were rowing against a downward swirl of water'.

In March 1956 there was a fateful meeting with Cecil King who, not altogether happily, began the discussion with 'Well, now to your poor, weakling child.' King's decision was final. His support would cease at the end of June. For

Lehmann, it was an intensely miserable situation; he was rejected again by those who controlled his future.

It looked for a time as if Lehmann might have to sell either no. 31 or Lake Cottage in order to raise funds to continue, extreme measures that he might or might not have taken if no alternative had presented itself. Hope came from other sources. Ian Parsons suggested that Chatto and Windus might assume responsibility for the magazine, then Alan Pryce-Jones proposed that *The Times* might be willing to take it on. Both ideas fell through. It looked as if another end had been reached, and on 6 April Lehmann broke the news to Barbara and his current assistant James Wright. Barbara, true to form, burst into tears and cried 'What *again?*', behaving in 'a very unhelpful, complaining and lamenting manner' that deteriorated into lengthy sulks.

An apparently wholly altruistic benefactor was Robert Maxwell, 'The Captain', with whom Lehmann had lunch at the Pergamon Press offices in Fitzroy Square, where Maxwell had 'created an amazing organisation ... this strange attraction between us, mysterious and indefinable, worked again; he was obviously eager and reluctant to help at the same time; and finally said he'd see us through to the end of the year'. He told Maxwell, 'You are a swell, and I am very, very grateful.'

Even with Maxwell's promise, keeping the magazine afloat remained a struggle, and without the unexpected boost to his morale *The Whispering Gallery* had brought 'I would be deep down in the pit of melancholy, bitterness and despair'. As it was, he was at the end of his tether, needing so much 'to possess my own life'.

It was almost entirely through Lehmann's own efforts that the magazine not only survived King's disappearance but seemed to flourish after it. Subscriptions rose, advertising increased, and people assured Lehmann that the magazine was much better – though he believed it was no different to what it had been before. By the autumn he had at last managed to strike a deal with Heinemann who agreed to publish and distribute, an agreement that ensured the magazine's survival from the issue of January 1957. The magazine moved to new premises at 36 Soho Square, where two rooms were allocated, cramped but friendly, in a house also occupied by Rupert Hart-Davis's publishing firm. The move took place in November 1956, with Barbara looking reasonably thunderous throughout.

Once again, Lehmann had wrenched success from the claws of disaster, and could take pleasure from the knowledge that for the present he felt himself to be at last in unique control and ownership. It was Hughes who one day suggested that Lehmann might consider once again beginning a publishing house of his own. 'David, my dear' Lehmann replied, 'having been *betrayed* by Leonard Woolf – *abandoned* by Allan Lane – *kicked* out, *ruined* by Purnell, *stabbed* in the back – and *thrown* out by Cecil King – I think I've had enough. Wouldn't you say? Wouldn't you say so? Isn't it perhaps enough for one little life, for one little Eton schoolboy?'

\*

In August 1957 Jeremy Kingston fell in love with the Anglo-Indian actor Rashid Karapiet, soon christened by Lehmann 'the Pakistani Witch'. Kingston's life was changing. His first radio drama had been accepted; in November 1958 his play *No Concern of Mine* was staged at the Westminster Theatre. As well as Lehmann being a sometimes inconsiderate lover, Kingston realised 'Socrates and his pupil is an admirable relationship when the pupil is young. When he is adult and wishes his own life, and when Socrates pursues him for his body – no longer.'

Lehmann felt deeply insulted, though it seemed for a time he might withstand the developments: 'you have emerged with a free hand to be promiscuous and go with anyone you like and yet can keep our relationship on the same level' he told Kingston, agreeing that he should stay on as his secretary. In November Kingston told Lehmann everything was over between them, but the following May he turned once again to Lehmann for whom it was 'almost harrowing to be shown how much he missed and minded. Incredible though it seems, this may really portend a return.' Two weeks later Lehmann wrote that Kingston had indeed come back 'after deciding that he cannot live without me'. But it was not to be. In July, after 'a terrible sequence of days' Kingston finally resolved the break, plunging Lehmann into despair.

Lehmann thought it might be easy enough to find a replacement in his affections. It certainly seemed essential that he should do so. But it was not until the summer of 1959 that a relationship promised substantially to answer his needs. He wrote to the Belfast-born writer Kenneth Martin, aged nineteen, shortly after the publication of his second novel *Waiting for the Sky to Fall*, and they met a few days later for lunch.

To Martin, Lehmann seemed 'old, and prematurely aged, balding and over-weight, but also with the lofty, piercing, sometimes imperious manner of an elder statesman of letters. The role was partly assumed, covering a prickly sensitivity: John's glory days were over.' But the pattern was in place to be repeated, and a brief affair was begun, followed by a friendship that lasted until Martin moved to America in 1970. He was a different type to many of Lehmann's lovers: tall and slim, with legs that he seemed to manage with difficulty, a long chin and long, articulated hands, the whole carried off with an easy precocious grace. Precocity, for a boy who two years before, at seventeen, had published his first novel, *Aubade*, might have been expected.

Martin was never physically attracted to Lehmann, but was drawn by his fame and status and the literary benefits that might come of knowing him. The boy was immediately enfolded. In July he spent a lugubrious weekend at Lake Cottage, upsetting Lehmann by getting up early and settling down to some writing. An affronted Lehmann told him 'In twenty-five years of pederasty, I've never had to eat breakfast by myself.' Nevertheless, Martin was taken off to Vienna for a few days, all part of a courtship that seemed hasty: gifts, paintings, and the offer of a ring. 'I was told by others that he was in love with me, and I suppose I knew it,' Martin remembers, but again, the pattern repeating, Lehmann did not make the depth of his feeling known to the object of his devotion. Indeed, alone at the cottage with Martin, he could not stop talking about how he had been abandoned by Spencer and Kingston. 'Why did he let himself get stolen away by that Pakistani witch?' he asked. Hoping to stem the flow, Martin suggested it might have been because Kingston had fallen in love with Rashid Karapiet. After a silence, Lehmann said 'The world isn't as simple as that, Kenneth.'

Their temperaments were ill matched; the union of a nineteen-year-old boy on the threshold of a writing career, and a man of 52 at the centre and peak of the literary world was something to test the most resilient Socratic principle. Lehmann's demands on Martin, whose main intent was the writing of a third and fourth novel, were not alleviated by the fact that Lehmann 'drank steadily and heavily, particularly in the evening before, during and after dinner'. On one occasion when Martin was invited to Egerton Crescent for drinks, Lehmann agreed that he might use his telephone to read an article he had written for the *Daily Telegraph* to one of its editors. He had got a little way through this call when Lehmann began shouting 'This is not a public telephone! This is not a public telephone!' Embarrassed, Martin left hastily.

Lehmann's love, too, soon grew cold. By September 1959, he was regretting 'the disastrous mistake with Kenneth Martin'. Parting was assuaged in January when, trailing echoes of what had happened with Kingston, Martin apparently returned to his old place in his life 'vowing that he was a different person now, had learnt a great deal' followed by the final collapse a few weeks later. As always, the pain did not prevent Lehmann from continuing the friendship, the only writer from Martin's past who stayed faithful to that spirit. In this he was generous. Thirty years later, Martin understood that

> It would be hard to underestimate the psychic injury being gay then caused. The concept of mutuality between queer lovers was rare. Queer people used to say that the only queer relationships that seemed to work were those between partners who were very different: in age, class, race. I'm fairly certain it was at least partly because queers had internalised society's message and hated themselves: neither partner could feel that anyone like himself was lovable, so he loved somebody very different. John loved young Austrians, or a nineteen-year-old like me from a totally different class who had a lot of class anger in him. And when he didn't have love or the illusion of it he met some pretty chancy working class hustlers or near hustlers at the bars and clubs.

# 15

# Too Late For Anything But The Truth

'Thinking of the London Magazine,' Lehmann wrote in late August 1957, 'of the future and its release – perhaps: the only things worth doing are worth doing with panache and zeal.' Was Lehmann distancing himself from the magazine? There is surely the suspicion that he could not bring to it that zeal and panache that was necessary. Sonia Orwell wondered whether he should go on with it; was he losing money? (He was.) If it ceased, she told him that the losers would be the poets, both the established and the novice. 'You started nearly ninety per cent of the new poets off – then the Americans, and the foreign authors.'

Lunching at the White Tower with Alan Ross, Lehmann listened as Ross told him how, since the demise of John Lehmann Ltd., there seemed to be no publishing house that was at once exciting, international, avant-garde and classical. They discussed the uncertain future of the magazine. Ross suggested that his wife Jennifer might be able to offer financial assistance. Lehmann noted that 'Alan suddenly starting to write good poetry at last has so oddly and so delightfully transformed our relationship, – back to something near what it once was.' We may imagine Barbara's despair when in early 1958 Lehmann decided that if £10,000 was not forthcoming the London Magazine would close with the June issue. It may be that he hoped the offer would not materialise.

Lehmann longed for the freedom to write, to achieve his creative potential before it was too late, and was already convinced that if the magazine was to continue it must become a quarterly. He was unwell, listless, not eating, not sleeping. He underwent X-rays and medical tests, but nothing was diagnosed. He considered selling Egerton Crescent, which was becoming a drain on his resources. Throughout this period, he was reworking the memoirs of Jack Marlowe started so many years before, remarking that Marlowe had made two discoveries. 'First, that it is *ambiguity* that attracts him, and, through many variations, always has: never the 100% m.[masochist], nor the out-and-out S.[sadist]; but always when the former is modified by, strangely blended with traits of the f.[first] – whether of manner, temperament, complexion or feeling.' His second discovery was that

... a persistent central problem for him, as absorbing as problems of poetic creation, has been the creation, maintenance and continual refreshment of a harmonious social network, a web of friends, both intimate and less intimate, having many interests in common, tastes and judgement approximating; to bring them continually together to increase intimacy, to exchange ideas, to create an *accord* that is an atmosphere into which new people can be brought with their own contribution, and to profit from it. This is, he [Marlowe] thought, surely the essential of civilized society, against which the decay of the possibilities of private entertaining militates today.

A new period of disruption with Rosamond was begun when her daughter Sally died suddenly from poliomyelitis in June 1958. Lehmann was moved when Beatrix, who was staying at Lake Cottage, left at once to be with her sister, for relations between her and Rosamond had been decidedly cool. It was one of Lehmann's first thoughts that Sally had been the Lehmann to whom he would have left books and pictures. Her husband, Patrick (P. J.) Kavanagh, came to lunch a few days later. He would come to remember Lehmann as 'ludicrously pompous'. They talked of Sally's death, of Kavanagh's plans for the future, and Kavanagh told Lehmann how fond Sally had been of her uncle. Lehmann found it impossible to speak, and later, only with great difficulty, told Kavanagh that he had considered Sally his natural heir. To Kavanagh, it must have seemed that Lehmann was controlled and dispassionate; after he had left, Lehmann broke down.

Lehmann would never come to terms with Rosamond's reaction to Sally's death. She became, in Lehmann's eyes, a spiritualist, in a desperate and passionate attempt to bring her daughter back into a world that lived around her. It was an attitude with which Lehmann had not the slightest sympathy. A tragedy that might have brought them closer together, instead widened the dreadful gap between them.

*

In September 1958 the financial deal between Jennifer Ross and Lehmann that ensured the future of the *London Magazine* was signed. The office was moved to 22 Charing Cross Road. Despite the financial security that now supported the magazine, Lehmann only felt 'excessive strain, self-doubt, dissatisfaction'. Various crises still presented themselves, and were overcome. By October 1959 he was telling Ross 'how tired and nervously low I often felt, how much I thought I needed a rest after twenty-five years of editing and publishing, and time to travel and read and above all to write'.

It was not until 1961 that he finally relinquished control and editorship to Ross, who had considerately waited long until Lehmann made his own decision to stand aside. He told Ross that he wished his name to appear in each forthcoming issue as the magazine's Founding Editor, and was displeased when

Ross argued that the break between their regimes should be complete; he did not want Lehmann's name to hover over the future. Ross asked to see Lehmann's final foreword: 'It's very important, as I know you'll agree, that the change doesn't go off at half cock, and the change must be a real one, so that we substitute something new, rather than carry on in your own imposing shadow.' All this was eminently sensible, but could hardly have met with Lehmann's approval. In his parting words, Lehmann finally accepted that he was handing on his 'worn blue biro with confidence and curiosity'.

Lehmann recommended that Barbara was kept on at the magazine, and Ross, hoping she would decline his invitation, asked her if she would like to work for him. 'No, I would *not*,' she replied. She subsequently kept a photograph of Ross in which she stuck pins, and put a curse on his books whenever she came across them in shops. As her retirement gift Leonard Cooper recalls Lehmann presenting her with 'a very small plant in a very small pot', but there were other gifts, including a painting of Chelsea by John Minton, of whom she had been so fond. In the difficult years ahead, Lehmann offered to finance a foreign holiday for her. Whatever allegations of ingratitude are levelled at him, it must be to her that the final verdict is given.

My heart is so full ... You have been *very* good to me, dear John ... I shall always remember the look and smile you give me when you come in at the office door: I can't believe I shall never see that again; that I shall never go through the manuscripts with you again, or listen, as I used to do with so much fascination, to your comments on the 'Private Pile'.

It was a separation that ended Barbara's life. 'Who will look after you now?' she asked Lehmann. 'Who will feel for you, as I do, admire your absolute integrity, understand a little of your inner difficulties, love you and be proud to work for you, as I have done? I hope you will miss me, but not too much, not as I shall miss you. My dear, dear friend, don't forget me, don't turn me right out of your life. In losing my work for you, the greater part of me has been torn away.' For a time she worked, terrified of the ruling Norah Smallwood, at Chatto and Windus, where the hours were too long. Tired in mind and body, she told Lehmann 'The truth is that I ought never to work for anyone but you.' In 1965 she was taken on for £800 a year as a reader-editor at the Lutterworth Press where she was sternly rebuked for letting through a reference to a girl wearing jeans; only jodhpurs, her superior tersely informed her, would have been permissible ('fantastic, almost fanatic in 1966' she complained). She had hoped for better, for 'something that would retrieve my life, and make it seem less of a failure'. Charles Osborne, 'that faithful friend', who had joined the staff of the *London Magazine* in 1958 and stayed with Ross as assistant editor until 1966, helped her to a temporary job at the Arts Council in 1970, and the following year she worked for the conductor Neville Marriner.

Barbara continued to do occasional secretarial work for Lehmann, but he did not ask her to prepare the typescript of *In the Purely Pagan Sense;* neither did he ever give her a copy, and Lettice eventually had to buy one in a shop. When Lehmann asked Lettice what Barbara had thought of it she said 'You had better ask her yourself.' He never did. Up to the year of her death she made the annual pilgrimage to Capetanakis's grave at Norwood; at the last, she found it bare and defaced. One evening after washing up the dishes she turned to Lettice and said 'Why is it one ends up doing the things one likes least?'

In May 1981 Leonard and Barbara were planning to see a performance of *Elijah* at the Albert Hall, but she was feeling poorly that evening, and Lettice took her place. The next morning Lettice went into her room and found her dead. Lettice told Lehmann, 'I could not have written all my books without the sympathetic encouragement enhanced by the keen edge of her criticism.' She remembered that the weekend before Barbara died Lehmann constantly telephoned her on the slightest of pretexts, as if aware that something was wrong. 'I shall always really belong to you,' she had told him. If there was tragedy in their relationship it was Lehmann's, not Barbara's; one feels, again, that the depth of his feelings had not found its proper expression.

*

For both Lehmann and Barbara the passing of the *London Magazine* was a sort of death. From the day he left it, Lehmann never again mentioned it to Ross. The world of which he had been the centre seemed to be crumbling. He visited Henry Yorke, now very deaf, the muscles of his face gone, shuffling about his room like a shell-shock case. 'One must abdicate from sex, John, it's no good,' he murmured. Lehmann knew that Yorke had abdicated from everything, including literature. As Lehmann was leaving, Yorke insisted 'Don't have anything to do with what Alan is up to at the London Magazine. Pay no attention – you've done what you've done.' Lehmann noted 'I left with a despairing feeling of catastrophe and collapse.' Edith Sitwell, also in decline, could offer nothing more cheerful: she seemed transparent, she mumbled, she cried, Lehmann trying to comfort her as best he could.

Isherwood encouraged him to look forward when they discussed the problems of middle age 'and my finishing with publishing and editing, and the curious ambiguous feeling it left me with – half immense relief, half confusing loss'. He knew that what lay ahead was ' a really strenuous life ... even if in a different direction, never letting the intellectual muscles grow flabby'. The fact that the fabric of life around him was so changing was something beyond his control.

He and Plomer went to see *Beyond the Fringe*, laughing and crying until they sweated, as the holy cows of British life were one by one swept away. But they were shocked by a sketch about the war. 'Nothing I have ever seen,' said Plomer, 'has made me realise the gulf between our generation and the present generation than this. They have no idea what was narrowly missed. They don't want to'; decent, dependable Plomer was so often the friend with whom Lehmann could agree. Moving away from the laughter engendered by the four bright boys of intimate revue, Lehmann was aware that 'in spite of all that is so much better and healthier ... the promise of 1945 has been horribly lost in complacency, vulgarity and exploitation of all that's lowest'.

Of course, it was poetry that must now take him, consume him. He must not disappoint the expectation: 'All my life, it seemed to me as I thought about poetry, I have been waiting for the moments when the visible will roll up like a blind, and reveal the invisible, the truth.' He sought it in Greece, in Pompeii and Rome. Instead, his creativity had been poured into a second volume of autobiography, his account of the war years, an enterprise that had gone stale on him. *I Am My Brother* was published in 1960. John Betjeman congratulated him on a work that was 'an unconscious record of a most generous and perceptive man'; Charles Causley felt it to be 'deeply moving, courageous, of the utmost interest – and not only to those of us to whom your work as editor meant so much during the war'.

In 1962 his volume of family history, *Ancestors and Friends*, was generally welcomed, but was scarcely gripping. It seemed almost as if he might be consigned to a life of committee meetings, of writers' delegations, of the Alliance Française in Great Britain, of PEN gatherings, of congresses and inter-cultural literary conferences, at so many of which he was so often the dedicated delegate. At least such work brought just rewards, such a number of them that he qualified almost as a prophet without honour in his own country: Greece named him Officer, Gold Cross, Order of George I, in 1954 (and, in 1961, Commander of the Order); he was named Officier Légion d'Honneur in 1958; Grand Officier, Étoile Noire, 1960; was awarded the Prix du Rayonnement Française, 1961, and made Officier, Ordre des Arts et des Lettres in 1965. Brian McColgan remembers Lehmann's intense disappointment at receiving the CBE in 1964; his ambition was to have the Order of Merit. For six years from 1952 he had been Chairman for the British Council's Editorial Advisory Board, and from 1962-8 was a member of the Anglo-Greek Mixed Commission.

At the State Banquet for the visit to London of President De Gaulle in 1960, Lehmann was glad that he had been given the Étoile Noire 'to cover my nakedness'. Rassine helped him to dress for the occasion, fixing ribbons and medals. From one of the balconies of Buckingham Palace, Lehmann watched the fireworks exploding over London in De Gaulle's honour. There was a reception at Lancaster House, at which Lehmann was the co-host, and gave a speech in French. He noticed De Gaulle's lips moving, as if he was always about to prompt him. Official functions, at which Lehmann was the representative literary panjandrum, proliferated. In August 1963 he was in Moscow for a conference on the contemporary novel, as Vice-President of the European Community, a non-political society of writers formed a few years earlier by the Italians. William Golding and Angus Wilson appeared for the distinguished English novelist.

Unexpectedly, Lehmann found himself in Leningrad, one of a party invited to lunch at Nikita Khrushchev's glass and concrete villa bordering the sea at Pitsunda. Khrushchev delivered a homily on communist policy and capitalist reactions, 'forcible, intransigent party-line stuff (and in fact quite unacceptable to us), but spiced with sly digs and animal anecdotes (typically Russian we had decided some days before.) I had the impression that he was speaking as if the Chinese were breathing down his neck.' Khrushchev emphasised the danger of the personality cult, adding that Stalin had been 'an elephant'. 'I know I'm provoking you,' he told them, 'but it will give you a better appetite for lunch.' Jean-Paul Sartre and Simone de Beauvoir listened grimly as Khrushchev spoke of Hungary. He escorted them around his beach park, bordered with oleanders and hibiscus, and invited them to bathe. Lehmann declined. They dined lavishly on caviar, smoked salmon, Caucasian trout, roast duck, vodka and forty-year-old brandy. Wilson was furious with Lehmann, who had forgotten to tell him he was invited; he attacked Lehmann 'like a wildcat, hysterically'. In Moscow, Lehmann noticed that for the Russians the phenomenon of strip-tease had become a symbol of decadent western culture, and oddly enough got mixed up with Proust, Joyce and Kafka in some of the old guard speeches defending socialist realism. Not surprisingly, Lehmann recorded having to endure long stretches of paralysing boredom.

In June Lehmann was in Vienna, perhaps the place most likely to awaken in his mind questions that had never satisfactorily been answered. '1963 – What is that meaning to me?' he wondered.

> Partly, of course, the recognition that I am no longer young, that the shadow of the end of my life should soon begin to fall on me. But it also means, I believe, that I am getting closer to the point where I can penetrate the mysteries; when reflection and experience provide – begin to provide – a far richer opportunity for this than ever before; in a new period in which I am without designs on the world. Coming back to Vienna, I am aware, as never before, of the obscure gap in my life, which now seems so far away as to be almost mythical.

Still the stress in Lehmann's sexual life would not diminish. There seems always to have been a number of young men in various stages of withdrawal from it, just as others whose names would feature throughout many of Lehmann's journals were arriving. The circles they moved in may well have been those of the rough trade, and they certainly brought with them problems that Lehmann could well have done without, but they often had characteristics that were, if not altogether endearing, characterful.

One such was Dennis Sturrey, a Cockney who had had the childhood of a

London street urchin and kept a house in Battersea in which at various times he harboured any number of waifs and strays. An epileptic and a heavy drinker, Sturrey (christened by Lehmann 'Pussycat'), worked as a builder, and was good at what he did. He also had charm, and when at Lake Cottage he might as well be found cleaning the drains or fixing a wall as sleeping with his employer. Lehmann was struck by 'the extraordinary *goodness* of his nature, his generosity, his sweetness of temper, his wish to think the best of everyone'. They were in the South of France together for six days in spring 1959, six days of unclouded happiness during which Sturrey was tender, anxious for Lehmann's enjoyment, and passionate that Lehmann should read Dickens to him at night until he fell asleep.

There seems to have been a sort of goodbye to Sturrey in June 1959, at a picnic supper they spent together, during which Lehmann presented him with the latest electric drill, complete with its attachments. Sturrey was delighted, and immediately began to drill holes in pieces of wood and to sand surfaces. 'We'll always be muckers, John,' he said, and Lehmann wanted it to be so. 'I shall not, cannot let go entirely' Lehmann realised, and indeed he did not, for their sexual friendship lasted many more years. By October Lehmann suspected the intensity of their affair was over. The passionate concern he felt for Sturrey is obvious: 'The way things have gone wrong again and again since his household broke up has upset me deeply; and since I see no hope of him changing – or even perhaps understanding how, as my feeling for him has grown, my misery at his promiscuity has become uncontrollable – I must try to break with him. I shall go to pieces if I don't.'

Of more importance in Lehmann's life was Douglas Stoker, born and raised in Glasgow, and a sexual partner, friend and employee of Lehmann's for thirty years. He was ten when his father, a consultant dental surgeon, died, leaving the family in financial difficulties. It was Douglas, as the eldest of two sons, who was expected to protect and maintain the family. The pressure was too much for him, and at seventeen he ran away from home.

Dark-haired, physically attractive, with an athletic build, Stoker was soon living, as his partner Bruce Cruickshank recalls, 'to all purposes as a rent-boy. He spread himself around. He had a couple of rooms in Eaton Square where he was kept by various wealthy men in the manner to which he became accustomed.' Stoker was highly intelligent, a voracious reader, a young man who might have achieved much. His bouts of heavy drinking disfigured his personality. He might not drink for weeks, but would then consume vast amounts of alcohol over a very short period, an act of self-destruction that would transform his personality. Cruickshank, an Australian who met Stoker in a Soho gay bar at the beginning of the 1960s, recalls that he would collapse on the floor of the Spartan Club from too much alcohol. Stoker had never had what might be termed a proper job, having been employed, when the need arose, for domestic duties; thus it was that he began 'dusting The Lehmann's ornaments' (he always referred to 'The Lehmann') – a task eventually handed on to a friend of Stoker's, Brian McColgan, whose relationship with Lehmann was platonic.

As well as the twice or thrice weekly visits to dust The Lehmann's ornaments, Stoker would have dinner with Lehmann one evening a week. Up to a few years before Lehmann's death, their relationship was sexual. It was Stoker, too, who accompanied Lehmann on much of his foreign travel. On the edge of the circle, Cruickshank said that

> Douglas felt there was a kudos in having a friendship with John. It brought him into contact with Auden and Isherwood and such people. But my impression was that John liked the kudos of it too. There was something slightly insecure about John. He felt that identifying with these people who had established themselves in the literary world would give him a certain status, and in this there was a parallel between John and Douglas. In a way, Douglas only lived for John when he was with him; it was as though John had no concept of people having a life of their own beyond his knowledge of them. It seemed to me that John had no idea how other people functioned.

In 1963, Stoker was taken by Lehmann to Vienna. In his journal Lehmann wrote

> Douglas: I could say of him that his gift has been to adapt himself to the needs of those he has chosen as his lovers; but he has not chosen them for that reason – for the reason of being able to adapt himself – but rather because of an intellectual and spiritual need in himself to associate himself with those who are questioning or exploring philosophically or poetically. All the more tragic, then, that his instability leads him to these repeated, self-destructive fugues; which even though I now understand them remain, partly at least, mysterious.

Eighteen months after their meeting, Stoker and Cruickshank began living together, at a flat off the Old Brompton Road, in the gloomy purlieu of Cornwall Gardens. It is perhaps this act that Lehmann refers to when he registers his 'baffled misery about Douglas'. The oppressive air of Cornwall Gardens was accentuated by having as one of its residents the novelist Ivy Compton-Burnett, whose rooms were filled with flowers that stood in vases on the floor because, according to Lettice Cooper, 'She thought one could see them much better like that. The whole effect was rather funereal.' And Colin Spencer, after paying several visits to Dame Ivy, told Lehmann that she always wore the same frock, and suspected that she had several copies of the same design.

Stoker was now ideally placed to make frequent excursions to Lehmann, for on 1 October 1964 Lehmann moved into the first-floor flat, no. 4, at 85

Cornwall Gardens. The move from Egerton Crescent, for the moment rented and subsequently sold for a mere £13,800, marked a change in Lehmann's life as assuredly as had the move to Egerton Crescent at the very end of the war. It brought with it an acknowledgement that his world was growing smaller. The accommodation at Cornwall Gardens was not particularly generous; not generous enough, apparently, for Rassine to be permanently housed there. We have no evidence of it, but it is possible that Lehmann simply told Rassine he must now find a home of his own. Beatrix was appalled, and offered to house him. Rassine was also assisted by Nadia Nerina and her husband, and eventually set up in a flat at Thurloe Place, conveniently close to Cornwall Gardens.

For Lehmann, the salon of Egerton Crescent became a thing of the past. The flat at Cornwall Gardens seemed to Cruickshank to reek of 'a tacky grandeur. Everything was very 1950s, coral red walls, deep greens. It was somehow disappointing, all rather run down and seedy.' Pamela Foster, taken there by Rassine in the late 1980s, found the atmosphere overbearing, with Lehmann at its centre, almost as if a stage set had been erected around him. The world that surrounded him there seemed in need of modernisation, as if the remnants of a past existence had been pushed into a smaller space.

The living room was L-shaped, dominated by his massive desk, behind which stood photographs of Odette Massigli and of Rassine in a mid-air splits. The sofa was yellow and tattered, with a coffee table in front of the fireplace. There was a chest of drawers, many cupboards filled with papers of long ago. The small dining table was round and wobbled. At the side of his armchair was a drinks table on which stood the gathered remnants of special offer gin and vodka and the bitter lemon with which he would top up guests' glasses. There was, already, the air of decay, a recognition that life was beginning to contract.

*

And still there was work to be done. The penetration of the mysteries might yet be accomplished through poetry, specifically through the prose poem 'Christ the Hunter'. Originally heard on the Third Programme in October 1964, 'Christ the Hunter' was intended to be heard rather than read. Conceived as poetry, it was a bringing together of 'meditations, diary entries, imaginary letters or monologues addressed to an intimate friend, dreams, invocations, resolutions, talkings to myself in the early morning, evocations of legend or history, notes towards a definition of belief, confessions'; in effect 'an attempt to write autobiography in a new way, the spiritual history of a brief space of months between spring and summer at a certain crucial point in the author's life'.

The title signalled no conversion to Christianity, for Lehmann's Christ is conqueror, musician, Orpheus, young Alexander, real in virility, the character of his being pagan as well as spiritual. This is a Christ who knows of sexuality, who expresses it in movement and intent, who uses his sexuality and rejoices in it. It is this Christ that strides through a 37 page prose poem that is Lehmann's most ambitious work and, somehow, one of his finest. That success does not come from his at last finding a unique manner of poetical expression, or a particularly individual voice; it cannot be said that finally Lehmann had won the battle he had fought with poetry.

It may be that 'Christ the Hunter' is little more than a rag-bag, jottings from the commonplace book of a philosophically muddled existence, stirrings of emotional hyperbole washed up with heroic classicism, but it has other functions. It is confessional as much as poem. Predominantly, this may be because we sense that its pages come out of an almost savage sense of regret and failure – though their purpose, according to Lehmann, is a rekindling of meaning in middle age, thoughts on heaven, poetry and love, carnal and divine.

It is the stated striving for renewal that sits at the core, and we await revelations. These will not come without reference to the ancient mysteries, against which Lehmann constantly measures the power of his own, modern, feeling, recognising the tragedy of his time against the ever widening separation between act and consequence. Lehmann is burdened by the belief that self-contentedness is not enough, that there is nothing fulfilling in emotional self-sufficiency: there must be dependence. Without questioning, he assumes that 'The meaning of life is in relationships. And every relationship that partakes of love is good.' The disappointment that must come with such happiness is not attempted; perhaps his undeniable knowledge of failure is too painful to contemplate, perhaps at last he accepts the likelihood of failure as a price to be paid. This, anyway, is the poetry of hope, of striving for perfection, of looking, surging forward with the virile, firm-thighed Christ.

Of course, Lehmann's ideal setting is a landscape of poetry, there being no suggestion that these vistas have radically altered since the beauty of Fieldhead revealed itself in his childhood. Now, the garden is no longer named, but remains at the centre of his imagination, and he is harnessed to it as its poet. Then we are at Alum Bay, beachcombing through days long gone, in the dimension of a resolutely pagan dream through which is seen

> ... the tip of a phallus in the moment of orgasm, huge genitals attached to a small body without head or legs, lips pressed between gigantic breasts, acts of the lewdest copulation.

Consciously, he unloads the furniture of a lifetime, cries out against cruelty to humankind and animal experimentation (he and Barbara had been obsessed with the horror of the dog sent into orbit in the Sputnik), the imprisonment of homosexuals, Vietnam, and the loss of friendship. Here is remembered Capetanakis, 'the poet the music of whose words was the refutation of his philosophy without hope', Gordon Hamilton and John Minton, bearing witness to 'the vision of a world remade ... in the image of the love of mother and son, nature and man, and of brother with brother, beyond the cold puritanism of our northern shores'.

Persistently compassionate, 'Christ the Hunter' pulls us back to its inspiration, Lehmann's visit to an early Christian tomb at Ostia in Rome, on whose walls is a bas-relief of Christ, but a Christ unheard of in the pulpits of England, a boy invigorated by searching, pulsing ahead, unfettered by apparent divinity or sacredness, borne up by youth, new limbs, flowing hair, unafraid or unconscious of that physical perfection that makes him desirable not only as symbol but object:

> He is that Christ who summons to new spiritual endeavour, whose challenge is to the established values of a world without vision, who calls us all, not to repentance but to thinking in a revolutionary way beyond the categories of conventional right or wrong, the master of paradox, the Hunter of living truth through the forests of seeming.

Thus does Lehmann's boundless Christ leap on in pursuit of truths, just as Adonis once pursued wild boar. He brings with him Orpheus and Eurydice; Ganymede ('the little bitch'), a sort of mythological rent-boy; Mary of Magdala in an amalgam with Mary of Bethany, as purity and prostituted love become equal in the presence of the death of God's son. Here, there can be no distinction between sexual and spiritual feeling. All is made one.

Renewal, restatement, restoration: all have their place in 'Christ the Hunter'. Rebirth can only come from a recognition of a flawed past, a life that is seen as having been of dubious worth, and is finished.

> I am making a bonfire in my own life too, and resolve to throw on it all the dead rubbish of a career that is over … Symbolically, I throw on the fire all the ill-typed, ill-written manuscripts I shall never have to read any more, and the falsely modest letters from their authors who ought never to have become literate …
>
> And I fill my wheelbarrow with shoddy evasions and pretences about human relations, the cultivation of valuable acquaintances and the neglect of friends in the blood, attitudes of respectability and certificates of approval from the establishment, and tip them on to the smoking pile.
>
> What a glorious blaze! The robin hops round, hoping to catch insects that crawl out of the flames.
>
> It is too late for anything but the truth.

Gone, too, is the possibility of Vienna and Toni, as the oracle river whispers its assurance that its waters 'are mixed with the waters of your childhood river for ever in your veins, but you will never come back to where you were. What you thought, what you hoped, what you loved, the causes and the people your heart once beat faster for are gone …The past is utterly the past.' Such intense valediction cannot be ignored, nor Lehmann's consciousness of the heart's misunderstandings.

A pot boiling over, 'Christ the Hunter' can barely contain its outbursts of feeling, and in the process Lehmann simply ploughs on, having no thought, it seems, of form, no regard of a sharper discipline. Christopher Levenson has criticised the inconsistency of its narrative and its lack of philosophical cohesion, noting that 'however moving or thought-provoking some of these passages are, it is difficult to see how their divergences cohere into a work of art, let alone a work of poetry'.

Yet, by its proclaimed nature, 'Christ the Hunter' exists outside either genre, branded by self-expression, allowed through experiment, another, new kind of autobiography, more honest and painful that any that had come before from Lehmann's pen. Any pain is gone at the poem's conclusion, when, unnamed but obvious, we are again at Fieldhead and, in a newer age, Lake Cottage, places reminding Lehmann that he is the patient spider poet. The hoped for renewal, it seems, is made stronger by a reunion with childhood obsession; now, the swans fly up at early morning, from the surface of the lake into the light of the sun, beating wings that might, that must, belong to angels.

If it was indeed the time for the truth, the truth seemed old. As we leave behind the varied beauties, extravagances, overstatements and half-baked relig-ions of 'Christ the Hunter', we must acknowledge that it did nothing to advance Lehmann's reputation as poet.

Lehmann seemed now to write almost as much autobiography as poetry. When his third volume, *The Ample Proposition,* appeared in 1966, its author had already moved into the shadows of the literary world. In every sense, the book seemed to be saluting something that was forever over.

The book's reception suggested that what he had to say was of little interest. Peter Quennell gently described Lehmann as 'a critic who will never become a cynic' and the book as 'almost alarmingly good-natured'. Geoffrey Grigson, that great enemy of Edith Sitwell, was scathing. Lehmann had been responsible for 'several literary ventures which in their time seemed to me no more than tepid'. *New Soundings* had 'coincided with the beginnings of the plunge of the Third Programme years ago into mediocrity'. If only, he complained, the book had vision, and 'if only *living* appeared under his touch, just a little of it'. Lehmann's reputation was fading; when it was not underrated it was ignored.

Part IV

# OLD FLAMES

# 16

# The Minor Cultural Monument

Early in 1969, Rex Warner, then a professor at the University of Connecticut at Storrs in New England, invited Lehmann to take part in a seminar about English writers in the thirties. Spender, too, was in America on a lecture tour, and joined them. Spender met Lehmann in New York and drove him to Storrs where they took part in a television discussion.

Lehmann was irritated by Spender's account of what he had done for students in Paris and Prague, 'but I saw that it didn't matter all that much to our audience: Americans treat Stephen as a *phenomenon*, not as a dispenser of wisdom, and therefore his quirks and irrelevancies fascinate them'. To Lehmann's evident satisfaction, Spender then misquoted Auden to cries of dismay from the audience. Lehmann and Warner had to leave early; Spender, left alone, told the gathering 'I didn't like to say this when Professor Warner and Mr Lehmann were here, but the Thirties were really a very *frivolous* decade.' Lehmann feigned amusement when told of Spender's coy admission, but, describing Spender's behaviour at Storrs to Connolly, Lehmann told him that Spender had been in 'an extraordinary feverish state'. Connolly was less sure. 'He was in an erotic frenzy, of course,' Connolly said. 'Instead of saying "Is there a Rothschild in the house?" as he used to, he probably said "Is there a queer student in the house? If so will he step outside." '

Lehmann's first lecture delivered to a room of American undergraduates went well, and he was immediately impressed by their stillness and attention. Then it was to Boston, always a place that filled him with a sense of the connections and reputation the Lehmanns had made there, where he met with his American publisher, William Abrahams. They drove out to the coast of Duxbury Bay, opposite Plymouth, to see John Malcolm Brinnin and his friend Bill Reed in their little clapboard house. 'It was like a home-coming for me, and touched deep springs. I could have cried when I thought of the jerry-built ugliness of so much of the English south coast.'

From Boston, he flew to Austin. A Texan called Harry Ransom had persuaded the trustees of the hugely wealthy University of Texas at Austin to found a Humanities Research Center, which was given Ransom's name. Five years earlier, Lehmann had sold a wealth of papers from *New Writing* to the Center, and now took the opportunity to visit it. He was lauded and given every courtesy, the prophet without honour in his own country hailed again, a survivor from another place and age.

Simply to see the respect and care awarded the papers of his life's work moved

Lehmann tremendously. In this temporary exile, he had been given back a worth – one that was keenly deserved. Two years before, he had written of 'an acute attack of the feeling that so often oppresses me now; that I am absolutely *nothing*, that anything I have ever done has been stripped off me, has totally disappeared, and I am naked – naked and empty.' He sat open-mouthed in the office of the Center's head, Warren Roberts, where there was furniture that had once belonged to Evelyn Waugh. Shown around the Center, he felt 'bewildered, almost entirely posthumous, and had to control an impulse to run away'.

Among those he met was a young man, Morris Fry, who for months had been cataloguing the Lehmann material, and who now told Lehmann of his admiration for 'Christ the Hunter'. Lehmann was immediately attracted; they had dinner together and 'we became more intimate, and a stronger and stronger sympathy developed between us ... I began to feel that he knows more about my life and activities than I can remember myself.' There was the Texas spring, the flowers, the mocking birds, the cardinal birds, a whole new collection of animals and plants that might bewitch his surroundings.

The possibility of Lehmann cementing all these new associations came when Roberts suggested that he might like to take up a visiting professorship. At last, another hint of revival seemed in the air. From Texas, Lehmann flew to Santa Monica to see Isherwood and his partner, Don Bachardy, finding it 'marvellously easy to pick up the old relationship ... perhaps better than ever before, because in this last lap of our lives I can allow no tension to come between us, and we seem to have even more to say to one another. We talk and talk and joke and fantasticate, more happily than ever, with Don beside us.' By Christmas, the offer of a visiting professorship at Austin for the Spring Semester had been made. Final terms were agreed in January 1970, with a fee of $14,000, and, unexpectedly, an invitation to fulfil the same post at San Diego University in the Fall of 1970, for $15,000. Rassine was marvellously enthusiastic and supportive, even if Lehmann's prolonged absences from London and Three Bridges brought with them more responsibility.

Lehmann was back in Austin by early February, supported on his arrival by Roberts and other personnel from the Harry Ransom: Tom Cranfill, Frank Lyell and the attentive Fry. Almost before his suitcase was unpacked, Lehmann was becoming fixed on Fry who 'has been incredible: in his sweetness, loyalty, devotion, passion. Something is happening to me that hasn't happened for years ... An almost bewilderingly impatient ardour.' Unexpectedly, Lehmann, in his sixties, had been plunged into a relationship that made heavy demands on his athleticism.

More prosaically, Lehmann rather learned the craft of professorship as he went along, and came to appreciate Rex Warner's advice that he must put forward an abstruse and intellectual-sounding project, preferably called Inter-Cultural Media Relationships. Lehmann was not unaware of the niceties of the academic profession, noting that 'the more gas and intellectual mumbo-jumbo there is in a theme, the better it pleases'; one of the students' 'projects' was recognised as 'a very skilfully cooked dish of *balls*'. In fact, Lehmann had a real empathy with the students, though he was a little shamefaced to realise he could remember the names of all the males, and not one of the females.

Inevitably, he was physically attracted to many of the boys he taught, and there is about his concern for them something of the passion he felt for the fate of the young men in the services throughout the war. In personal tutorials, they poured out their problems to him, and he, who had always flourished within the Socratic relationship, flourished anew, on what may have been countless occasions, with an untold number of handsome students. Barry, who wanted to be a golf professional, raved about the Beatles, and Lehmann, who saw the boy's quick intelligence, persuaded him to begin reading Isherwood. Another, Andrew, was preparing a dissertation on Edith Sitwell, no doubt assisted by Lehmann's portmanteau biography of the Sitwells, *A Nest of Tigers*, published the previous year. It had pleased Osbert Sitwell, and irritated Sacheverell Sitwell, who found the book 'idiotic' and Lehmann 'wooden-headed and humourless'; furthermore, Sacheverell pouted, he felt nothing like a tiger. Lehmann was fascinated by Andrew's insights, by the way his thoughts rebuked English criticism of Edith's poetry. He was worried only that an interest in the occult would destroy the boy's potential.

And, everywhere, there was Morris Fry. He drove Lehmann out to Llano, his birthplace, where an aunt had a neglected, rather mysterious house, and they stayed the night. Lehmann flew to Houston where he lectured on 'Working with Virginia Woolf', where 'a young man came in and looked at me with a kind of rapt enthralment out of blazing blue eyes' but 'alas, the young man vanished'. But it was Fry, fondly titled 'Chick', who filled Lehmann's consciousness, although 'Like all supremely happy love affairs, my love with Chick is almost impossible to chronicle. He said to me, "You are the complete sexual being. I have never known anyone like you." And "I am a completely different person since you arrived in Texas. I am transformed to happiness and confidence." He, for his part, has given me something I thought long beyond my reach.'

With brilliant success, Lehmann yet again was reinventing himself, but across this idyll as across the others that had presented themselves in such profusion through the years before there was the fact of his Englishness, the furniture of sixty years. These were times of a recurring dream, in which he returned to Eton, not young but white-haired, trying to reach the Master in College, with a confusion of boys running about. Within the dream, too, was a piece of lost luggage, which had been concealed, possibly by Beatrix, in a shed beyond the College's walls. He had dreamed of lost luggage before, dreams that sometimes turned to nightmares where his clothes and books were missing. The day before one of the luggage dreams he recalled feeling 'that I was no one, that everything had gone. Where was my career, where were my achievements, my reputation?'

Somewhere between reality and dream, he thought often of the cottage and Rassine, but when he returned to England in March for a week his nostalgia was for Austin, 'chiefly I think because of Chick', and his daily walks along University Avenue through the gambolling poppies, wisteria and roses to the fountains and shady lanes among which the English building lay hidden. When he returned to Austin it was to a welcome reception of his lectures and the comfort of new friends, but among the busyness of it all he was struck by an incongruity: 'What am I doing here? Who are these people who surround me, who act so strangely, talk so strangely? How can I stand anything so remote from my own world in which I have lived my life?'

In fact, Lehmann coped as he had always coped, with the struggle to establish reputation anew; no matter that so much of the fresh reputation was based on his past, on Bloomsbury and the writers of the thirties and the importance, not of himself, but of those with whom he had associated. The tensions would not lessen.

\*

On a day of blinding sunlight and thickly hot air, Chick drove Lehmann on the road to Llano, their way strewn with all kinds of wild flowers. Chick tried to find a road that ran beside Lake Travic, and was confused. Lehmann insisted they stopped by a stream. Chick relaxed, and Lehmann took photographs of him. Chick told him how his life was changing, and how important a part Lehmann was playing in the process. When they got back to Austin the sky exploded 'and then the full rain, satisfying and releasing'. The world awaited the splashdown of Apollo 13.

When he lectured at New Orleans in May, the students outside the hall were burning effigies of President Nixon, and 'I had the feeling that I was in a very strange dream'. Lehmann was sympathetic to the demonstrating students, thinking some of the Faculty's attitudes hysterical and fatuous; he saw that the Vietnam War was a bog that was turning into a quicksand. By the end of the year he was convinced that young Americans were 'bitter, unsatisfied, disaffected from the way things are run, this huge unsettled country, that has so little to anchor it to life ... And then I wonder whether it hasn't been like that for generations; whether the frightening divisions of today are perhaps another face of the frightening divisions of yesterday.'

Lehmann was to find that his graduate pupils were uninterested in any British writers they did not already consider to be 'great'. He eventually got them to admire Henry Green and Elizabeth Bowen, 'but at what cost in effort'. The struggle was all uphill, it seemed, and at every turn his consciousness of the in-fighting of the administrators.

Inevitably, his relationship with Chick became troubled, their meetings increasingly 'riddled with bitterness and disagreement'. In a letter that was not sent, Lehmann wrote that

> I just don't believe you can cease to be certain that I have from the beginning wanted nothing more than to show my love, my concern and my faith in you. In fact, that has, at bottom, been my whole life in Austin … I felt from the beginning that our relationship was balanced on three poles: your quite wonderful belief in and admiration for me (dangerous for me of course); my conviction that you have in you the seeds of some marvellous work, with all your gifts of intelligence and perception and empathy; and the passion of our feeling for one another. Please, please don't yield to the impulse of throwing it all away. You may – you will – have many lovers in your life; but as you have often told me you have never had one so understanding or so devotedly passionate in the past, think that perhaps you will never find one so devoted in the future.

How could Chick have known that, for Lehmann, the old pattern had begun its work? The perfection of love, and violence, the repeated sequence, the canker needing expression.

That autumn, Lehmann would reflect that 'I do not think I remembered often enough that in spite of his intelligence, sensitivity and imagination, I must often have seemed to him a strange being from another world, a puzzling cosmopolitan sophisticate.' For the present, there was restoration before Lehmann left for England. They drove, again, to Llano. By a stream they picked wildflowers, black-eyed susan, verbena, tiny hollyhocks and daisies. An armadillo sat on its haunches and stared at him. There were cardinal birds and, everywhere, butterflies of black and midnight blue.

In September 1970, Lehmann spent a few days with Chick in Austin, and again they visited the aunt's home in Llano, a house where Lehmann imagined he was an actor in a French film, before flying to San Diego for the Fall Semester. The campus at San Diego was even more chaotic and geographically confusing than at Austin, and the weather baking hot, though dry. He was found an apartment within ten minutes walk from the campus, a short distance but one that was already beginning to tax his strength. He plunged immediately into discussions about Virginia, the Hogarth Press and all of Bloomsbury. He was to deliver courses on Nonsense (embracing the work of Lewis Carroll and Edward Lear) and the Novel of Poetry and Symbolism. From his window he could see 'young Californians passing, tall, lithe, rangy, with straight limbs, golden locks and sun-burnt bodies: their beauty is staggering. This is the ideal type, that stands out from the many others, the type that my selective eye chooses' (even though he was startled to see many a dark root beneath those golden locks).

In San Diego Lehmann found the same attentive, genuinely interested students he had experienced at Austin. Through their expectation he gained confidence as a tutor. He read them comedy scenes from Henry Green's *Loving*, and 'they were truly in fits of laughter by the end'. But Lehmann could not warm to San Diego as he had to Austin; he found the place claustrophobic and the weather boring, the endless heat of day and the cold nights. He felt he had rather been abandoned to it all, in a way that he had not in Austin. Chick provided a welcome distraction when he came for four days, a happy, indeed blissful, reunion. Together, they prepared a goulash when Isherwood and Bachardy came from Santa Monica.

In late November, he stayed with Isherwood *en route* to lecturing at Berkeley University, and they visited Elsa Lanchester, 'very heavy in torso', who had an unnerving habit of appearing uninvited through hedges. Bachardy sketched him, later expressing irritation that Lehmann had not taken it seriously, refusing to keep still. Isherwood and Lehmann discussed E. M. Forster and the imminent publication of his novel about homosexuality, *Maurice*, which Forster had shown Lehmann in the early fifties. Looking at books about Forster, Isherwood said, 'Of course all those books have got to be re-written. Unless you start with the fact that Morgan was homosexual, nothing's any good at all.' The following day they drove to Santa Barbara to see more of Isherwood's gay friends. Bachardy, speeding demon-like along the crowded freeways, drove him to Los Angeles airport.

Lehmann stayed at Palo Alto in a flat shared by William Abrahams and Peter Stansky, where they spoke of the difficulties they were encountering with his ex-employee, Sonia Orwell: she had closed the Orwell archive to them, and was refusing their use of quotations for their forthcoming book. Abrahams launched a tirade against the disastrous attitude of widows to the archives of famous authors. The lecture went well, after which there was no time to sample San Francisco's homosexual underworld. Back at San Diego, there was Mark, who was invited for gin and tonics one morning. Mark was attractive and happily married, and had been invited to explain the mysteries of the Tarot to Lehmann, but Lehmann was much more interested in the emotional charge of their meeting, for 'this morning an extraordinary, deep, intuitive understanding seemed to declare itself between us, as if we were already lovers. A most disturbing, and in some ways thrilling experience. Perhaps I have been blind all the time to what has been there, right in front of my nose.' A few days later, Lehmann was being romanced by Alan Searle, Somerset Maugham's secretary, who became drunk and amorous when they met in Los Angeles to discuss the complexities of the Maugham estate.

He was back at Austin in January 1971, reunited with Chick, who was now working for the journal *Arion*, but in indifferent health. There were other young men, including Frank Lyell from the Center, who shared Lehmann's bed. And there was Frank Oatman, a graduate student in Lehmann's seminar in the spring of 1970 and a cousin of President Lyndon Johnson, who swiftly moved to the forefront of Lehmann's American life. Through Oatman, whose family welcomed Lehmann into their home, he was taken into spheres of Texan and American society he would not otherwise have known.

One day in the spring of 1971, Oatman drove him out to a canyon filled with cypresses and ferns, a grotto and deep caves, with rain pouring from springs above into a pool at the foot, trickling into a stream that made its way to the river. They ate the picnic Oatman had prepared, and he took off his T-shirt to show his honey-brown torso, telling Lehmann that it was here, many years before, that as a boy of fifteen he had first made love. 'Let's see what birds we can call up,' he said. Oatman put his hand to his mouth and produced weird calls. Almost at once in a canyon that had seemed so still and empty, birds were everywhere fluttering around them, cardinal birds and golden-crested warblers. For Lehmann, 'It was like an Orphic rite.' And Oatman became 'Lovely Golden Haired Frank', celebrated in the poem 'Canyon Weather'.

> Out of nothing and stillness
> Suddenly leaping, flittering
> Everywhere, everywhere birds
> Swooped, half shy, but twittering
>
> Calls that your fluting evoked
> Speaking a language that I
> Knew nothing of; yet half knew
> Like an ear that will not die
>
> In the depth of a poet's acceptance,
> And closer, with intimate wing,
> Rarest, that golden-cheeked bird
> Hovered and followed, a thing
>
> It seemed to me pure and unknown,
> A new creation of feather
> And song, enchanter, you drew
> To live in that canyon weather.

Soon, there was Lehmann's reunion with Mark. He spent an evening with the young man and his wife, both of whom he saw were devoted. When they left him, the wife kissed Lehmann: 'I'm sure she knows everything, and I was deeply touched.'

So much of his life was now found in this strange country. In March he was at the Armstrong Browning Library at Baylor University in Waco to see the Lehmann artefacts housed there. Years before, he had listened almost unbeliev-ingly when Alice had told him she considered selling some family portraits to a Browning collection at Waco. Here were Pen Browning's portrait of a reading

Abbé, and the portrait of Rudolf Lehmann, pictures that had faced each other high on the walls of Fieldhead's library, so associated 'with my earliest memories of that room of marvels'. Yet it was surely appropriate that fragments of Lehmann's life should have made their way to America; his own life, after all, had been fragmented there. The past, however, would never be escaped. In April 1971, after a quarrel that threatened to end their relationship, Lehmann sent Chick a letter that might as well have been a letter he had once written to Redgrave or Hart or Rassine or Kingston. It was a letter in which he acknowledged the damage that had been done to past friendships.

> We had had such a wonderfully happy day together. I was bursting with love for you, and the desire to express it, and then you suddenly seemed to switch off entirely. That's how it *seemed to me*, anyway. I have never been able to bear such reversals, and I found myself on one of those pitches of agony where I lose control. It couldn't happen if I didn't love you, concern myself with you all the time so much. I wonder if you really know that?

Here are old words, ancient tensions, aged pleas, made new. How can we avoid the feeling that Lehmann had somehow never moved on, never taken what was offered and settled for it, in his emotional life? Chick and Lovely Golden Haired Frank and Frank Lyell – 'the three closest to me' – waved him off from the airport back to England in May 1971, back to Rassine and Douglas Stoker. England now seemed such a temporary home, while the universities of America fought over securing his services. At first, it seemed he would not be asked back to Austin, but he had already been employed by San Diego for the Fall of 1971 for $9,000. Austin followed up with an offer for the whole of 1972-3 for a fee of $17,000.

*

That summer of 1971, Lake Cottage was a blaze of rhododendron and roses. Rassine was staying with Nadia Nerina and her husband on their yacht at Beaulieu. Lehmann was devoting much of his energy to the Royal Literary Fund. He had become President of the Fund in 1966, 'good and conscientious' according to his deputy and (in 1976) successor Janet Adam Smith, if becoming 'a bit pompous and thin-skinned'. He hardly endeared himself to Victor Bonham Carter, also of the Fund, who thought Lehmann's sexuality 'affected his normal character in as much as it made him aggressive and overbearing, unless he was "stood up to" – as I had to do, on more than one occasion'. The tedious workings of such organisations dragged on. He was seeing much of Douglas Stoker 'who has been in his sweetest form before and after his crack-up' (Stoker, like Fry and Oatman, was in poor health), promising that he would take him to California, as he planned to take Oatman on a Hellenic cruise that September. He worked at a memoir, never published, of Rudie, and revised his most recent poems.

Another student from Austin in his late twenties, David Wetsel (christened the 'Tiny Texan'), arrived in London that summer to stay with Lehmann. This new suppliant at Lehmann's feet brought with him the requisite problems that would bedevil their friendship: he suffered from depression and worrying physical ailments that made for a genuine despair. Lehmann summoned his doctor, Rex Warren, to examine the young man, hoping that he would cure him. Wetsel told Lehmann from Paris where he was teaching at the Sorbonne that he would not lose hope 'as long as there's someone in my life as concerned about me as you are'. Lehmann visited him in Paris, a meeting that Lehmann declared 'a miserable failure'. He was, said Wetsel, the one stable thing in his life.

Lovely Golden Haired Frank Oatman, the golden hair longer than ever, was about to holiday with Lehmann in Greece on a fifteen day cruise. 'You will be sharing an Upper Deck double cabin with Professor John Lehmann, C.B.E., F.R.S.L., (so the Passenger List says), so I hope you know about his disgusting morals,' Lehmann told him. In Athens they met Capetanakis's family. Oatman proved an intelligent and charming, and stunningly attractive, companion, but Lehmann was dismayed that he seemed to pass himself off as a teenager by consorting with them whenever he could – 'undignified and certainly inconsiderate of me'. Lehmann made tremendous demands on Oatman, not wanting him out of his sight for a moment; any disappearance was noted as a 'nasty incident'. He saw Oatman 'in a very bad light, displaying disloyalty to one whose guest he was as well as mutually (and happily) agreed boy-friend, and a ruthless lack of consideration'. Nevertheless, despite the endless waiting around for him to fix his hair, 'I truly believe I can still say I love him for many things – though I would never go on such a trip with him again.' After staying with Lehmann for a few days at Cornwall Gardens, Oatman returned to America, unwilling to become part of everything Lehmann had planned for him. He felt that Lehmann was possessive and was 'attempting to fit me into a British homosexual scheme, looking to me for a "secretary cum lover". I came to find the entire mind-set of John and his contemporaries, *vis-à-vis* homosexual relationships, sadly dated and misguided.'

By mid-September Lehmann was back at San Diego, accompanied by Douglas Stoker, teaching on Byron, Shelley and Keats, 'British Poets of Two World Wars' and taking a Poetry Workshop. Lehmann was disturbed by the sense of isolation that overcame him here, Stoker was drinking too much and suffering dizzy spells, and there was not the sympathy among the students that was so plentiful at Austin; instead, he was shown reverence by 'these creatures from Mars'. Inevitably, he was attracted to many of his male students, but 'Here I seem to have lost my radar detection flair for those who will and those who won't; made worse by my shyness when I don't know for certain.' At his lecture 'Lewis Carroll and Nonsense' there was not a drink to be had before, during or after, alcohol being banned on State property.

Lehmann felt at home, now, at Isherwood's house in Adelaide Drive, taking away an inscribed copy of his recently published *Kathleen and Frank*, and feeling a pang that he might never visit the house again. In late October, Stoker went back to London, missed for the 'love and kisses' he had provided, even if he seemed a different person, for 'the sober, self-controlled Douglas was a so much nicer person than the reckless, drunken zombie of yore'. Alone at last, the old facility of writing poetry began to return, poems that would find their way into *The Reader at Night*. How appropriate that one of these should be a tribute to his 'faithful correspondents', for on 10 December he noted 'How strange, in the last 24 hours, to have letters of love from Philip [Mansel], from Morris Fry, from David Wetsel, and from Frank Oatman.'

In his last week, in early 1972, he went from San Diego to Austin for a passionate reunion with Chick. And so to Lovely Golden Haired Frank, with whom 'I felt so immediately in rapport that I began to think I was really falling in love with him, danger, danger – we lay on the bed together, and I read him my new poems, which excited him – and then we kissed and fondled each other and he said "I love you so much" – how beautiful and adorable and understanding and sensitive he is, and how I wish *something* didn't come between us which is nothing to do with time and place – goodbye meetings with dear, amusing Frank Lyell, Tom Cranfill, and Warren Roberts – and so on in the early morning to Dallas, and New York.'

\*

In England young friends now also provided much of the company and stimulation, among them David Plante and Nikos Stangos, and Philip Mansel, in whom Lehmann took the closest interest. Mansel, whose grandmother Sylvia Campbell was a first cousin of Lehmann's, was at Eton in the mid-1960s when he invited Lehmann to speak at the college's Literary Society. It began a friendship that meant much to Lehmann, and that lasted until his death. Once more, Lehmann was in touch with youth, with new hope, and with a young man for whom books had a prime importance. Lehmann was thrilled to see that on the walls of his rooms at Eton were two blow-up photographs, of Virginia Woolf and of Isherwood and Auden about to leave for China. As always, Lehmann took the closest interest in Mansel's development. On leaving Eton, he arrived at Cornwall Gardens 'looking very sweet, almost too vulnerable and attractive: I fear for him'. That summer, they went to the film of *Cabaret*, Lehmann noting that while Liza Minnelli was as far from the original Sally Bowles as it was possible to be, Michael York, whom he thought bore a marked resemblance to himself when young, was 'Very dishy indeed'. York's charms were different to those of Mansel, who was now 'looking like a page boy out of a Botticelli painting'; his visits left Lehmann 'deeply, deeply disturbed'. He was to be one of Lehmann's faithful correspondents in the years of his exile, 'and complains if my letters to him are even a few days late. I find myself continually surprised by his mischievous sophistication – and his learning – only 18!'

Lehmann gave a party at the Garrick for Rassine's birthday, with Beatrix and the actress and writer Shelagh Fraser. Beatrix did her impression of a cleaning woman and convulsed everybody. Rosamond was doubtful about Fraser's social suitability but, having had dinner with Fraser and Beatrix, approvingly told Beatrix that she considered Fraser 'one of us'. There had been recent difficulties between Lehmann and Rosamond. Lehmann had written a generous appraisal of Day Lewis's life for the press. Rosamond wrote 'in the hope of easing my heart a little' that

> What stabbed me to the quick was – not so much the fact that you should pay Cecil a public tribute – though naturally I wish you hadn't felt compelled to – but that the whole thing reads like the record of an unbroken and delightful personal relationship. No doubt part at least of you feels it was so – but, considering the atrocious and irreparable hurt he caused me, you needn't have said so publicly.

Lehmann replied 'It seems to me unfair to suppose that one's own wounded feelings in a purely personal affair takes precedence over other people's feelings in the complex web of relationships.'

America, of course, had been mostly Spender-free; he and Lehmann met again at a party given by Christabel Aberconway in June. Talking about the difficulty of making a living, Spender said, 'I think sometimes I ought to have been a hustler.' This was a gift that Lehmann could not resist. 'You would have had a great success as a hustler, Stephen,' he replied, 'but I rather doubt whether your clients would have come back for a second night, because the experience would have been so much, so much, much more than they had bargained for. *Intellectually*, of course.'

Lehmann still thought of Vienna and returned there in October of 1972, inspired by an unconscious intuition to meet up with Sikyr's young nephew, Karli, a taxi-driver who had been involved in an accident a year earlier. To his horror, Karli's career had been ruined, and the scars of the crash had marked him for life. In an echo of all the concern he had poured out for the boys of Vienna forty years before, Lehmann wrote 'If only one could find some activity for him, that wouldn't lose him his pension. Only his girl-friend knows the whole story, his mother partly – and now me.' He called at the restaurant Sikyr ran, his old friend delighted and astonished to see him. No matter that Sikyr seemed to be living still in a dream world of unrealistic projects; Lehmann was overcome by the autumn colours of the trees, reds, yellows, orange, green-yellow and green.

Rassine was settling to the unique place he had in Lehmann's altered life. His flat at 12 Thurloe Place, ideal because their dog Rudy had no steps to climb, was a base from which Rassine operated between Cornwall Gardens and Three Bridges. He spring-cleaned for Lehmann, washed the kitchen ceiling and curtains and caught three mice. At Lake Cottage he picked 12lbs of grapes and 9lbs of pumpkin, storing some for Christmas pies. He made chutneys and apple jelly and took down the net curtains. In October 1971 he opened the Alexis Rassine School of Ballet in St Augustine's Church Hall at 117 Queen's Gate, with fourteen pupils aged from six to sixteen.

Lehmann was immensely proud of this achievement, but Rassine was not an interested teacher. 'He was too lazy,' Pamela Foster recalls. 'He used to sit on his chair and beat time with his cane. I said, "Why don't you get up and dance?" ' He spent more and more time at Three Bridges, reporting to Lehmann that 'everything is OK at your flat and cottage'. In America, Lehmann thought a good deal about Rassine, and how he looked after him 'with a care that is quite spontaneous, and a feeling that seems quite simply to go deeper than he has with anyone else'.

With the arrival of another handsome young man in Lehmann's life, Rassine was to face one of his greatest challenges. Thomas Urquhart-Laird came from Scotland in 1961 when he was eighteen. He tried, without much success, to become an actor. It was in the early 1960s that he first met Sturrey, Lehmann's 'Pussycat', at the Toucan, a homosexual pub in Soho run by an ex-Wing Commander. Ten years later, Urquhart-Laird moved into Sturrey's Battersea home and did occasional work in the building trade for him. Through Sturrey, Urquhart-Laird met Adrian Liddell Hart, 'a very sadistic character, well into S & M. I was at his flat one night. He grabbed me by the hair and said, "I'm going to beat the hell out of you." I pushed him off.'

One evening in the summer of 1972, Sturrey asked Lehmann if he might bring his young friend to dinner at Cornwall Gardens. After dinner, Sturrey said he would be sleeping with Lehmann and invited Urquhart-Laird to join them. He declined, but Lehmann had already taken a liking to the boy: 'He is highly strung, rather hysterical, has let himself go while living in [Battersea] with Pussycat – but sees what he is losing after quite some talking to by me – not a beauty, not an intellectual (very ignorant in many ways) but a perfectly adorable boy to be with.' At the time, Urquhart-Laird was involved with a girl. Lehmann and Sturrey 'got together to force the woman out. They wouldn't have minded if it had been a boy.'

A couple of weeks later Lehmann took Urquhart-Laird, christened Tommymouse, on holiday to Corsica, and in August he moved into Cornwall Gardens as Lehmann's new secretary-lover. What Rassine did not do, Tommymouse did. He cooked (after dining at the flat Connolly once left a card for him saying he had just dined at one of the best restaurants in London), shopped, dressed, read proofs, answered the telephone, did the decorating, bought the daily supplies of the cheapest cigarettes (Embassy Royals) and slept with his employer (who in turn had been christened 'Huggy Bear' by Tommymouse). A real affection developed between them. 'I loved him', Urquhart-Laird tells me. It was not easy, this role somewhere between servant and partner. Jonathan Fryer recalls that on the arrival of Lehmann's guest, Tommymouse would be 'summarily dismissed. He seemed to resent it rather, understandably.' Rosamond was displeased, and her dignity offended by a stranger leaning over her at the dinner table to ask 'Soup, Rosamond?' On her visits she was usually 'on Cloud Nine', and was always trying to extract information from Urquhart-Laird: 'there was malice there, really'.

Rassine was a greater and more constant problem than Rosamond, but the two men were necessarily thrown together. There was never a friendship between them; they grew to tolerate one another, sharing the preparation of meals at Lake Cottage. Even when Lehmann was in America Urquhart-Laird's life could hardly be called his own, for Rassine was regularly calling in at Cornwall Gardens. On his visits, he kept an eye out for anything suspicious. In April 1974 he was not slow to report to Lehmann that 'I popped into your flat – and found Tom having some friend called Steve cooking in the kitchen for all I know he may be living there too – so much for your trust in him. I was livid – but didn't say anything. I shall do your balcony garden next week – it's a mess at the moment.'

Urquhart-Laird had also to hold his place when the literary distinguished came to dinner, and seemed capable of doing so. He grew fond of Plomer, whom he knew briefly, and Paul Dehn and Roy Fuller – 'lovely men'. Spender was initially cool towards him. Isherwood and Bachardy were friendly, and Bachardy made a pass at him. Flirting might be acceptable, but Lehmann, himself sexually greedy, 'didn't like the idea of me going with other people at all'. It was left to the discerning to determine the nature of their association. When abroad (and there were many holidays taken together) Urquhart-Laird was introduced either as Lehmann's secretary or as his nephew. Many remarked on the obvious family resemblance.

Perhaps more intimately than any other since Rassine, Urquhart-Laird came to know Lehmann as the domestic animal, but 'He was a terrible martinet. If you returned two minutes late from drinking with friends, there would be trouble. He was picky about food, and you had to keep a chart of what wine had been drunk and when.' Work was alleviated by increasingly infrequent trips to the theatre ('too expensive') and cinema. They saw *Everything You Always Wanted To Know About Sex And Never Dared Ask* and laughed until they were in agony. There were only two television programmes Lehmann enthused over, *Starsky and Hutch* and *Alias Smith and Jones*, both of which Lehmann was convinced were about gay relationships that had been made heterosexual for public consumption.

Against all this, ran Lehmann's feeling 'of being washed up; of nobody wanting my poems or my books; of having difficulty in arranging American teaching assignments; of wondering how I am going to live through this decade'. The parties at Cornwall Gardens were not as grand as they had once been, and he was left with the sensation of emptiness. 'Why is it all dust and ashes,' he wondered, 'compared with the old days? Perhaps it is those years in America that has shifted my focus.' Urquhart-Laird remembers that at this time Lehmann went into a deep depression that lasted for several weeks. He needed to be reminded, sometimes, of past glories, physical as well as professional. A few months later, in Paris, where he spent much time with his cousin Philip Mansel, the porter at his usual hotel told him he hadn't changed at all in seventeen years. 'You're a flatterer,' said Lehmann. 'No, it's true,' said the man. 'How do you manage it?' 'Perhaps not getting married,' said Lehmann. 'That's it, that's it,' the porter shouted. 'Not getting married! That's the answer!' The woman at the desk smiled, and lowered her eyes.

\*

The knowledge of his mortality was strong in Lehmann as he approached his seventies. What would become of Rassine after his death? He began to sell off parts of the grounds at Lake Cottage, itself valued at over £75,000, to raise money so that Rassine might be left with a roof over his head. Alan Ross advised Lehmann to sell up at Three Bridges and buy somewhere cheaper, but could not penetrate Lehmann's obstinate devotion to places he loved. There was hope that the book about 'Jack Marlowe' would bring about a reverse in fortune. Isherwood read extracts and approved, 'definitely encouraging, in sober fashion'.

Beside the high hopes he began to have for the novel, he was negotiating for a book of the letters between himself and Isherwood, concerned that 'it may easily be fucked up if *not* done in our lifetime'. Urquhart-Laird and he were kept busy preparing the material, but the project was eventually abandoned, though much of the work was utilised for Lehmann's last book, his memoir of Isherwood.

Connolly, another survivor from an earlier age, came to lunch with him at the Garrick. He was pasty-faced, drank only Perrier water with lemon and seemed nervous when Lehmann confessed to keeping a private journal. They discussed bisexual marriages. Lehmann told how Sturrey had been buggered by his two brothers-in-law on the eve of his wedding. Connolly was unshaken. 'Well,' he said, 'there's nothing like starting one's marriage the way it's going to go on.'

Lehmann was shortly to write a tribute to Connolly on his seventieth birthday, feeling as he prepared it that it was 'difficult not to be influenced as one writes by his selfishness, his jealousy, his conceit, while admitting his loyalty (or at any rate probationary loyalty) to those who come within the penumbra of his nostalgia (and that I believe includes me.) To recognise his unique gifts as a stylist without hiding his weakness for being "funny" – which to my mind spoils so much of his writing. He would sell his grandmother for a luxury weekend at a millionaire's villa – and write with modest satire about it afterwards. How I love his chuckles, how his capricious rudeness repels me.'

The meeting with Connolly was followed by a visit to Wormwood Scrubs, a regular destination of Lehmann's, where an ex-guardsman boyfriend was serving a sentence for the killing of a prostitute. It had been a violent murder, the man having pushed a broken bottle into the woman's vagina. Despite the revulsion Lehmann would have felt at such a crime, he nevertheless kept in touch with his old lover, who told Lehmann he would forever have the mark of Cain on him. And there is something in the two meetings, with Connolly and the killing boyfriend, that somehow typifies the unmatched levels of Lehmann's life. He seems never to have turned his back on a friendship, and was strenuous in his efforts to maintain it.

Lehmann recognised the inevitability of the loss of those he had known for so many years, but the death of William Plomer in September 1973 was a cruel shock. Since they had met over forty years before at the Hogarth Press, Plomer had shared many of the secrets of Lehmann's life. In letter after letter, written in his brown or mauve ink (for Plomer deplored the typewriter), Plomer had confirmed the strength of their friendship, had helped Lehmann with the difficulties that plagued him throughout the war, had supported him through the *New Writing* series and the life of the *London Magazine*. Without Plomer, there was bound to be more darkness; it was a sure sign, beyond the accumulated losses of Forster, MacNeice, Osbert and Edith Sitwell, and Day Lewis, that the days were shortening.

> He is absolutely irreplaceable. He should have lived at least another ten years ... I can hardly conceive that there will be no more of those treasured talks together, his absurd wit and gaiety and sensitivity so absolutely unique. We agreed, quietly and confidentially about so many things – the madder and more destructive phenomena. He was a perfectly loyal friend, always could be relied on for a shrewd and sober estimate of what one did; a natural sceptic but always so warm-hearted. I can't go on more now.

Rosamond accompanied him to the Brighton crematorium for his friend's last gathering. Lehmann was pleased that she had chosen their flowers so well. Plomer's beloved Charles was 'very emotional, but bore up well'.

Within a few days, Auden was dead of a heart attack. To Lehmann, it seemed confirmation of 'The end of a chapter of our youth: I feel a chill in the air.' He thought of Auden's face, 'as if it had been left in a laundry basket and never ironed', at the meetings he remembered in New York at the disordered flat in St.

Mark's Square, in Vienna at the Mozart Café, and at Cornwall Gardens. He had tried to explain Auden to his Austin students as a mixture of Saint and Doctor. Before the end of the year, Elizabeth Bowen, too, was dead, and Henry Yorke, a death that had dismayed him horribly. Lehmann the littérateur had hoped, since Yorke's last novel, *Doting*, published in 1952, that he would produce another great work, but for the last twenty years there had been only illness and silence: 'And now it is all over. I am haunted by his haggard, unshaven face, the sudden look of horror that would cross it in the intervals of joking (and what a good friend to me he was.)'

It had been a bad year. The negotiations to sell Lake Cottage eventually collapsed. There was a plan to write a book about Salzburg, which he visited in October, chauffeured by Karli. He broke his ankle there and the book fell through. There was also the shock and disappointment of Isherwood suddenly stopping the book of their letters on which Lehmann had worked so diligently. Among the close literary friends from the past, Isherwood seemed to Lehmann probably the most enduring; how baffled he must have been by this sudden change of mind. Wasn't Isherwood dismissing the importance of their friendship? He wondered if, as Urquhart-Laird suggested, Bachardy was behind Isherwood's decision. With such a run of bad news, Lehmann prophetically feared that 'Stephen will survive us all, and have the last word.'

# 17

# Speaking of England

Lehmann returned on March 22 1974 to lecture at Austin, his second home, as he called it, though already there is a note of regretfulness in what he confides to his journals. This second home, the welcoming attentions of Chick, of Lovely Golden Haired Frank, of the Tiny Texan, were guaranteed to bring a feeling of 'renewed youth; just a dream really, I think, though I was happy here, and found new adventures of many sorts, – and new achievements'. American academia again welcomed him with equally open arms. He took up his post as Beckman Professor at the University of California at Berkeley from 1 April to 30 June for a fee of $10,000, taking a senior seminar in Virginia Woolf and a graduate course on the British Novel of Poetry and Symbolism. There would be yet more periods spent in America as a Visiting Professor.

Lehmann's dampened excitement on returning was undoubtedly partly due to the events of the previous year, and also to his poor health. Even before he had broken his ankle in Austria, he had been walking badly. He suffered terribly from gout, and found he could not walk far, one of the reasons why he considered his apartment at San Diego, so far from any shops, inconvenient. Urquhart-Laird remembers that when he first met him in the early seventies, Lehmann was in no way enfeebled, but he already had a slight tremor – despite the fact that the tremor would eventually worsen, Lehmann, unlike Rudie, would not suffer from Parkinson's disease.

It is perhaps not surprising that his increasing disability did not put a stop to Lehmann's sexual profligacy. No sooner had he arrived at Berkeley than a new friend took him to a San Francisco gay bar and, later, a gay restaurant. The next night, Lehmann was taken to a sea-hotel on the north coast to meet with other new gay friends, one of whom was a Stanford drama student called Douglas. At the end of the evening, Lehmann's perhaps over-ambitious host suggested that Lehmann should bed down in a sleeping-bag arrangement with five or six others. Lehmann insisted on taking a separate room and offered to share it with the attractive Douglas 'who blossomed when we went to bed ... and who proved, well, everything; and a secret; as if he had made up his mind to be seduced by me'. Naked on the bed, his hair black, his eyes brown, his skin the colour of burnt sugar, Douglas seemed a legendary figure, a Roman in a Pompeian wall-painting. On meeting his students, Lehmann was alarmed that the majority of Virginia Woolf students were female, but there was one 'very highly strung dishy young man to whom I take a great liking'.

Throughout May, he made progress on the memoirs of Jack Marlowe. He was sitting on the lavatory when the conclusion of the book came to him and thought 'it will really do; but much depends on how I work up the intervening material'. The manuscript was eventually completed in January 1975, after four years of intermittent but steady work. Rosamond asked 'Is it funny sometimes? I hope so!' There were sympathetic friends who cheered his progress with the book, including Bill Brown, who

> ... belongs to that well-travelled, well-read, sophisticated generation that came to maturity after the war, as the war was ending, when everything was there to be experienced and everyone picked the fruits that were there hanging on the tree ... the present generation seems utterly tame beside them – a different *kind* of human beings.

He nevertheless worked to bring to these different beings an understanding of Bloomsbury, of Virginia Woolf through *Orlando* and *The Waves*, and of Henry Yorke, entrancing his class with 'Mr Jonas' and readings from *Loving*.

In June, he was in New York, invited to examine Virginia's various typescripts of *Between the Acts* at the Berg collection, reminding the Berg's imperious librarian that he was the only person who could positively identify the definitive version. He went through Virginia's diaries for 1937 and 1938, remembering the events that had led to his renewed association with the Hogarth Press. Work was progressing well on a book he was writing about Virginia. He thought how much his life had been enriched by having known people of such visionary power as Virginia, Edith Sitwell and Capetanakis, convinced that it had been something more than mere chance. David Wetsel came from Boston and stayed the night. They visited Ned Rorem, and saw Bernstein's operetta *Candide*, but his relations with Wetsel were 'rather like those of a fond uncle who visits his nephew at Eton, gives him strawberries and cream and a big tip on departure ... And yet what uncle would be listening to harrowing sexual confessions and melancholy speculations, or would be hugging him and fondling him with love kisses in bed?'

Chick made his first visit to Cornwall Gardens in September, a happy time marred only by Lehmann being 'still under the shock of Tommymouse's disappearance, and inexplicable stab-in-the-back'. There was a miserable holiday in Spain, terrible food and weather, and then England again, and the first visit of the autumn to Lake Cottage. There is something in Lehmann's description of this scene that might be of a mediaeval warlord visiting a fifedom he had almost forgotten about; there is a remoteness about it all, as if he had suddenly lighted on the place which others have tended in his long absences (as, of course, Rassine had). The cottage was warm, with paraffin heaters at work, and logs Rassine had chopped ready for burning. The kitchen was filled with marrows, squashes, trays of ripening tomatoes, pears and pumpkins. On the lake were a pair of wild ducks, their presence infuriating the resident moor-hens.

*

Against a background of England in the grips of 'the creeping advances of the closed society of socialism', the dispiriting reports of old friends weighed on Lehmann's mind. David Carver, the President of PEN for whom Lehmann had always had a great fondness and respect, died that year, an event he felt had been sent down by a vengeful god. William Sansom seemed in decline. At a painful meeting of the Royal Society of Literature Sansom rambled incoherently on, removing his dentures to illustrate a point.

Connolly's death at the end of the year affected Lehmann perhaps more than might have been expected. 'I didn't think I should mind as much as I am minding,' he wrote,

> ... he had become so much mellower in the last few years, so much more of a friend, and I think continually of the many times in fifty years our lives intersected. There were so many things he was the ideal person to talk over with: that I shall miss especially.

Such final admiration did not stop Lehmann feeling indignant at the begging letters that followed from the Cyril Connolly fund, expecting 'to bail Cyril's widow out of a mess that Cyril selfishly and recklessly created when living very well himself with a very large salary'. At the Royal Literary Fund, Osbert Lancaster told him that Connolly had been one of those people who believed the world had owed him a living and, incredibly, the world had agreed. In fact, Lehmann was growing unhappy with his work for the Fund, plagued by the 'manic' Victor Bonham Carter, 'who having very nearly wrecked the Authors' society, seems now intent on wrecking the R. L. F. I felt like saying to him: 'You have cast yourself in the role of Hercules cleaning out the Augean Stables; but there *are* no Augean Stables'.

Jonathan Fryer first met Lehmann in 1975 when he was researching a biography of Isherwood. He was struck by the fact that, at a time when Isherwood was breaking off from his English friends and Lehmann was upset that behind his back Isherwood was referring to him 'basically as a silly old fart', Lehmann was being extraordinarily protective. Isherwood had adopted a mantle of honest self-expression and sexual disclosure, but

> John was completely the opposite. He had this carapace which covered a very complex inner self which at first view was quite intimidating. It was slightly old-fashioned but very upper-middle-class British reserve with a headmasterish tone which gave the false impression that the only impor-

tant thing was to behave correctly, and to realise the importance of the great literary endeavour to which he was so married. It was only later that I realised the person within was quite different.

The biographer in Fryer found Lehmann irritatingly reticent in conversation: 'I felt because he'd spent a lifetime covering up his own life that he thought he should cover up Christopher's, whereas Christopher wanted my book about him to be as shocking as possible.' It seemed that the coldness and official demeanour disguised a vulnerable, warm man, and the self-protecting device had the effect of giving off inaccurate signals to those he met. As his confidence in Fryer's company grew, Lehmann found it impossible to hide the disappointment he had felt with Isherwood. To Fryer it was obvious that

> John was in love with Christopher in the broadest sense. He desperately admired him. He wanted Christopher to be the brother he had never had. Christopher was looking for the perfect son that he had never had, so they were quite incompatible. And of course Christopher was absolutely ruthless, such a manipulator of people, and John was a victim of that.

*

Lehmann's bitterness had three sources. One was the way in which other writers and friends whom he had helped had moved on to greater success and left him behind. Another was the lost reputation of his poetry, which he knew had been forgotten or, even worse, overlooked. Another was the inescapable feeling that his family, notably Rosamond, had somehow let him down. Lehmann knew how strongly she disapproved of his life, but 'he didn't feel guilty; he felt that Rosamond was not playing the game'. Rosamond's interest in spooky things might be ridiculed but here too there was a dilemma, for Lehmann himself was fascinated in astrology, and had his horoscope drawn up. Both he and Fryer were Geminis, which seemed to both of them to justify the fact that each thought they had two distinct personalities.

By this time Lehmann was publishing work that made his new-found American reputation as a professor seem all the more desirable. He was ready to make an uncluttered assessment of any shred of reputation that was left.

> I reconcile myself to the fact that I have become a kind of minor cultural monument; I am what I am, what I have done; and it's out of that that everything must stem. Nothing else matters – in fact, to hell with the rest.

The stuff he was commissioned to write seldom rose above the bread and butter. In 1970, there had been a dull parish history, *Holborn*, financed by the local council. With Derek Parker he edited the *Selected Letters of Edith Sitwell*.

Parker would sometimes work at Cornwall Gardens, where Lehmann cooked Wiener schnitzel for lunch. Lehmann was very much a sleeping partner in the enterprise, and pocketed the majority of the shared advance.

*The Reader at Night*, a slim collection of new poems, would not have appeared at all without the persistence of Paul Davies who ran the Basilike Press in Toronto. 250 copies were produced in 1974, of an elegant volume that recalled the early days of the Hogarth in its handset pages, and John Lehmann Ltd. in its physical beauty. When he first saw the book, Lehmann declared 'This is the nicest thing that has ever happened to me as a writer.' Happily, it is a collection that confirms Lehmann as a poet who has grown with satisfaction into an old age. We open its pages wanting to find something at least of a settled quietude, we need to know he has acquired some autumnal understanding.

If we long to see that Lehmann is not exempt from the deepest feeling there is material enough here, in his tribute to Virginia Woolf as 'The Lady of Elvedon', and in the little portraits he gives 'To my Faithful Correspondents in England' (and how the title itself tells of his estrangement). Here is the hired professor, wanted in old age not only as an exported relic of a glorious age of English literature, but also still physically desired; the idol of young American men making their way to him with a purpose that suggests he has almost a Paul Bunyan-like charisma. Beyond all this stand the Faithful Correspondents: Roy Fuller and Beatrix 'like a double Angel of light and darkness' who has walked with him 'On that long pilgrimage that could not be / But stones, thirst, mirage'; and Plomer.

In 'Photograph' – a great outpouring at the beauty of Chick in what must be one of his most effective poems – the realisation of a divide of years between an elderly man and his young lover provokes a challenge to the sanctity of everything that Fieldhead has meant. Love is so felt that it strikes at the core of his personality. It becomes possible to contemplate another beginning, made desirable by whatever Lehmann felt: lust, infatuation, love, the degrees and interpretation of adoration.

> I pore over the photograph, and see
> You standing there, nostalgia in your gaze
> For the wild scene of childhood wanderings
>     Where the lone cowboy's shadow goes
>
> Always before you in my imaginings;
> And though half one man's lifetime separates
> Two dreaming children, each captive to a river,
>     I feel I could exchange my roots
>
> And become you by the sheer power of love,
> Bound up with armadillos, mocking birds,

And the burnt mountain where the Indians fought,
In the empathy of where one's raised.

How strange this minute square of photograph
Should contain all our history; I read,
Tears forming, but of joy, convinced of what
Lives here and cannot be betrayed.

Increasingly, it was the past that claimed Lehmann's time as a writer. *Virginia Woolf and her World* appeared in 1975, competent and attractive but almost irrelevant to scholarship. Such books cannot have been his first choice; too often, it was a struggle to get into print. The memoirs of Jack Marlowe, *In the Purely Pagan Sense*, had begun a round of publishers in 1972, even before its final revision. After rejections from Macmillan, Constable and W. H. Allen, it was taken up by Blond and Briggs in 1976 with an advance of £1,000 and published that September.

\*

Did Lehmann have hopes that *In the Purely Pagan Sense* would bring him a new celebrity in literature? Did he envisage fresh sprigs of success through notorious – if slightly coy as to identities – disclosure? Isherwood, who had just completed *Christopher and his Kind*, had a tête-à-tête with him at which they discussed their respective, and as yet unpublished, books. Lehmann's journal notes with pride how effusive Isherwood was in praise of *In the Purely Pagan Sense*. With typical robustness, Lehmann then launched on a reasonably devastating list of criticism against Isherwood's effort. But there were clearly doubts in Lehmann's mind about how this (supposedly, but undeclared) fourth volume of autobiography, clumsily obscured as fiction, would be received. Central to his belief was that the book 'is all done for *truth*'

> If one sets out to write a serious, candid account of what it has been like to live a homosexual life in our time … one must, to make a full picture (which has not been done before) give the full physical details of sexual attraction and intercourse; otherwise it would be just a tract or veiled confession … Not a fig-leaf left in place.

For the Attic Dionysic festivals, had not Aristophanes written bawdy farces, full of phallic innuendo, with all the quality of the tragedies that preceded them? Interviewed by Peter Burton and Denis Lemon just before publication, he seemed almost surprised that some passages of the book might offend the most genteel of his readers. Whatever he expected, he decided to escape its publication by booking a holiday to Greece with Urquhart-Laird.

No welcome awaited *In the Purely Pagan Sense*. There was no mention that the book had an intent, or that it was a work of an intelligent mind, or that it had any kind of worth. Rather than establishing a fresh perspective, the book confirmed Lehmann's reputation in the critical view as a resolutely minor figure, the author of yesterday's book. The only claim to notoriety came from its talent to embarrass; if the book brought any new perception of Lehmann, it was that he could not write. The depressing catalogue of critical complaint (the book was one of indescribable tedium, oddly blank, two dimensional, numbingly repetitive) seemingly had no end.

A wholehearted critical destruction might have been preferable to a faint dismissal. After comparing Lehmann's confessions with those of Ackerley and, more stingingly, of Isherwood, David Leitch was most struck by the fact that all the boyfriends in the book were little more than prostitutes, and Lehmann's relationship with them based on the inequality of the classes – what Lehmann would probably have identified as Socratic. 'I fear,' Leitch wrote, 'the liberated "gays", far from acknowledging this homo-hero of dad's generation, will only turn and rend him asunder.' The book, perhaps, gave too much away about those whose world had seemed so closed, mysterious, physically only guessed at. The caravan had moved on. But from Lehmann's perfectly valid perspective it was a blindingly accurate account of a British homosexual's life in the first half of the twentieth century.

It is easy to pour scorn on *In the Purely Pagan Sense* because it has no existence as a novel. The book is full of dull thuds, badly managed changes of gear, and betrays Lehmann's lack of feeling for the human voice and, more damagingly, for the human predicament. Any idea of structure or a novelistic plot is abandoned to a catalogue of Marlowe's and Lehmann's sexual life, through fellatio, intercourse, sado-masochism and his attempt at heterosexuality with Odette Massigli. Here, she is Oriane, but the transformation is transparent, as it is for so many of the characters: on they come, flickering across the pages in poorly-fitting masks – Rassine as Dmitri Pavlenko, Hart as Rickie, Redgrave as Torquil, Dyer as Chuck, Kingston as Simon. John Mellors in the *Listener* found the boys 'in (and often out) of their *lederhosen* become as indistinguishable and characterless as girls in a high-kicking chorus'.

What the novel does, with disappointing irregularity, is to let in glimpses of light on Lehmann's understanding of himself, glimpses that suggest he was never self-deluding. He recognises that what he found so appealing in his partners was a pagan, uncluttered earthiness, their lack of knowledge of the literary world through which he moved. They were as much antidote as gratification. The relationship between himself and his lovers was transitory but meaningful. He recognises the growing desperation, in middle age, of his searching. To some it may seem that *In the Purely Pagan Sense* has the unhappy result of separating life from sex; to others it may seem that Lehmann has perfectly judged the integration of the two, unbothered by any particularly penetrating psychology, or indeed any psychology.

If there is a key to the purpose of it all it is in Marlowe's 'pursuit of illumination through sex'. Perhaps we need know no more. This belief necessitates equating lust with love, for it is lust with care. It is a directness of statement that distinguishes the text, as in the flagellation scenes, where Lehmann argues that such activity does not preclude emotional involvement. Eight years before, J. R. Ackerley's *My Father and Myself* – a book Lehmann disliked – had proved that a homosexual identity could be disclosed with clinical but piercing impressionistic style. Style, dismally lacking in *In the Purely Pagan Sense*, had no place there. Peter Burton suggests that 'It isn't always great works of art that have the greatest effect. The value of the book is in its honesty. It's the statement itself, not the quality of it, that's important.'

If *In the Purely Pagan Sense* is a failure it may be because Lehmann does not suggest the apparently invisible intention he has in its writing. Towards the book's close, Marlowe meets a young foot guardsman.

> I asked him how I could give him pleasure, whereupon he said, in a strangled voice, 'Take me in your mouth, Jack!' I leaned over and, putting my hand on his bottom and my left leg between his legs, took the tip of his cock gently between my lips. He flung his head back, shutting his eyes, and uttered a gasp of delight …

For Lehmann this (almost the penultimate sexual act of *In the Purely Pagan Sense*) represented 'a ritual, a summing-up image of phallic worship', a confirmation of the first stirrings of homosexual desire felt in childhood. But he makes no attempt to imbue the action with any symbolism, leaving the reader to see it as simply one more adventure.

We cannot be certain whether Lehmann ever regretted the book's publication – and how are we to regard it; as a late assertion of his sexual power, as an act of tremendous bravery or foolishness? It shifted a perception of Lehmann's character and, rather than bringing him into the modernity of experience, it removed him a little further from it.

Rosamond, predictably, was incensed, raging at Lehmann 'like a jealous wife who has caught her husband out in squalid delinquencies'. In forbidding her brother the truth, however, she would have stopped the sudden revelations that make *In the Purely Pagan Sense* an important document: Lehmann's love for Kingston, the depth of his political concern, his commitment to Rassine (who at the end of his life described it as 'a beautiful book') and, occasionally, that light of self-understanding.

> My experience has been that awareness of perfection having been reached in a love relationship has all too often been followed by disaster. I refuse

to see this as a fatal pattern in my life; but later reflection has led me to think that my personality may tend, as my happiness increases, to have an almost overpowering effect on the person involved with me in the relationship. Without knowing quite why he is doing it, or giving at any rate wrongly rationalised explanations, he runs suddenly for cover to someone less complex and less dominant than myself.

There is the sound of truth, and there are other truths in the book, often brutal and promiscuous. The truths are not always completely honest. The tangled relationships that filled Lehmann's life are simplified here, one lover obligingly quitting the book before another arrives, a conscious manipulation of something unmanageable. But what emerges so strongly is the lack of any connection. We might say that disconnection is at the centre of the book, unjoined as it is. As a fourth volume of autobiography, it seems unable to lose itself in elegiac celebration (compare the first hundred pages of *The Whispering Gallery*); it is bereft of sympathy and the altering force of beauty. There is a separation between what emotion might be capable of and what must be done to enact the sexual event. It is as if the small boy wetting the bed at last cries out the fact, confesses his dirtiness, the detail of his stigmata. In exposing himself he runs the risk that understanding will be withheld. It is too late to feel that the truth had better not be told.

The past so often offered itself up as a stranger to Lehmann. He looked through letters of his life in pre-war Vienna, as if the years he had spent there had belonged to another person. He was horrified to visit Alum Bay. Where as children he and Rosamond and Beatrix and Helen had clambered on to the beach from the cliffs, there was a non-stop chair-lift to take them up and down. No longer could children scrape the coloured sands from the cliff face. Now, they were presented with a tray of different coloured sands and a spoon with which they might fill a bottle.

*

Lehmann clung to what he could of the past, old friends, gatherings at which the German champagne had the desired effect. The writers that arrived at the door of Cornwall Gardens grew older, and fewer. Isherwood visited, a little stiff but his eyes still twinkling away, on Lehmann's sixty-ninth birthday. The next day, there was the annual summer party at Cornwall Gardens, the room filled with rhododendrons brought up from Lake Cottage. There is no record of when the final laburnum party was held.

For his seventieth birthday, a party at the Garrick was organised by Miles Huddleston, at which a Festschrift called 'The Cross and the Gauntlet' was presented. The tributes of prose and poetry assured him of the respect and admiration that was still held for him: an unpublished recipe of 'Scrambled Eggs

Variation 77' from 'your ever affectionate cookery author' Elizabeth David; Thom Gunn wrote out his first poem that Lehmann had accepted for 'New Soundings' – the first of Gunn's work that had ever been taken by an editor outside Cambridge; Elizabeth Hepworth wrote to remember the achievement of *Penguin New Writing* 'which did so much to lift all our hearts during those ghastly years'. David Hughes celebrated 'the fact that you were born and that you entered to such good and lasting effect my life and so many others'. Adrian Liddell Hart wrote that he owed Lehmann 'a reply to your "Letter to a friend at sea," 1941'.

Norah Smallwood raised a toast to 'one who has done more to encourage, and guide, poets and writers than any of his generation'. Spender sent his poem, 'Lost Days', dedicated to Lehmann. Rex Warner could think of 'No more gracious a host or a companion, No more loyal a friend or better fellow.' Veronica Wedgwood told him that long before she had been invited to one of his parties at Egerton Crescent, she had 'followed eagerly the earliest issues of New Writing which introduced me to the best and most adventurous writing in contemporary literature, both English and foreign'. Subsequently, he had helped her develop her critical skills. 'You gave me confidence as a writer in a world of writers,' she explained, 'one minor example of what your discriminating and exhilarating influence has done for writers over more than four decades of English literature.'

Included in the Festschrift's leaves is the most poignant, indeed tragic, of the many contributions, Rosamond's 'Letter to my Brother'. It left no doubt of her love for him, and of the shadows that had crossed it through their lives. It remains almost unbearably honest, painful and moving. 'Dear John,' she wrote

> May all be mirth,
> Feast intellectual, culinary as well,
> To celebrate your seventy years on earth.
> But should a sister swell
> However proud, this hearty PUBLIC chorus?
> Accept instead a (semi-) private page,
> A backward glance with the long sight of age.
> Let us remember how, the prospect all before us,
> Softly sweet Thames began to run
> Beside our parents' second daughter,
> And not long afterwards beside their son.
> Since then, how many bridges, how much water
> Since you and I
> Set out! ... Let's not philosophize or specify.
>
> The prospect dwindles now; and the running tide
> Upon which we have travelled – sometimes side by side

Slackens ... And yet, how stealthily, still hurries us along;
Will bear away toys, trinkets, relics, prizes,
Pomps, medals, masks, and other old disguises;
Will sweep us out of Time and end our song.
Alone then, bearings lost, how will it be
For us? – how shall we fare? ...
Striving to breathe an unaccustomed air,
Facing at last our hidden selves may we
Take hands again; laugh again; agree,
If not before, after we reach the sea.

\*

Lehmann had seemed to settle into a sort of contentedness, at least when in London, with Tommymouse. It may be that Urquhart-Laird might have gone on living at Cornwall Gardens, but the drinking he had begun during Lehmann's long absences in America effectively ended their relationship in 1978. 'It has been painful to find Tommymouse in difficulties again,' Lehmann wrote in March 1977, 'also suffering from black-outs. In fact I am perturbed for the future.'

The death of the beloved Rudy accentuated the bonds. As always, the death of an animal had a tremendous effect on Lehmann. 'Quite often, recently, I have had thoughts and recollections of Rudy; and always have been on the verge of tears. One is, I feel sure, always more deeply affected by a death one has seen. Which is one reason why I wanted to spare Alexis [from being present]' Parting from Urquhart-Laird was another sort of death; but there had been so many. Urquhart-Laird recalls 'We decided to split up. It was a shared decision, really. John cried his eyes out, one of the very few times I ever saw him cry. I went off to sort my drinking out in my own way.' He telephoned Lehmann once or twice. They never met again.

Urquhart-Laird's disappearance left Lehmann rudderless for the first time in years. It was clear that Lehmann, whose health was steadily failing, needed to find secretarial help. He advertised in *Gay News* for 'a young literary aspirant', and, at the ensuing interviews, made pertinent notes: one was 'in spite of beard, very feminine – too much', another '*Is* gay but *not* pansy – difficult chap to have around.' Michael Bloch met Lehmann at the table of a Faber employee, Charles Orwin, that summer, and offered himself 'as a lark' as secretary. The duties seemed manageable: two hours three mornings a week for £5 an hour, but

John was an exacting and irascible employer, who would be seriously annoyed if one turned up five minutes late and would ask one to retype a letter if it contained a single mistake. He was something of a bully, and full of tiresome eccentricities: one of my tasks was to do the shopping and he

257

insisted on my going out to buy the minimum requirements for that day, two bananas, ten cigarettes, six postage stamps, and would lose his temper if I ever suggested it might be easier for him to make bulk purchases. Also, I had been hoping to meet interesting friends of his in the literary world, but although he invited them to lunch quite often, I was rarely asked to stay on and meet them.

Bloch also noticed Lehmann's disappointment, a lack of fondness for the human race, his jealousy of contemporaries – even his jealousy of Bloch himself, when the young secretary began to have books published. This evident lack of generosity was contradicted if Bloch asked for advice about writing or personal problems, on which occasions he was 'always patient and generous'.

In the autumn of 1978 Bloch entertained Lehmann at Cambridge while he was researching his biography of Rupert Brooke. Bloch gave a tea party in his rooms in King's Parade at which interested students were invited to meet Lehmann. These included 'a very handsome undergraduate called Keith Tanner. John behaved badly, concentrating all his attention on Keith and ignoring everyone else.' Probably to Lehmann's satisfaction, Tanner became the new secretary, a post he subsequently passed to Christopher Hawtree. Barbara Cooper was still occasionally called in to do secretarial work. She typed Rassine's memoirs, concocted by Rassine and Lehmann and called *Once a Bluebird*, but no publisher showed interest. One dismissed the manuscript as 'marginal'. It was a clear sign that Rassine's career, too, had slipped into an obscurity; now, they shared decline.

\*

Despite Lehmann's concern for his sister's health, Beatrix continued her career as a distinguished actress throughout the 1970s, even if she still railed at often being cast as older women. One such memorable role was as the centenarian recluse Miss Bordereau in Redgrave's adaptation of *The Aspern Papers* at the Queen's Theatre in 1959, 'where I quiver in my bath chair and innumerable shawls like the Princess Tingle-Tangle'.

In 1979 she was forced to withdraw from her final role, that of the Dowager Lady Monchensey in a revival of Eliot's *The Family Reunion*, when she was taken ill at her hotel in Manchester with what appeared to be a stroke. Slowly, she seemed to rally, but she collapsed at home that summer. When the ambulance arrived, her collie Merc ran downstairs and hid. Rassine, out of his love for Beatrix, one of the most faithful of his friends, eventually cared for the dog until its death two years later. Beatrix had never deserted Rassine, even if for years she had been obliged to listen to his endless chatter of 'old films and parties with rich, rich people with brains like peas'. At the Hospital for Nervous Diseases, Beatrix was diagnosed as having a brain tumour. An operation was performed. She lapsed into a coma. Lehmann and Rosamond closed ranks against all outsiders, issuing instructions that none except family should see her. To Shelagh Fraser it seemed that 'John and Rosamond wanted, regally, to keep her to themselves.' Those who nursed Beatrix ignored the injunction, and welcomed all visitors.

It was during this period that a Canadian professor, Trevor Tolley, was paying his first visit to Lehmann, and, on leaving, murmured that it had been kind of Lehmann to see him during what must be an anxious time. 'He looked me in the eye,' Tolley recalls, 'and, after some deliberation, said, slowly and with decided emphasis, "Terribly trying". This underplaying of personal feeling I came to feel was very characteristic of him. George Barker had said that nobody knew John Lehmann; and I came to feel that, for most of his acquaintances, this was probably true, because of this masking reticence.' After three months of coma, Beatrix died on 31 July. She was seventy-six. Lehmann and Rosamond's hostility to her circle continued throughout the funeral arrangements; Fraser, for one, found it impossible to attend.

Perhaps Beatrix's only real professional failure had been never to win popularity. It was surely the traits in her personality – forthright honesty, wide and passionate intelligence, unalterable belief and, in her case, a devotion to communism – that had led to her so often being overlooked. How difficult now to capture the power and significance of her achievements, the armoury of qualities she brought to a catalogue of roles begun in London in 1924. Whatever she did was touched by her penetrating intelligence, made unique with a style at once ethereal, haunting and deeply idiosyncratic.

Her view of humankind was as individual as the parts through which she reflected it: through Lavinia in Eugene O'Neill's *Mourning Becomes Electra* (1938) and Abbie in his *Desire Under the Elms* (1940) – 'I rather hate O'Neill. He's so smug, like a matron in an institute, sure of superiority, blind to reality'; through distinguished work at Stratford with Redgrave – 'no knowledge of character or acting, just a great gift for the outer shell'; through Madame St. Pe in Anouilh's *The Waltz of the Toreadors* (1956) – 'quite, *quite* impossible to play: charades, funny lines, *no* consistency'. Eric Shorter regretted the death of 'that fine, fiery actress [who] left such vivid memories of her mysterious, intimidating power to suggest, with her big dark eyes and gravelled voice, a host of sinister or sardonic characters'.

While tributes were paid elsewhere, her death prised wider the chasm that had separated Lehmann from Rosamond. It seemed as if they were only united in their unhappiness at the bequests their sister had made. Rosamond was displeased that Lehmann had written an obituary notice for the *Daily Telegraph* without consulting either Helen or herself, possibly (and if so justifiably) on the grounds that it was exceedingly badly written and lacked any sense either of fondness or *gravitas*. But worse was to come. Lehmann expected to organise a memorial service, but Rosamond would have none of it. She maintained that

Beatrix had had no Christian belief and had led what was essentially a pagan existence (at Violet Hammersley's Mass at Brompton Oratory Beatrix, typically, had mocked 'The endless props and the priest swigging away at the cheap wine', reducing Rosamond to giggles).

When Lehmann pointed out that such an occasion would be for the benefit of 'the living' Rosamond humourlessly responded that, so far as she could see, his definition of 'life' applied merely to those who still breathed and walked about the earth. 'Frankly,' Lehmann replied, 'I don't think your spiritualistic beliefs are relevant to our problem. I respect them, of course, but do not share them. I remain a sceptic and an agnostic – but not an atheist.' Rosamond railed in indignation against once again being branded as a spiritualist, insisting that her beliefs were Christian. Lehmann's riposte was cold.

> I am sorry you were so indignant that I spoke of your 'spiritualistic beliefs'. It was not meant to be derogatory in any way, as I thought I made clear. But someone who claims to be in communication with the dead has always been to me a spiritualist. Such attempt at communication is not, to the best of my knowledge, officially countenanced by any of the main branches of the Christian religion we know. However, in future I shall only refer to your 'psychic beliefs'. Not that the occasion is likely to occur, as I will not be lectured or abused about it, and the subject must now be dropped.

Rosamond's response to this was to suggest that perhaps he did not miss Beatrix as much as she did. Beneath this comment, Lehmann wrote 'I could not answer this terrible letter.' Plans for some sort of secular gathering to commemorate Beatrix lumbered ineffectively on for what seems years, with Lehmann making himself unpopular by interfering with various proposed schemes: it seems not to have occurred to him or Rosamond that the moment for doing the proper thing had passed.

In 1980 Trader Faulkner was asked by Lehmann, whom he found 'very dry ... aloof and grand', to undertake a biography of Beatrix, but his synopsis was turned down by Rosamond who forbade any mention of Beatrix's sexuality, and Faulkner withdrew from the project. At a meeting with Rosamond, Faulkner took a dislike to her 'very imperious' manner, not helped by the fact that throughout the three hours of the interview he was not offered so much as a cup of tea. There is comicality in such meanness, but there is no pleasure to be had from the behaviour of Lehmann and Rosamond following Beatrix's death.

\*

The lack of any private journals for the last decade of Lehmann's life make it almost impossible to chart the sequence of his physical decline. Deafness and gout were constant problems, as was his lameness. It was probably in 1977 that he underwent a hip replacement, but the operation was not a success, and not helped when he subsequently had a fall. The second hip was replaced in February 1978 at Nuffield Hospital, but did nothing to alleviate Lehmann's lameness. Anna Woodhouse, Rosamond's grand-daughter, remembers the operations as being successful, but he refused to work through any physiotherapy. Two days after Christmas 1981, he was driving his Ford Escort on the M25 in thick fog when it was involved in a collision. The car was written off, and Lehmann charged with driving without due care and attention. He pleaded guilty, and never drove again.

Lehmann now had a perpetual tremor. Rosamond offered to 'pay for a neurological treatment ... though I think I ought to pay for it myself. I know there are wonderful remedies now for Parkinson's, but this, they all assure me, is a benign (!) tremor and quite different.' Despite all their difficulties, Rosamond's proffered kindness must have moved Lehmann. She was clearly made deeply unhappy by the divisions between them. On visits to Cornwall Gardens, Lehmann would constantly snipe at her. 'No John,' she wrote,

I am not in the least mentally unbalanced – the recent family anxieties have considerably worn me down. What you call my 'complaints' are in the nature of laments. Nowadays I approach your door with apprehension and leave it in deep depression – having failed once again to penetrate the wall you have erected between us of recent years – Coldness, suspiciousness, defensiveness. I tell myself 'at all costs don't provoke one of his explosions' ... You may not realize how we worry about your crippled state, also about your shaking hands. You bear it stoically, but it is very sad for you.

On 9 May 1984 Lehmann told Eric Oliver 'I was so glad to know you were prepared to come and help look after me when Alexis had to be away.' Could he come for two nights, with all expenses paid? 'I have not been very well for a large part of this year,' he told Fryer, 'and have been shamefully neglecting my friends.' A summons to a gathering at Cornwall Gardens grew rare, as did excursions beyond it.

Infirm as he was, there was a holiday with Stoker in Venice and Vienna that September; it was almost certainly the last. For the next three years, Oliver made regular pilgrimages to Cornwall Gardens from Hove, hanging Lehmann's pictures upside down and, in his absences, sending obscene postcards to 'Dear very big Blue-Eyes'. One can scarcely imagine Oliver's nursing skills; there is something fairly tragic in the fact that Lehmann sought them.

In the spring of 1985 Lehmann was 'horribly ill' and after a mild stroke was admitted to Unsted Park in Godalming, where he received speech therapy. He was complaining in August that 'I have been pretty well cleaned out by my Unsted Park and other charges connected with my disabilities' and asked for time to pay the fees of £655. He asked Lloyds Bank for an overdraft of £5,000 against the lease of Cornwall Gardens.

Lehmann's physical shrinking belied his continuing vitality of mind and his capacity for hard work. In conditions that must often have been extremely difficult he produced a string of books: *Edward Lear and His World* in 1977, *Thrown to the Woolves* (his account of his association with the Hogarth Press) in 1978, a book about Rupert Brooke in 1980, a disappointing and brief study of *English Poets of the First World War* in 1981, and *Three Literary Friendships* (between Byron and Shelley, Rimbaud and Verlaine, and Robert Frost and Edward Thomas) in 1983. Still, Lehmann battled against the fact that he was not the equal of the people he admired and wrote of. And always the sense, as he had once, perhaps unfortunately, admitted to himself, he only half-believed in himself.

If, like his father, Lehmann had to suffer ten years of poor health, he at least remained mentally sound, and productive. How many years before, home from Cambridge, had he lifted his father in his arms, cupped his body against his own, and climbed the staircase at Fieldhead to put Rudie to bed? Now, Eric Oliver must have performed, with a good deal less affection, something of the same duties for Lehmann. Apparently in a constant muddle of dates, Oliver must have been a reluctant presence. Only the fact that he was paid for his attendance can have lured him from his daily trips to Brighton's gay beach, of which he was an *habitué*.

\*

Lehmann spent his final months at Cornwall Gardens while Lake Cottage began its own decline. There is an irony in the fact that his final secretary was a woman, Rachel Gould, who typed letters to which he added his barely readable signature. Until the end, Jeremy Kingston thought he never lost 'his sense of gaiety. Even then, he was a very human, affectionate, jolly, sometimes frivolous human being'. Roy Fuller, a faithful friend, undertook, in 1985, the co-editing with Lehmann of an anthology of pieces from *Penguin New Writing*. For Lehmann, it was a last opportunity to show how brightly his influence had shone through English writing of the 1940s. Fuller wanted the selection to embrace the lesser known writers whom Lehmann had helped to publication, but Lehmann would have none of it: he insisted on names whose glory might reflect on himself. Not agitated by his old friend's dictatorial attitudes, Fuller remained devoted, taking a 53 bus to Westminster and a tube to Gloucester Road when the Pope (as the Fullers called Lehmann) summoned him to the Vatican (Cornwall Gardens). The whisky, Fuller remembered, was the brand that was on offer at the local supermarket, the 'pink champagne' a fizzing *vin rosé*, offered and consumed in the hope of attaining a party atmosphere.

The parties grew less, the company less distinguished, the conversation, against Lehmann's deafness, less flowing. But, whatever else had gone, Lehmann never lost his belief in the supreme importance of the literature he had served. When William Caskey, an ex-boyfriend of Isherwood's and a man much respected by Lehmann, was found dead in his Athens flat in 1980, his body had laid undiscovered there for several months. Fryer recounted all this to Lehmann, and

suddenly the façade completely collapsed, and one saw the very real humanity and the very real tenderness that was there ... I remember John suddenly looked down and went quite pale and said, 'Oh my God, whoever got all the letters?' It wasn't that he felt his own letters would have anything compromising in them; he had this enormous concern for literary property. He knew that Caskey had Isherwood letters and had had a long correspondence with Stravinsky and various others. That concern was something very, very dear to his heart.

There were periods when Lehmann's years fell away from him. He rang Fryer and took him to lunch at the Chanterelle in the Old Brompton Road. He was in sparkling form, as if he had forever emerged from his slow decline. For two hours he rattled off anecdotes and memories. Fryer told a friend about the lunch, and said 'Isn't it amazing?' The friend said, 'It *is* amazing. You took him to the Chanterelle and *he* paid?' Philip Mansel remembers the dignity with which Lehmann coped with his physical debility, never complaining. On one of the last occasions David Hughes saw him, he asked Lehmann how his sex life was. 'Old flames, dear boy,' said Lehmann.

In the early spring of 1987 Miles Huddleston had arranged to call at Cornwall Gardens early one evening. He noticed lights through the uncurtained window, but was unable to get an answer from the doorbell. Huddleston rang Lehmann from a nearby pub. He had fallen on his way to the door. He said he would wait on the floor until help arrived at 8.30 p.m. He had managed to pull a book of his own poems from a nearby shelf. 'Dear boy,' he said, 'I think they're rather good.'

\*

John Lehmann died on 7 April at the Devonshire Hospital, 26 Devonshire Street. After his death, Lettice Cooper, perhaps also speaking for Barbara, made a tribute that still rings with truth. John had cared more for good writing than for anything else in the world. He had a very deep love for England, and always wanted English writers to do well, to do better, always urging them on. Always she remembered John as lonely and imperious. He was the centre of the writing world. It was she who recalled that at a PEN meeting at the Savoy, all the foreign writers spoke of Lehmann 'as if they were speaking of England'.

The cremation was at Golders Green, a gloomy, damp day. Rassine, taken by

Mansel in his car, was withdrawn and dignified; he had been concerned that he could not find a pair of black shoes that would be comfortable and suitable, for his feet were terribly deformed after years of dancing. To Mansel, Rosamond seemed 'calm and queenly'. After the service the little party repaired to the house of Anna Woodhouse, for sandwiches and champagne – it was almost certainly French. John Lehmann had been allowed to slip out of life almost unnoticed.

# 18

# The Bone Standing Out

Remembering Rosamond's insistence that there should be no memorial service for Beatrix, it is not surprising that none was held for their brother. It did not seem a time for tribute; the obituarists did not mourn. Spender had been approached by Trevor Tolley, to write a piece for the book he was compiling as an eightieth birthday tribute for Lehmann, and began drafting it. Remarkably, Spender admitted that through the long history of their bad feeling for one another, there had nevertheless been respect and, even, love. Having confessed as much, Spender scratched through these words, telling Tolley that he was simply unable to write about Lehmann. Tolley never told Lehmann of the others who had refused to pay him tribute.

At his last meeting with Lehmann in 1986, Tolley, fearing that Lehmann might not live to see the finished book, gave him a typescript of it. Not for the first time 'John showed what may have been something of a proclivity for looking a gift-horse in the mouth', criticising much of its content: J. K. Johnstone's essay on Bloomsbury was 'a bit dull' and mostly about Virginia Woolf; Paul Davies's celebration of *The Reader at Night* was 'a bit long'; he did not see why Jeremy Reed should have included two of his own poems; the book as a whole was 'too Canadian'. Despite Tolley's efforts, no British edition could be arranged. The book appeared as a posthumous tribute at the end of 1987, launched in Canada by a speech from Roy Fuller who regretted the fact that a salute to so distinguished an English figure should have had to be published there. It was a final rejection of all that Lehmann had done for the literature of his country over fifty years.

The circle that had surrounded Lehmann was fast diminished in the next few years. Isherwood, too, died in 1987. Rosamond died in March 1990, properly acknowledged as having fulfilled the Lehmann destiny of intermittent greatness. Adrian Liddell Hart died in 1991, collapsing at the Beefsteak Club, a drink in his hand and a cigarette, no doubt, at his lips. Lettice Cooper, the sharer of Barbara's life, died in July 1994, having spent her last years with her brother in Coltishall. Eric Oliver died in April 1995, buried by a cheery vicar who assured the mourners that the departed had gone to 'that great nudist beach in the sky'. Three months later, Spender, having indeed had the last word, was dead.

And what of Lehmann's friends? We know that many went on to successful careers. Jeremy Kingston became a drama critic for *The Times*; Colin Spencer, Christopher Hawtree, Kenneth Martin, and Michael Bloch were among those who became writers, David Hughes a distinguished novelist, Miles Huddleston a notable publisher, Charles Osborne a writer and critic, Frank Oatman a poet and the co-author of two major books on ornithology. The *London Magazine* flourishes still under the editorship of Alan Ross, who has proved himself in every way Lehmann's natural successor. Almost forty years as its editor has not diminished Ross's commitment. In the best sense, although Ross has made the *London Magazine* his own, it remains the most tangible and living memorial to Lehmann's achievements.

Much as one would like to know the fate of Shakespeare Fred and Panda and Frank Beresford and the like, we cannot. We do not know the destinies of so many of Lehmann's lovers, but, occasionally, they are brought into a focus that reminds one that they had lives of their own. So, let us remember Douglas Stoker. Many years before, Lehmann had vouchsafed two paintings to Stoker's care. In his last years, he wrote to Stoker asking for their return. Stoker had sold them. Lehmann was outraged, and wrote a letter that Bruce Cruickshank describes as 'vitriolic, an outpouring of years of resentment. They never spoke to one another again.' Stoker, certainly, has a tragedy about him. Handsome, witty, intelligent, he was yet unable to harness his talents to anything by which he might have left a mark. Something in Stoker inspired Lehmann to friendship and love. Lehmann may have been excited by Stoker's physical attraction, and touched by things that seemed almost a mirror image of his own life. His father died when Stoker was only ten. To escape family pressure, Stoker ran away from home at seventeen. He suffered from enuresis until the end of his life, wetting the bed two or three times a week.

Cruickshank recalls that Stoker was not in the least affected by Lehmann's death. His own health was precarious. In his last existing letter to Lehmann, in 1987, he reported that there was slight damage to his brain, a result of his chronic drinking bouts. A few days after Christmas 1988, Stoker took his Norfolk terrier, Gillie, for a walk by the river at the back of the flat he shared with Cruickshank in Elm Hill, Norwich. Some time later, Stoker hammered at the door of the flat. He had suffered a stroke outside, had rung the bell to summon help, and then staggered up the steep flight of steps to the top floor flat. Cruickshank laid him on the bed, and said he would telephone the doctor. Stoker said, 'No, I feel better now,' and died.

For ten years after Stoker's death, Cruickshank kept the letters Lehmann had written him throughout the long course of their friendship. Only a few weeks before I wrote asking if he would speak to me about Stoker's role in the Lehmann story, Cruickshank had sorted through the letters and destroyed them all. A few photographs survive, Douglas displaying a magnificent torso at Cannes, Douglas in white bathing trunks, Douglas smiling behind sun-glasses on a beach, Douglas standing on steps in Greece, Douglas looking a little uncomfortably at the camera as he stands between Isherwood and Lehmann. We look at them, seeing what Lehmann saw, and I think of their conversation, their intimacies, their knowledge. Cruickshank tells me that Stoker had a piece of a tooth missing. The tooth had smashed because Adrian Liddell Hart, for some long forgotten reason, had once hit him in the mouth with a bottle.

\*

The bulk of Lehmann's estate, including Lake Cottage, was left to Rassine. He was persuaded to search for Lehmann's private journals; one by one, they came to light, rescued from drawers and cupboards. The contents of Cornwall Gardens were packed up and sent to Three Bridges, where they were stacked in the sitting-room, its red curtains always closed against the light. With his legacy, Rassine might have lived in comfort, even luxury, for the rest of his days, but he had been taught not to touch Lehmann's belongings. Eric Oliver made an attempt to retrieve the Denton Welch possessions that had supposedly been handed to Lehmann for safe-keeping in 1950, including a Welch painting, 'The Cat', but Rassine would not relent. He continued to teach at his school, the music played on a wind-up gramophone, but he had tired of it, and gave it up around 1989.

Pamela Foster had not seen Rassine since they had danced together at the Casino in 1938. She had married and emigrated to Canada in mid-career, but was now living close to Rassine off the Old Brompton Road. Her remarkable career seemed as forgotten as his. She had partnered Massine in *A Bullet in the Ballet*, spent three months dancing with Anton Dolin, was with the Ballet Rambert and in a Julian Wylie extravaganza entitled *Leg Theory*. She played Salome at the Albert Hall, and the Fairy Queen in pantomimes with Dorothy Ward and Shaun Glenville ('always drunk'). Now, she had an antiques stall at Camden Passage, and Rassine and she went 'antiquing'.

They both adored dogs. Rassine's last years were no doubt cheered by Foster's witty and extravagant personality, by visits to her mews house with its décor of purple and turquoise, and her tussle with advancing years ('I can't open any-thing, nowadays. I rush out into the street and ask perfect strangers, "*Would* you be so kind as to open this for me?" '). She telephoned Rassine every morning, perhaps after he had read his daily chapter from the Bible, something he always did. On Sundays she would pick him up in her car ('Alexis never learned to drive. He was too terrified.') and they would go to Hackney Flower Market and then antiquing at Brick Lane. Foster recalls 'Physically, I can't imagine him ever having been attractive. There were times when I could have killed him. He was very tight about money, not generous. But he was a real friend. When my last dog died I went round to see him and he got out the whisky and we howled.'

Cornwall Gardens was sold. More and more days were spent at Three Bridges where he was a local eccentric, pottering in the garden with his bonfires, going down to the shops for a newspaper on his bicycle. Beyond the gates of the cottage lived a married couple, Jean and Gordon Watson. It was Jean (who called

Rassine Alex) who was to provide a friendship the like of which he could never have had before. 'He never talked about his art,' she remembers. 'You don't realise, he'd say, you don't understand. We talked washing powders. We were from different worlds. I mean, what you see is what you get.' There were frequent break-ins at the cottage, but the burglars would steal alarm clocks and inexpensive trinkets, unaware of the fortune that lay stored in the sitting-room. Jean would go over to the cottage to check that all was well when Rassine was away; there were times when he looked after her Dalmatian. She was never asked inside.

One day, when Rassine was walking along Chaucer Road (the roads of Three Bridges, like the trees at Lake Cottage, are named after the poets), he was knocked down by a red-haired boy on a bicycle. He maintained that it was this fall that marked the start of his final illness. It was also the beginning of a stronger friendship with Jean: 'I used to nag him all the time.' For the last eighteen months of his life, she was at last allowed into the cottage, but only into Rassine's bedroom. Years before, he told her, he had wanted to move into the larger bedroom at the back of the property, but Lehmann had said he could not. He had written to Lehmann to ask if he might do so. As a concession, Lehmann told him he might sometimes go into the sitting-room. Even now, he did not move.

Rassine had a photograph of Lehmann that hung above his old brass bedstead. The cottage was riddled with damp, its roof leaking, carpets rotting, curtains falling away from the walls. There was no heating except for an electric bar in his bedroom. The once glorious garden had become a wilderness. As Rassine's cancer of the bowel progressed, he became increasingly less mobile. A few old friends from the ballet world made the expedition to Three Bridges, but such visits were notable by their rarity. When Nadia Nerina and her husband came they enquired if Jean was Rassine's charwoman. In her inimitably direct manner, Jean left them in no doubt that she was not. Faithfully, Foster went down to see him and kept in touch. He spent the Christmas of 1991 with her, arriving with a tiny suitcase, and stayed a week in the guest room that has steps out to a little garden.

It was Jean who washed him, shaved him and cooked for him. He had neglected himself horribly; everything 'smelled to high heaven'. One of the nurses who came in to tend him wondered how Jean could bear to spend time there. To Jean, 'not many saw him as a human being. Even when he was as ill as that, he still had a vicious tongue. He still wanted to be top dog.' When she took him a plate of eggs and chips he threw it to the floor. 'I said, all right Alex, you can lie there and rot.' A few days later he came to her door bearing a peace offering of mouldy apples from the garden. She would spend most of her evenings with him, sitting on his bed and singing with him, 'Call Round any Old Time' and the songs of Nat King Cole. 'Lilli Marlene' was another favourite of Rassine's, and 'Strangers in the Night'.

## 18. The Bone Standing Out

In his last weeks, he was taken to Guildford Hospital and then moved to St. Catherine's Hospice in Crawley, where he took a childlike delight in being given whisky. He died on 25 July 1992, one day before his seventy-third birthday. The nurses put a red rose on the pillow by his face.

The Watsons attended his funeral, with a nurse and a woman who picked blackberries in Rassine's garden. There were no other mourners. The estate was left to Jean. Her response, when the solicitor informed her, was probably unprintable. She was warned not to go into the cottage because 'instruments' had been found there, a pram, dummies and rattles and other impedimenta. Jean took it in her stride: 'Perhaps they used to play Mums and Dads, but so what?' She was advised to have the cottage demolished, but 'I didn't want to do that. I wanted to keep it going for John and Alex.' Now, the thin, overgrown path to the front door has been widened. The garden has been cut back, and nature tamed. In the cottage, the damp has almost been conquered, and the interior transformed with a brio that Rassine would have marvelled at. His lilliputian greenhouse still stands, close to a wooden shed behind which is propped his bicycle, rusted. Beyond is a foxhole where six cubs are being reared, fed by Jean, although 'I know I shouldn't do it.' The lake is home to seventeen ducks, and the moorhens, a different generation, are still there.

*

John's archive was sold to the Princeton University Library in New Jersey. Today, it is seldom brought up from the vaults, and then only for the attention of a student who is interested in Virginia Woolf or Stephen Spender. Here are paintings, drawings, locks of hair, a lucite 'Imperial Tobacco Award for Radio, 1976' given to Beatrix, Rudie's brass buttons, Nina Lehmann's blue velvet lap desk, bells, candlesticks, gramophone records, home movie reels, a silver goblet won by John at the 70 yards Swimming Race at Summer Fields in 1920, diaries, ration books, theatre programmes, postcards from long forgotten holidays, and an untold number of letters: the catalogue is endless, and the bulk of John's life organised and undisturbed. Those wanting to understand John's life must search here, read the letters from writers famous and unknown, from lovers hopeful or weary, from friends faithful and tired. Sometimes, life leaps up from the pages, with an assurance of old happiness. But where to find the truth? Is it at the lake where the resonance of their lives, John's and Alexis's, is felt the most strongly? Carlotta, the singing dog, has her tombstone here. Elsewhere, merely ghosts.

How can we know the accumulated mysteries of forty-seven years? Is it impossible to think of Alexis, beloved Alyosha, only as an adjunct to John's life, a life he had, literally, danced himself into? Perhaps, for John, there was a final untangling of the web that had obscured the possibilities of ecstasy. Had there, for either of them, been at last the recognition of 'love, the bone standing out, the most insubstantial has become the most concrete'? In 1940 Alexis had told him 'Our friendship will go on just as long as you want it to.' Who can deny that Alexis had always been constant? And who can argue with the fact that, at the end, he was there?

Listen: the swans have taken off from the lake that now lies open to the sun beyond the pines. They are flying into the morning, high high up, with long necks outstretched, and I can hear the pulsing of angels' wings.

# Acknowledgements

Those who have contributed to the book by writing letters or speaking to me (and to Martin Taylor) are many. Michael Bloch described his life as Lehmann's secretary; Peter Burton discussed Lehmann's publishing achievements; Leo Cooper spoke of his aunts Lettice and Barbara, and I was fortunate to meet Barbara Cooper's brother, Leonard Cooper, who told me much that would otherwise be unknown. Only through an extraordinary chain of circumstances did I learn of the existence of Douglas Stoker, and only through the co-operation and kindness of Bruce Cruickshank did I learn more of him. I must also thank Brian McColgan, Stoker's friend and for a period a Lehmann employee. Michael De-la-Noy was a welcoming host and an authoritative source of information on Denton Welch. One of the great pleasures of writing this book was meeting the remarkable Pamela Foster, who probably deserves a biography of her own. I am grateful to Jonathan Fryer who spoke of his friendship with Lehmann. My visit to David and Judy Gascoyne on the Isle of Wight (where I was also privileged to meet Edward Upward) was another delight, as any who have experienced Judy's hospitality will testify. Other meetings with associates and friends of Lehmann were usually not only informative but pleasurable, and here I must thank Miles Huddleston, David Hughes, Francis King, James Michie and Alan Ross. Jeremy Kingston has provided not only generous information but support; nothing seemed to be too much trouble. Graham Lee provided useful, professional information on the subject of enuresis. Colin Spencer's recollections of Lehmann were helpful and illuminating. Grateful thanks must be given to Liebie Trope, Alexis Rassine's niece, who incurred frightening postal charges to send me information on Rassine's family background, and photographs, from South Africa. Thomas Urquhart-Laird was generous in giving an honest and instructive portrait of Lehmann in later life. Jean Watson was a breath of fresh air to the tired biographer, giving me a tour of Lake Cottage and its garden: she could not have been more forthright.

I am also most grateful to William Abrahams, Professor Peter Alexander, Don Bachardy, the late Professor Quentin Bell, Olivier Bell, Victor Bonham Carter, the late Lettice Cooper, Alex Danchev, Ann Douglas, Pip Dyer, Gavin Ewart, Trader Faulkner, Shelagh Fraser, the late Roy Fuller, Tony Garrett, Valerie Grove, Thom Gunn, Sir Rupert Hart-Davis, Christopher Hawtree, Geoffrey Hedger, Jack Hewit, Chris Hopkins, Julie Kavanagh, P. J. Kavanagh, Ludovic Kennedy, Moira Kennedy, Derek Law, the late Laurie Lee, Mark Le Fanu,

Gweno Lewis, Dr Philip Mansel, Kenneth Martin, Frank Oatman, Kate O'Brien, the late Eric Oliver, Charles Osborne, Derek Parker, Roland Philipps, the late Alexis Rassine, Ned Rorem, Dr George Rylands, Tom Sargant, Elizabeth Saville, Janet Adam Smith, the late Sir Stephen Spender, Anthony Thwaite, Gore Vidal, Robert Waller, Ella Whitehead, and Anna Woodhouse. To those many others who gave assistance and support in many ways whose names are not (through my inefficiency) found here, I offer my thanks.

Corin Redgrave has kindly given permission for me to quote from his father's letters. I am grateful to the University of Sussex for allowing me to quote from the correspondence of Leonard Woolf. David Hughes has kindly allowed me to quote from his correspondence with Lehmann. I am indebted to Lady Selina Hastings and Lord Milford for allowing me to quote extracts from the letters and writings of Rosamond Lehmann, and to Lord Milford for allowing me to quote from the correspondence of Wogan Philipps. Alan Ross has kindly allowed me to quote from a letter he wrote to Lehmann. Jeremy Kingston has generously given me access to his diaries. My thanks are due to Olivier Bell for giving me permission to quote from the letters of her late husband, Professor Quentin Bell, to Lehmann. For permission to quote from letters between Lehmann and Adrian Liddell Hart, and from other letters in their possession, I am indebted to The Trustees of the Liddell Hart Centre for Military Archives. Any scholar writing about Lehmann owes much to Professor A. T. (Trevor) Tolley, whose work has so often in the preparation of this biography been an inspiration to me. For his assistance, and his generosity in allowing me to use his bibliography of Lehmann's work, I am most grateful. Lehmann's literary executors had the foresight to photocopy his extensive personal journals before their despatch to America, an act without which the writing of this book would have been almost impossible.

I must thank the Liddell Hart Centre for Military Archives at King's College, London, for their helpfulness, as well as the London Library, Norfolk County Library, the New York Public Library, the Harry Ransom Humanities Center at the University of Texas at Austin, the New York Public Library, the University of Princeton at New Jersey, the University of California at Berkeley and Eton College Library.

The late Martin Taylor was commissioned to write the biography of John Lehmann, and embarked on an assiduous programme of research and interviews. Sadly, he died after spending several years of assembling material for the book, but without having written a word of it. Following his death, Peter Parker suggested me to Robin Baird-Smith as a suitable biographer of Lehmann. To both, I give my thanks. I am also greatly indebted to David Goudge, who made it possible for me to bring back to Norfolk the enormous Lehmann archive that Martin Taylor had collected during his research. These circumstances have greatly facilitated the writing of this book, but I have of course followed my own path and feelings in conducting further research.

## *Acknowledgements*

Finally, I must as always thank those who have been most concerned with the daily development of the manuscript, Terry Dunning and Michael King. I could not have written it without their understanding, patience, practical assistance, and forbearance in the face of a sometimes apparently obsessed biographer. If the book has any virtues, they are theirs. The vices in the book are mine.

Adrian Wright
Poringland, June 1998

# Bibliography

**Books written and edited by John Lehmann (compiled by A. T. Tolley)**

## Poetry

*The Bud, Burial, Dawn, Grey Days, The Lover, The Mountain, Ruin, The Gargoyles, Turn Not, Hesperides.* Privately printed, 10 broadsheets, 1928.
*A Garden Revisited and Other Poems.* London: Hogarth Press, 1931.
*The Noise of History.* London: Hogarth Press, 1934.
*Forty Poems.* London: Hogarth Press, 1942.
*The Sphere of Glass and Other Poems.* London: Hogarth Press, 1944.
*The Age of the Dragon: Poems 1930-1951.* London and New York: Longmans, Green, 1951; New York: Harcourt, Brace, 1952.
*Collected Poems 1930-1963.* London: Eyre and Spottiswoode, 1965.
*Christ the Hunter.* London: Eyre and Spottiswoode, 1965.
*Photograph.* London: Poem-of-the-Month Club, 1971.
*The Reader at Night and Other Poems.* Toronto: Basilike, 1974.
*New and Selected Poems.* London: Enitharmon, 1985.

## Fiction

*Evil was Abroad.* London: The Cresset Press, 1938.
*In the Purely Pagan Sense.* London: Blond and Briggs, 1976.

## Other

*Prometheus and the Bolsheviks.* London: The Cresset Press, 1937; New York: Knopf, 1938.
*New Writing in England.* New York: Critics Group Press, 1939.
*Down River: A Danubian Study.* London: The Cresset Press, 1939.
*New Writing in Europe.* Harmondsworth and New York: Allen Lane/Penguin, 1940.
*The Open Night.* London and New York: Longmans, Green, 1952; New York: Harcourt, Brace, 1952.
*Edith Sitwell.* London and New York: Longmans, Green, 1952; revised edition, 1970.
*The Whispering Gallery.* London and New York: Longmans, Green, 1955; New York: Harcourt, Brace, 1955.
*The Secret Messages.* Stamford, Conn.: Overbrook Press, 1958.
*I Am My Brother.* London: Longmans, Green, 1960; New York: Reynal, 1960.
*Ancestors and Friends.* London: Eyre and Spottiswoode, 1962.
*The Ample Proposition.* London: Eyre and Spottiswoode, 1966.
*A Nest of Tigers: Edith, Osbert and Sacheverell Sitwell in Their Times.* London: Macmillan, 1968; republished as *A Nest of Tigers: The Sitwells in Their Times.* Boston: Little, Brown, 1968.
*In My Own Time: Memoirs of a Literary Life.* Boston: Little, Brown, 1969; revised

and condensed version of *The Whispering Gallery, I Am My Brother,* and *The Ample Proposition.*

*Holborn: An Historical Portrait of a London Borough.* London: Macmillan, 1970.

*Lewis Carroll and the Spirit of Nonsense.* Nottingham: University of Nottingham, 1974.

*Virginia Woolf and Her World.* London: Thames and Hudson, 1975; New York: Harcourt Brace Jovanovich, 1975.

*Edward Lear and His World.* New York: Scribners, 1977; London: Thames and Hudson, 1977.

*Thrown to the Woolfs: Leonard and Virginia Woolf and the Hogarth Press.* London: Weidenfeld and Nicolson, 1978; New York: Holt, Rinehart and Winston, 1979.

*Rupert Brooke: His Life and Legend.* London: Weidenfeld and Nicolson, 1980; republished as *The Strange Destiny of Rupert Brooke.* New York: Holt, Rinehart and Winston, 1981.

*The English Poets of the First World War.* London: Thames and Hudson, 1981; New York: Thames and Hudson, 1982.

*Three Literary Friendships: Byron and Shelley, Rimbaud and Verlaine, Robert Frost and Edward Thomas.* London: Quartet Books, 1983.

*Christopher Isherwood: A Personal Memoir.* London: Weidenfeld and Nicolson, 1987. New York: Henry Holt, 1988.

### Books edited by John Lehmann

Fox, Ralph. *A Writer in Arms.* Edited by Lehmann, C. Day Lewis and T. A. Jackson. London: International, 1937.

*The Year's Poetry.* Edited by Lehmann, Denys Kilham Roberts and Gerald Gould. 3 volumes. London Lane, 1934-1936.

*Poems for Spain.* Edited by Lehmann and Stephen Spender. London: Hogarth Press, 1939.

*Poems from New Writing, 1936-1946.* London: Lehmann, 1946.

*French Stories from New Writing.* London: Lehmann, 1947; republished as *Modern French Stories.* New York: New Directions, 1948.

*Demetrios Capetanakis: A Greek Poet in England.* London: Lehmann, 1947; republished as *Shores of Darkness: Poems and Essays.* New York: Devin-Adair, 1949.

*Shelley in Italy: an Anthology.* London: Lehmann, 1947.

*English Stories from New Writing.* London: Lehmann, 1951.

*Pleasures of New Writing.* London: Lehmann, 1952.

*Modern French Stories.* London: Faber, 1956.

*The Chatto Book of Modern Poetry 1915-1955.* Edited by Lehmann and Cecil Day Lewis. London: Chatto and Windus, 1956.

*The Craft of Letters in England: a Symposium.* London: The Cresset Press, 1956; Boston: Houghton Mifflin, 1957.

*Coming to London.* London: Phoenix House, 1957.

*Italian Stories of Today.* London: Faber, 1959.

Sitwell, Edith. *Selected Poems.* London: Macmillan, 1965.

*Selected Letters of Edith Sitwell 1919-1964.* Edited by Lehmann and Derek Parker. London: Macmillan, 1970.

*The Penguin New Writing 1940-1950.* Edited by Lehmann and Roy Fuller. Harmondsworth: Penguin, 1985.

## Periodicals edited by John Lehmann

*New Writing* 1936-1939
*Folios of New Writing* 1940-1941
*Penguin New Writing* 1940-1950
*Daylight* 1941
*New Writing and Daylight* 1942-1946
*Orpheus* 1948-1949
*The London Magazine* 1954-1961

# Source Notes

Abbreviations have been used as follows: JL (John Lehmann), DC (Demetrios Capetanakis ) and ALH (Adrian Liddell Hart).

Lehmann's Diaries were catalogued after his death, as follows:

1. 31 July 1923 – 9 September 1923 [An Account of a journey through eight weeks, and the divers places, people, and adventures encountered on the road. Volume I 1923]
2. July 1924 – September 1924
3. 7/8 February 1933 – 2 March 1933
4. 15 April 1934 – 22/23 May 1934 [Diary: Expedition to Russia, Spring 1934]
5. May 1935 – December 1935
6. 25 January 1936 – 1 December 1936
7. End September 1936 – July 1937
8. August 1937 – 26 October 1937
9. 18 September 1938 – February 1939
10. 1 September 1939 – 23 November 1939
11. 30 November 1939 – 5 May 1940
12. 10 May 1940 – November 1940
13. 25 January 1941 – 2 June 1941
14. 6 June 1941 – 6 October 1941
15. Early October 1941 – 21 February 1942
16. 12 January 1943 – 23 May 1943
17. 25 June 1944 – 31 December 1944
18. January 1945 – August 1945

B1. 23 February 1949 – 25 February 1950
B2. 30 March 1950 – 9 October 1950
B3. 21 October 1950 – 16 May 1951
B4. 23 May 1951 – 26 November 1951
B5. 5 January 1952 – 26 August 1952
B6. 4 September 1952 – 23 March 1953
B7. 30 March 1953 – 17 September 1953
B8. 23 September 1953 – 9 May 1954
B9. 1 August 1954 – 10 April 1955
B10. April 1955 – New Year 1956
B11. 10 January 1956 – 23 June 1956
B12. 8 July 1956 – 20 July 1957
B13. 14 August 1957 – 15 September 1958
B14. 20 September 1958 – 5 April 1960
B15. August 1961 – June 1962
B16. 18 September 1962 – Summer 1964
B17. 11 June 1966 – 19 July 1969
B18. 23 October 1969 – 25 May 1970
B19. 22 September 1970 – 12 April 1971
B20. 23 May 1971 – 15 October 1972
B21. Christmas Day 1972 – December 31 1973
B22. Spring 1974 – Spring 1975
B23. January 25 1976 – March 14 1977
B24. March 28 1977 – 4 June 1977

## Chapter One

| | |
|---|---|
| 'River Garden' | *Collected Poems*, p. 11 |
| I was born to this house | *Collected Poems*, 'The House', p. 106 |
| It is possible | *Ancestors and Friends*, p. 121 |
| had done excellent / preparing | Charles Darwin, *The Origin of Species*, 1868 |
| Keep for me | *Ancestors and Friends*, p. 71 |
| a very genuine anxiety | Henri Delaborde speech to Académie des Beaux-Arts, October 1883 |

forced to descend / vein of — Kurt Günzl, *The British Musical Theatre*, Macmillan, Volume I, p. 866

always the same — *Ancestors and Friends*, p. 178
My dear Padrona — Wilkie Collins to Nina Lehmann 26.10.1866
The thing is quite amazing — *Ancestors and Friends*, p. 223
Will you mention? — Charles Dickens to W. H. Wills 26.9.1860
they persevered — Janet Wills to W. H. Wills Jan [n.d.] 1856
I have done — R. C. Lehmann to Frederick Lehmann 5.6.1878
playful or tender — *History of Punch*, p. 142
fearfully busy — R. C. Lehmann to Frederick Lehmann 22.1.93
cheered / one of the most — R. C. Lehmann to Alice Lehmann 30.6.1897
is not the temper — *Punch*, November 1899
a certain masterfulness — *Punch*, 30.1.29

### Chapter Two

a focus of harmony — *The Whispering Gallery*, p. 89
And I remember — George Allsop to JL 21.1.50
the perfect pattern — *The Whispering Gallery*, p. 88
Sometimes Be's voice — Trader Faulkner, unpublished proposal for biography, n.d.

A cat — *The Whispering Gallery*, p. 31
set in motion — Ibid. p. 25
I saw your Father's hand — *Collected Poems*, 'The House', p. 112
It is never the same — Ibid. p. 109
And I am also haunted — *The Whispering Gallery*, p. 63
a crusader — *Ancestors and Friends*, p. 38
If I could remember — *Collected Poems*, 'The House', p. 106
a special romance — JL and Rosamond Lehmann, *Return Journey*, radio script

And Peggy as waitress — R. C. Lehmann, *Punch*, 27.5.14
One of the marks — R. C. Lehmann, *Punch*, 26.8.14
There is love — R. C. Lehmann, *Punch*, 28.10.14
But John — R. C. Lehmann, 'The Lean-To Shed', *The Vagabond and other Poems*, John Lane: The Bodley Head, 1918, p. 61

the searching appraisal — Rosamond Lehmann, *Invitation to the Waltz*, p. 50
took his trousers down — *In the Purely Pagan Sense*, p. 10-11
Already he showed signs — L. A. G. Strong, *Green Memory*, Methuen, 1961, p. 211-212

### Chapter Three

a clever little animal — L. A. G. Strong, *Green Memory*, Methuen, 1961, p. 185

Cambridge / the telephone — Usborne, Richard, *editor*, *A Century of Summer Fields*, Methuen, 1964, p. 74

You are to write — Alice Lehmann to JL n.d.
I went up — R. C. Lehmann to JL 5.5.17
I miss you — R. C. Lehmann to JL 19.5.17
Oh Well Beloved — Beatrix Lehmann to JL 16.3.18
the whole web — *The Whispering Gallery*, p. 86

## Source Notes

| | |
|---|---|
| A charming boy | E. H. Alington to R. C. Lehmann 17 December, n.d. |
| John was settled | Margaret Alington to Alice Lehmann n.d. |
| 'The Milky Molar' | R. C. Lehmann, *Punch*, 26.2.19 |
| a shining light / never likely | E. H. Alington to R. C. Lehmann 1921, n.d. |
| extremely sophisticated | 'And yet I was very happy', *A Century of Summer Fields*, Methuen, 1964, p. 147 |
| 'The penis peeps through' | Jeremy Kingston in conversation with Martin Taylor |
| timeless symbolism / the spacious | *The Whispering Gallery*, p. 100 |
| All that was | Ibid. p. 101 |
| 'Well, Johnny Lehmann | Ibid. p. 98 |
| notorious among us | Ibid. p. 97 |
| a philosophic darkness | Ibid. p. 101 |
| the real object | Ibid. p. 110 |
| 'That's the boy | Diary B17, p. 68 |
| It is curious | Diary 2, p. 12 |
| the sentimental strands | Diary 1, p. 15 |
| all of which | Diary 1, p. 35 |
| Feverish | 'Aunt Jane', *College Days*, No. 11, 29.11.24 |
| It was orrible | 'The man in the Corner', *College Days*, No. 13, 30.11.25 |
| just, but severe / and sustained | *The Whispering Gallery*, p. 97 |
| I'm a rowing failure | JL to Alice Lehmann 8.3.26 |
| a perpetual round | Ibid. |
| more acquaintance | H. K. Marsden to Alice Lehmann 9.8.26 |
| a mean-spirited / He was not | Michael Meredith in conversation with author |

### Chapter Four

| | |
|---|---|
| a great release | *The Whispering Gallery*, p. 136 |
| Knives and circles | JL to Alice Lehmann 22.1.28 |
| a romantic | Dadie Rylands in conversation with the author |
| and my mind | *The Whispering Gallery*, p. 155 |
| The river | Ibid. p. 156 |
| profoundly disillusioned | Ibid. p. 139 |
| Trinity was too large | Ibid. p. 140 |
| a great untidy | Ibid. p. 141 |
| It worried me | JL to Julian Bell 3.11.31 |
| He was a hesitant | *The Whispering Gallery*, p. 143-44 |
| the most detailed arguments | Ibid. p. 146-147 |
| I think there is | Peter Stansky and William Abrahams, *Journey to the Frontier*, Constable, p. 60 |
| a bit of a cold fish | JL to Martin Thompson 17.6.83 |
| very disappointing / monstrously | JL to Alice Lehmann 10.2.29 |
| Tall, slim | *The Whispering Gallery*, p. 151 |
| not long / deserve | Dadie Rylands to JL 13.3.29 |
| My dear, you must | Ibid. |
| But I will try | Michael Redgrave to JL 21.3.29 |
| You seem so straight | Ibid. |
| I am very fond | Dadie Rylands to JL 22.3.29 |
| There is a bird | Michael Redgrave to JL 22.3.29 |
| O you do love me | Michael Redgrave to JL 26.3.29 |

| | |
|---|---|
| I feel it | Ibid. |
| Our love is beautiful | Michael Redgrave to JL 13.4.29 |
| I grow to love you | Michael Redgrave to JL 29.5.29 |
| It would be foolish | Michael Redgrave to JL 13.6.29 |
| terrible injury / Suddenly | Michael Redgrave to JL 18.6.29 |
| But now I know | JL note on letter from Michael Redgrave 20.6.29 |
| You have grown up | Dadie Rylands to JL 10.7.29 |
| I honestly care | Michael Redgrave to JL 15.9.29 |
| One cannot / Your danger | Michael Redgrave to JL 28.12.29 |
| the bad temper / for you | Michael Redgrave to JL 11.1.30 |
| too false | JL (unpublished manuscript) n.d. |
| Was R. C. L. | JL to Alice Lehmann 20.5.28 |
| We were alone | *The Whispering Gallery*, p. 157 |
| He seems to me | JL to Alice Lehmann 1.2.29 |

## Chapter Five

| | |
|---|---|
| Lehmann may do | Virginia Woolf, *Diaries*, 10.1.31 |
| In order to write | *The Whispering Gallery*, p. 198 |
| a giraffe | Ibid. p. 173 |
| Several of the poets | Ibid. p. 182 |
| formalized reminiscences | *Cambridge Review*, 20.11.31 |
| almost unbrokenly descriptive | *Manchester Guardian*, 29.10.31 |
| Very tall and slim | *The Whispering Gallery*, p. 176 |
| youth had started | Ibid. |
| In England | Ibid. |
| like a slowly tolling bell | Ibid. p. 177 |
| the author is perfectly calm | JL, Report to Leonard Woolf, u.d. |
| I'm afraid this correspondence | Lytton Strachey to JL 5.11.31 |
| I knew him quite well [& paragraph] | JL in conversation with Denis Lemon and Peter Burton, 1976 |
| What can I say | Quentin Bell to JL n.d. |
| Dear dearer | Quentin Bell to JL n.d. |
| I have given some | Quentin Bell to JL 8.2.32 |
| had created the illusion | *The Whispering Gallery*, p. 199 |
| His behaviour | Leonard Woolf to Rosamond Lehmann 7.9.32 |
| of endless horror [etc] | Beatrix Lehmann to Rosamond Lehmann 1931 u.d. |
| it is queer / Perhaps | Beatrix Lehmann to Rosamond Lehmann 6.10.32 |
| and I was *real* glad | Beatrix Lehmann to Rosamond Lehmann 29.10.32 |
| I am terribly glad | Wogan Philipps to JL 1932, u.d. |
| your family | Wogan Philipps to JL 16.9.32 |
| as those which / you have been | Frank Beresford to JL 30.8.32 |
| already to go away | Ibid. |
| a penniless / If you are | Wogan Philipps to JL 16.9.32 |
| Well I'll say | Frank Beresford to JL n.d. |
| I have kept away | Fred Turner to JL 2.8.33 |
| for your friendship | Fred Turner to JL 1933 u.d. |
| and I think | Fred Turner to JL 24.7.34 |
| I have been a liar | Fred Turner to JL 18.2.36 |
| that job | Fred Turner to JL 7.4.39 |
| On the one hand | *Thrown to the Woolves*, p. 42-43 |
| they could not have | *The Whispering Gallery*, p. 207 |

| | |
|---|---|
| looked more exquisite | Diary 3, p. 2 |
| I find it very exciting | Ibid. p. 5 |
| a point from which | Ibid. |
| inevitable confession / obstacle | Ibid. |
| the most successful | Ibid. p. 4 |
| Willi vamping | Ibid. p. 9 |
| I feel absolutely sick | Ibid. p. 11 |
| in the same way | Ibid. p. 4 |
| His childish (& paragraph) | Ibid. p. 11 |
| I've reached a period | Ibid. p. 8 |
| Abandoned Woman | Ibid. p. 2-3 |
| this idea | Ibid. p. 11 |

### Chapter Six

| | |
|---|---|
| How is it possible | *The Whispering Gallery*, p. 215 |
| He started to kiss me | *In the Purely Pagan Sense*, p. 68 |
| be careful | Beatrix Lehmann to JL 1933 u.d. |
| I'm afraid | JL to Beatrix Lehmann 13.2.33 |
| we astonishingly deluded | *The Whispering Gallery*, p. 218 |
| We discuss the future | Diary 4, p. 1 |
| Toni is immensely excited | Ibid. p. 7 |
| Toni and I talk hard | Ibid. p. 18 |
| a sort of tom-cat | Ibid. |
| as pleasant | Ibid. |
| the enormous complexity | Ibid. p. 19 |
| amazing new civilization | Diary 5, p. 2 |
| I felt I could | *The Whispering Gallery*, p. 221 |
| There only remained | *Down River*, p. 44 |
| The living truth | *The Whispering Gallery*, p. 226 |
| A mile away | Ibid. p. 227 |
| as dead / He will never | Dylan Thomas, *Bookman*, December 1934 |
| rank and file | George Stonier, *New Statesman*, 27.10.34 |
| much of this book | *Daily Worker*, 24.10.34 |
| I suddenly seemed | Diary 5, p. 17 |
| the *second* / the collapse | Diary 6, p. 5 |
| in that time | Ibid. p. 13 |
| feeling always | Ibid. p. 23 |
| It was a dreary | Pip Dyer in conversation with Martin Taylor |
| a secondary affair (& paragraph) | Ibid |
| not grown less egocentric | Diary 7, p. 1 |
| I had already chosen | *The Whispering Gallery*, p. 283-284 |
| supremely corrupt | Diary 8, p. 20 |
| I know that I can't | Ibid. p. 18 |
| with all the force | Diary 9, p. 23 |
| lyrically happy | Ibid. p. 2 |
| Toni and I / happiness | Ibid. p. 26 |
| on her side | Ibid. p. 28 |
| But most of all | Ibid. p. 29 |
| a dawning sense | Diary 9, p. 33 |
| For God's sake | Ibid. p. 34 |
| I shouted to him | Ibid. |

| | |
|---|---|
| Pip managed it | Ibid. p. 35 |
| while Wystan | Ibid. p. 35-36 |
| his bad luck / vivid picture | Ibid. p. 40 |
| Wanted | Ibid. p. 49 |
| as I cannot leave | Clothilde Schweiger to JL 15.10.39 |
| an astonishing insult | JL to Clothilde Schweiger 21.10.39 |
| closely following | Diary 9, p. 54 |
| with all its warmth (& paragraph) | Diary 10, p. 10 |

## Chapter Seven

| | |
|---|---|
| a time of great tension | Diary 7, p. 13 |
| clear press prejudices | Ibid. |
| I had not | Ibid. |
| did you feel | *Prometheus and the Bolsheviks*, p. 252 |
| remain in the steady | Diary 8, p. 25 |
| My journalist life | Ibid. p. 18 |
| the vivid human appeal | *The Whispering Gallery*, p. 261 |
| My response / inarticulately aware | Ibid. p. 249 |
| it hung awry | George Garrett, 'Fishmeal', *New Writing 2*, p. 71 |
| One must see | Diary 9, p. 3-4 |
| an unexpected look | *Evil was Abroad*, p. 99 |
| since it amounts | Robert K. Martin, 'Appeals from across some frontier: the novels of John Lehmann', *John Lehmann: A Tribute*, edited by A. T. Tolley |
| in so narrow | *Evil was Abroad*, p. 36 |
| ideas in the void | Ibid. |
| to know more | Ibid. p. 37 |
| the tangle between | Ibid. p. 41 |
| tackle seriously | Ibid. p. 152 |
| a direct door | Ibid. p. 10 |
| had started earlier | Ibid. |
| there were two processes | Ibid. |
| pursuit of illumination | *In the Purely Pagan Sense*, p. 75 |
| entirely without protection | *Evil was Abroad*, p. 109 |
| The great sin | Ibid. p. 195 |
| a protest | Ibid. p. 179 |
| How was it | Ibid. p. 251 |
| a child that strays | Diary 9 p. 18 |
| immature, the technique | Richard Church, *John O'London's Weekly*, 7.10.38 |
| under-emphatic | Frank Swinnerton, *Observer*, 2.10.38 |
| Many readers | L. A. G. Strong, *Spectator*, 21.10.38 |
| The shutting [& paragraph] | Diary 9, p. 19 |
| natural traitor | Diary 9, p. 36 |
| a grasping business man | Ibid. p. 41 |
| a streak of genius | Ibid. p. 48 |
| tomorrow (& paragraph) | Robert Waller in conversation with the author |
| mass-hysteria | Diary 11, p. 29 |
| impossible to have | Diary 10, p. 47 |
| I know | Diary 11, p. 68 |
| one of the few | Diary 10, p. 77 |
| so many | *I Am My Brother*, p. 45 |

## Source Notes

| | |
|---|---|
| To breed the kind | Virginia Woolf, 'The Leaning Tower', *Folios of New Writing*, Autumn 1940, p. 19 |
| the violence | Ibid. p. 26 |
| inconsistent / the embittered | Louis MacNeice, 'The Tower That Once', *Folios of New Writing*, Spring 1941, p. 37 |
| leaders in thought [& paragraph] | B. L. Coombes, 'Below the Tower', *Folios of New Writing*, Spring 1941 p. 31 |
| all his / will lack | Ibid. p. 34-36 |
| a near-fanatical loyalty | *I Am My Brother*, p. 144 |
| She was more like | Leonard Cooper in conversation with the author |
| because there was | Lettice Cooper in conversation with Martin Taylor |
| all the credit | Ibid. |
| every firm | James Michie in conversation with the author |
| not above / willing | Leo Cooper in conversation with the author |
| moods | JL to Christopher Isherwood 27.12.39 |
| I miss you | JL to Christopher Isherwood 6.9.39 |

### Chapter Eight

| | |
|---|---|
| Of medium height | *In the Purely Pagan Sense*, p. 137-8 |
| And now | Diary 11, p. 32 |
| some great synthesis | Ibid. p. 34 |
| Alexis did a very unexpected thing | Ibid. p. 33 |
| the supreme example | Ibid. |
| To feel, like a stabbing wound | Ibid. p. 59 |
| Is it Pride? | Ibid. |
| turn down the tap | Ibid. p. 70-71 |
| Our friendship | Ibid. p. 71 |
| Young writers in the airforce | Diary 12, p. 45 |
| I am still looking | Diary 13, p. 56 |
| And by poetry | Ibid. p. 61 |
| in a more eternal way | Ibid. p. 71 |
| to think in four dimensions | Ibid. p. 72 |
| all the charm | Diary 14, p. 22 |
| And I wake this morning | Ibid. p. 18 |
| and all the other horrors | Diary 12, p. 59-60 |
| that rock-bottomness | Ibid. p. 60 |
| Why hadn't I learnt | Ibid. p. 70 |
| great revolutionary truth | Ibid. p. 77 |
| How strange, how quickly | Diary 11, p. 69 |
| Did what took place | JL to ALH 16.11.40 |
| You say that all roads | JL to ALH 17.2.41 |
| Sailors don't care | JL to ALH 19.3.41 |
| in an acutely normal state | JL to Nigel Nicolson 19.10.80 |
| amazed and deeply moved | Diary 13, p. 44 |
| I could see her so well | Ibid. p. 49 |
| Hush, the red fungeses | 'The Lady of Elvedon', *The Reader at Night* |
| senseless, inexplicable | Diary 13, p. 12 |
| stoic humanism | Ibid. p. 14 |
| with Alexis laughing on the bed | Ibid. p. 29 |
| it made no difference | Ibid. p. 37 |
| threw some light | JL to ALH 30.4.41 |

| | |
|---|---|
| an attempt to regain | Diary 13, p. 60 |
| And I keep on | Ibid. p. 65 |
| When I remember | ALH to JL 3.6.41 |
| with joy and unhappiness | Diary 13, p. 75 |
| He's mad / Stephen sniggering | Diary 14, p. 53 |
| lead in my heart | Diary 13, p. 79 |
| transposed and blended | *I Am My Brother*, p. 266 |
| Great were our plans / Till I was | 'The Summer Story', *Collected Poems*, p. 67 |
| I was only not strong | JL to ALH 8.7.41 |
| I have this unhappy knack | JL to ALH 14.7.41 |
| I've been very lucky | JL to ALH 6.8.41 |

**Chapter Nine**

| | |
|---|---|
| He grew enthusiastic / He is modest | Diary 13, p. 49 |
| greater strength / works I have felt | Ibid. p. 11 |
| but I also felt | DC to JL 21.7.41 |
| how out of the world | Diary 14, p. 39 |
| I am quite convinced | DC to JL November 1941 u.d. |
| My desire | Ibid. |
| away from you | DC to JL u.d. |
| really astounding | Edith Sitwell to JL 28.5.43 |
| The stranger left | 'Detective Story', *Demetrios Capetanakis*, p. 19 |
| I know | DC to JL 12.10.42 |
| He was the most discreet | Panayotis Canellopoulos, 'My friend Demetrios Capetanakis', *Demetrios Capetanakis*, p. 173 |
| Sometimes the way | Diary 14, p. 23 |
| ghastly psychological tangle | Ibid. p. 51 |
| You evidently have | Basil Liddell Hart to JL 10.11.51 |
| Please don't think | Jessie Liddell Hart to JL 3.7.42 |
| slipped into a region | Diary 14, p. 54 |
| and after that | Ibid. p. 66 |
| live for an evening | Ibid. p. 43 |
| 'There, I'm crying | Ibid. p. 47 |
| Why did he begin | Ibid. |
| adventures | Ibid. p. 70 |
| sublime experience | Diary 15, p. 2 |
| blinded with tears | Diary 14, p. 79 |
| a demonstration / desperately | Ibid. |
| there is something | Diary 15, p. 21 |
| Why do you look [& paragraph] | Ibid. p. 24-26 |
| my major personal problem | Ibid. p. 30 |
| if you will | JL to ALH Diary 15, p. 40-41 |
| When I see you | Ibid. |
| H.M.S. Adrian | Ibid. p. 42 |
| pulpit attitude | Diary 14, p. 7 |
| complex and baffling | Diary 15, p. 48-49 |
| 'I was left | Ibid. p. 51 |
| the simpler peoples | Ibid. p. 53 |
| how they gripped | Ibid. p. 56 |
| It was wonderful | JL to ALH 14.12.41 |
| one must believe | Diary 15, p. 59-60 |

| | |
|---|---|
| indeed the violence | Ibid. p. 60 |
| one side a boy | Ibid. p. 65 |
| quiet, roomy | Ibid. p. 73 |
| There was a week-end | Ibid. p. 77 |
| extremely unpleasant | JL to ALH 28.4.42 |
| in more ways | Ibid. |
| monster spermatozoa | JL to ALH 3.7.44 |
| How I agree | ALH to JL July 1944 u.d. |
| I think you have still | JL to ALH 21.12.50 |
| If people think / Not only | ALH to Basil Liddell Hart 2.2.51 |
| a cause of embarrassment | Basil Liddell Hart to JL 6.11.51 |
| I was mad at you | JL to ALH 25.11.51 |
| I'm going to beat | Thomas Urquhart-Laird in conversation with Martin Taylor |
| still on | JL to ALH 24.1.80 |
| Not again | Diary 15, p. 78-79 |

### Chapter Ten

| | |
|---|---|
| sketch map / may be all | *New Writing in England*, p. 6 |
| specifically | Ibid. |
| the collapse of Austria | Ibid. p. 62 |
| keep it alive | Diary 12, p. 26 |
| something fated | Ibid. p. 74 |
| in a shady flood | Diary 13, p. 27 |
| higgledy-piggledy | Ibid. p. 24 |
| the almost total failure | Ibid. p. 31-32 |
| conscript prose | Andrew Sinclair, *War Like a Wasp*, Hamish Hamilton, 1989 |
| continual train-journeys | *I Am My Brother*, p. 106-107 |

### Chapter Eleven

| | |
|---|---|
| I have no political axe | JL to Foreign Office 4.6.39 |
| careful to emphasise | JL to Leigh Ashton 1940 u.d. |
| his pale and ardent face | *I Am My Brother*, p. 152 |
| in sudden clear / He spoke | Diary 16, p. 57 |
| it had grown | Ibid. p. 6 [typescript] |
| only the forehead | Ibid. p. 10 |
| the stuffing | Ibid. p. 19 |
| a fascination | Ibid. p. 20 |
| a startled ferret [& paragraph] | Ibid. p. 24 |
| Leslie, recite me | Ibid. p. 24-25 |
| giving one of her | Ibid. p. 25 |
| old Mandarins | Ibid. p. 27-28 |
| to an almost pathological | Ibid. p. 28 |
| the insincerity | Ibid. |
| utter lack | Ibid. |
| If I were you | Ibid. p. 9 |
| instantly the great | Richard Church, *John O'London's Weekly*, 8.12.42 |
| seems to have squeezed | *Time and Tide*, 23.1.43 |

| | |
|---|---|
| new town / In whose blood-throb | *Forty Poems*, p. 37 |
| To all these boys | Diary 16, p. 32 |
| It made me think | Ibid. p. 30 |
| where *we* | *Ibid. p. 29* |
| ceaseless, energetic | Roy Fuller to JL 10.2.60 |
| moved by | Ibid. |
| conjured up / a boy | Diary 17, p. 29 |
| not as fucking awful | Hamish Henderson to JL 30.3.44 |
| looking longer | Diary 10, p. 26 |
| an experience of the void | Ibid. |
| fluttering / I like him | Diary 13, p. 51 |
| I believe in you | DC to JL November 1941, u.d. |
| destructive passion | DC to JL March 1942, u.d. |
| I want you | DC to JL 9.3.42 |
| You are life to me | DC to JL Easter 1942, u.d. |
| You saved my life | DC to JL n.d. |
| triumphed, but I could | Panayotis Canellopoulos, 'My Friend Demetrios Capetanakis', *Demetrios Capetanakis: A Greek Poet in England*, p. 175 |
| I am experiencing | DC to JL 15.2.44 |
| had to suffer | DC to JL 26.2.44 |
| the best thriller | Ibid. |
| Yes, we can | DC to JL 26.2.44 |
| I must thank you | DC to JL 3.3.42 |
| it was life | Panayotis Canellopoulos, 'My friend Demetrios Capetanakis', *Demetrios Capetanakis: A Greek Poet in England*, p. 176 |
| destined to be | Edith Sitwell, 'The Poetry of Demetrios Capetanakis', Ibid. p. 35 |
| This knock / And now | 'Lazarus, Ibid. p. 34 |
| mysterious reserves | Barbara Cooper, unpublished ms |
| You know | DC to JL 11.5.42 |
| The ageless ambiguity | Demetrios Capetanakis, 'Abel', *Demetrios Capetanakis: A Greek Poet in England*, p. 24 |
| Those whom / I knew | Barbara Cooper to JL 8.3.56 |
| You know that | Barbara Cooper to JL 8.3.48 |
| To penetrate that room | 'To Penetrate That Room', *Collected Poems*, p. 26 |
| so terrible | Diary 17, p. 7-8 |
| and as that is the case | 'Ben' to JL 9.4.45 |
| extremely gay | 'David' to JL 2.9.45 |
| enchanting with perhaps | 'David' to JL 28.6.49 |
| it shocks me | George Stonier, *New Statesman*, 28.4.45 |
| a charming lilt | *Listener*, 10.5.45 |
| what Mr. Lehmann | *Tribune*, 9.2.45 |
| the death or murder | Diary 18, p. 26 |
| disappointed | JL, unpublished typescript, n.d. |

**Chapter Twelve**

| | |
|---|---|
| the pictures, the books | Diary 18, p. 43 |
| one of a generation | Diary B4, p. 31 |
| The secret | 'The House', *Collected Poems*, p. 110 |

| | |
|---|---|
| a sombre spirit | Diary B4, p. 32 |
| involved some patronising | James Michie in conversation with the author |
| a huge, immovable | David Hughes in conversation with the author |
| like a scurge | AR to JL 6.3.42 |
| Your loving Hunky | AR to JL 4.5.43 |
| like dancing | AR to JL 30.1.45 |
| I think it's very fair | AR to JL 14.2.45 |
| It fills me | Rosamond Lehmann to JL 9.2.40 |
| got the impression | Diary 18, p. 35 |
| another fearful landmark | Diary B1, p. 67 |
| like a Victorian clergyman | Diary B1, p. 25 |
| She cannot believe | Diary B1, p. 76 |
| burst into a long | Diary B2, p. 5 |
| 'After all, | Ibid. |
| horrible and useless | Beatrix Lehmann to JL 28.4.36 |
| cheap, stinking | Beatrix Lehmann to JL 15.2.37 |
| I'd rather go to Russia | Beatrix Lehmann to JL 26.8.39 |
| *before* decisions are made | Leonard Woolf to JL 4.10.43 |
| tart little flimsies | JL to Leonard Woolf 6.10.43 |
| I cannot agree | JL to Leonard Woolf 12.10.43 |
| I scarcely trust / I feel | JL to Leonard Woolf 15.10.43 |
| absolutely / grossest rudeness | Leonard Woolf to JL 23.10.43 |
| the moment I express | Ibid. |
| I am horrified | JL to Leonard Woolf 20.7.43 |
| unintelligible | Leonard Woolf to JL 17.5.43 |
| takes life and himself | Leonard Woolf, *The Arrival Not the Journey that Matters*, p. 449 |
| I miss you / There isn't | Barbara Cooper to JL 24.6.49 |
| whimsy stories | Barbara Cooper to JL 13.6.49 |
| very quiet | Barbara Cooper to JL 17.6.49 |
| I long for mid-July | Barbara Cooper to JL Ibid. |
| A recklessly audacious | *The Ample Proposition*, p. 23 |
| The deep need today | *Orpheus*, No. 1, p. vi |
| gilded nuts [& paragraph] | *Orpheus*, No. 2, p. v |
| the impresario | Diary B1, p. 38 |
| the consolidation | Diary B1, p. 62 |
| partly because of | Diary B1, p. 46 |
| 'Everyone imagines | Diary B1, p. 59 |
| more doll-like / more perhaps | Ibid. |
| 'She'll die young | Diary B2, p. 4 |
| I had run my race | Diary B2, p. 76 |
| If I ever write | Diary B1, p. 78-79 |

**Chapter Thirteen**

| | |
|---|---|
| I have only known | [The Faun] to JL 6.8.52 |
| after my shot | Diary B5, p. 68 |
| boiled right over | Ibid. |
| has always been | Diary B5, p. 81 |
| I pleaded / I hated | Ibid. |
| the harmony was so perfect | Diary B6, p. 6 |
| wishing I could get past | Ibid. p. 11-12 |

| | |
|---|---|
| how much I'd had | Ibid. p. 4 |
| I suddenly realised | Ibid. p. 5 |
| climbing pine-forests | Ibid. p. 8 |
| in a war-shattered city | Ibid. p. 10 |
| I don't know | JL to Rosamond Lehmann February 1950 u.d. |
| I was in touch | *The Ample Proposition*, p.128 |
| It had become | Diary B4, p. 24 |
| a breach of trust | Ibid. p. 20 |
| I am hypersensitive [etc] | JL to Rosamond Lehmann June 1952 u.d. |
| Shock, shame, humiliation | Rosamond Lehmann to JL 5.3.58 |
| You do not like | JL to Rosamond Lehmann 1958 u.d. |
| disastrous | Diary B8, p. 39 |
| the old, old complaint | Ibid. p. 40 |
| sank to the bottom | Ibid. |
| incapable of grasping | Ibid. p. 41 |
| There can be few people | *The Times* 15.12.52 |
| the departure of one | Ibid. |
| The small people | The *Bookseller* 13.12.52 p. 1613 |
| like a dripping sponge / hopeless | Diary B6, p. 43-44 |
| so full of warmth | Ibid. p. 42 |
| I have never | Ibid. |
| there was an enormous narrowing | David Hughes in conversation with author |
| I've a strange feeling | David Hughes to JL 24.4.50 |
| OUR radio / rather like | David Hughes to JL 5.11.51 |
| reached a kind | *New Soundings* Introduction to Programme 5 |
| O for a life | Ibid. |
| the problem / there was never | *The Ample Proposition*, p. 194-195 |
| I always thought | David Hughes to JL 28.8.52 |
| that mixture | Diary B6, p. 47 |
| people are always | Peter Burton in conversation with author |
| the pretentiousness | Diary B7, p. 49 |
| Yes, it can really happen | 'Sunrise: Amalfi', *Collected Poems* p. 113 |
| to rise | *I Am My Brother*, p. 213 |
| the sensitiveness | Diary B7, p. 12 |
| The Air Force boy | 'Out of Time, *Collected Poems* p. 119 |
| I watched the peasants | 'Greek Landscape with Figures', *Collected Poems* p. 126-127 |
| a sort of Buxton-cum-Cheltenham | *I Am My Brother*, p. 225 |
| The traveller returned | Demetrios Capetanakis, 'Return', *A Greek Poet in England*, p. 26 |
| and now | Diary B8, p. 36 |
| in the deep green | Ibid. p. 5 |
| an evening on the tiles | Diary B10, p. 9 |
| I could not | Barbara Cooper to JL 20.6.53 |
| I want to make it | Ibid. |
| her judgement | Diary B7, p. 64-65 |
| Well, you've been able | Diary B8, p. 9 |
| the real point | Diary B9, p. 47 |
| thinks of everything [etc] | Ibid. |
| his intellectual | Richard Eberhart, *New York Times* 26.4.53 |
| still about objects | The *Listener* 17.1.52 |
| Poets, one might say | *The Open Night*, p. 128 |

| | |
|---|---|
| with that curious feeling | Diary B8, p. 38-39 |
| bearing in mind [etc] | Diary B9, p. 21-22 |
| to discriminate [etc] | Ibid. p. 22 |
| I also know | Ibid. p. 71 |
| a nasty disappointment | Diary B10, p. 11 |
| obsession with the idea | Ibid. p. 24 |

**Chapter Fourteen**

| | |
|---|---|
| it was the most | Colin Spencer in conversation with Martin Taylor |
| John was the most | Ibid. |
| a lovely, warm | Ibid. |
| You've got the cornerstone | Ibid. |
| like a champagne bottle | Ibid. |
| such a monster | Ibid. |
| 'First come | Ibid. |
| matchsticks and old wool | Diary B2, p. 47 |
| proved herself | Ibid. |
| there is something | Ibid. |
| and she has to be soothed | Diary B11, p. 51 |
| What more can one say? [etc] | Ibid. |
| Last night Odette | Ibid. |
| Perhaps that means | Ibid. p. 53 |
| with undiscovered shores | Ibid. p. 58 |
| Perhaps | Ibid. |
| his other self | Ibid. |
| even more painfully | JL to Odette Massigli 1956 u.d. |
| she unexpectedly asked | Diary B11, p. 40 |
| Alex has been | Ibid. p. 72 |
| a ballet dancer | Gore Vidal, *Palimpsest*, Andre Deutsch, 1995 p. 176 |
| I should have been | Diary B11, p. 39 |
| Yes, I'm afraid I am | Diary B12, p. 27 |
| It has all happened | Ibid. p. 26 |
| my own master [etc] | Ibid. p. 51 |
| succeeded in wounding me | Ibid. p. 30 |
| This is my test | Jeremy Kingston, Diaries, 18.7.56 |
| Jeremy's explosion | Diary B12, p. 17 |
| Oh, you don't need | Jeremy Kingston in conversation with Martin Taylor |
| I am a Royale | Ibid. |
| I am not merely Jeremy | Jeremy Kingston, Diaries, June 1957 |
| a genial and elderly child | Ibid. December 1956 |
| Socrates and his pupil | Ibid. September 1957 |
| you have emerged | Ibid. |
| almost harrowing | Diary B13, p. 55 |
| after deciding | Ibid. p. 60 |
| a terrible sequence of days | Ibid. p. 64 |
| I've been fighting [etc] | Jeremy Kingston, Diaries, October 1956 |
| We had decided | Ibid. September 1956 |
| the mouth | Jeremy Kingston in conversation with Martin Taylor |
| Would you say | Jeremy Kingston, Diaries, June 1957 |

| | |
|---|---|
| quite rightly | James Michie in conversation with author |
| full of guttural laughter | David Hughes in conversation with author |
| a person who wished | James Michie in conversation with author |
| like a great meringue | Alan Ross in conversation with author |
| She kissed John | Jeremy Kingston, Diaries, December 1956 |
| I think I could stand | Lettice Cooper in conversation with Martin Taylor |
| it didn't give the magazine [etc] | David Hughes in conversation with author |
| there is not nearly | JL to Lionel Fielden 2.2.55 |
| somehow the look | David Hughes in conversation with author |
| has no other criterion | Diary B10, p. 30 |
| a young assistant | Cecil King to JL 26.5.55 |
| the creative impulse [etc] | Diary B10, p. 45 |
| sweet-tempered and able | Ibid. p. 50 |
| a classical document | G. S. Fraser, the *Observer* |
| It is the poet | Guy Ramsey, *Daily Telegraph* |
| intellectual ardour | Rose Macaulay [unattributed], *Times Literary Supplement*, 30.9.55 |
| | |
| The discerning reader | Stephen Spender, *News Chronicle*, 29.9.55 |
| the bland, sane | Cyril Connolly, *Sunday Times*, 26.9.55 |
| who really care | Diary B10, p. 81 |
| What *again*? [etc] | Diary B11, p. 37 |
| created an amazing organisation | Ibid. p. 69 |
| You are a swell | JL to Robert Maxwell 30.5.56 |
| I would be deep | Diary B11, p. 79 |
| to possess my own life | Diary B12, p. 4 |
| at last in unique control | Ibid. |
| David, my dear [etc] | Jeremy Kingston, Diaries, February 1957 |
| old, and prematurely aged | Kenneth Martin to Martin Taylor 12.12.93 |
| In twenty-five years | Jeremy Kingston, Diaries, July 1959 |
| I was told by others | Kenneth Martin to Martin Taylor 12.12.93 |
| Why did he let himself [etc] | Jeremy Kingston, Diaries, July 1959 |
| drank steadily and heavily | Kenneth Martin to Martin Taylor 12.12.93 |
| This is not a public telephone! | Ibid. |
| the disastrous mistake | Diary B14, p. 47 |
| vowing | Ibid. p. 58 |
| It would be hard | Kenneth Martin to Martin Taylor 12.12.93 |

**Chapter Fifteen**

| | |
|---|---|
| Thinking of the London Magazine | Diary B13, p. 9 |
| You started nearly ninety | Ibid. p. 23-24 |
| Alan suddenly started | Ibid. p. 25 |
| First, that it is | Ibid. p. 45 |
| a persistent central problem | Ibid. |
| ludicrously pompous | P. J. Kavanagh to author 21.5.98 |
| excessive strain | Diary B14, p. 46 |
| how tired and nervously low | Ibid. p. 53 |
| It's very important | Alan Ross to JL 12.12.60 |
| No, I would *not* | Alan Ross in conversation with author |
| a very small plant | Leonard Cooper in conversation with author |
| My heart is so full | Barbara Cooper to JL 1.3.61 |
| Who will look after you now? | Ibid. |

## Source Notes

| | |
|---|---|
| The truth is | B. Cooper to JL 7.10.65 |
| fantastic, almost fanatic | Barbara Cooper to JL 29.9.66 |
| that faithful friend | Barbara Cooper to JL 27.2.70 |
| You had better ask her | Lettice Cooper to Martin Taylor in conversation |
| Why is it one ends | Ibid. |
| I am quite sure | Lettice Cooper to JL 22.5.81 |
| I shall always really belong | Barbara Cooper to JL 1.3.61 |
| One must abdicate from sex | Diary B15, p. 19-20 |
| I left | Ibid. |
| any my finishing / a really strenuous | Diary B15, p. 16 |
| Nothing I have seen | Ibid. p. 21-22 |
| in spite of all | Ibid. p. 22 |
| All my life | Diary B15, p. 24 |
| an unconscious mood | John Betjeman to JL 20.2.60 |
| deeply moving | Charles Causley to JL 17.2.60 |
| to cover my nakedness | Diary B14, p. 75 |
| forcible, intransigent party-line | Diary B16, p. 44 |
| an elephant | Ibid. |
| I know I'm provoking | Ibid. p. 45 |
| like a wildcat | Ibid. p. 58 |
| strip-tease | Ibid. |
| 1963 / Partly, of course | Diary B16, p. 66 |
| extraordinary *goodness* | Diary B14, p. 29 |
| We'll always be muckers | Ibid. p. 42 |
| I shall not | Ibid. |
| The way things have gone | Ibid. p. 54 |
| to all purposes | Bruce Cruickshank in conversation with author |
| dusting the Lehmann's ornaments | Ibid. |
| Douglas felt there was a kudos | Ibid. |
| Douglas: I could say | Diary B16, p. 67 |
| baffled misery about Douglas | Ibid. p. 9 |
| She thought | Lettice Cooper in conversation with Martin Taylor |
| a tacky grandeur | Bruce Cruickshank in conversation with author |
| meditations, diary entries | 'Christ the Hunter', Foreword |
| an attempt to write | Ibid. |
| The meaning of life | 'Christ the Hunter', p. 20 |
| the tip of a phallus | Ibid. p. 25 |
| the poet the music | Ibid. p. 31 |
| the vision of a world remade | Ibid. |
| He is that Christ | Ibid. p. 16 |
| the little bitch | Ibid. p. 39 |
| I am making a bonfire | Ibid. p. 28 |
| are mixed with the ashes | Ibid. p. 41 |
| however moving | Christopher Levenson, 'The Poetry of John Lehmann, *John Lehmann: A Tribute*, p. 57 |
| a critic | Peter Quennell, *Sunday Telegraph* |
| several literary ventures [etc] | Geoffrey Grigson, *New Satesman* |

### Chapter Sixteen

| | |
|---|---|
| but I saw | JL, *A Posthumous Life in Texas*, typescript |
| I didn't like to say | Ibid. |

| | |
|---|---|
| much as I had always admired | Diary B18, p. 47 |
| an extraordinary [etc] | Diary B17 p. 68-69 |
| It was like a home-coming | Ibid. |
| an acute attack | Diary 17, p. 31 |
| bewildered, almost entirely | JL, *A Posthumous Life in Texas*, typescript |
| we became more intimate | Ibid. |
| marvellously easy | Ibid. |
| has been incredible | Diary B18, p. 19 |
| the more gas / a very skilfully | Ibid. p. 37 |
| idiotic / wooden-headed | Sarah Bradford, *Sacheverell Sitwell*, Sinclair-Stevenson, 1993, p. 414 |
| | |
| a young man came in | Ibid. p. 33 |
| Like all supremely happy love | Ibid. p. 35 |
| that I was no one | Diary B17, p. 43 |
| chiefly I think | Diary B18, p. 41 |
| What am I doing here? | Ibid. p. 44 |
| and then the full rain | Ibid. p. 49 |
| I had the feeling | Ibid. p. 58 |
| bitter, unsatisfied | Diary B19, p. 47 |
| but at what cost | Ibid. p. 76 |
| riddled with bitterness | Diary B18, p. 59 |
| I just don't believe | Ibid. p. 60 |
| I do not think | Diary B19, p. 18 |
| young Californians passing | Ibid. p. 21-22 |
| they were truly in fits | Ibid. p. 25 |
| very heavy in torso | Ibid. p. 34 |
| I felt that at any moment | Ibid. p. 41 |
| this morning | Ibid. p. 44 |
| Let's see what birds | Diary B19, unpaged |
| It was like an Orphic rite | Ibid. |
| Out of nothing and stillness | 'Canyon Weather', *The Reader at Night* |
| I'm sure she knows | Diary B19, p. 65 |
| with my earliest memories | Ibid. p. 71 |
| We had had | Ibid. p. 85-86 |
| good and conscientious [etc] | Janet Adam Smith to author 19.4.97 |
| affected his normal character | Victor Bonham Carter to author 30.3.97 |
| who has been in his sweetest form | Diary B20, p. 15 |
| as long as there's someone | David Wetsel to JL February 1972 u.d. |
| a miserable failure | JL to David Wetsel 2.5.72 |
| You will be sharing | JL to Frank Oatman 8.7.71 |
| undignified | Diary B20, p. 22 |
| nasty incident | Ibid. p. 23 |
| in a very bad | Ibid. p. 22 |
| I truly believe | Ibid. p. 25 |
| these creatures from Mars | Ibid. p. 34 |
| Here I seem | Ibid. p. 41 |
| love and kisses / the sober | Ibid. p. 36 |
| How strange | Ibid. p. 55 |
| I felt so immediately | Ibid. p. 59-60 |
| looking very sweet | Diary B17, p. 67 |
| Very dishy indeed | Ibid. p. 86 |
| looking like / deeply | Ibid. p. 74 |

| | |
|---|---|
| and complains | Diary B18, p. 30 |
| in the hope / What stabbed me | Rosamond Lehmann to JL 1.6.72 |
| It seems to me unfair | JL to Rosamond Lehmann u.d. |
| I think sometimes [etc] | Diary B20, p. 77 |
| If only one could find | Ibid. p. 98 |
| He was too lazy [etc] | Pamela Foster in conversation with author |
| with a care | Diary B19, unpaged |
| a very sadistic character | Thomas Urquhart-Laird in conversation with author |
| He is highly strung | Diary B20, p. 81 |
| got together to force | Thomas Urquhart-Laird in conversation with Martin Taylor |
| I loved him | Thomas Urquhart-Laird in conversation with author |
| summarily dismissed | Jonathan Fryer in conversation with author |
| 'Soup, Rosamond? | anonymous source in conversation with author |
| on Cloud Nine / there was malice | Thomas Urquhart-Laird in conversation with Martin Taylor |
| I popped into your flat | Alexis Rassine to JL April 1974 u.d. |
| lovely men | Thomas Urquhart-Laird in conversation with Martin Taylor |
| He wouldn't stay faithful | Ibid. |
| He was a terrible martinet | Ibid. |
| of being washed up | Diary B21, p. 4-5 |
| Why is it all dust | Ibid. p. 15-16 |
| You're a flatterer [etc] | Ibid. p. 33 |
| definitely encouraging | Ibid. p. 19 |
| it may easily | Ibid. p. 20 |
| Well, there's nothing | Ibid. p. 25 |
| difficult not to be influenced | Ibid. p. 66 |
| He is absolutely irreplaceable | Ibid. p. 76 |
| very emotional | Ibid. p. 78 |
| The end of a chapter / as if | Ibid. p. 83 |
| And now it is all over | Ibid. p. 90 |
| Stephen will survive | Ibid. p. 91 |

### Chapter Seventeen

| | |
|---|---|
| renewed youth | Diary B22, p. 3 |
| who blossomed | Ibid. p. 16 |
| very highly strung | Ibid. p. 19 |
| it will really do | Ibid. p. 36 |
| 'Is it funny sometimes? | Ibid. p. 65 |
| belongs to that well-travelled | Ibid. p. 38 |
| rather like those | Ibid. p. 42-43 |
| still under the shock | Ibid. p. 47 |
| the creeping advances | Ibid. p. 80 |
| I didn't think | Ibid. p. 61 |
| to bail Cyril's widow | Ibid. p. 81 |
| manic / who very nearly | Ibid. p. 59 |
| basically as a silly | Jonathan Fryer in conversation with author |

| | |
|---|---|
| John was completely | Ibid. |
| he was terribly coy | Ibid. |
| the guardsman syndrome [etc] | Ibid. |
| he didn't feel guilty | Ibid. |
| I reconcile myself | Diary B18, p. 25 |
| This is the nicest thing | Diary B22, p. 37 |
| Like a double Angel [etc] | 'To my Faithful Correspondents in England', *The Reader at Night*, unpaged |
| I pore over the photograph | 'Photograph', *The Reader at Night*, unpaged |
| It is all done for *truth* [etc] | Diary B23, p. 54 |
| I fear | David Leitch, *New Statesman*, 10.9.76 |
| Gor blimey | *In the Purely Pagan Sense*, p. 52 |
| in (and often out) | John Mellors, *Listener*, 16.9.76 |
| pursuit of illumination | *In the Purely Pagan Sense*, p. 75 |
| It isn't always | Peter Burton in conversation with the author |
| I asked him | *In the Purely Pagan Sense*, p. |
| a ritual | Diary B23, p. 54 |
| a gross error | Jonathan Fryer in conversation with author |
| like a jealous wife | Diary B23, p. 60 |
| My experience | *In the Purely Pagan Sense*, p. 242 |
| which did so much [& paragraph] | Festschrift for John Lehmann, m.s. |
| Dear John / May all be mirth | Rosamond Lehmann, 'Letter to my Brother', Festschrift for John Lehmann, m.s. |
| It has been painful | Diary B23, p. 76 |
| Quite often, recently | Final Diary [unnumbered], p. 17 |
| in spite of beard | annotated interview list, typescript |
| as a lark | Michael Bloch to author 17.4.98 |
| John was an exacting | Ibid. |
| always patient | Ibid. |
| a very handsome undergraduate | Ibid. |
| where I quiver | Beatrix Lehmann to JL 1959 u.d. |
| old films and parties | Beatrix Lehmann to JL 7.10.70 |
| He looked me in the eye | Trevor Tolley, typescript memoir of Lehmann |
| I rather hate O'Neill | Beatrix Lehmann to JL 1.5.40 |
| no knowledge | Beatrix Lehmann to JL 1947 u.d. |
| quite, *quite* impossible | Beatrix Lehmann to JL 6.10.53 |
| that fine, fiery actress | Eric Shorter, *Daily Telegraph*, 13.8.79 |
| The endless props | Beatrix Lehmann to Alexis Rassine 15.2.64 |
| Frankly | JL to Rosamond Lehmann 15.9.79 |
| I am sorry | JL to Rosamond Lehmann 25.9.79 |
| I could not answer | JL note at bottom of letter from Rosamond Lehmann 3.10.79 |
| very dry / very imperious | Trader Faulkner in conversation with Martin Taylor |
| I am *all right* | JL to Jonathan Fryer 22.7.81 |
| pay for | JL to Rosamond Lehmann 4.6.83 |
| No John [etc] | Rosamond Lehmann to JL 1.6.83 |
| I have not been | JL to Jonathan Fryer 31.5.84 |
| horribly ill | JL to John Denny 20.4.85 |
| I have been | JL to Unsted Park 10.8.85 |
| his sense of gaiety | Jeremy Kingston in conversation with author |
| suddenly the façade | Jonathan Fryer in conversation with author |
| calm | Philip Mansel in conversation with author |

**Chapter Eighteen**

| | |
|---|---|
| somehow failed [etc] | *The Times*, 8.4.87 |
| less than enthusiastic | Trevor Tolley, memoir of John Lehmann, typescript |
| John showed [& paragraph] | Ibid. |
| that great nudist beach | Peter Burton in conversation with author |
| vitriolic | Bruce Cruickshank in conversation with author |
| No, I feel better | Ibid. |
| always drunk [& paragraph] | Pamela Foster in conversation with author |
| He never talked [etc] | Jean Watson in conversation with author |
| love, the bone standing out | *Christ the Hunter*, p. 51 |
| Our friendship will go on | Diary 11, p. 71 |
| Listen: the swans have taken off | *Christ the Hunter*, p. 52 |

# Index